ShutterBox Vol.3

Tavisha/Wired Psyche – Story and Illustrations
Rikki Simons – Writer, Tones, and Letters

Tavisha and Rikki Simons – Front Cover
Raymond Makowski – Graphic Designer
Suzanne Waldman – Copy Editor

Rob Tokar – Editor
Chris Buford – Digital Imaging Manager
Jennifer Miller and Mutsumi Miyazaki – Production Managers
Jill Freshney – Managing Editor
Jeremy Ross – Editorial Director
Ron Klamert – VP of Production
Mike Kiley – Publisher and E.I.C.
John Parker – President and C.O.O.
Stuart Levy – C.E.O.

A  Manga

TOKYOPOP Inc.
5900 Wilshire Blvd. Suite 2000
Los Angeles, CA 90036

E-mail: info@TOKYOPOP.com
Come visit us online at www.TOKYOPOP.com

ISBN: 1-59816-005-2

First TOKYOPOP printing: August 2005
10 9 8 7 6 5 4 3 2 1
Printed in the USA

SHUTTERBOX

BOOK THREE: ENTRY EXAM

BY

TAVISHA
AND
RIKKI SIMONS

TOKYOPOP®

HAMBURG • LONDON • LOS ANGELES • TOKYO

M. U.   S.E.

AN INTRODUCTION BY THE WIRED PSYCHE

Here now, this essay lengthens, dear reader, for we enter into the third chapter of our story of the ShutterBox Exchange Student, Megan Amano: this tale of how a seemingly simple girl from Earth changed our afterlife, our life between life, forever. For some time now, we here in this afterlife have been searching for a human capable of describing our tale to you in the mortal world below. At first, we beseeched a snobbish throng of clients and tested foolish academics of terrestrial colleges... but being that our realm here within the ninth level of imprecation is only communicable to you in the shortest bursts of time, the professors failed us in a most blustering fashion.

The five senses dwell within your human skin, humans reside within the nine dimensions, the nine dimensions are tucked into the universe, and the universe lies inside the infinite multiverse... Your five senses stab out to feel and think through your first four dimensions, the first three of which are wholly yours, yet the fourth, Time, overlaps into Immiserriah, the world of waste, in much the same way Immiserriah's seventh dimension, Wasteful Time, overlaps into our world of Merridiah. Merridiah, where we muses live, is Evolution. There can be said to exist a tenth dimension, and that dimension is Progressive Time to our Merridiah, but it is entirely morphological, belongs wholly to the larger structure of the multiverse, and only blindly binds itself to our world when it is natural to do so... which is only when a ShutterBox Exchange Student is in our midst. So and such, as Time begets Wasteful Time and Wasteful Time is struck down by Evolution, an artist cursed with a nearly schizophrenic sense of their own work

was needed to translate our tale in full. A comic book artist, preferably a Gemini, we soon discovered, was the only person truly capable of receiving us. Thus we have whispered our tale to Tavisha for many years, and she has been so kind as to force her Virgo husband's hand in writing it all down... and now, such delight! He is ours, for he can no longer resist our soundless caterwauls, our little bites that probe beneath his temple; perhaps he shall go mad? That is a concern for another Time...

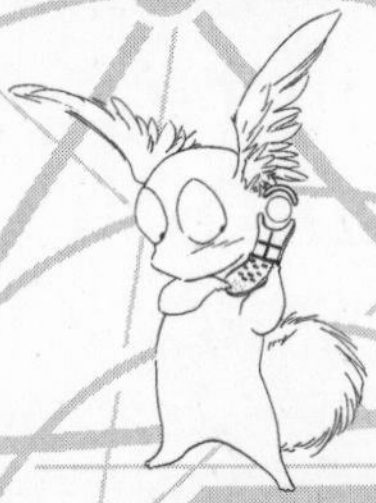

Ours is a story of a conflict with cruelty. Cruelty muddles the human condition and is generated by waste. Its only intention is to nourish more waste. Cruelty saturates the mortal populace, and even in our search to find appropriate tellers of our tale, we muses found ourselves surrounded by human advocates of the wasteful and cruel. We, the tired and tried muses of Merridiah, find there to be hardly anything more loathsome than the foolish, unnecessary scribbling of literary critics, especially those old buffoons of heavy brow who sit at head in places of higher education, that is: the professors and their lapdog academics who exalt the aesthetic structure of writing above all else in canonical works. Our good advice is squandered upon them. They curse the writing that happens because of purity of adoration, and the fervent need of the honest writer to contribute to the literary ages, whether pulp or higher. There are those who adore reading and thus engage in this most ancient of communicative arts with honest aplomb. Often, these worshippers of the creative pen choose to give back to the medium that has sustained them mentally, and they are compelled to write fiction with an almost giddy melancholy, which is purity at its best. Then there are those who approach the literary world with their insults in hand, swinging lies blindly to enlighten the so-called unintelligent. They flail about with words like "tripe" and "pedestrian" to punish

the ignorant via mean-spirited example. We solicited this seemingly elevated class of academia, but being that these arrogant plutocrats of the erudite mind were too busy focusing on any means to justify and nurture said cruelty, these self-proclaimed authentic readers and masters of the Western canon were only destined to fail us by their unconscious design. Of course, Damien would probably disagree.

Cruelty is the Enemy and we have an example of how love of aesthetic alone can lead to the destruction of the written word...

Displayed here upon our make-believe stage are the lives of two real comic book creators: here they struggle for a decade and more to make their thoughts known. They suffer under the gaze of relatives who refuse to understand their life-style, they sleep badly, worry and fret, sometimes in poverty, sometimes not, hoping for the time when their vision is finally understood, and in being understood: loved. The academic world too looks upon them with wolves' tongues hanging, waiting for failure as proof of the comic creators' choice of the wrong sort of fiction: their penny-dreadful comic books. Yet, if the actual boring day-to-day lives of the artist and her writer were penned in prose, as an examination of a life-style, packed with plenty a dribbling metaphor (much like this introduction) in a nineteenth century style or some-such, academia would give an approving nod... but ideally, their story should also take place on a farm if it were to be prize worthy (or it should concern a war between heaven and hell for it to be noticed by comic book accolades). This is why we muses waste our time in the halls of higher learning. They fail to see that the wretched

lives of our two penny-servants need not flowery text to make what is already made — and although a flowery text is a fragrant gift, its scent can only be inhaled if a breeze finds an unblocked nose. We, the beleaguered muses of Merridiah, raise your mortal hand with pen and mind set at center, not just so that you may play in arduous exercises of clever sentence structure alone, as the academics would have you think. Sentence structure is subjective to the language it is born from, and what may be so very clever in English, can seem entirely dimwitted when translated to German, French, Chinese, and to the unknown lands of etceteras. With this said, it can be assumed, and rightly so, that the dramatic and, indeed, comedic interpersonal relationships between characters is most important of all. For every brilliant rhyme or culturally astute metaphor lost in translation, there is a character and their stimulating plot that wins the immortality of years as "easy as pie" and as easily as this cheap cliché shall die at the borders of those nations who do not know what a pie is and why it seems to be in a mind of all things cinched. Of course, Thomas would probably disagree.

If cruelty is the Enemy, then what springs from the soul of the generous right-minded? Science fiction and fantasy is your friend. Science fiction and fantasy exults a poetry of thought that moves within the realm of the fantastic, to guide you, dear reader, past the prison of the present. It is no surprise then, that most comic books are science fiction and fantasy and that the Japanese counterpart to the Western comic book, the manga, whose plots often swim in the circles of the scientifically and spiritually absurd, the seemingly nonsensical made tantalizing by a very human desire for a more interesting version of their dear old universe, should in turn be the medium in which we muses choose to relate our tale. We know that Adrien would agree.

In the making of these ShutterBox books, the work goes on for Tavisha and Rikki. They toil for us in all manner of servitude, through half-lit days and withdrawn nights. At least they now have a new cat for a friend: six toes on the left foot and seven on the right, a blue body as long as a snake and lank as a ferret, little Pippi Poppenstocking helps comfort them for us as only a monstrous cat can. They work, not entirely alone now... but at least they work for us.

Being that this is the third part of six, we feel it only fair, dear reader, that we illustrate here, in words and in pictures, what has come before.

<u>Megan Amano</u>
Mortal Age: 18.
Birthday: May 25.
Blood Type: O+.
Soul: possibly new.

Megan was a young photography student attending Santa Monica Community College. She began having very real and troubling dreams the night she saw a suicidal young man named AJ Crandall walk fully clothed into the ocean and vanish in the fog. Since then, Megan's curious therapist, Petier Troia seemed to provide little comfort from Megan's dreams, dreams where she visited with the deceased AJ in a tranquil summer-set meadow. Events took a turn for the bizarre during one troubled sleep. Megan found herself enlisted as a living ShutterBox exchange student at Merridiah University of Spiritual Education. She returned to Merridiah University on December 25th to begin her education as a living Muse. When she once again met the brothers AJ and Dane, she also learned that her therapist, Petier Troia, was in actuality Headmaster Petier Troia, probably the most important muse in all of Merridiah.

Damien "Dane" Crandall
Mortal Age: varies.
Birthday: usually August 8.
Blood Type: varies.
Soul: old.
University position: the
Angel of Death Unbalanced.

Adrien "AJ" Crandall
Mortal Age: varies (never
more than 18).
Birthday: usually August 8.
Blood Type: varies.
Soul: old.
University position: the
Angel of Childhood's End.

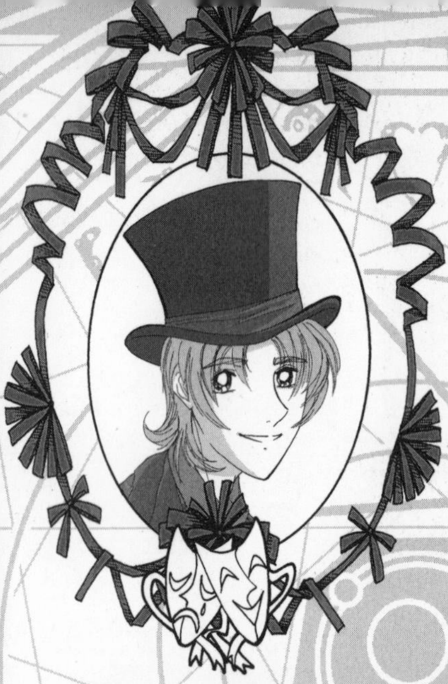

Thomas Kelly Jenkins
Age: varies.
Birthday: Usually February 5.
Blood Type: varies.
Soul: flippantly median.
University position: Muse, "Student Disembodied President."

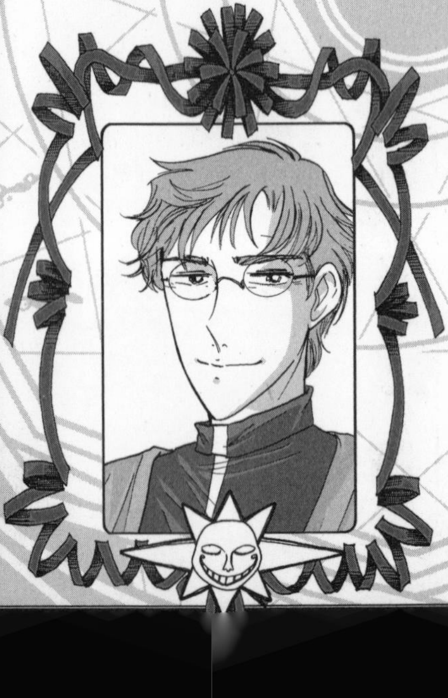

Petier Troia
Age: never more than 35.
Birthday: Usually September 4.
Blood Type: forgotten.
Soul: possibly very old.

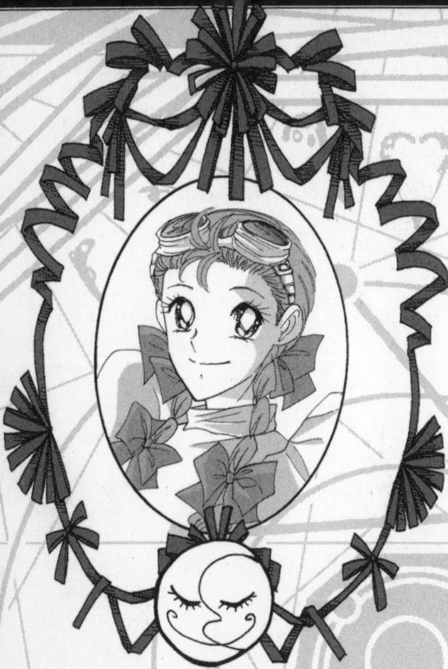

Dagny Gilhooley
Age: 18.
Birthday: February 29.
Blood Type: A.
Soul: new.
University position: First Aide to ShutterBox, Megan Amano.

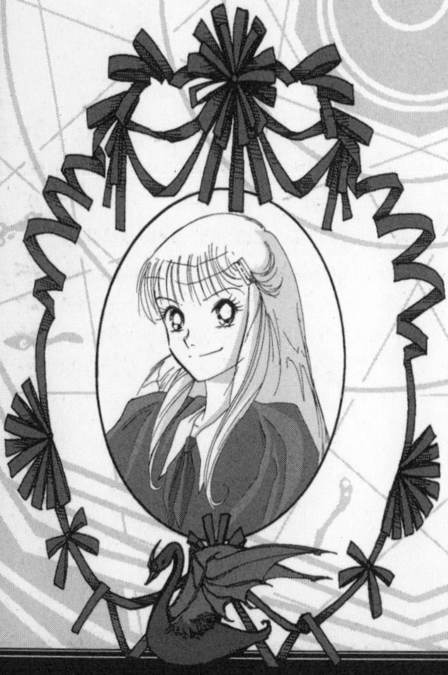

Caroline Egolatry
Age: never more than 18.
Birthday: possibly sometime in November.
Blood Type: varies.
Soul: old.

The Banshee
Age: 16,832.
Birthday: June 6.
Blood Type: Ammonia.
Soul: very old.

We now begin this third part of six. May the telling of the tale further free you of the corruption of the banshees and the otherwise sad horror of living. Eternally Nocturnally Yours, The Inhabitants of Merridiah, speaking through this Wired Psyche.

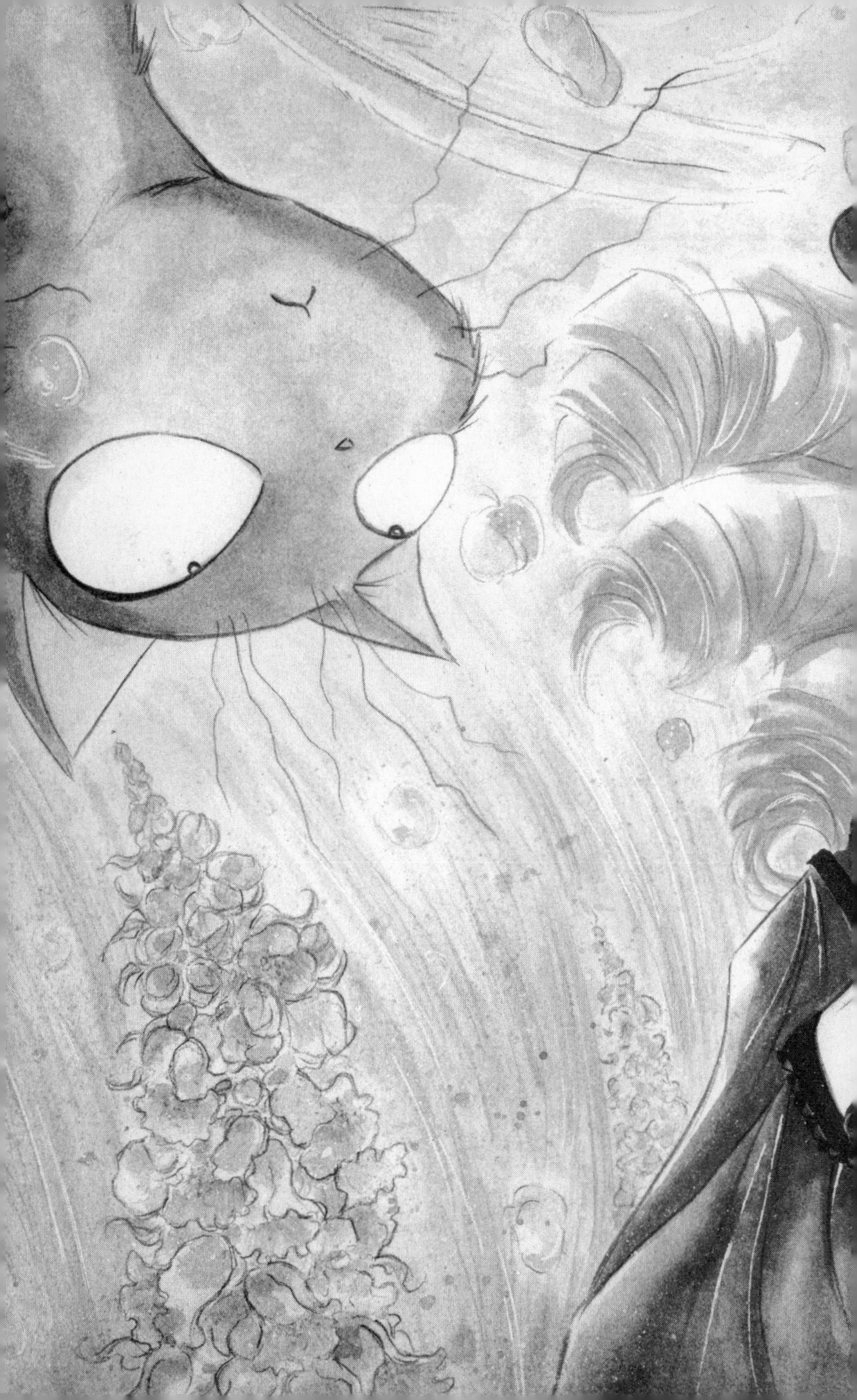

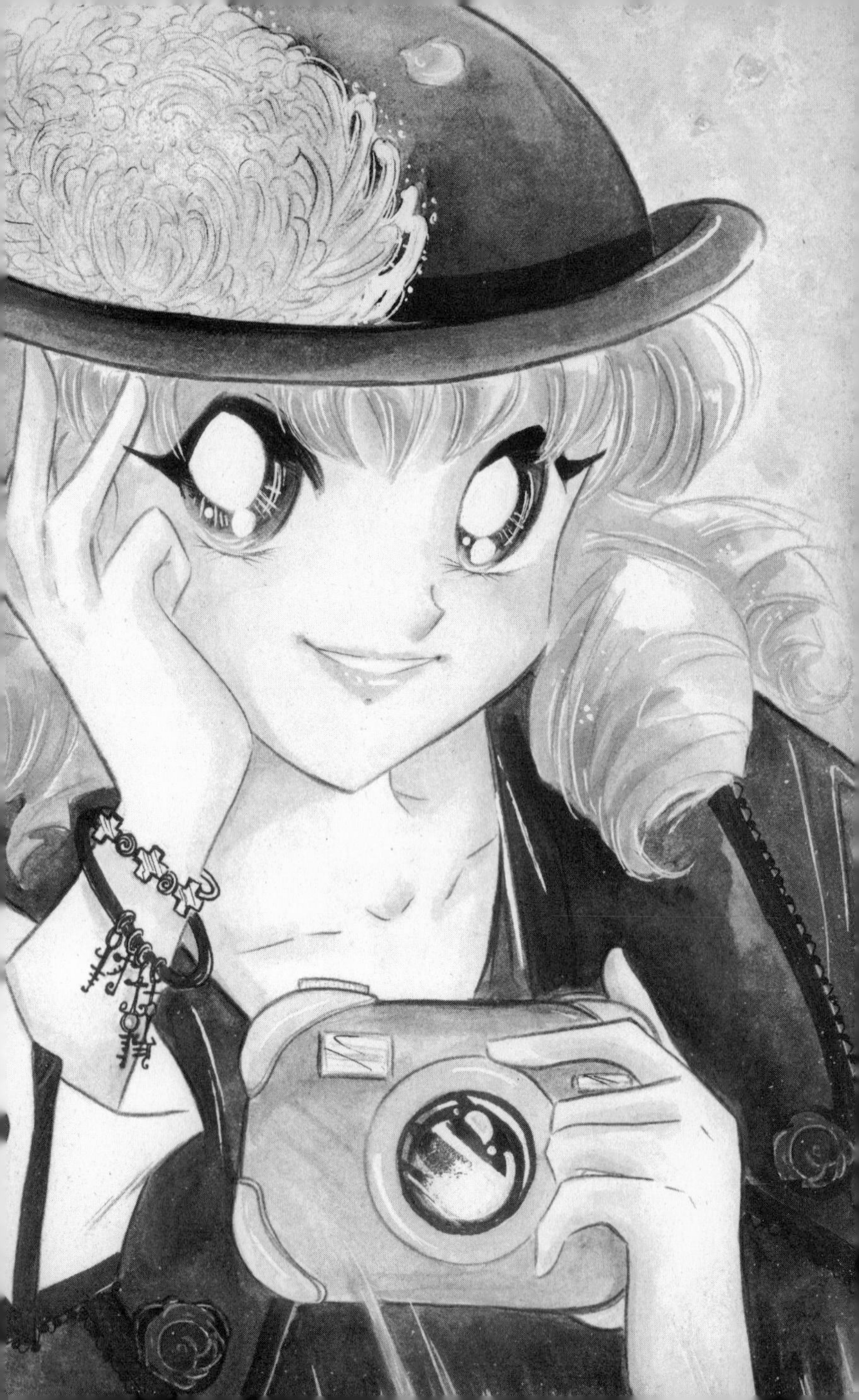

Chapter One:

What is Miserablism

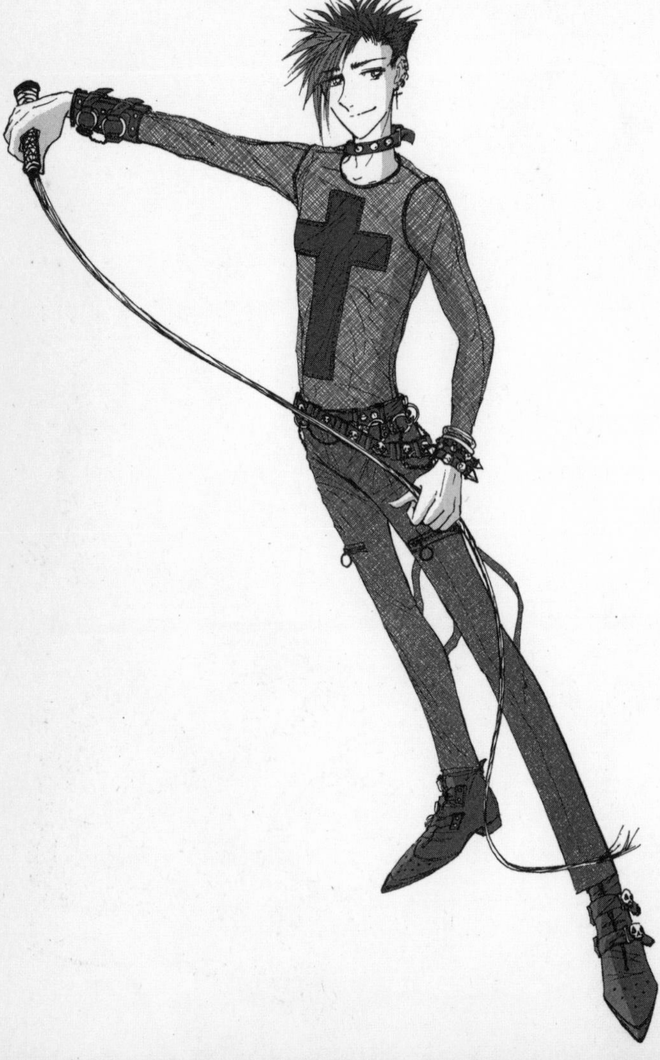

bauhaus
BOYS DON'T CRY
THE CURE
THE SISTERS OF MERCY
JOY DIVISION
DEAD•CAN•DANCE
MORRISSEY

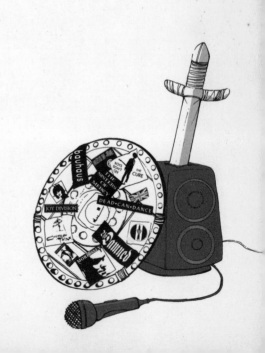

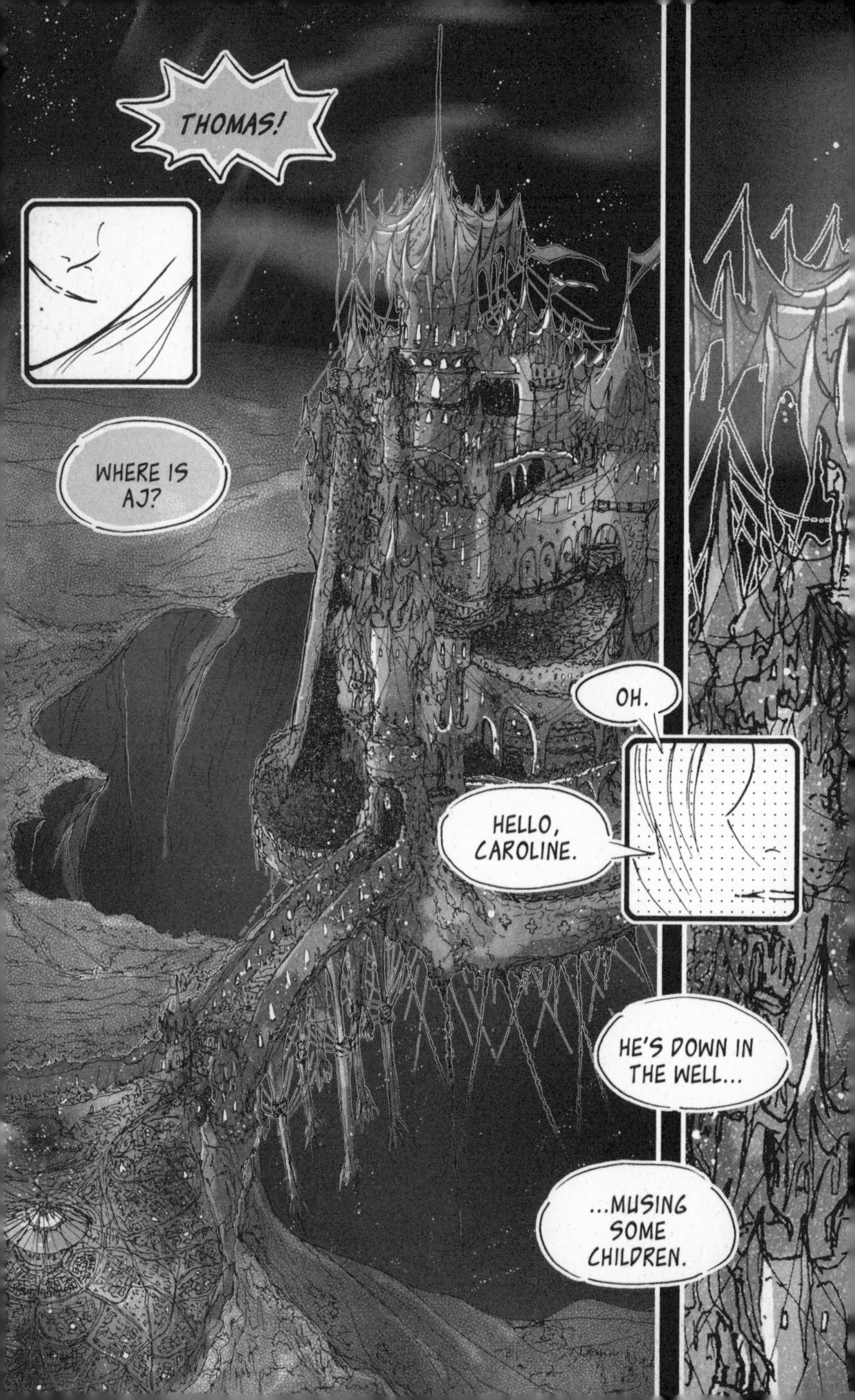
THOMAS!
WHERE IS AJ?
OH.
HELLO, CAROLINE.
HE'S DOWN IN THE WELL...
...MUSING SOME CHILDREN.

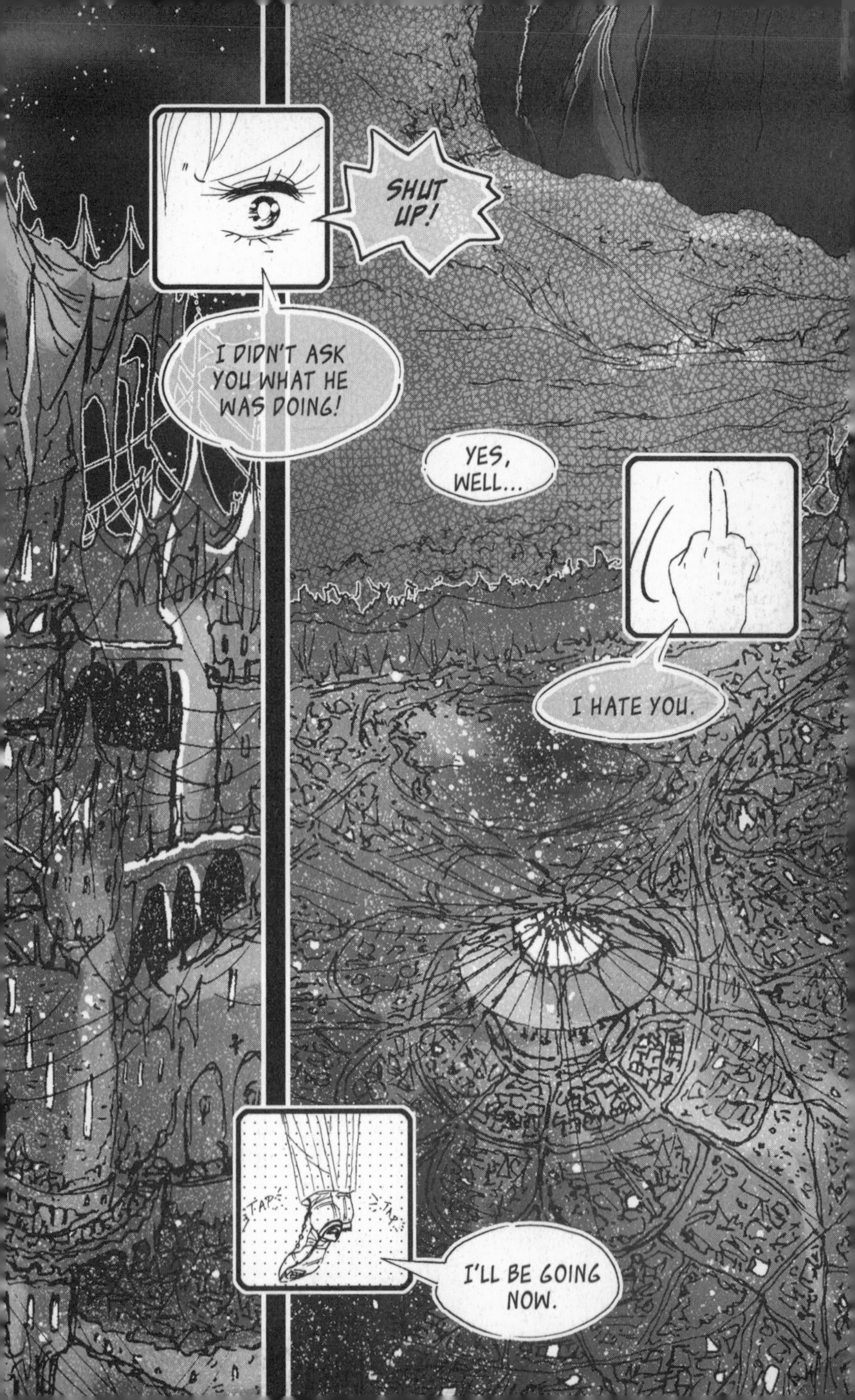
SHUT UP!
I DIDN'T ASK YOU WHAT HE WAS DOING!
YES, WELL...
I HATE YOU.
TAP
TAP
I'LL BE GOING NOW.

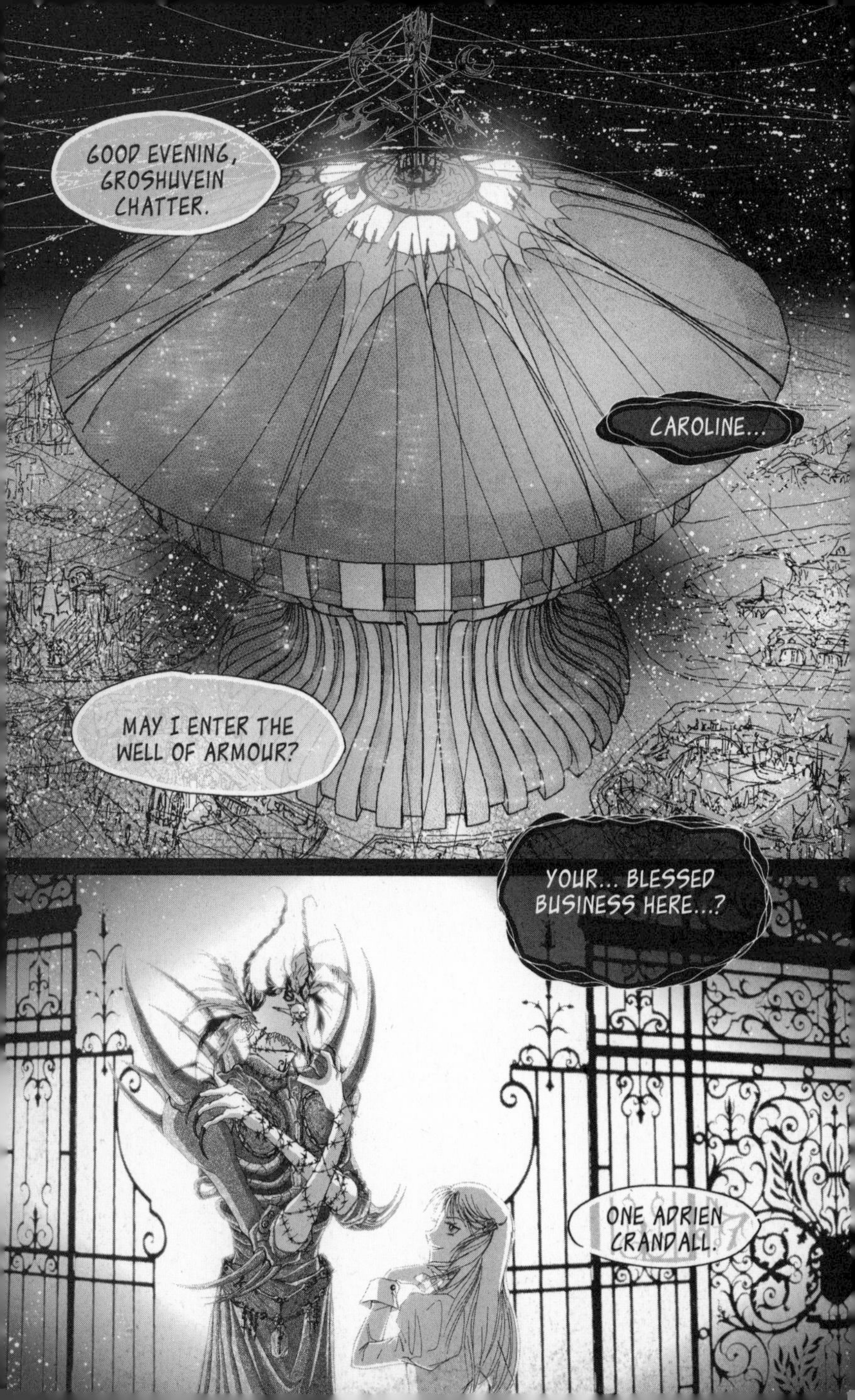
GOOD EVENING, GROSHUVEIN CHATTER.
CAROLINE...
MAY I ENTER THE WELL OF ARMOUR?
YOUR... BLESSED BUSINESS HERE...?
ONE ADRIEN CRANDALL.

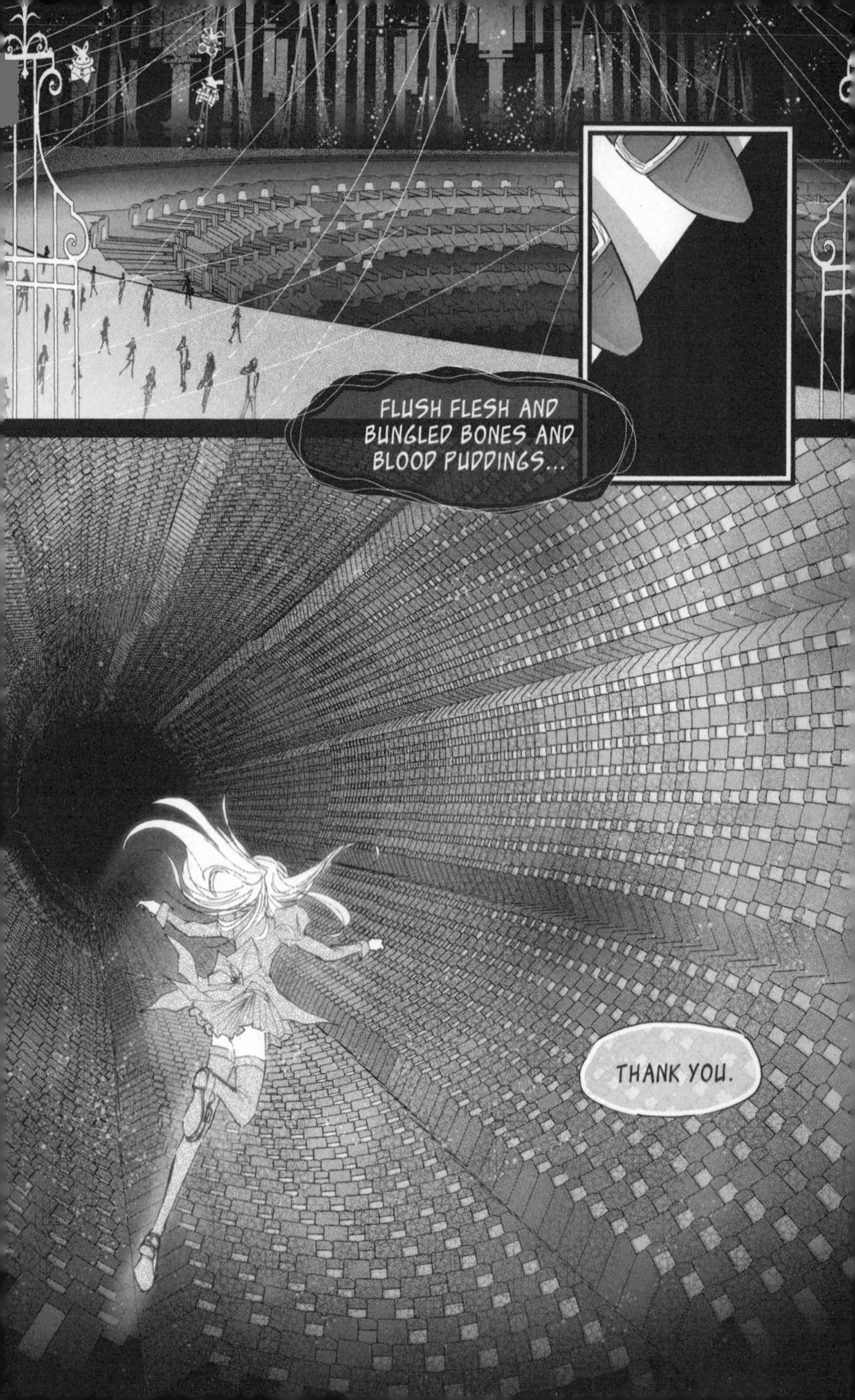
FLUSH FLESH AND BUNGLED BONES AND BLOOD PUDDINGS...
THANK YOU.

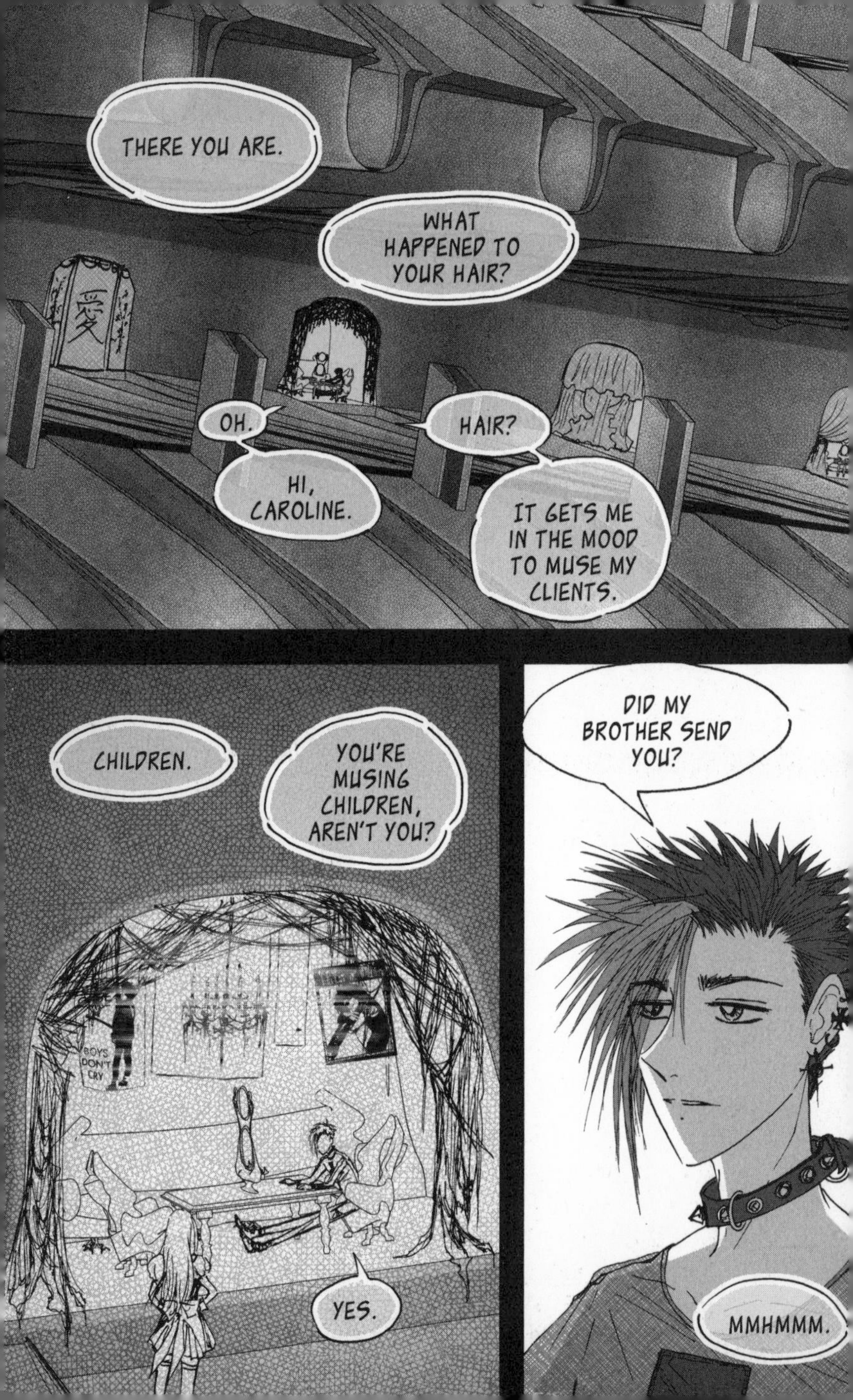
THERE YOU ARE.
WHAT HAPPENED TO YOUR HAIR?
OH.
HI, CAROLINE.
HAIR?
IT GETS ME IN THE MOOD TO MUSE MY CLIENTS.
CHILDREN.
YOU'RE MUSING CHILDREN, AREN'T YOU?
BOYS DON'T CRY
YES.
DID MY BROTHER SEND YOU?
MMHMMM.

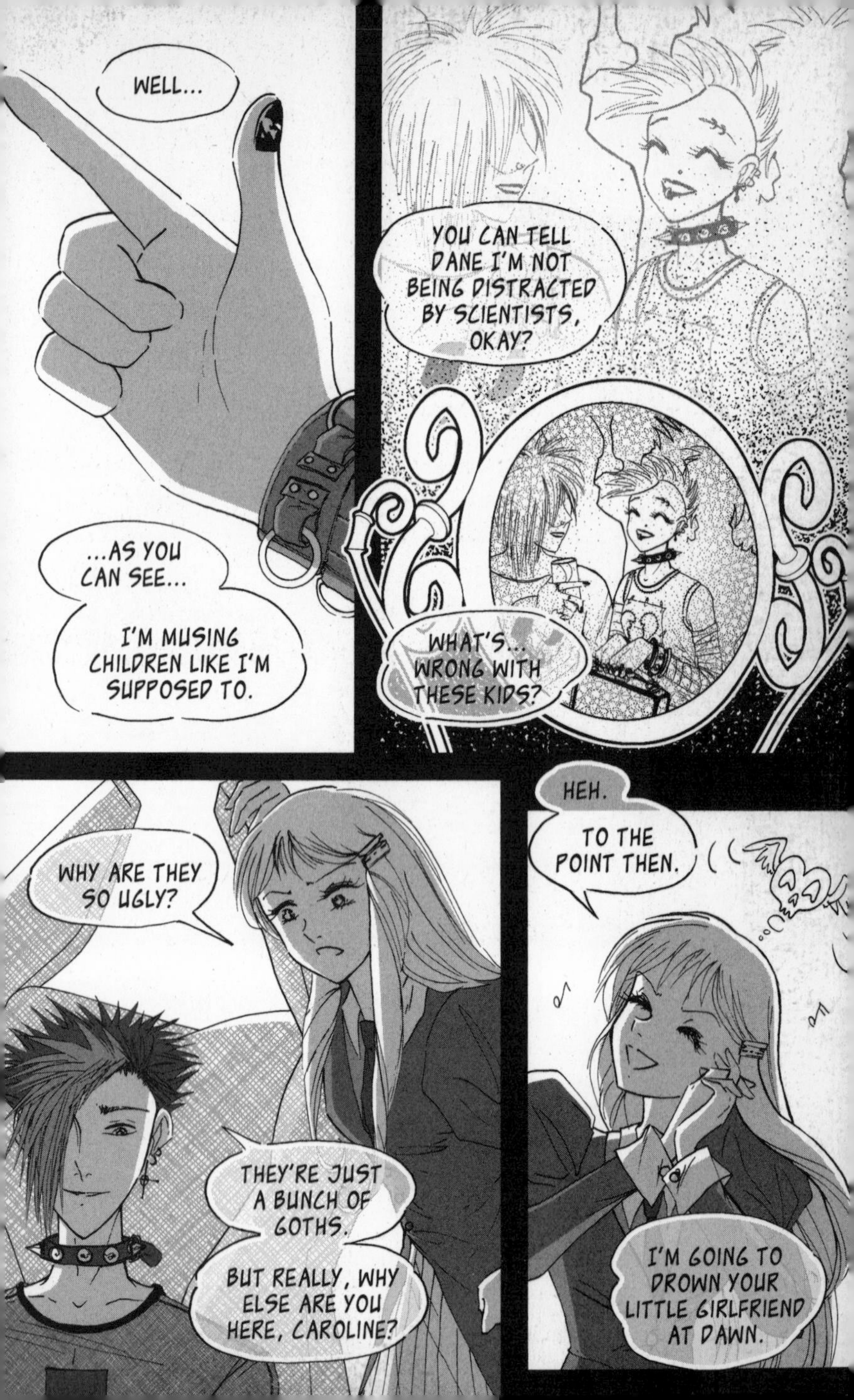
WELL...
...AS YOU CAN SEE...
I'M MUSING CHILDREN LIKE I'M SUPPOSED TO.
YOU CAN TELL DANE I'M NOT BEING DISTRACTED BY SCIENTISTS, OKAY?
WHAT'S... WRONG WITH THESE KIDS?
WHY ARE THEY SO UGLY?
THEY'RE JUST A BUNCH OF GOTHS.
BUT REALLY, WHY ELSE ARE YOU HERE, CAROLINE?
HEH.
TO THE POINT THEN.
I'M GOING TO DROWN YOUR LITTLE GIRLFRIEND AT DAWN.

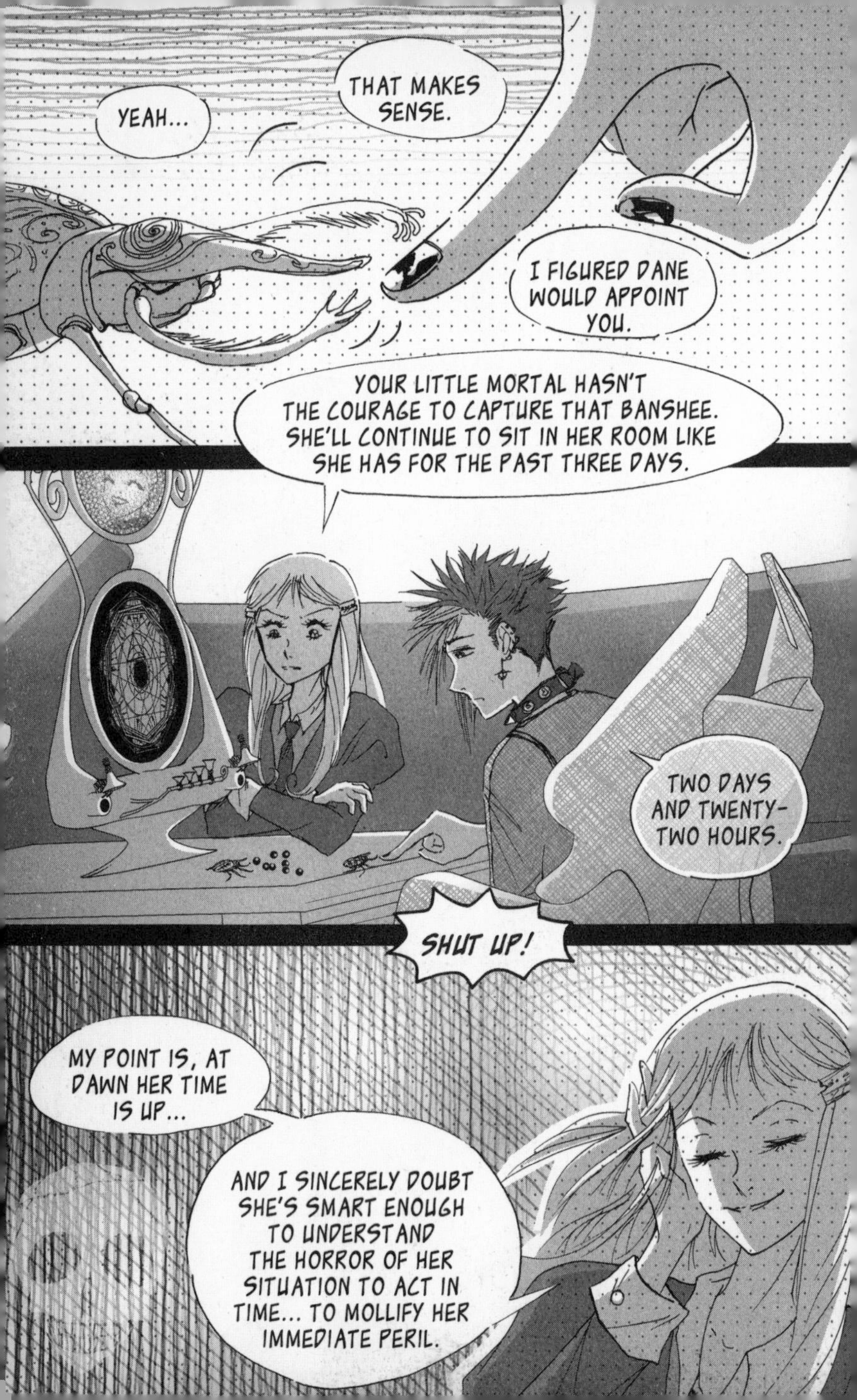
YEAH...
THAT MAKES SENSE.
I FIGURED DANE WOULD APPOINT YOU.
YOUR LITTLE MORTAL HASN'T THE COURAGE TO CAPTURE THAT BANSHEE. SHE'LL CONTINUE TO SIT IN HER ROOM LIKE SHE HAS FOR THE PAST THREE DAYS.
TWO DAYS AND TWENTY-TWO HOURS.
SHUT UP!
MY POINT IS, AT DAWN HER TIME IS UP...
AND I SINCERELY DOUBT SHE'S SMART ENOUGH TO UNDERSTAND THE HORROR OF HER SITUATION TO ACT IN TIME... TO MOLLIFY HER IMMEDIATE PERIL.

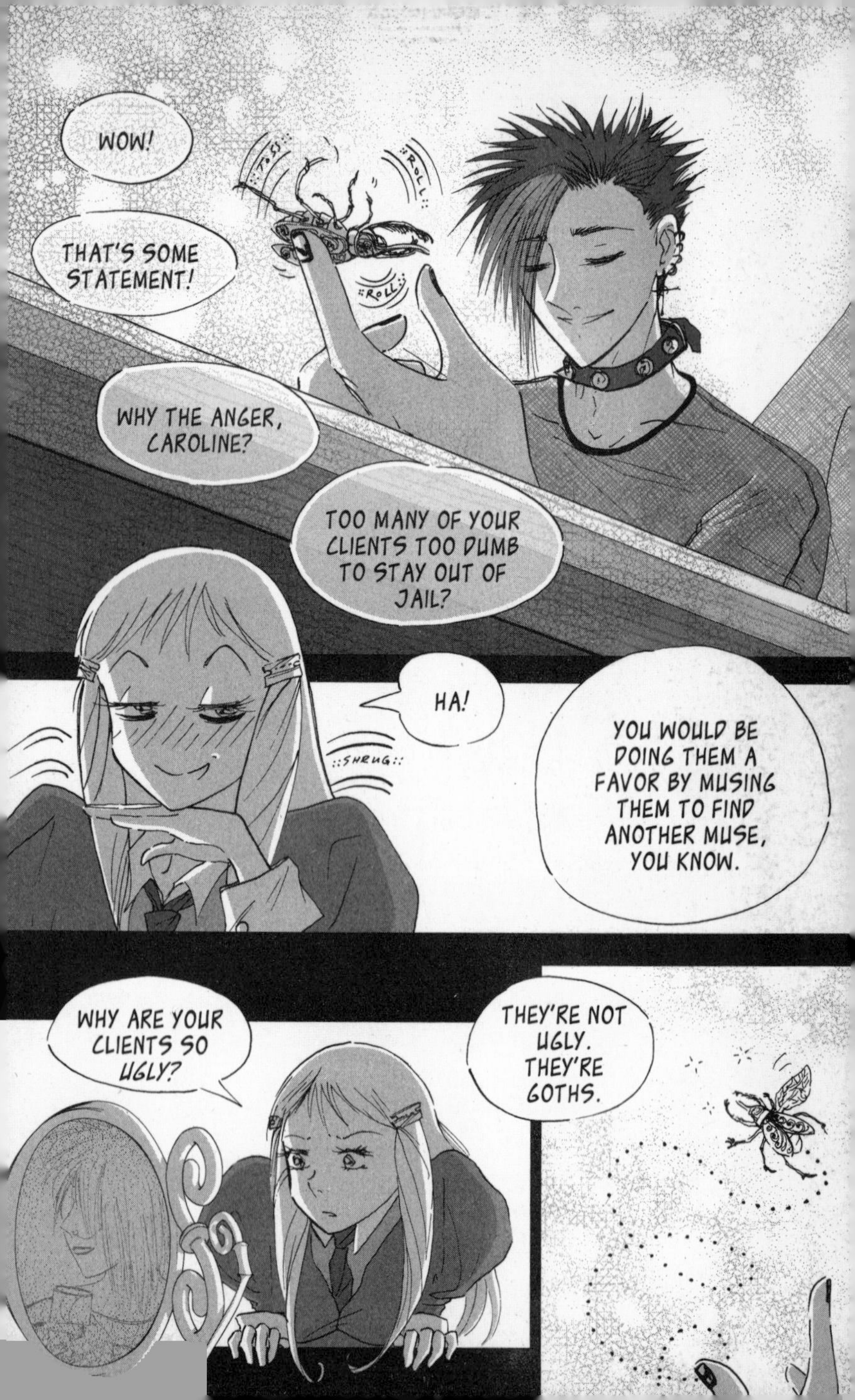
WOW!
THAT'S SOME STATEMENT!
::TOSS::
::ROLL::
::ROLL::
WHY THE ANGER, CAROLINE?
TOO MANY OF YOUR CLIENTS TOO DUMB TO STAY OUT OF JAIL?
HA!
::SHRUG::
YOU WOULD BE DOING THEM A FAVOR BY MUSING THEM TO FIND ANOTHER MUSE, YOU KNOW.
WHY ARE YOUR CLIENTS SO UGLY?
THEY'RE NOT UGLY. THEY'RE GOTHS.

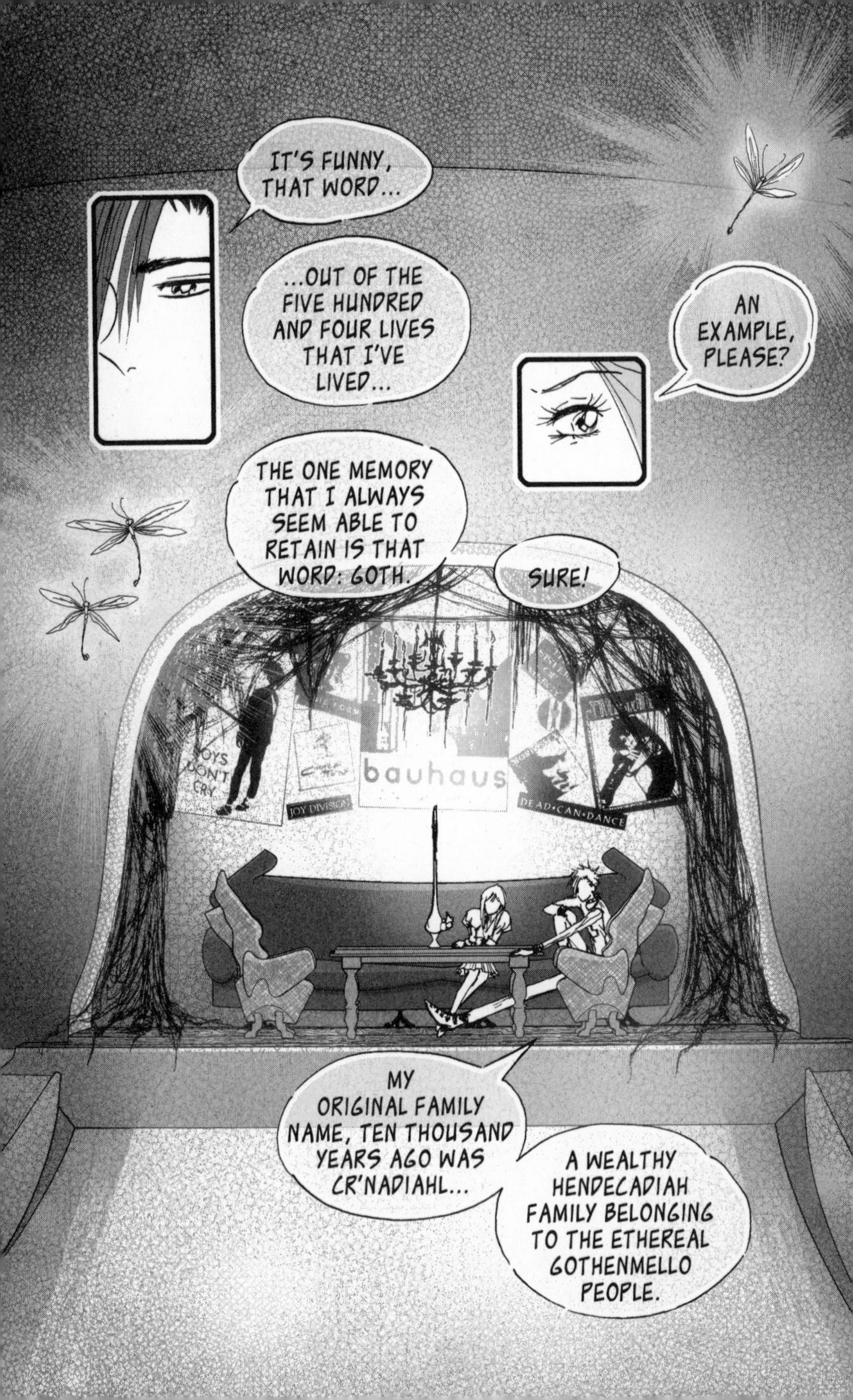
IT'S FUNNY, THAT WORD...
...OUT OF THE FIVE HUNDRED AND FOUR LIVES THAT I'VE LIVED...
AN EXAMPLE, PLEASE?
THE ONE MEMORY THAT I ALWAYS SEEM ABLE TO RETAIN IS THAT WORD: GOTH.
SURE!
BOYS DON'T CRY
JOY DIVISION
bauhaus
DEAD·CAN·DANCE
MY ORIGINAL FAMILY NAME, TEN THOUSAND YEARS AGO WAS CR'NADIAHL...
A WEALTHY HENDECADIAH FAMILY BELONGING TO THE ETHEREAL GOTHENMELLO PEOPLE.

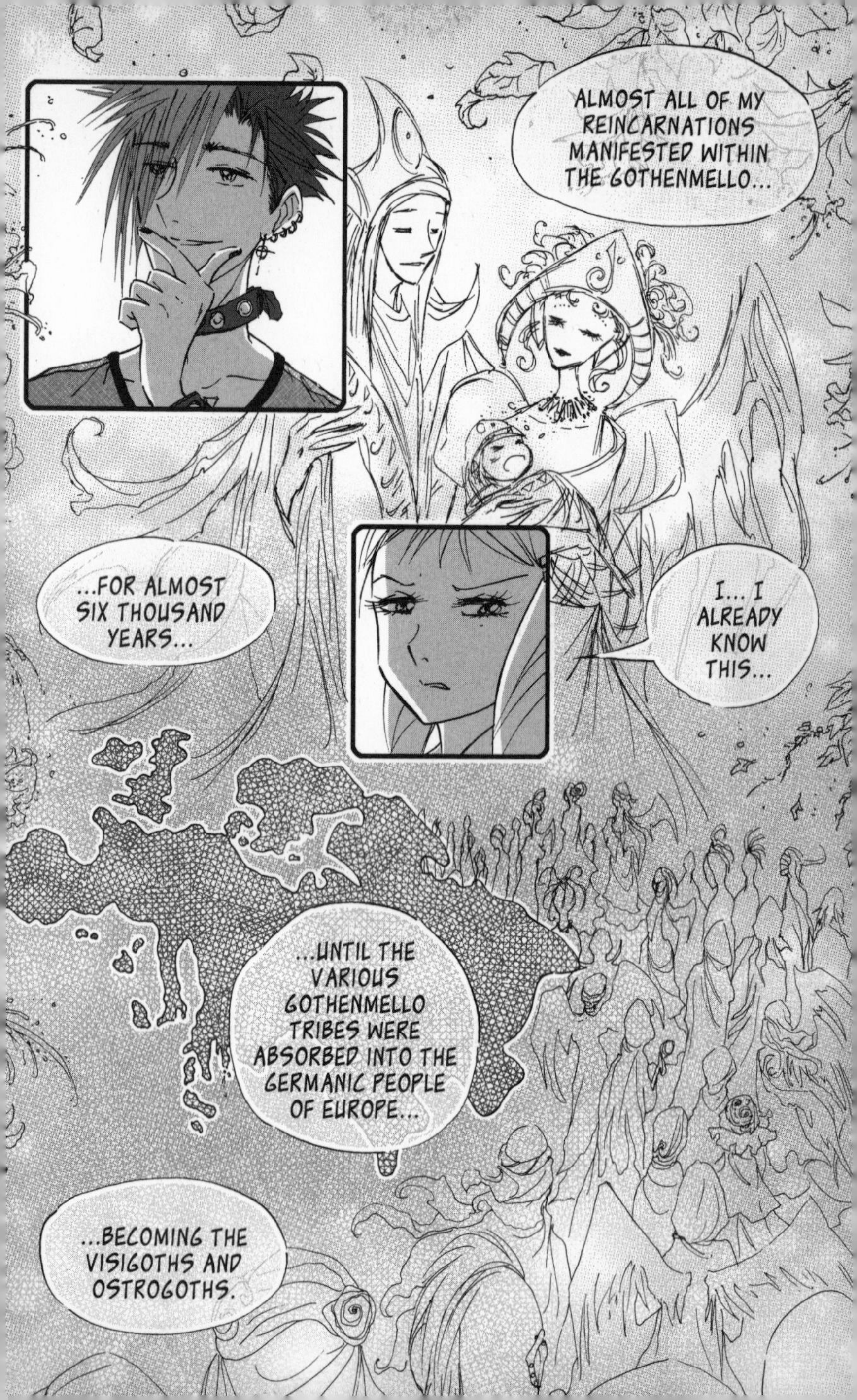
ALMOST ALL OF MY REINCARNATIONS MANIFESTED WITHIN THE GOTHENMELLO...
...FOR ALMOST SIX THOUSAND YEARS...
I... I ALREADY KNOW THIS...
...UNTIL THE VARIOUS GOTHENMELLO TRIBES WERE ABSORBED INTO THE GERMANIC PEOPLE OF EUROPE...
...BECOMING THE VISIGOTHS AND OSTROGOTHS.

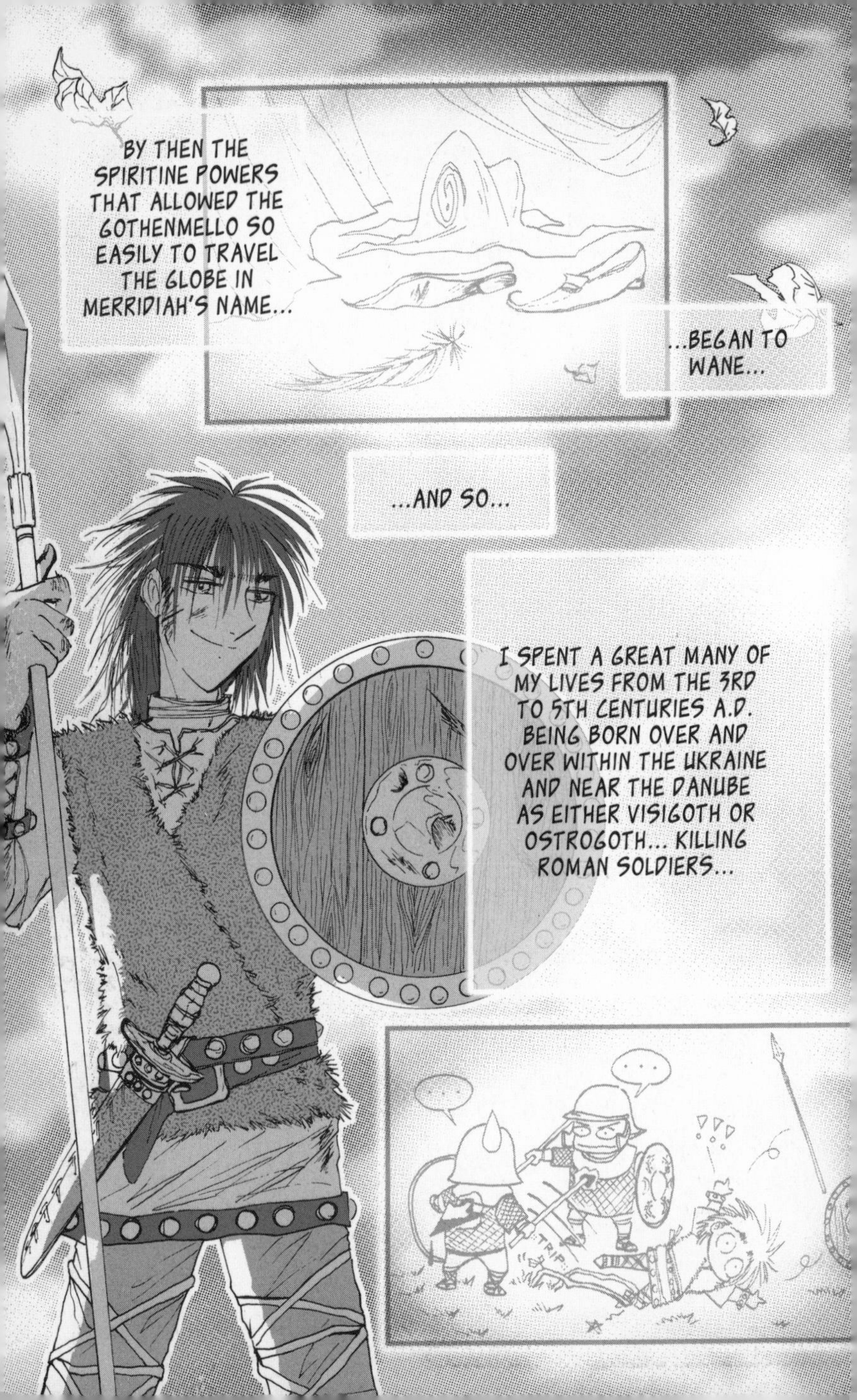
BY THEN THE SPIRITINE POWERS THAT ALLOWED THE GOTHENMELLO SO EASILY TO TRAVEL THE GLOBE IN MERRIDIAH'S NAME...
...BEGAN TO WANE...
...AND SO...
I SPENT A GREAT MANY OF MY LIVES FROM THE 3RD TO 5TH CENTURIES A.D. BEING BORN OVER AND OVER WITHIN THE UKRAINE AND NEAR THE DANUBE AS EITHER VISIGOTH OR OSTROGOTH... KILLING ROMAN SOLDIERS...
TRIP

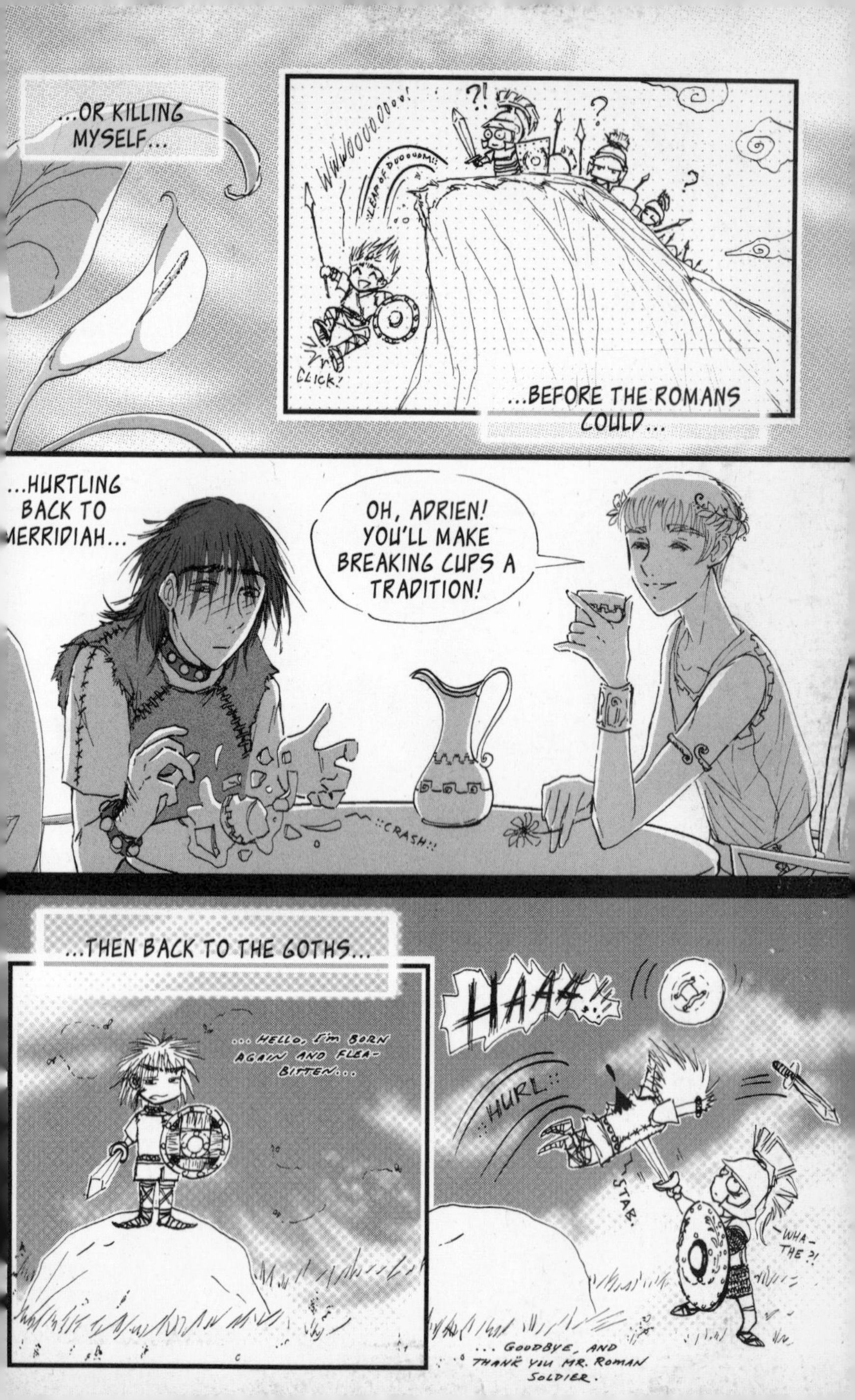
...OR KILLING MYSELF...
?!
?
LEAP OF DOOOOOM!!
CLICK!
...BEFORE THE ROMANS COULD...
...HURTLING BACK TO MERRIDIAH...
OH, ADRIEN! YOU'LL MAKE BREAKING CUPS A TRADITION!
CRASH!!
...THEN BACK TO THE GOTHS...
...HELLO, I'm BORN AGAIN AND FLEA-BITTEN...
HAAA!!
HURL
STAB.
WHA- THE?!
...GOODBYE, AND THANK YOU MR. ROMAN SOLDIER.

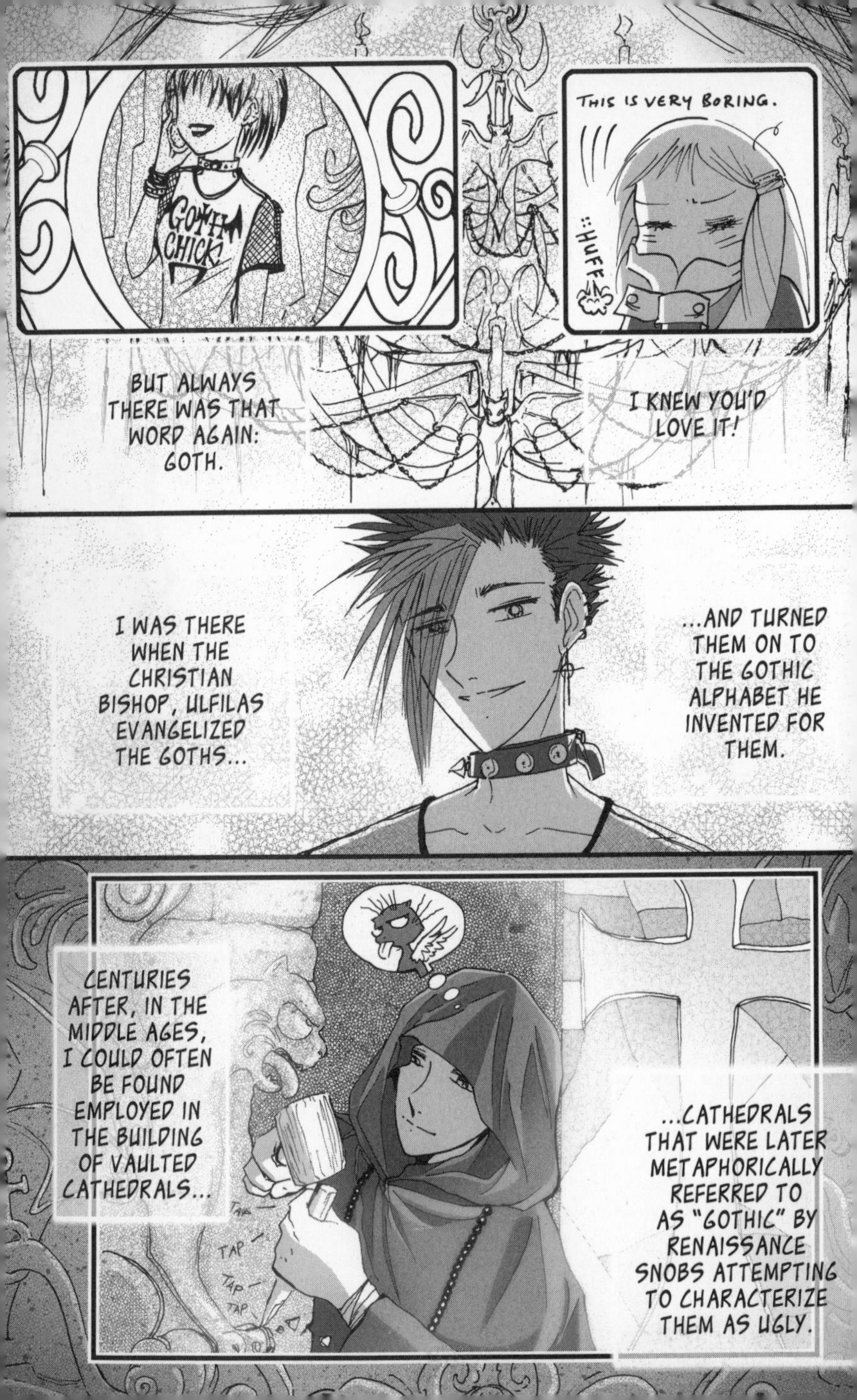
GOTH CHICK!
THIS IS VERY BORING.
::HUFF::
BUT ALWAYS THERE WAS THAT WORD AGAIN: GOTH.
I KNEW YOU'D LOVE IT!
I WAS THERE WHEN THE CHRISTIAN BISHOP, ULFILAS EVANGELIZED THE GOTHS...
...AND TURNED THEM ON TO THE GOTHIC ALPHABET HE INVENTED FOR THEM.
CENTURIES AFTER, IN THE MIDDLE AGES, I COULD OFTEN BE FOUND EMPLOYED IN THE BUILDING OF VAULTED CATHEDRALS...
TAP
TAP
TAP
TAP
...CATHEDRALS THAT WERE LATER METAPHORICALLY REFERRED TO AS "GOTHIC" BY RENAISSANCE SNOBS ATTEMPTING TO CHARACTERIZE THEM AS UGLY.

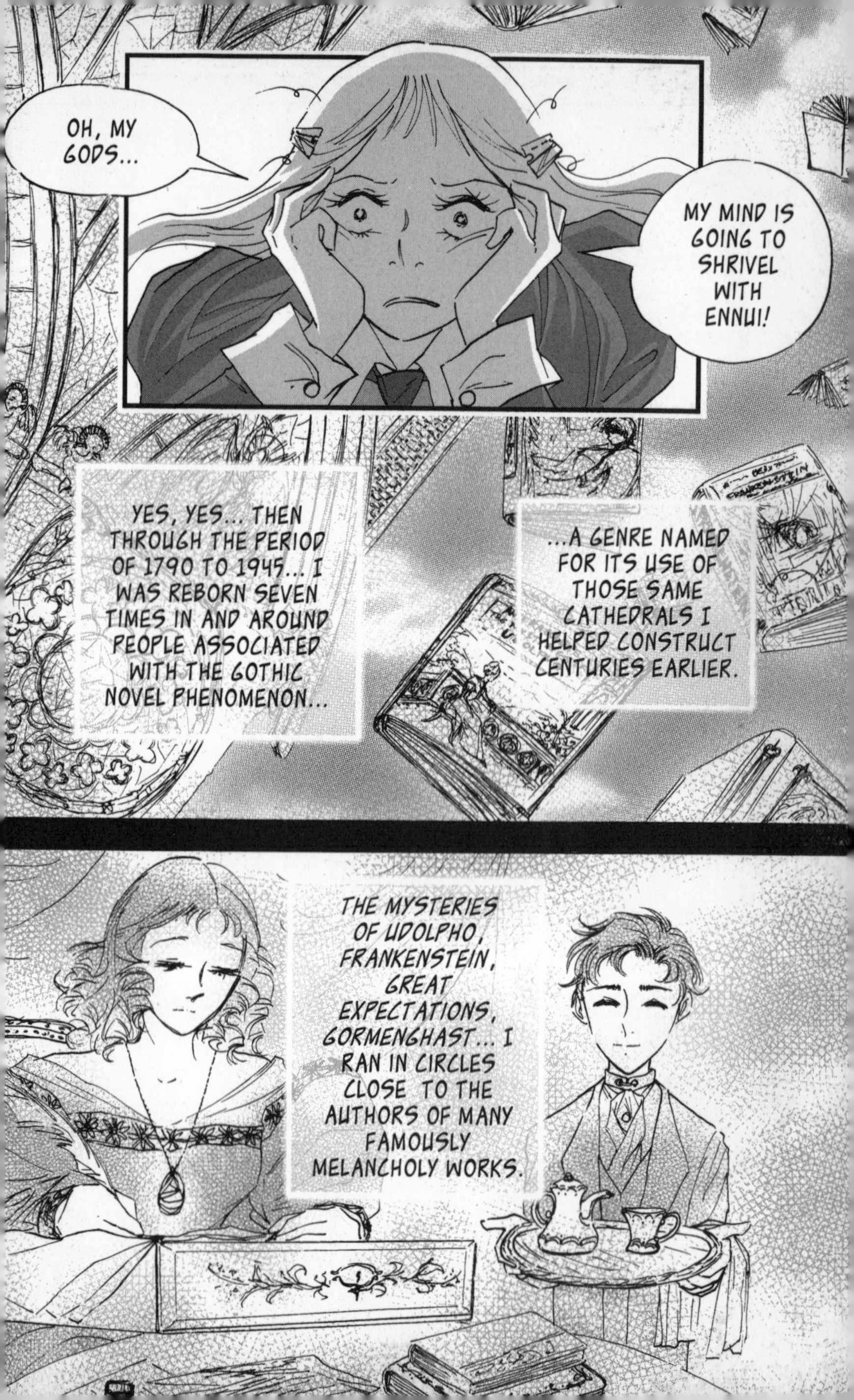
OH, MY GODS...
MY MIND IS GOING TO SHRIVEL WITH ENNUI!
YES, YES... THEN THROUGH THE PERIOD OF 1790 TO 1945... I WAS REBORN SEVEN TIMES IN AND AROUND PEOPLE ASSOCIATED WITH THE GOTHIC NOVEL PHENOMENON...
...A GENRE NAMED FOR ITS USE OF THOSE SAME CATHEDRALS I HELPED CONSTRUCT CENTURIES EARLIER.
THE MYSTERIES OF UDOLPHO, FRANKENSTEIN, GREAT EXPECTATIONS, GORMENGHAST... I RAN IN CIRCLES CLOSE TO THE AUTHORS OF MANY FAMOUSLY MELANCHOLY WORKS.

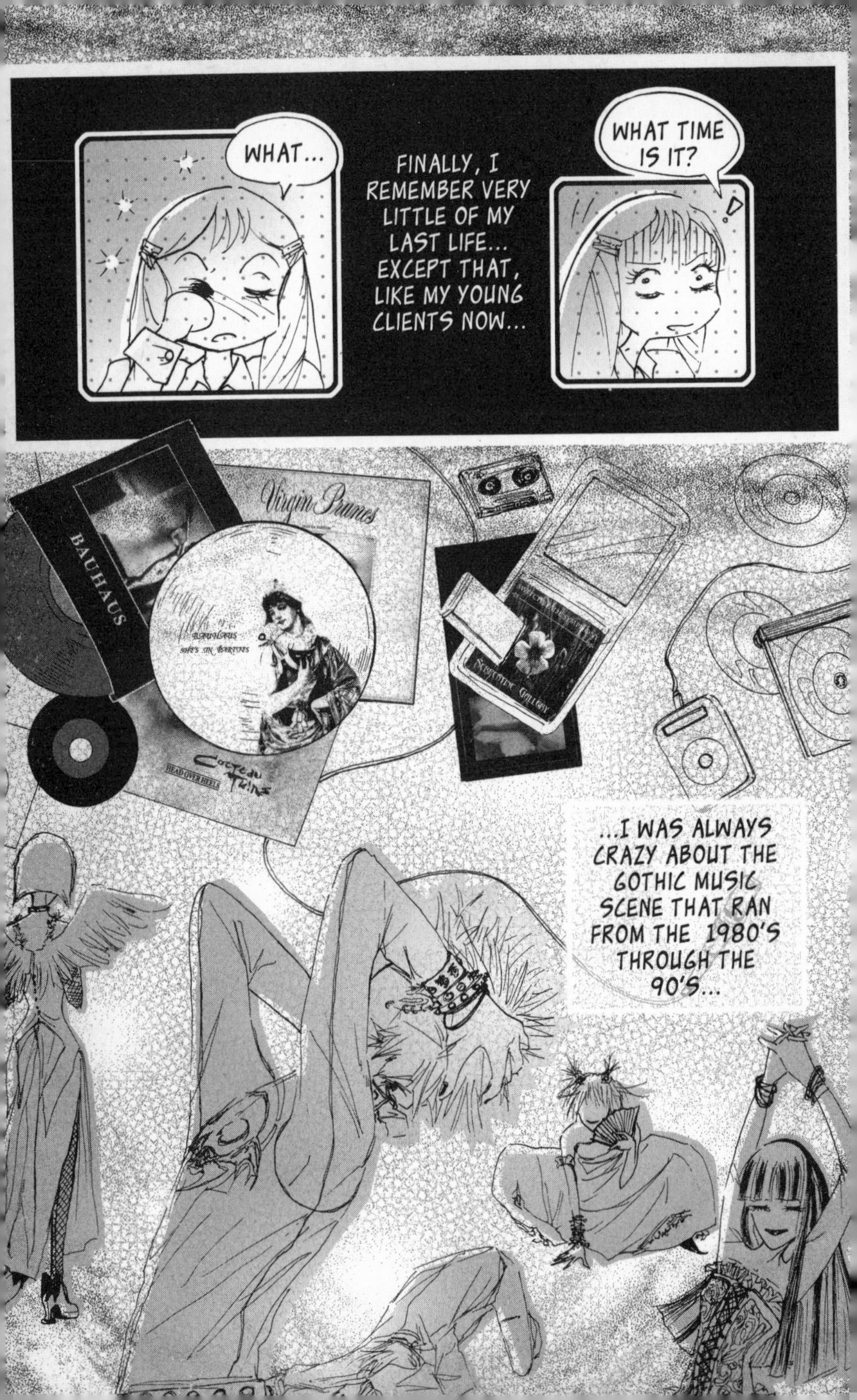

WHAT...
FINALLY, I REMEMBER VERY LITTLE OF MY LAST LIFE... EXCEPT THAT, LIKE MY YOUNG CLIENTS NOW...
WHAT TIME IS IT?
!
BAUHAUS
Virgin Prunes
Cocteau Twins
HEAD OVER HEELS
...I WAS ALWAYS CRAZY ABOUT THE GOTHIC MUSIC SCENE THAT RAN FROM THE 1980'S THROUGH THE 90'S...

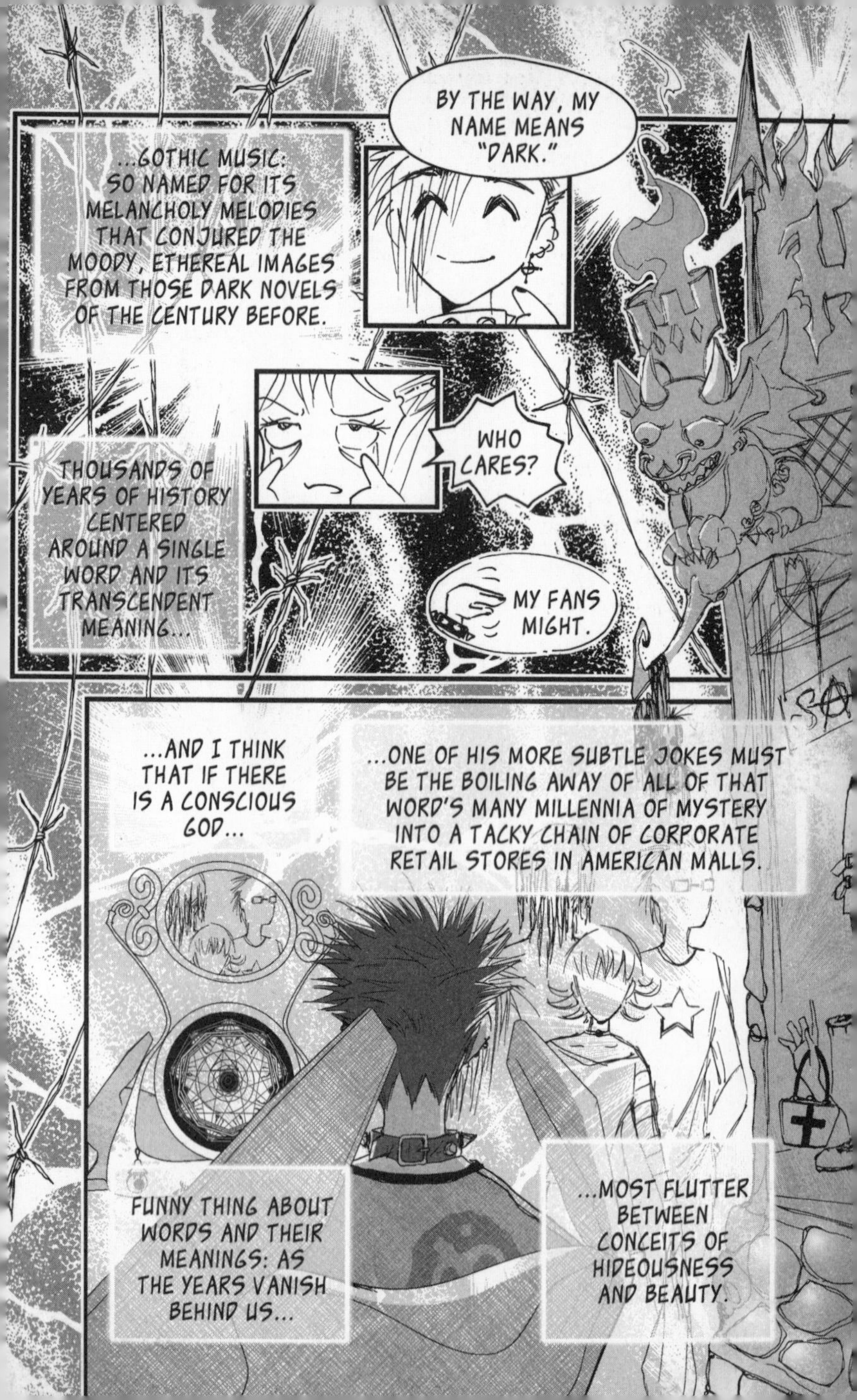
...GOTHIC MUSIC: SO NAMED FOR ITS MELANCHOLY MELODIES THAT CONJURED THE MOODY, ETHEREAL IMAGES FROM THOSE DARK NOVELS OF THE CENTURY BEFORE.
BY THE WAY, MY NAME MEANS "DARK."
WHO CARES?
THOUSANDS OF YEARS OF HISTORY CENTERED AROUND A SINGLE WORD AND ITS TRANSCENDENT MEANING...
MY FANS MIGHT.
...AND I THINK THAT IF THERE IS A CONSCIOUS GOD...
...ONE OF HIS MORE SUBTLE JOKES MUST BE THE BOILING AWAY OF ALL OF THAT WORD'S MANY MILLENNIA OF MYSTERY INTO A TACKY CHAIN OF CORPORATE RETAIL STORES IN AMERICAN MALLS.
FUNNY THING ABOUT WORDS AND THEIR MEANINGS: AS THE YEARS VANISH BEHIND US...
...MOST FLUTTER BETWEEN CONCEITS OF HIDEOUSNESS AND BEAUTY.

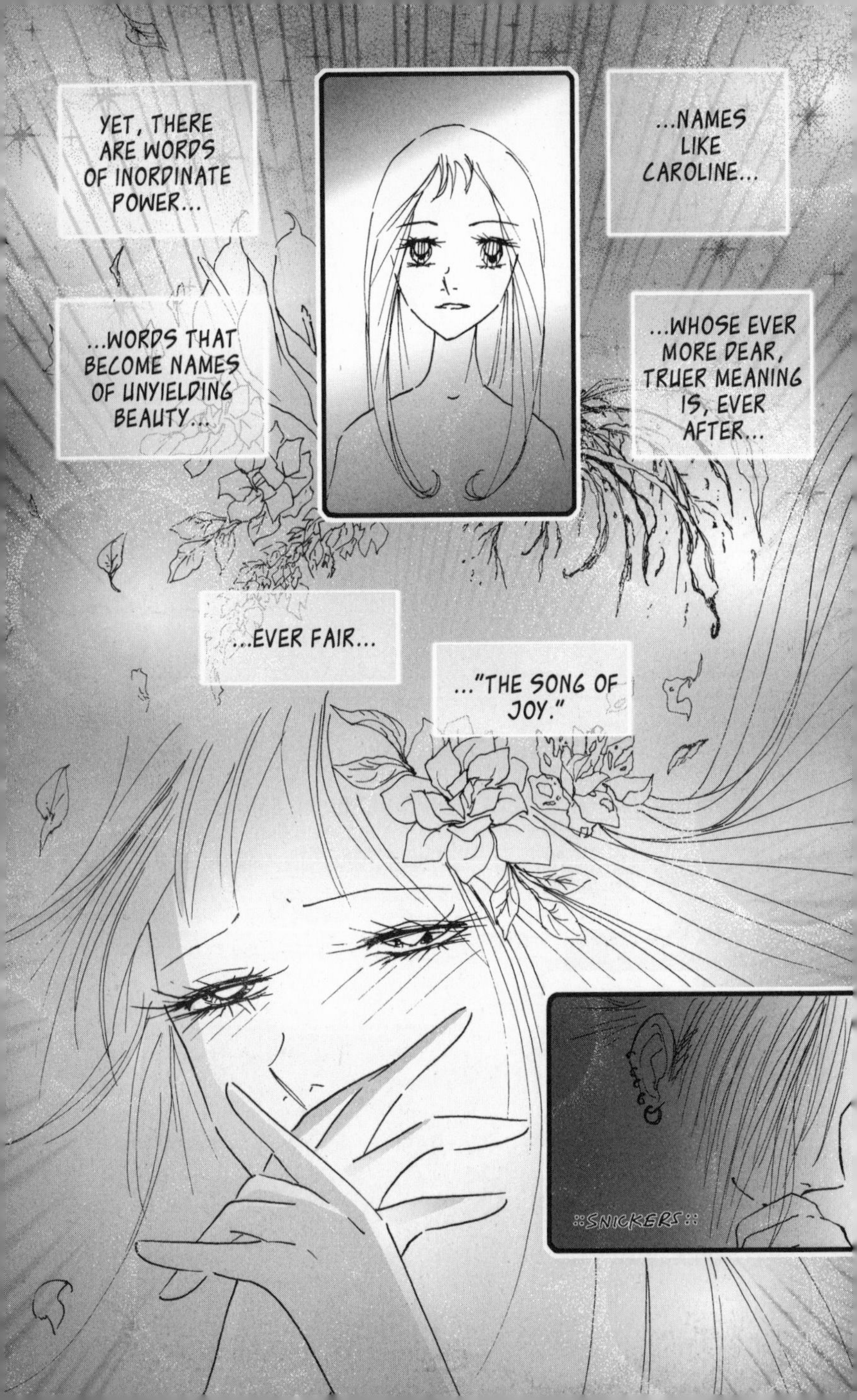
YET, THERE ARE WORDS OF INORDINATE POWER...
...NAMES LIKE CAROLINE...
...WORDS THAT BECOME NAMES OF UNYIELDING BEAUTY...
...WHOSE EVER MORE DEAR, TRUER MEANING IS, EVER AFTER...
...EVER FAIR...
..."THE SONG OF JOY."
::SNICKERS::

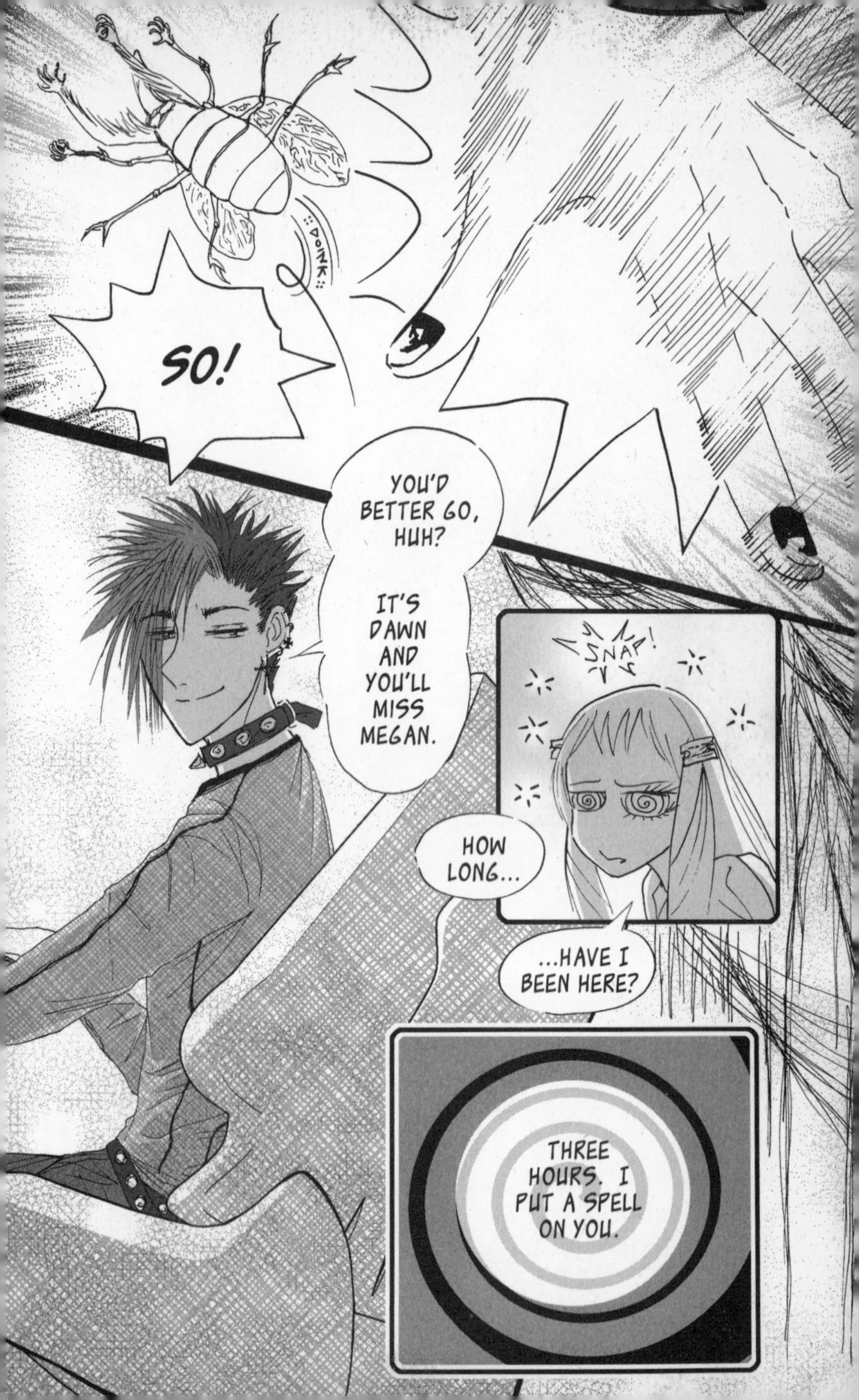
:: DOINK ::
SO!
YOU'D BETTER GO, HUH?
IT'S DAWN AND YOU'LL MISS MEGAN.
SNAP!
HOW LONG...
...HAVE I BEEN HERE?
THREE HOURS. I PUT A SPELL ON YOU.

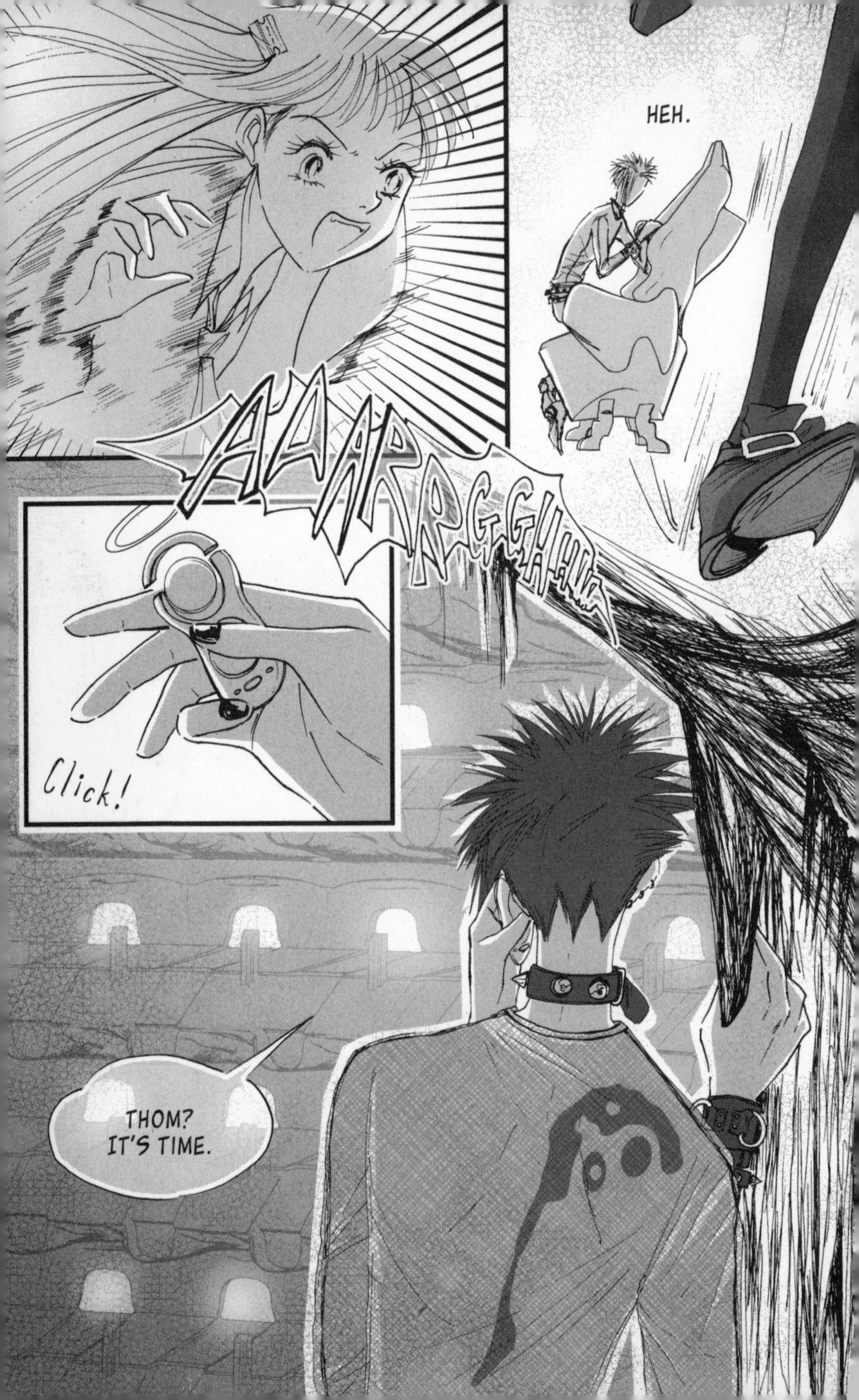
AAARRGGHHH
HEH.
Click!
THOM?
IT'S TIME.

CHAPTER TWO:

WHAT IS

DECOHERENCE

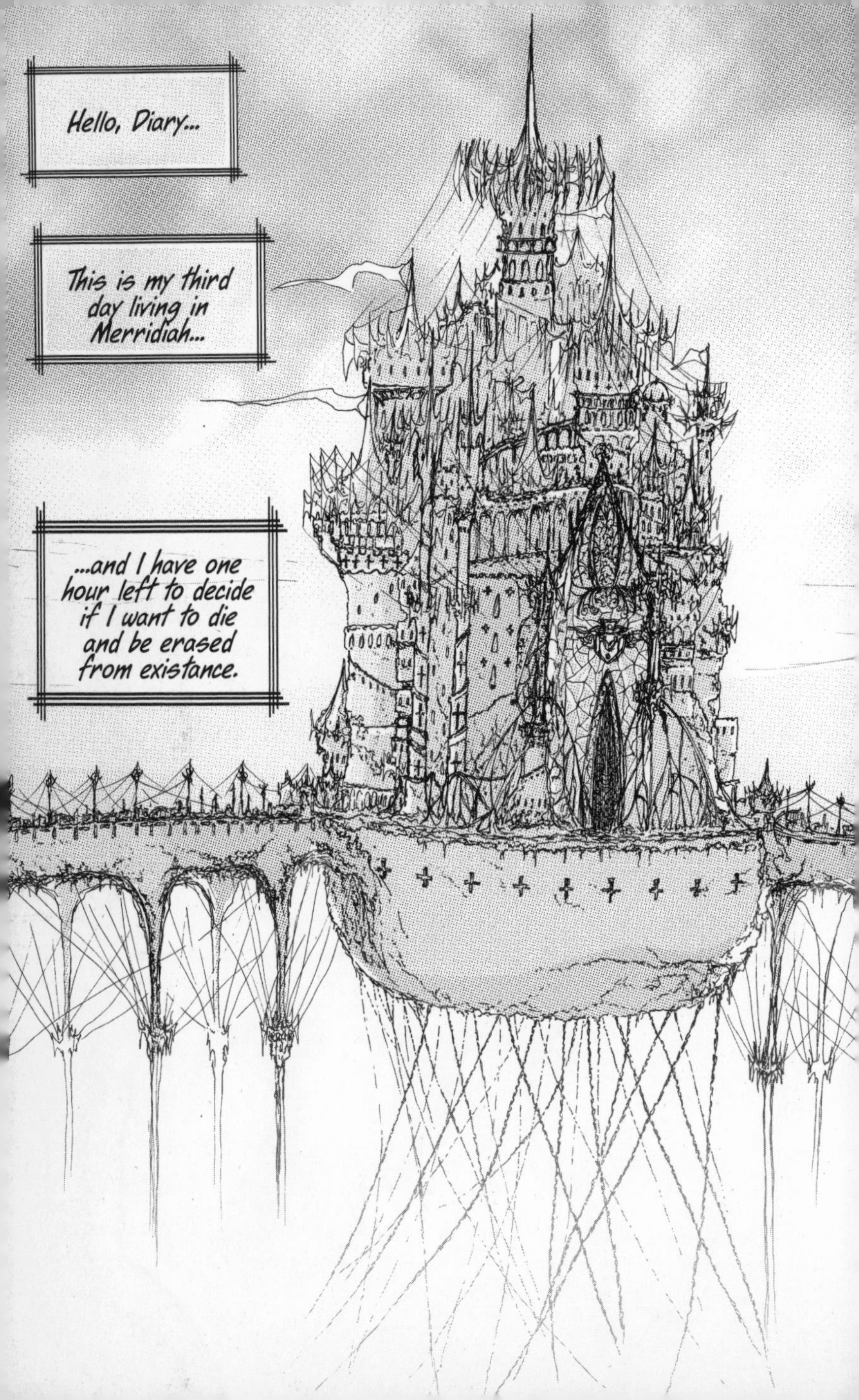
Hello, Diary...
This is my third day living in Merridiah...
...and I have one hour left to decide if I want to die and be erased from existance.

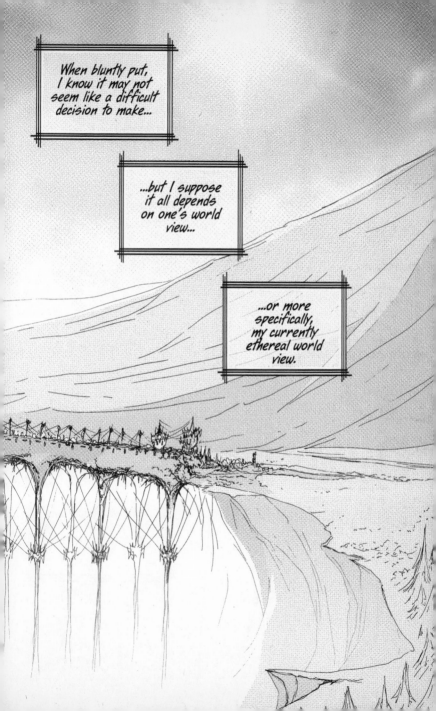

When bluntly put, I know it may not seem like a difficult decision to make...

...but I suppose it all depends on one's world view...

...or more specifically, my currently ethereal world view.

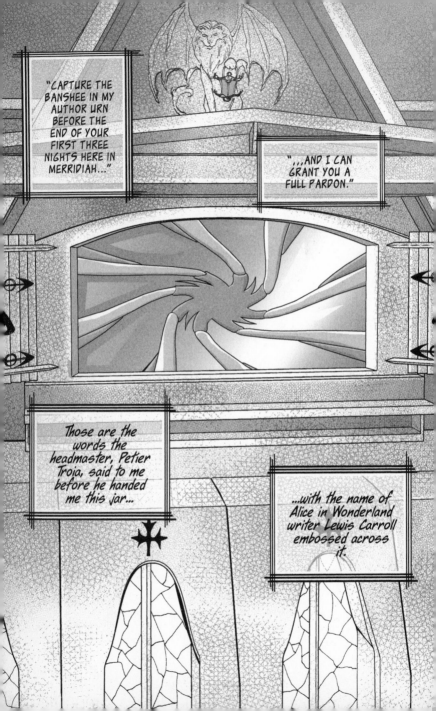

"CAPTURE THE BANSHEE IN MY AUTHOR URN BEFORE THE END OF YOUR FIRST THREE NIGHTS HERE IN MERRIDIAH..."

"...AND I CAN GRANT YOU A FULL PARDON."

Those are the words the headmaster, Petier Troia, said to me before he handed me this jar...

...with the name of Alice in Wonderland writer Lewis Carroll embossed across it.

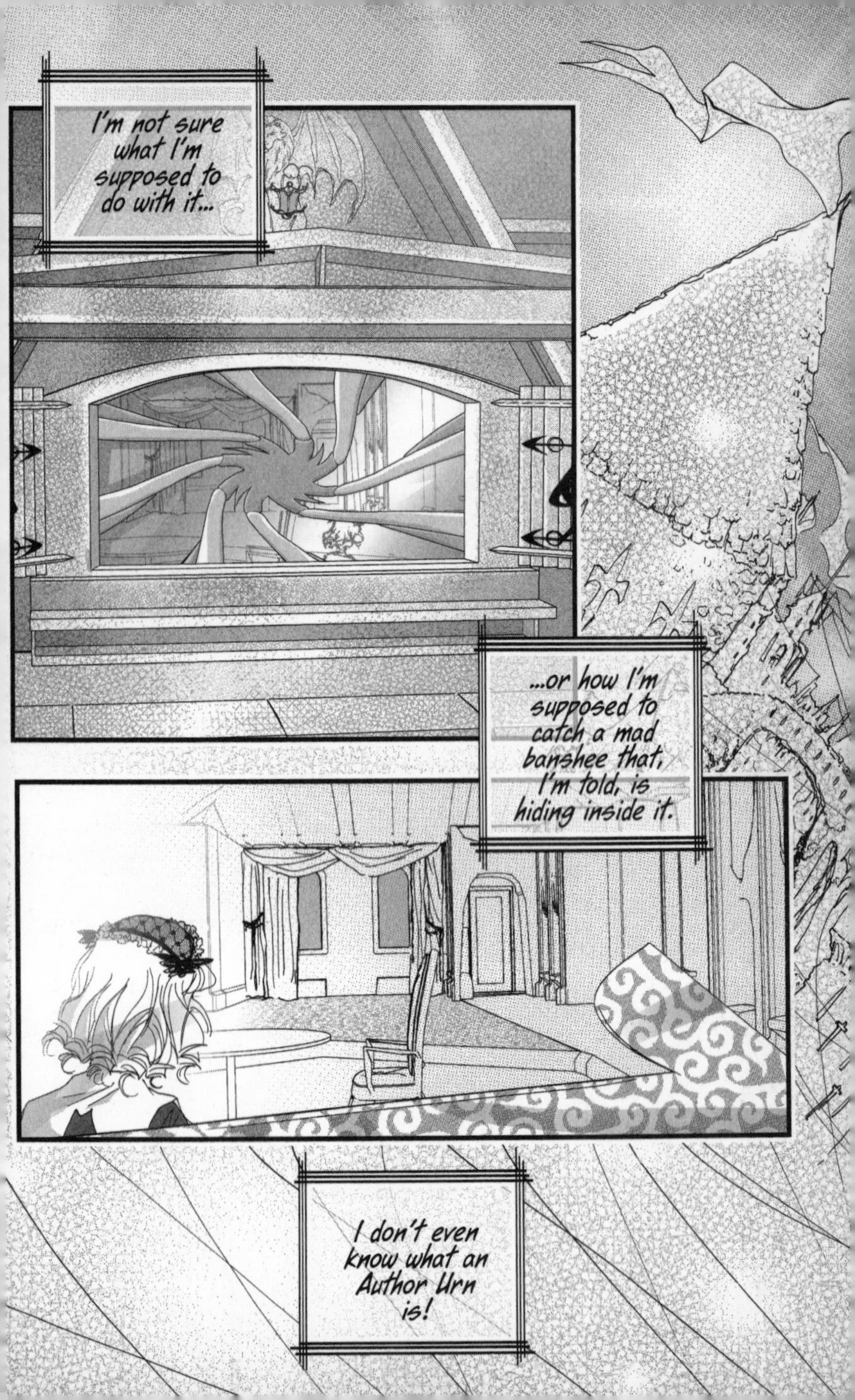
I'm not sure what I'm supposed to do with it...
...or how I'm supposed to catch a mad banshee that, I'm told, is hiding inside it.
I don't even know what an Author Urn is!

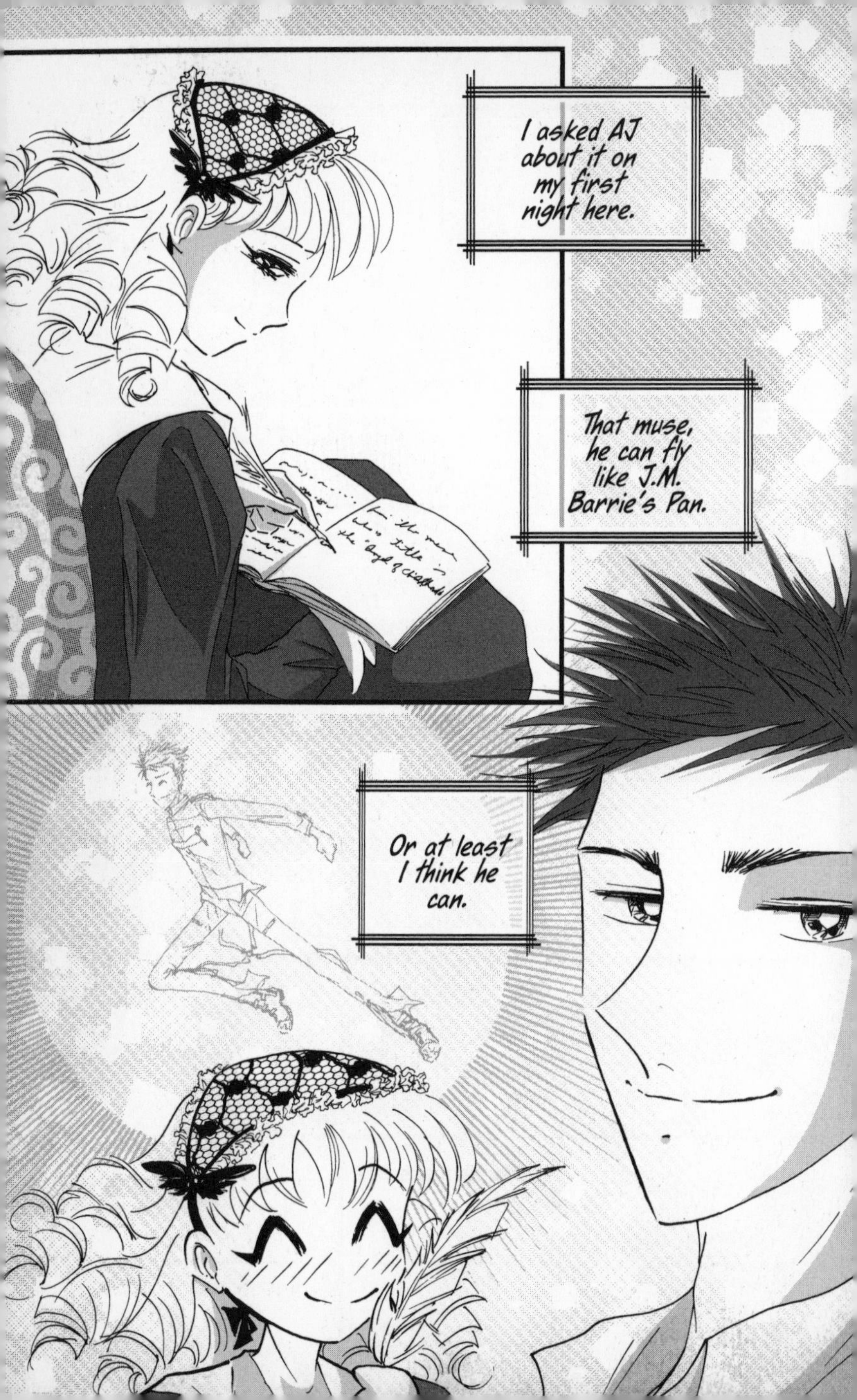
I asked AJ about it on my first night here.
That muse, he can fly like J.M. Barrie's Pan.
Or at least I think he can.

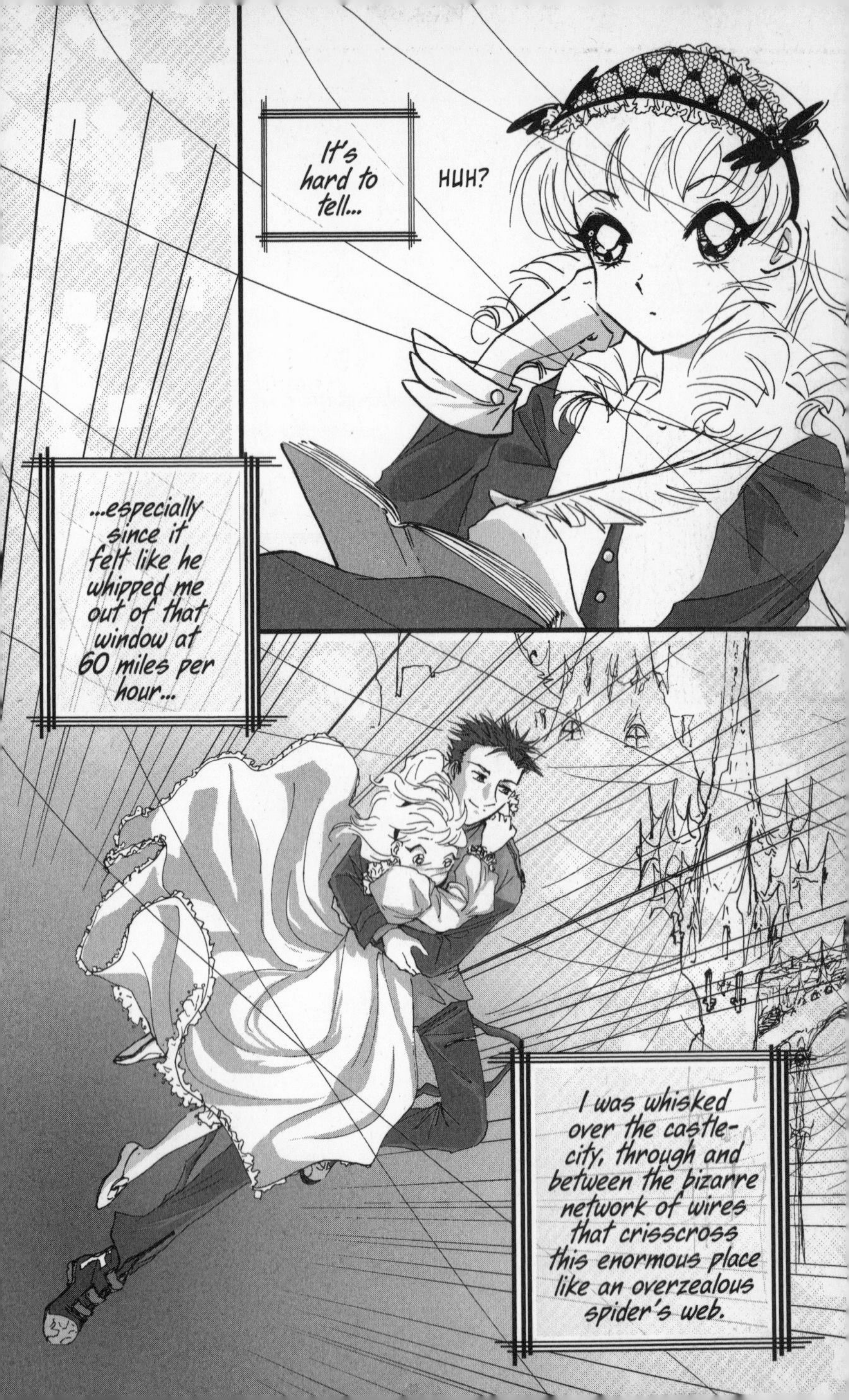
It's hard to tell...
HUH?
...especially since it felt like he whipped me out of that window at 60 miles per hour...
I was whisked over the castle-city, through and between the bizarre network of wires that crisscross this enormous place like an overzealous spider's web.

That's when I clung on for dear-what-remains-of-my-life...

life," whilst the winds ripped and rushed... I were a

...whilst the winds rushed through me as if I were already a ghost.

That's odd, I usually never use "whilst" in my writing because it reminds me of my mean ol' British grandmother.

It's strange that it's ceased to bother me now...

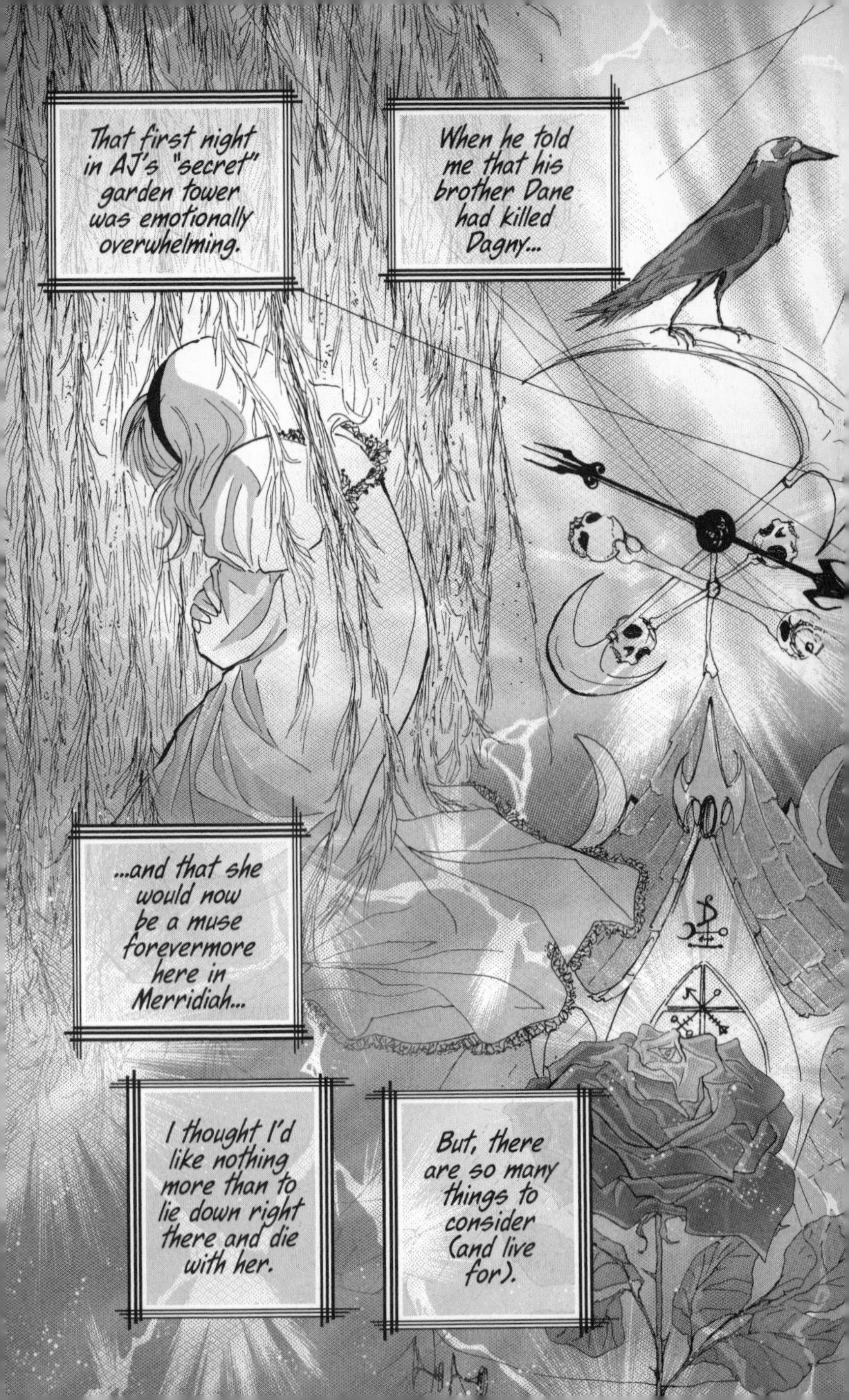
That first night in AJ's "secret" garden tower was emotionally overwhelming.
When he told me that his brother Dane had killed Dagny...
...and that she would now be a muse forevermore here in Merridiah...
I thought I'd like nothing more than to lie down right there and die with her.
But, there are so many things to consider (and live for).

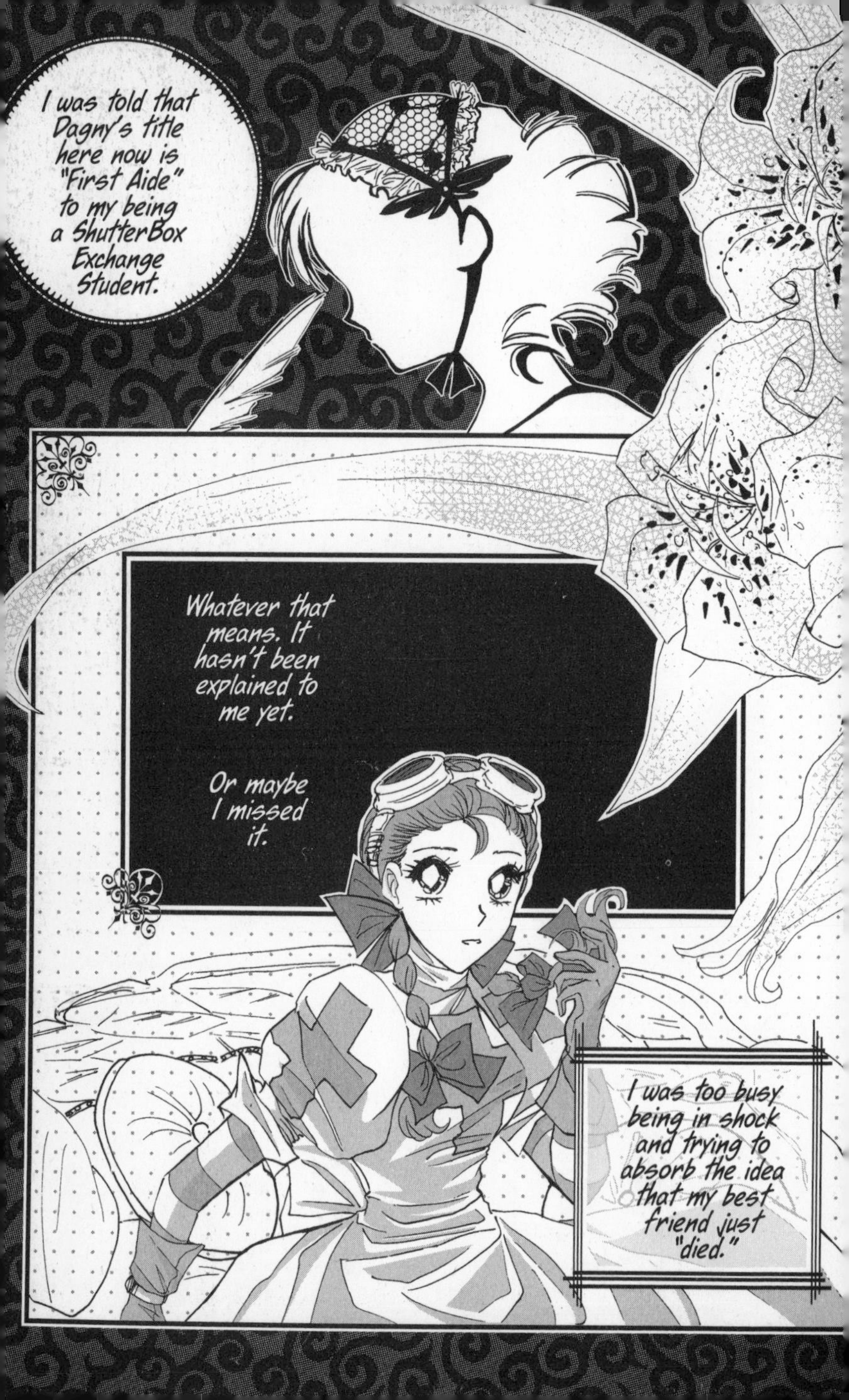
I was told that Dagny's title here now is "First Aide" to my being a ShutterBox Exchange Student.
Whatever that means. It hasn't been explained to me yet.
Or maybe I missed it.
I was too busy being in shock and trying to absorb the idea that my best friend just "died."

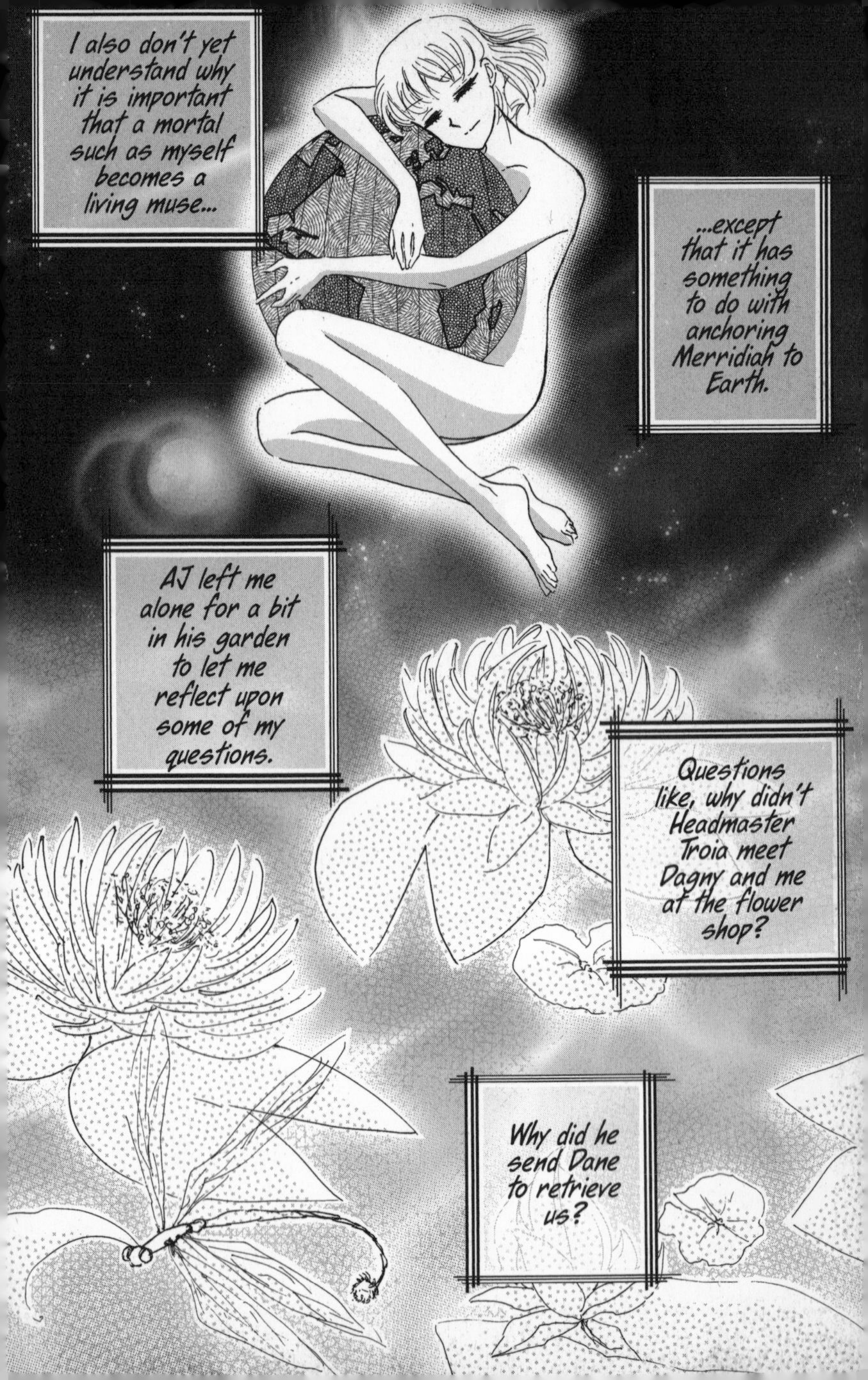
I also don't yet understand why it is important that a mortal such as myself becomes a living muse...
...except that it has something to do with anchoring Merridiah to Earth.
AJ left me alone for a bit in his garden to let me reflect upon some of my questions.
Questions like, why didn't Headmaster Troia meet Dagny and me at the flower shop?
Why did he send Dane to retrieve us?

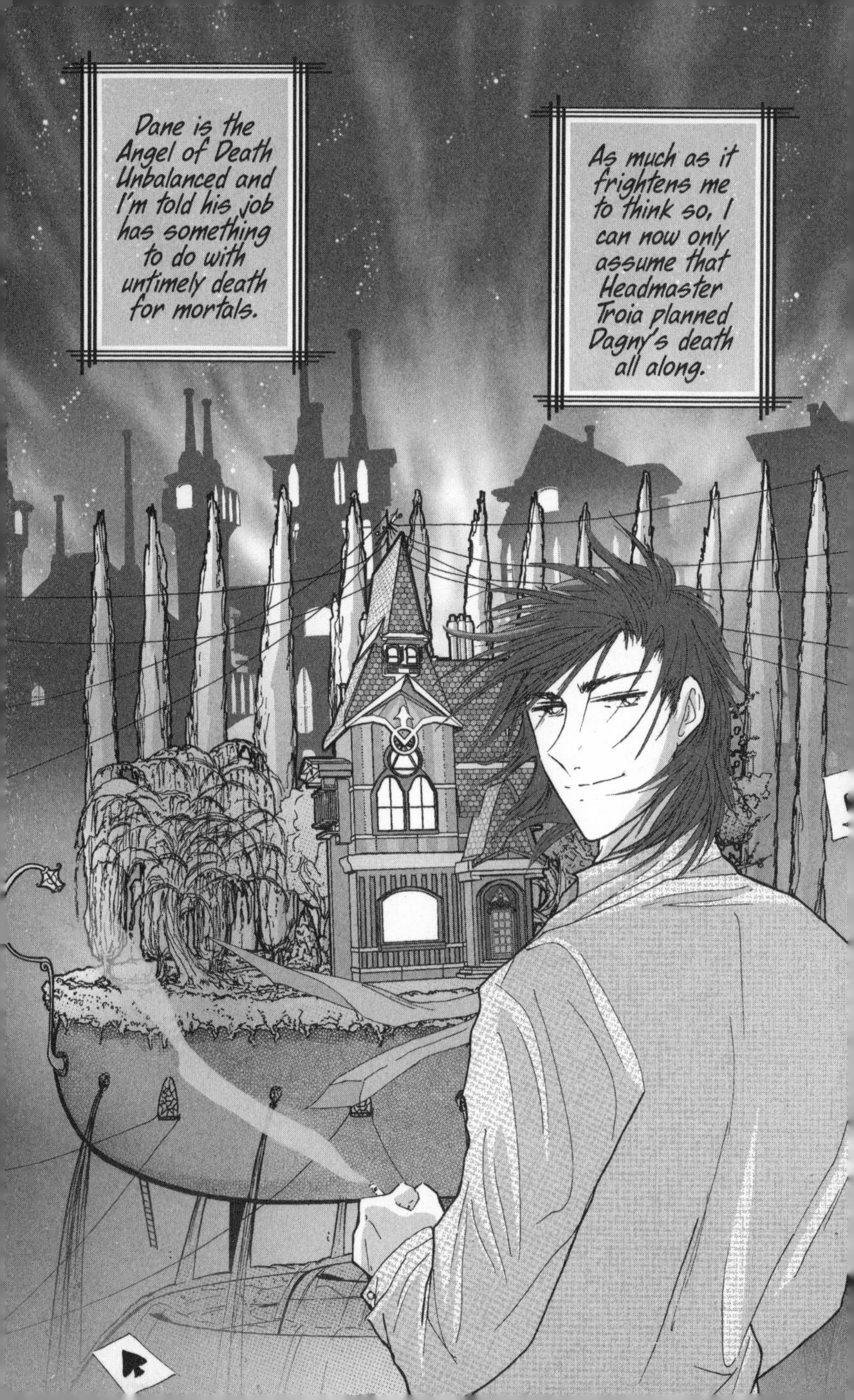
Dane is the Angel of Death Unbalanced and I'm told his job has something to do with untimely death for mortals.
As much as it frightens me to think so, I can now only assume that Headmaster Troia planned Dagny's death all along.

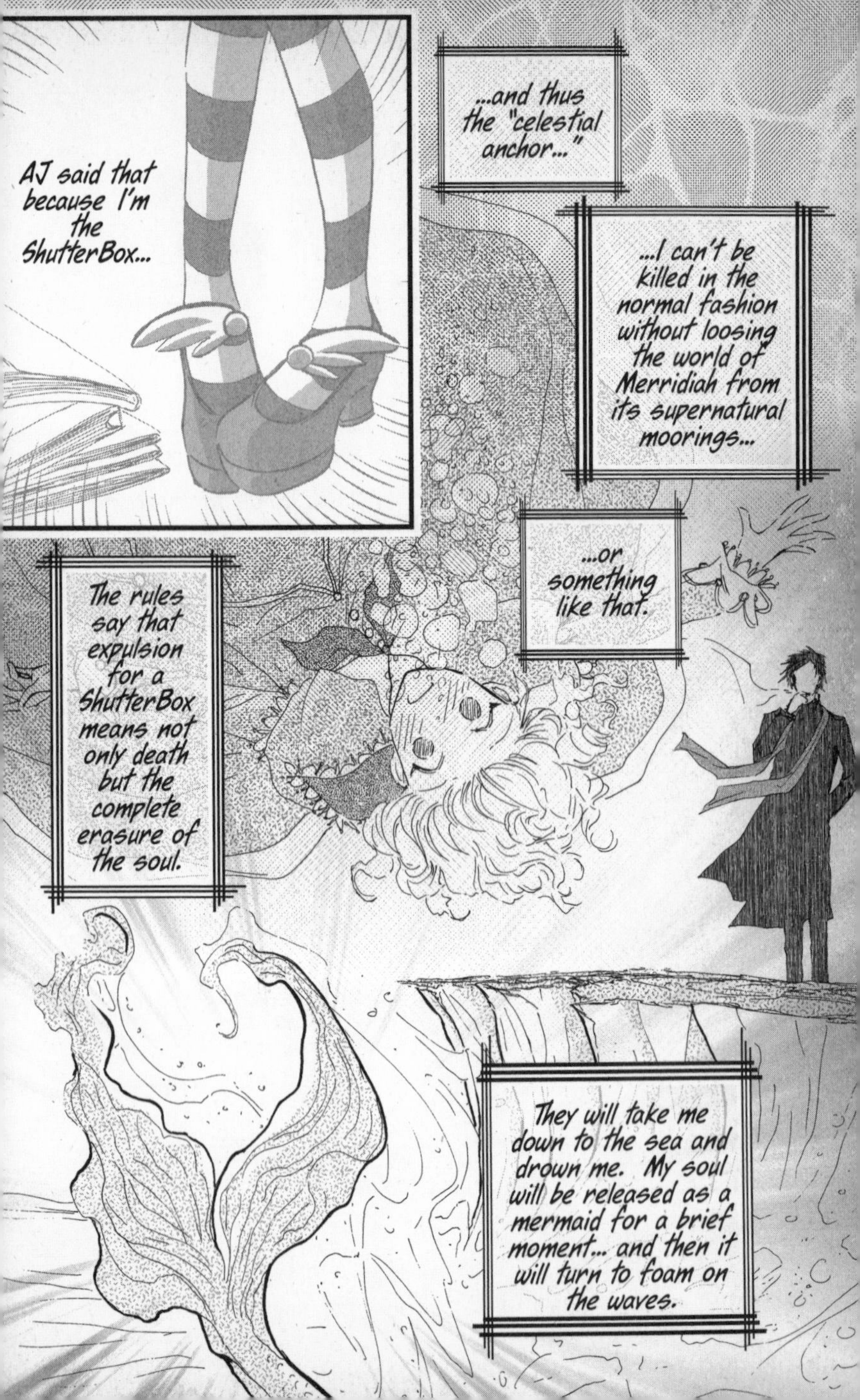
AJ said that because I'm the ShutterBox...
...and thus the "celestial anchor..."
...I can't be killed in the normal fashion without loosing the world of Merridiah from its supernatural moorings...
...or something like that.
The rules say that expulsion for a ShutterBox means not only death but the complete erasure of the soul.
They will take me down to the sea and drown me. My soul will be released as a mermaid for a brief moment... and then it will turn to foam on the waves.

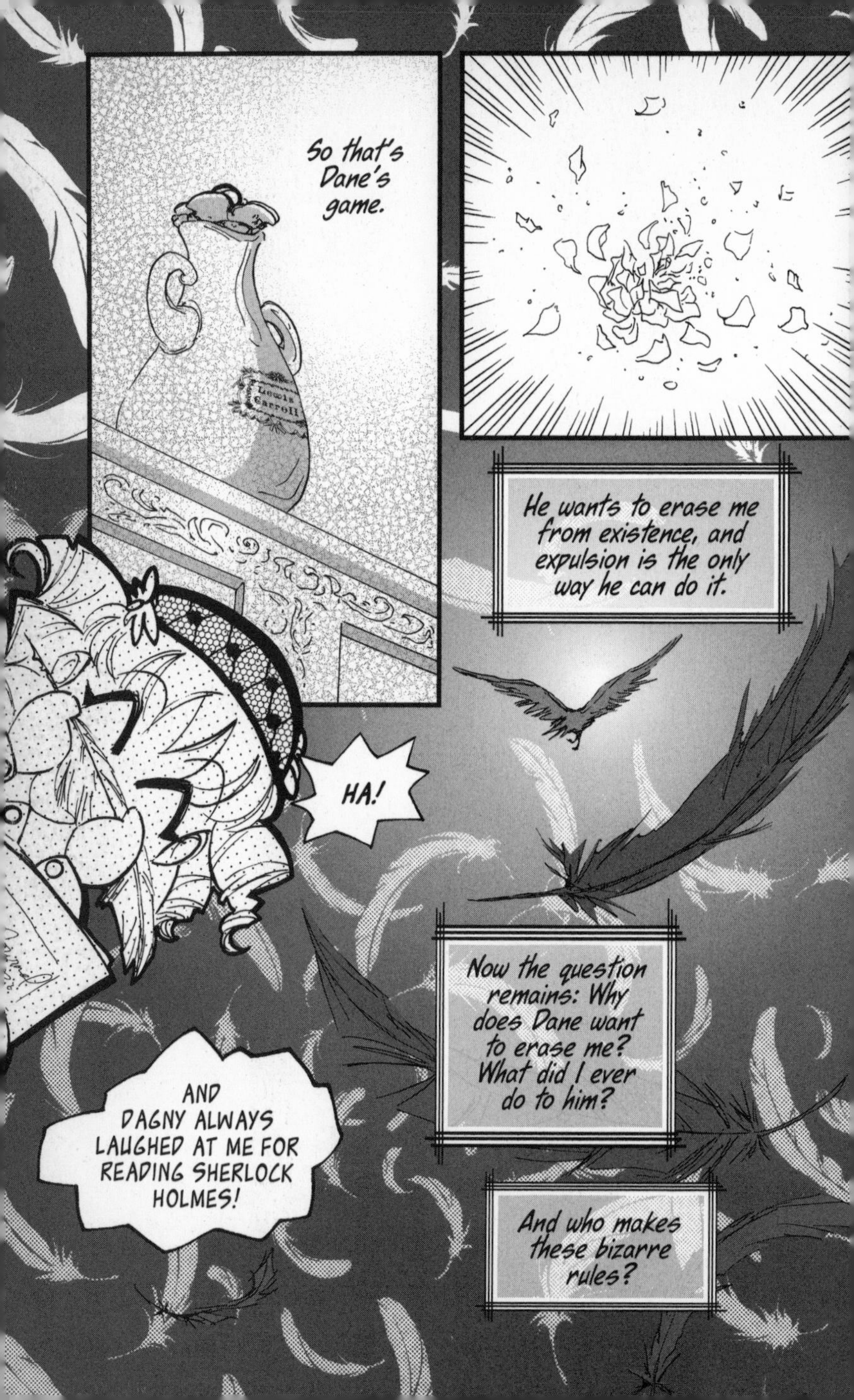
So that's Dane's game.
Lewis Carroll
He wants to erase me from existence, and expulsion is the only way he can do it.
HA!
Now the question remains: Why does Dane want to erase me? What did I ever do to him?
AND DAGNY ALWAYS LAUGHED AT ME FOR READING SHERLOCK HOLMES!
And who makes these bizarre rules?

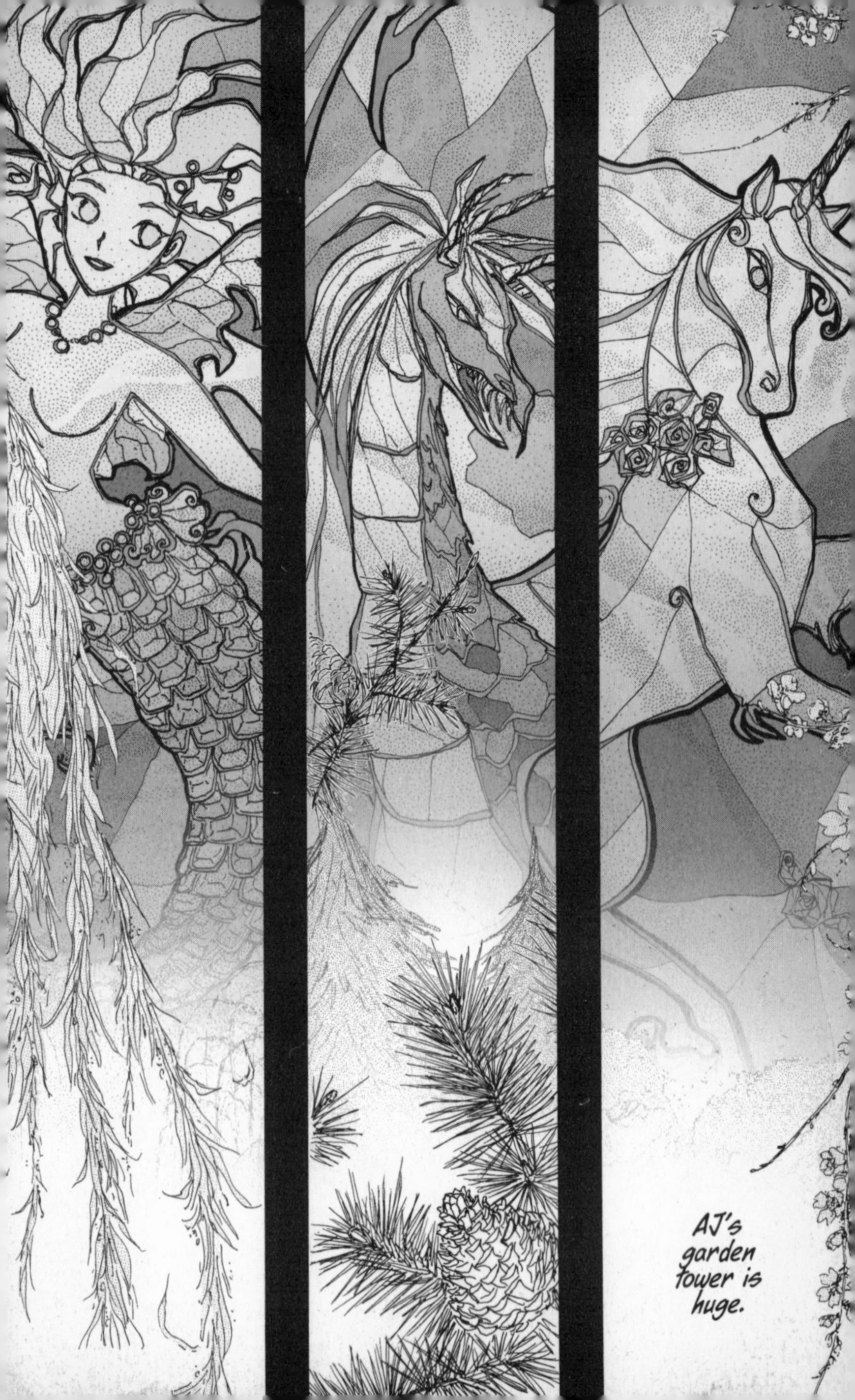
AJ's garden tower is huge.

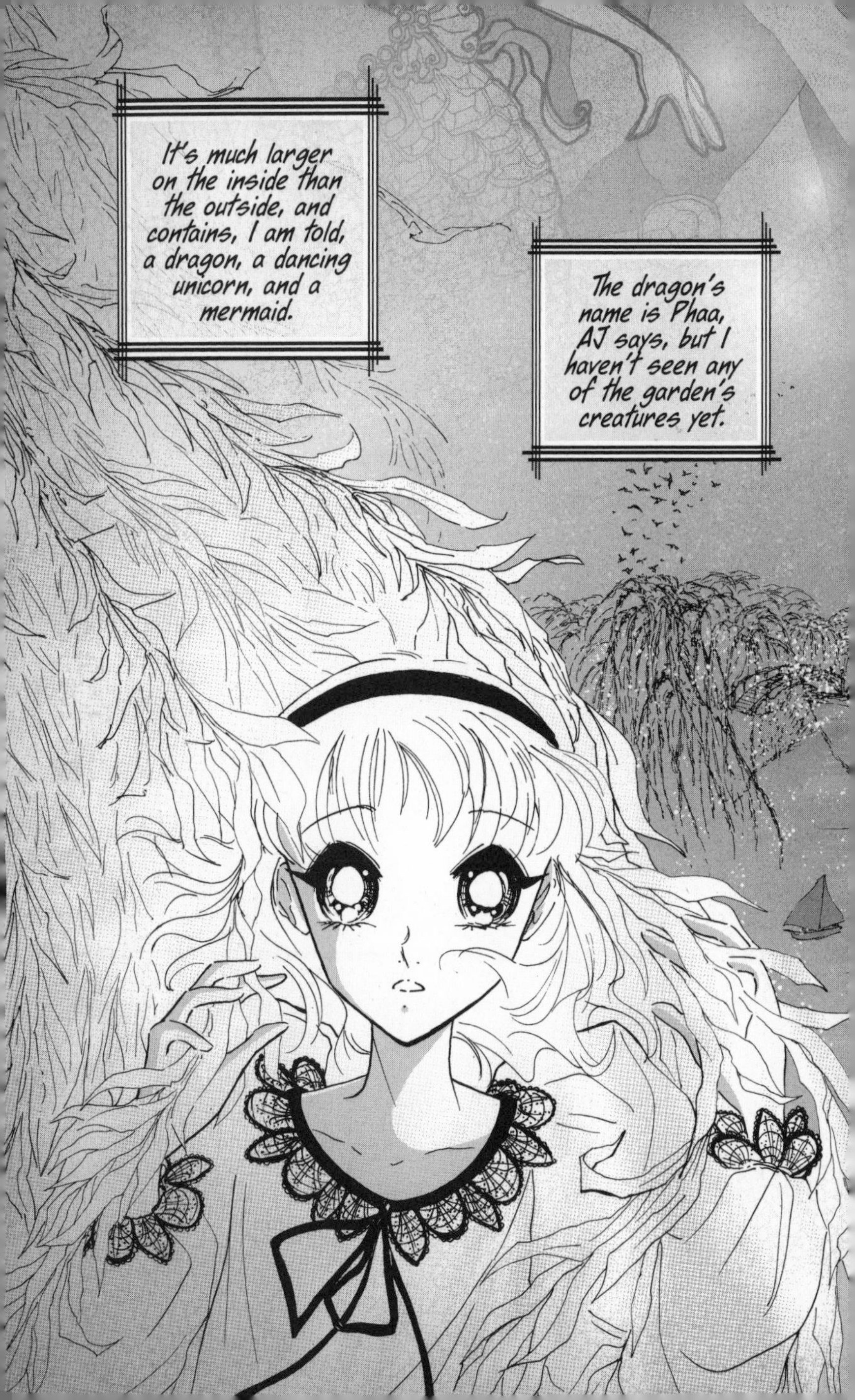
It's much larger on the inside than the outside, and contains, I am told, a dragon, a dancing unicorn, and a mermaid.
The dragon's name is Phaa, AJ says, but I haven't seen any of the garden's creatures yet.

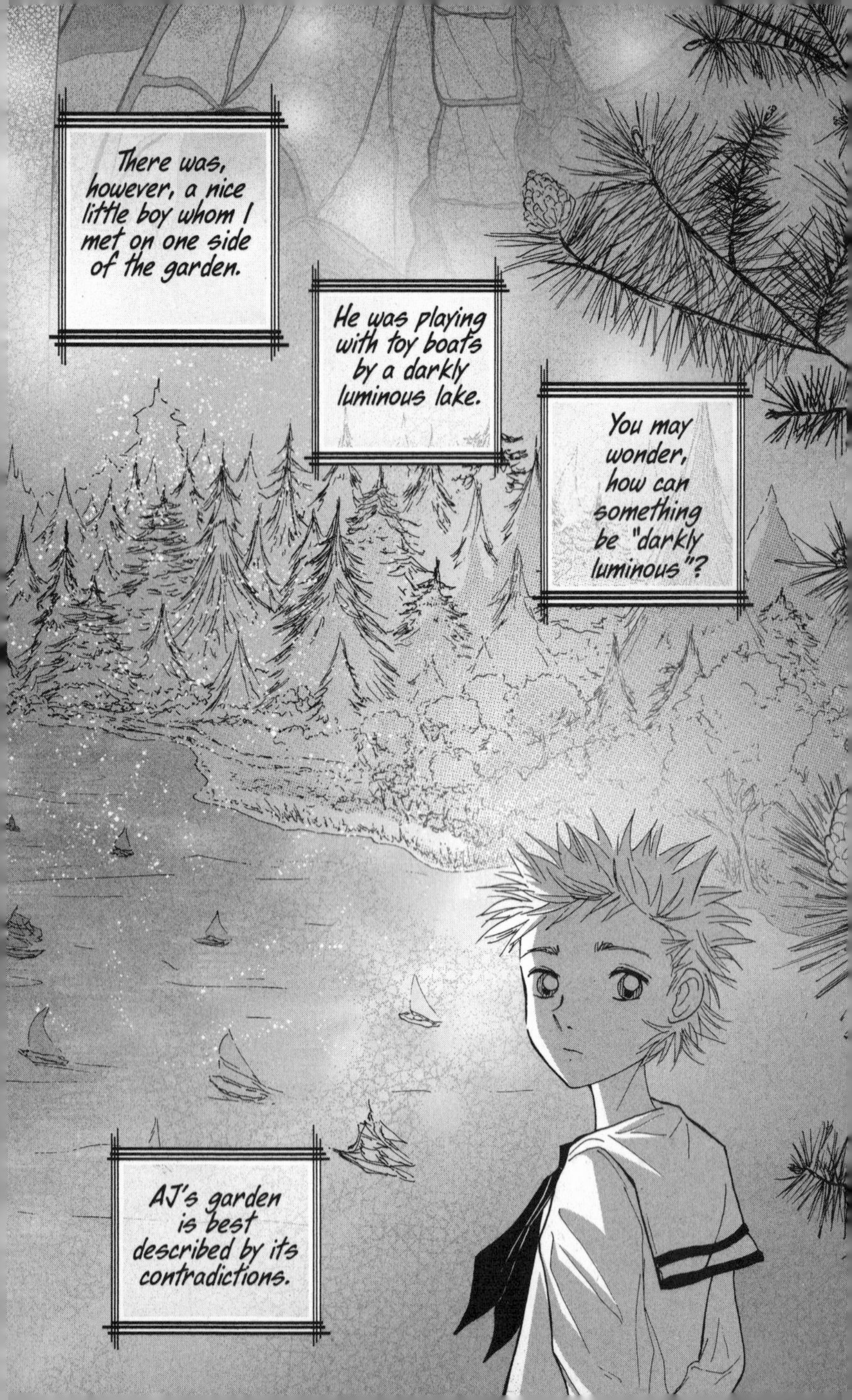

There was, however, a nice little boy whom I met on one side of the garden.
He was playing with toy boats by a darkly luminous lake.
You may wonder, how can something be "darkly luminous"?
AJ's garden is best described by its contradictions.

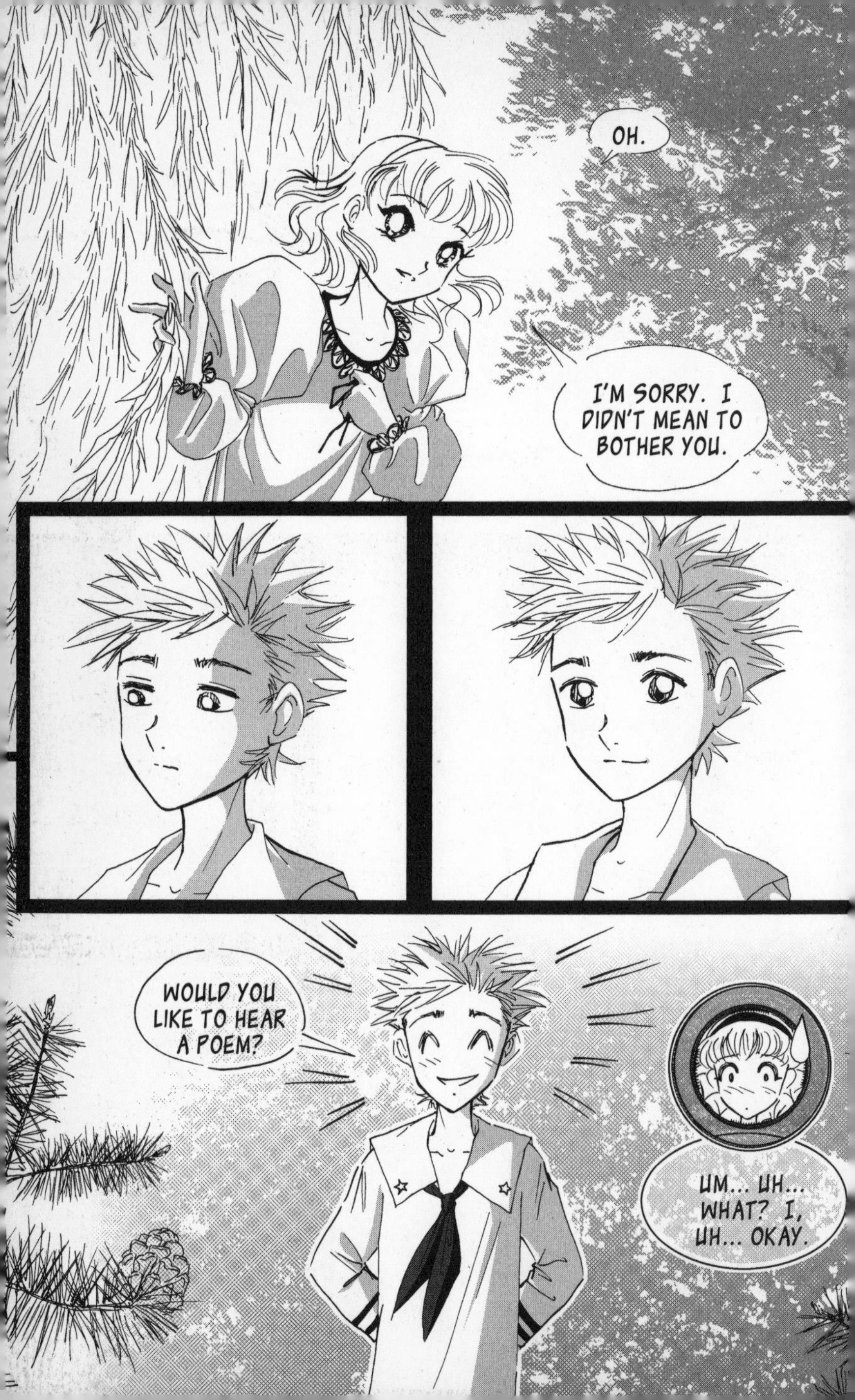
OH.
I'M SORRY. I DIDN'T MEAN TO BOTHER YOU.
WOULD YOU LIKE TO HEAR A POEM?
UM... UH... WHAT? I, UH... OKAY.

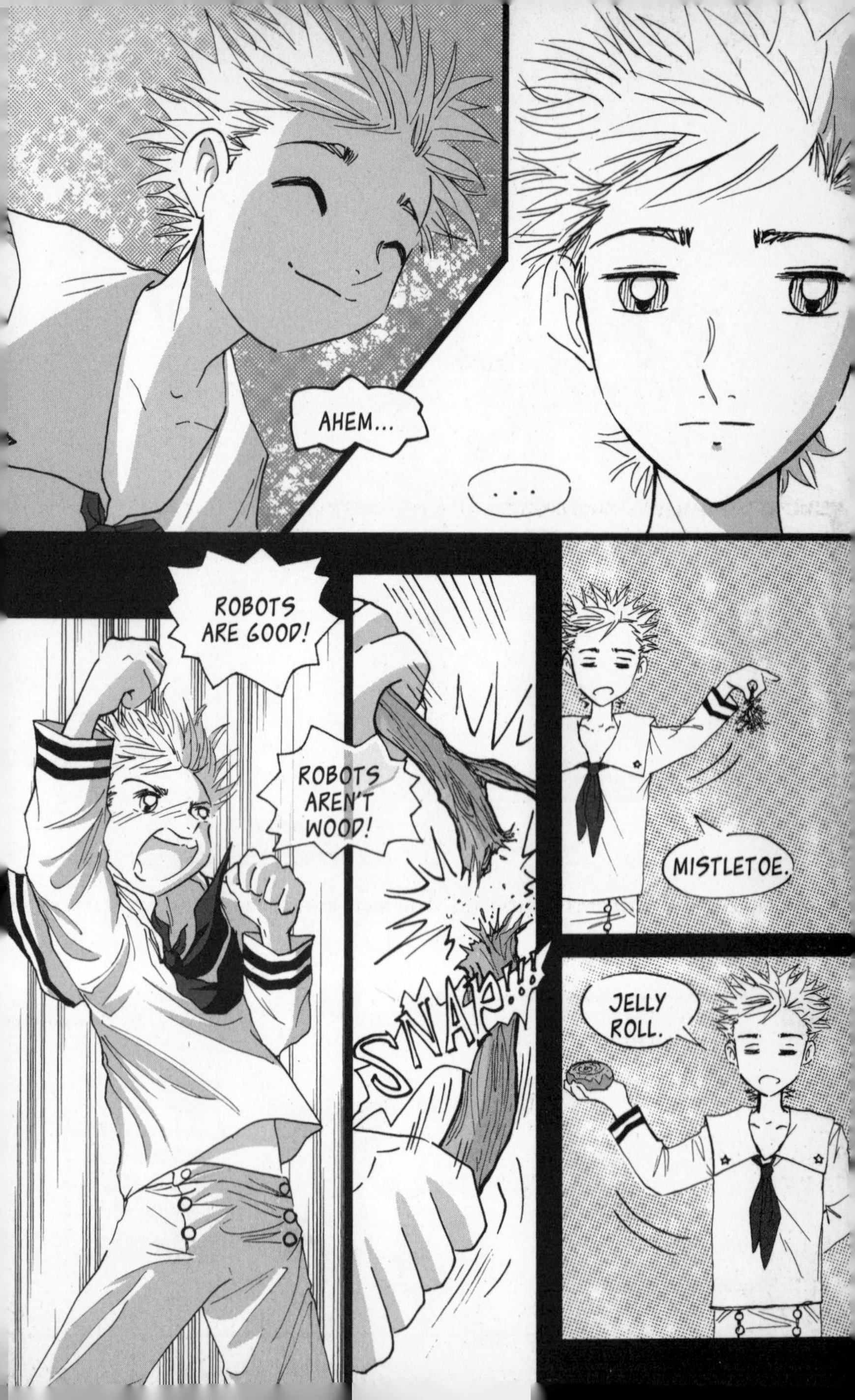
AHEM...
...
ROBOTS ARE GOOD!
ROBOTS AREN'T WOOD!
SNAP!!!
MISTLETOE.
JELLY ROLL.

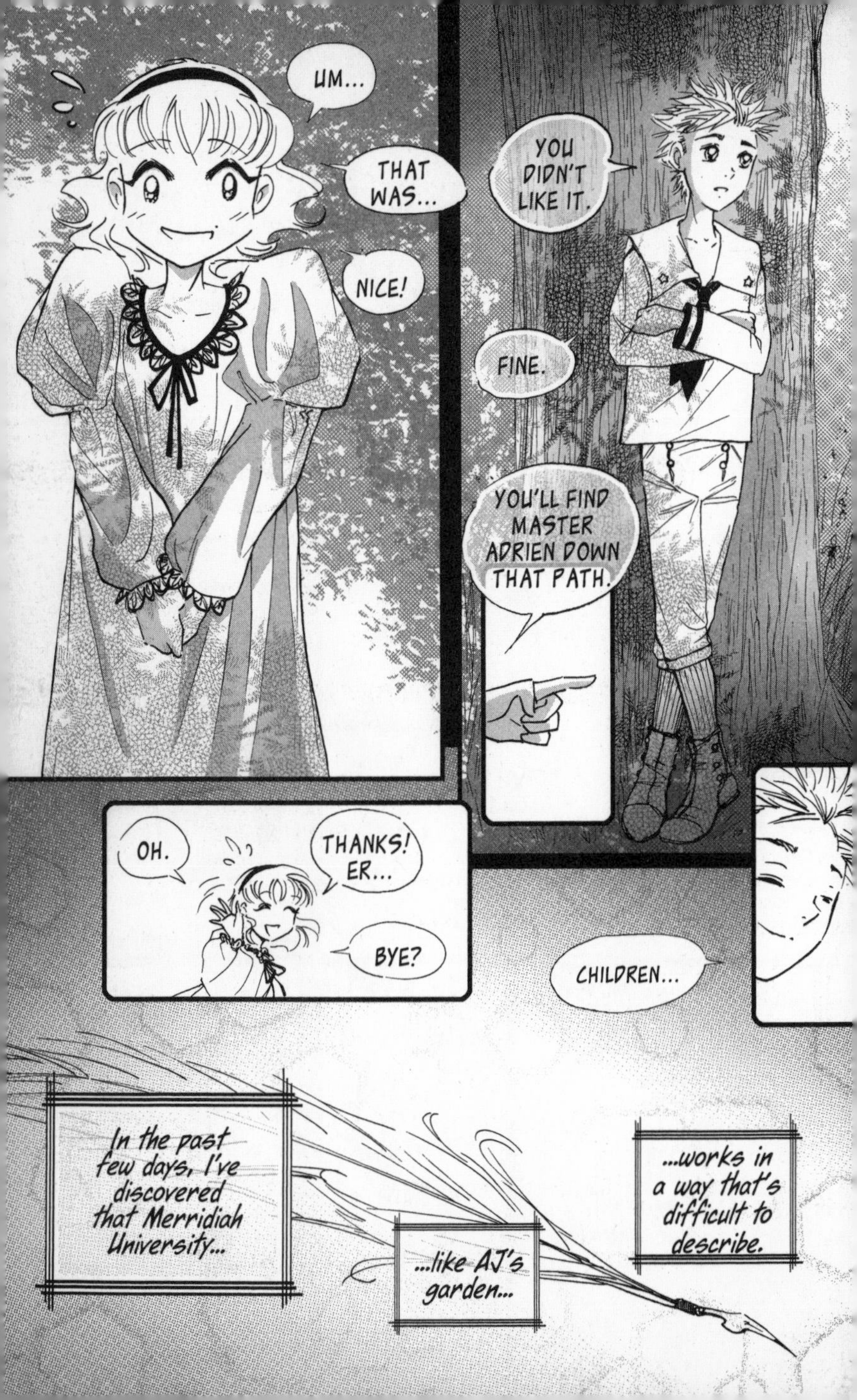
UM...
THAT WAS...
NICE!
YOU DIDN'T LIKE IT.
FINE.
YOU'LL FIND MASTER ADRIEN DOWN THAT PATH.
OH.
THANKS! ER...
BYE?
CHILDREN...
In the past few days, I've discovered that Merridiah University...
...like AJ's garden...
...works in a way that's difficult to describe.

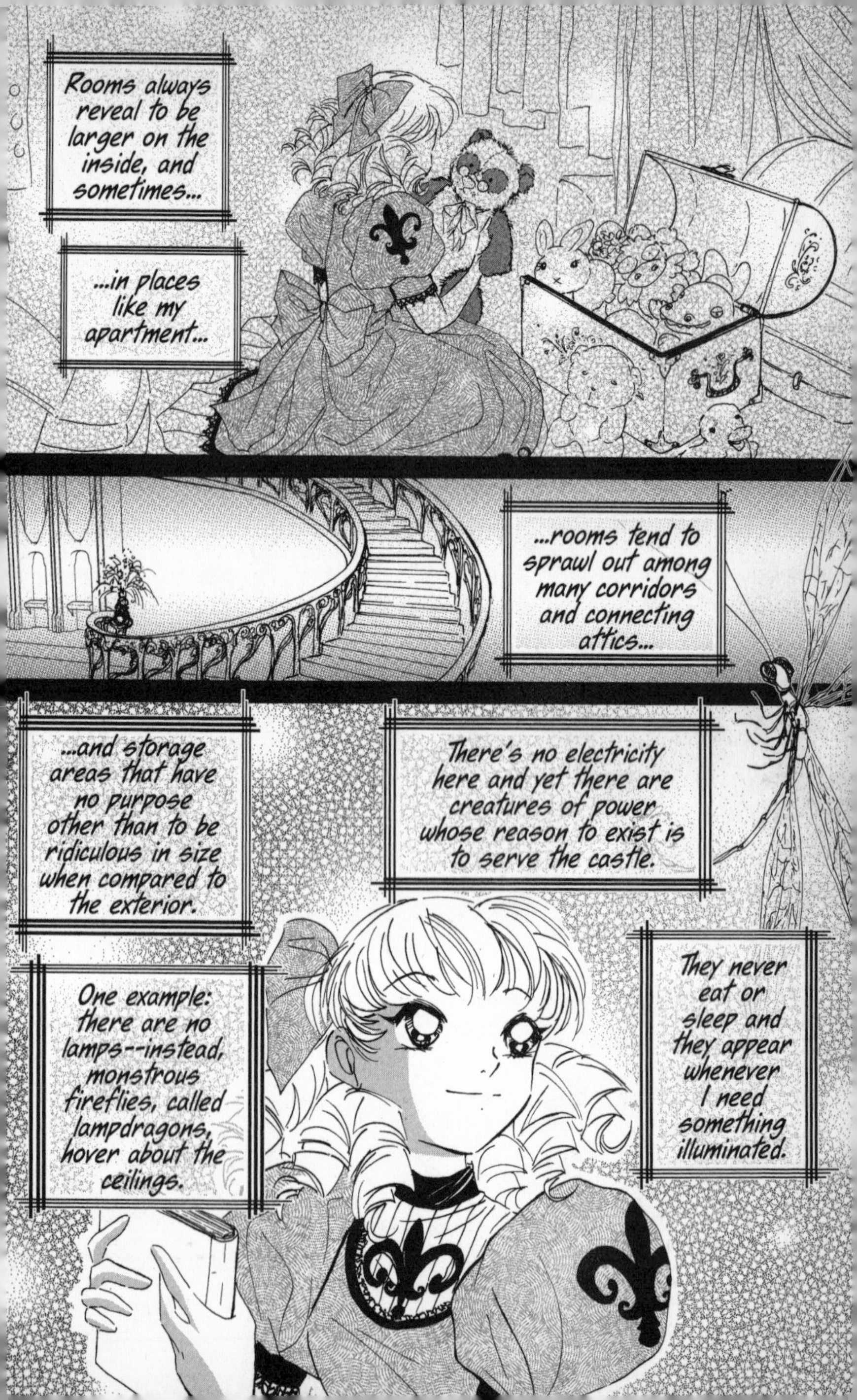
Rooms always reveal to be larger on the inside, and sometimes...
...in places like my apartment...
...rooms tend to sprawl out among many corridors and connecting attics...
...and storage areas that have no purpose other than to be ridiculous in size when compared to the exterior.
There's no electricity here and yet there are creatures of power whose reason to exist is to serve the castle.
One example: there are no lamps--instead, monstrous fireflies, called lampdragons, hover about the ceilings.
They never eat or sleep and they appear whenever I need something illuminated.

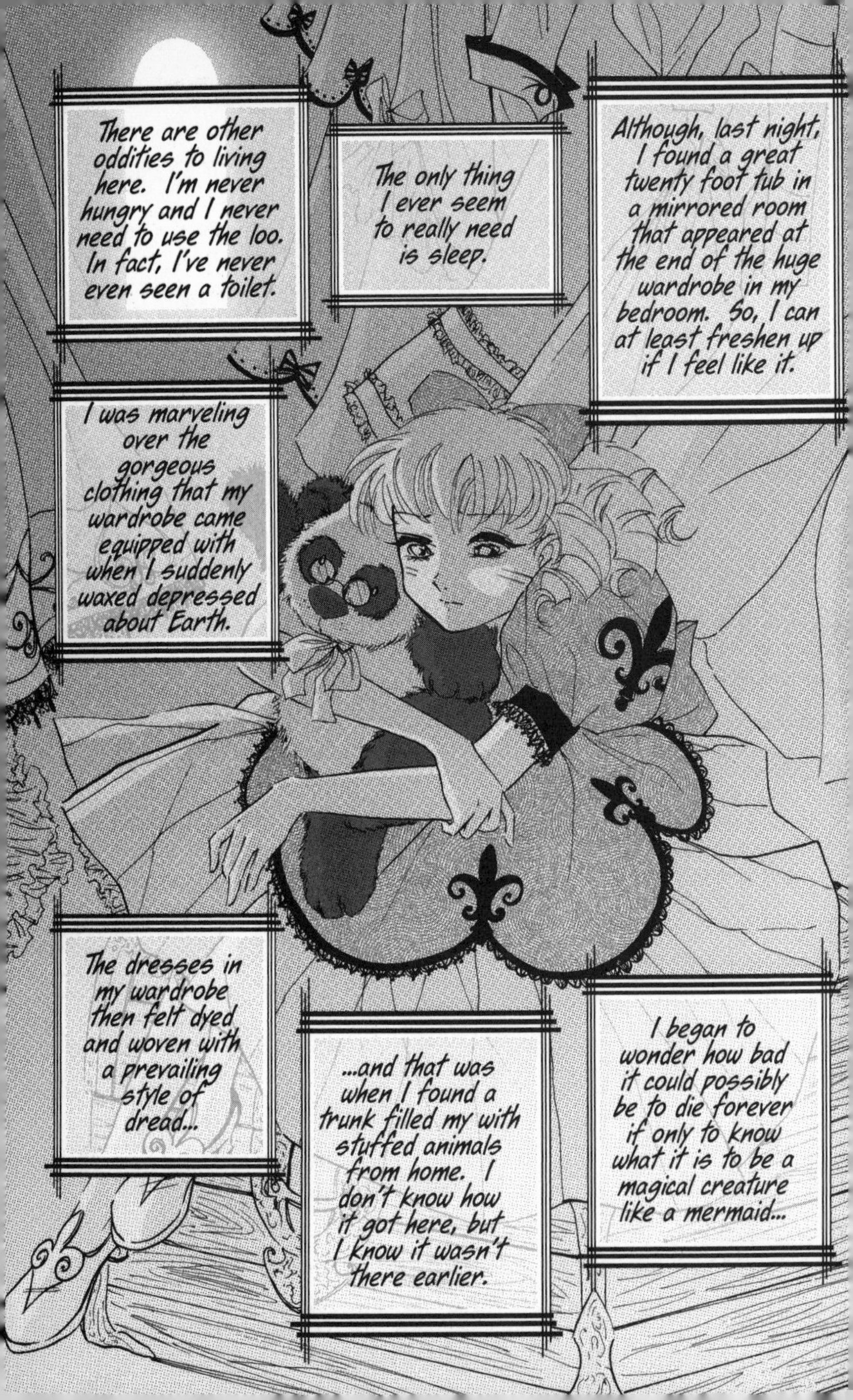
There are other oddities to living here. I'm never hungry and I never need to use the loo. In fact, I've never even seen a toilet.
The only thing I ever seem to really need is sleep.
Although, last night, I found a great twenty foot tub in a mirrored room that appeared at the end of the huge wardrobe in my bedroom. So, I can at least freshen up if I feel like it.
I was marveling over the gorgeous clothing that my wardrobe came equipped with when I suddenly waxed depressed about Earth.
The dresses in my wardrobe then felt dyed and woven with a prevailing style of dread...
...and that was when I found a trunk filled my with stuffed animals from home. I don't know how it got here, but I know it wasn't there earlier.
I began to wonder how bad it could possibly be to die forever if only to know what it is to be a magical creature like a mermaid...

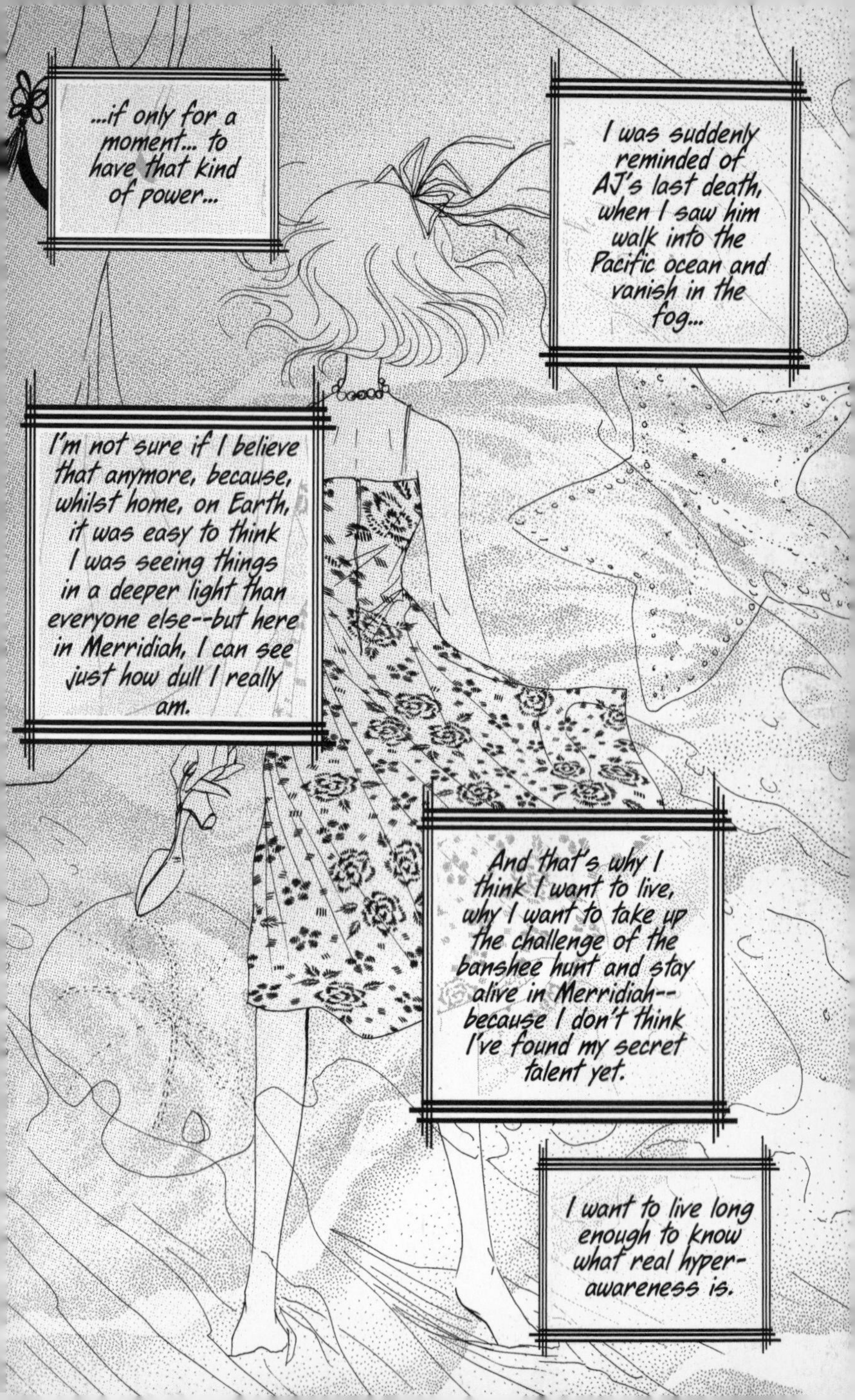
...if only for a moment... to have that kind of power...
I was suddenly reminded of AJ's last death, when I saw him walk into the Pacific ocean and vanish in the fog...
I'm not sure if I believe that anymore, because, whilst home, on Earth, it was easy to think I was seeing things in a deeper light than everyone else--but here in Merridiah, I can see just how dull I really am.
And that's why I think I want to live, why I want to take up the challenge of the banshee hunt and stay alive in Merridiah--because I don't think I've found my secret talent yet.
I want to live long enough to know what real hyper-awareness is.

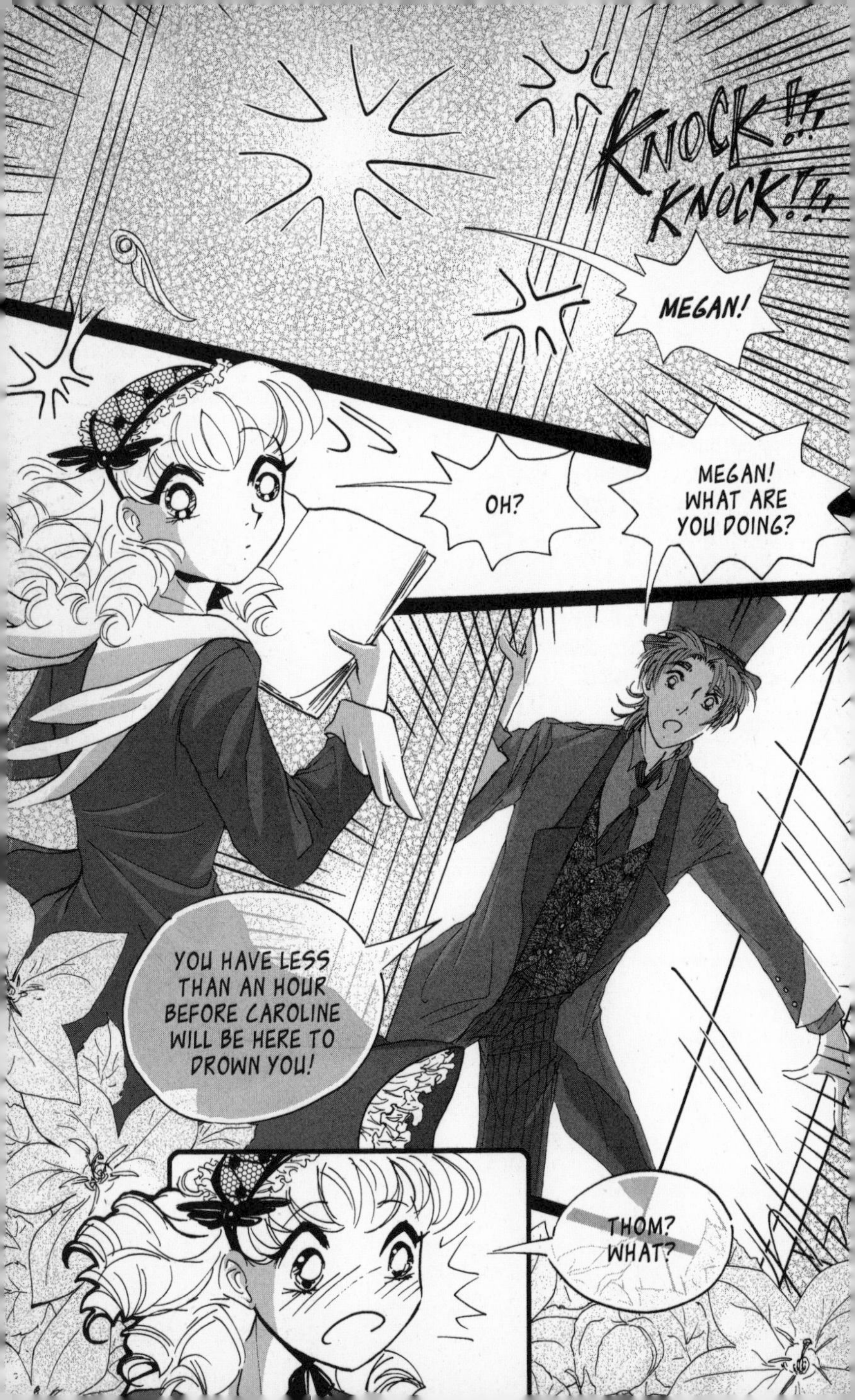
KNOCK!!
KNOCK!!
MEGAN!
OH?
MEGAN! WHAT ARE YOU DOING?
YOU HAVE LESS THAN AN HOUR BEFORE CAROLINE WILL BE HERE TO DROWN YOU!
THOM? WHAT?

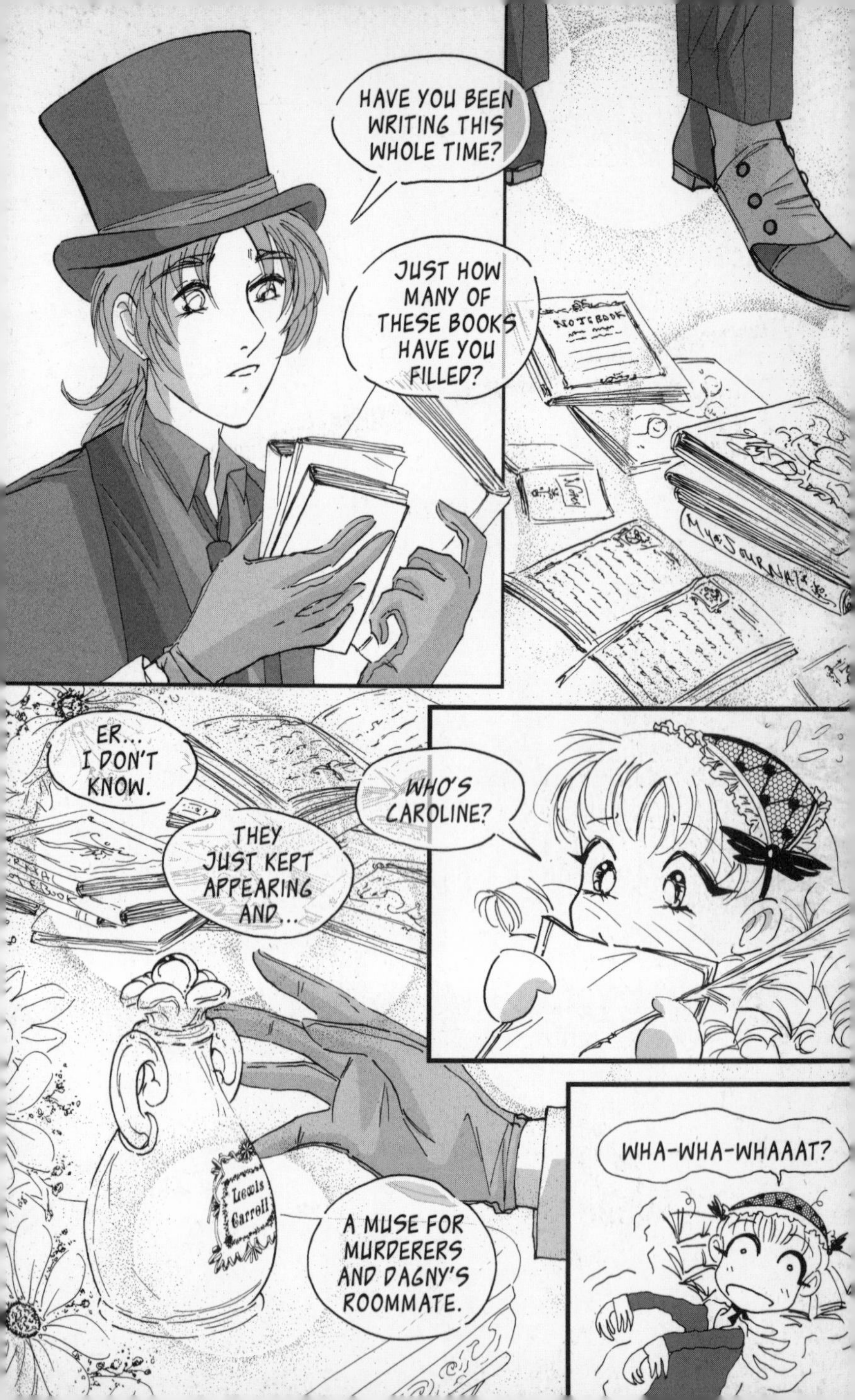
HAVE YOU BEEN WRITING THIS WHOLE TIME?
JUST HOW MANY OF THESE BOOKS HAVE YOU FILLED?
ER... I DON'T KNOW.
THEY JUST KEPT APPEARING AND...
Lewis Carroll
A MUSE FOR MURDERERS AND DAGNY'S ROOMMATE.
WHO'S CAROLINE?
WHA-WHA-WHAAAT?

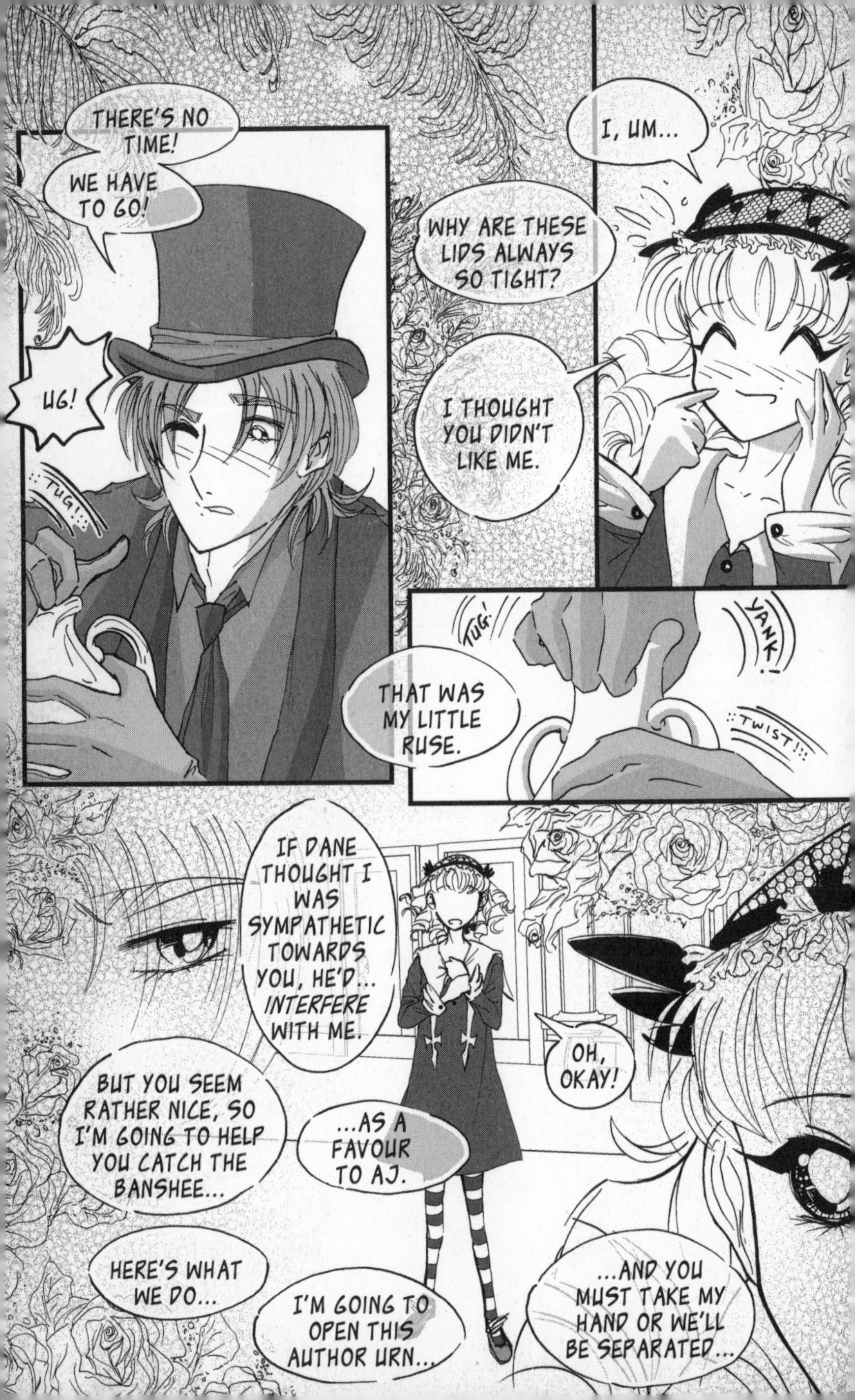
THERE'S NO TIME!
WE HAVE TO GO!
UG!
::TUG!::
WHY ARE THESE LIDS ALWAYS SO TIGHT?
I THOUGHT YOU DIDN'T LIKE ME.
I, UM...
TUG!
THAT WAS MY LITTLE RUSE.
YANK!
::TWIST!::
IF DANE THOUGHT I WAS SYMPATHETIC TOWARDS YOU, HE'D... *INTERFERE* WITH ME.
OH, OKAY!
BUT YOU SEEM RATHER NICE, SO I'M GOING TO HELP YOU CATCH THE BANSHEE...
...AS A FAVOUR TO AJ.
HERE'S WHAT WE DO...
I'M GOING TO OPEN THIS AUTHOR URN...
...AND YOU MUST TAKE MY HAND OR WE'LL BE SEPARATED...

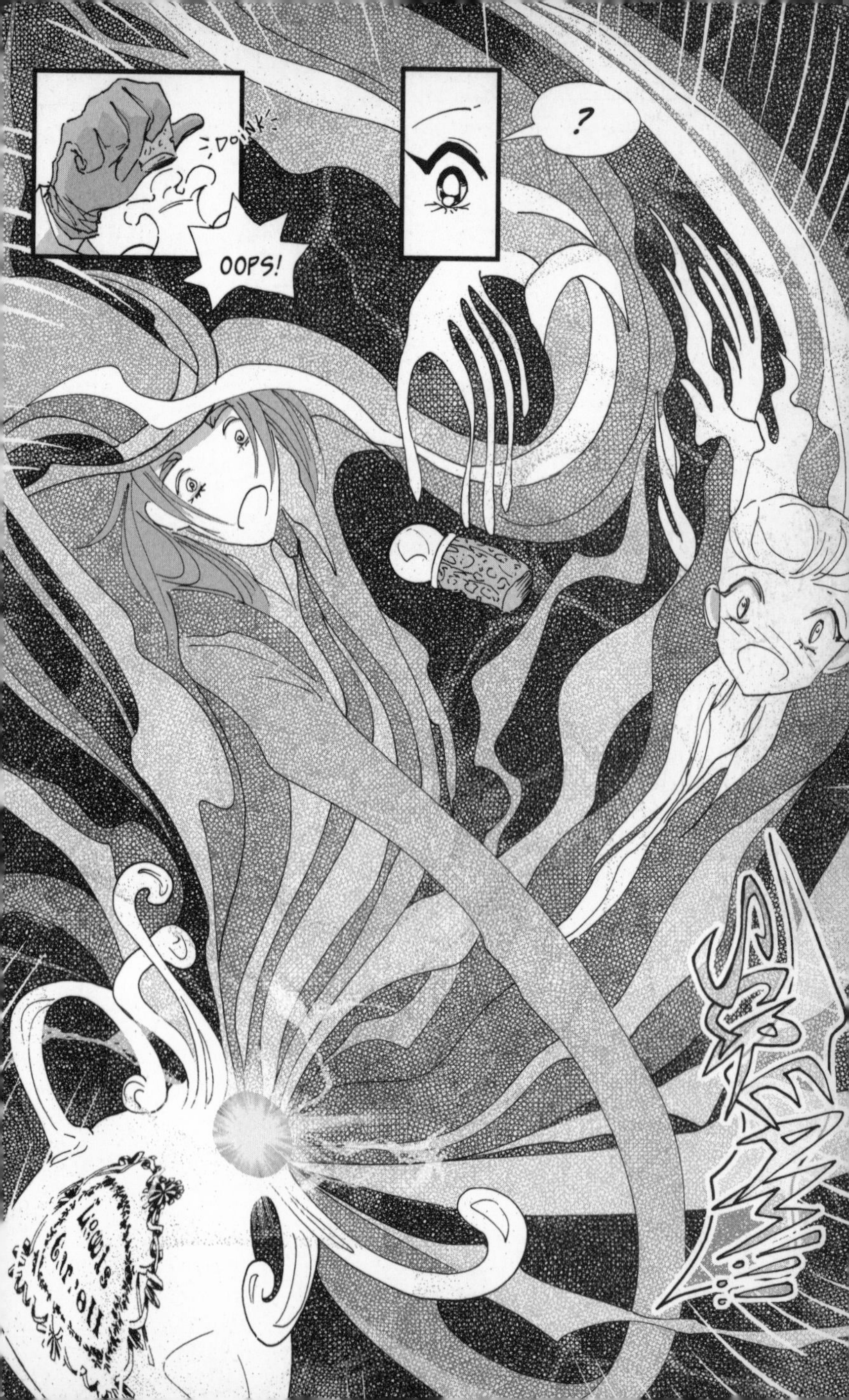
DOINK
OOPS!
?

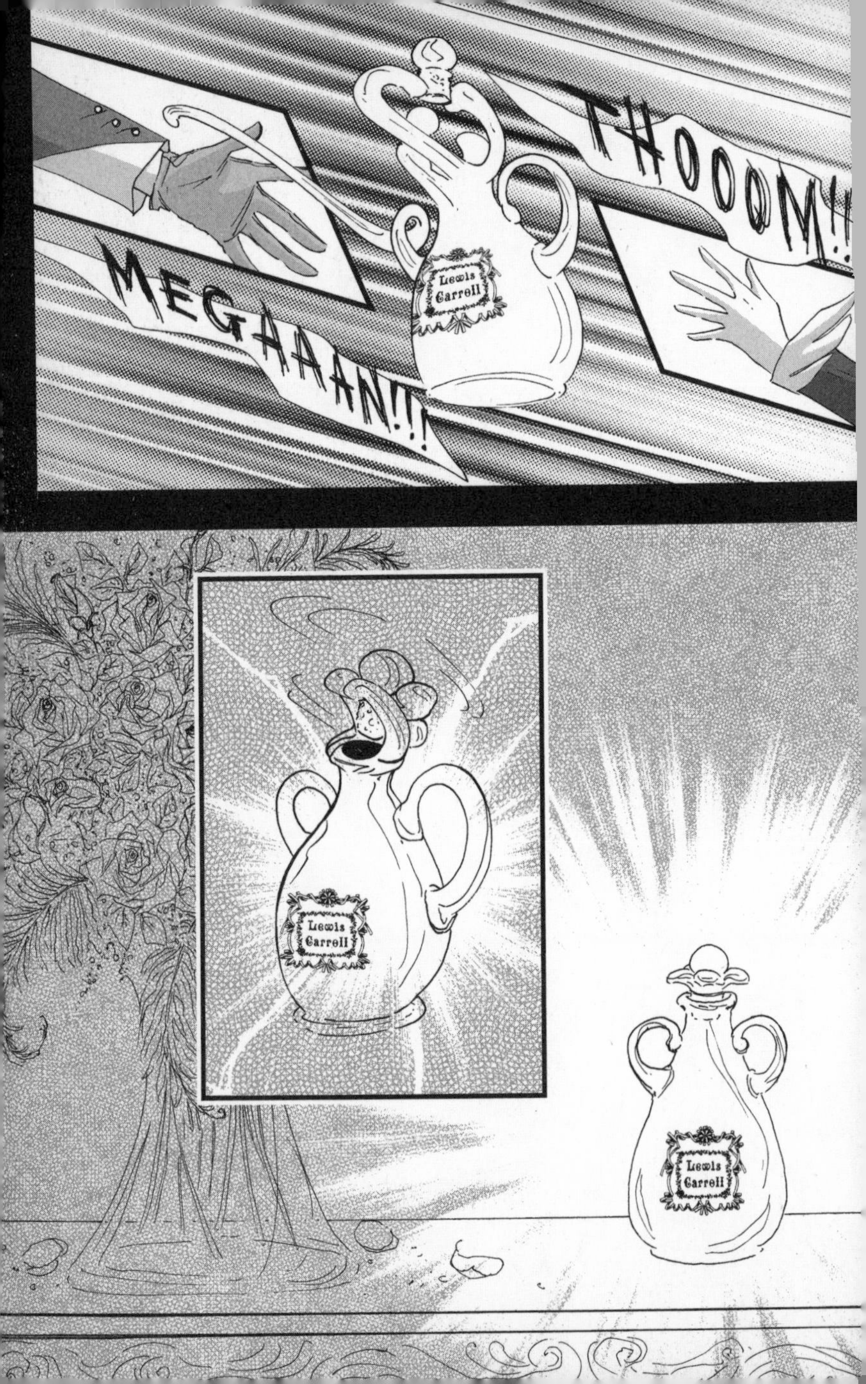
MEGAAAN!!
Lewis Carroll
THOOOM!!
Lewis Carroll
Lewis Carroll

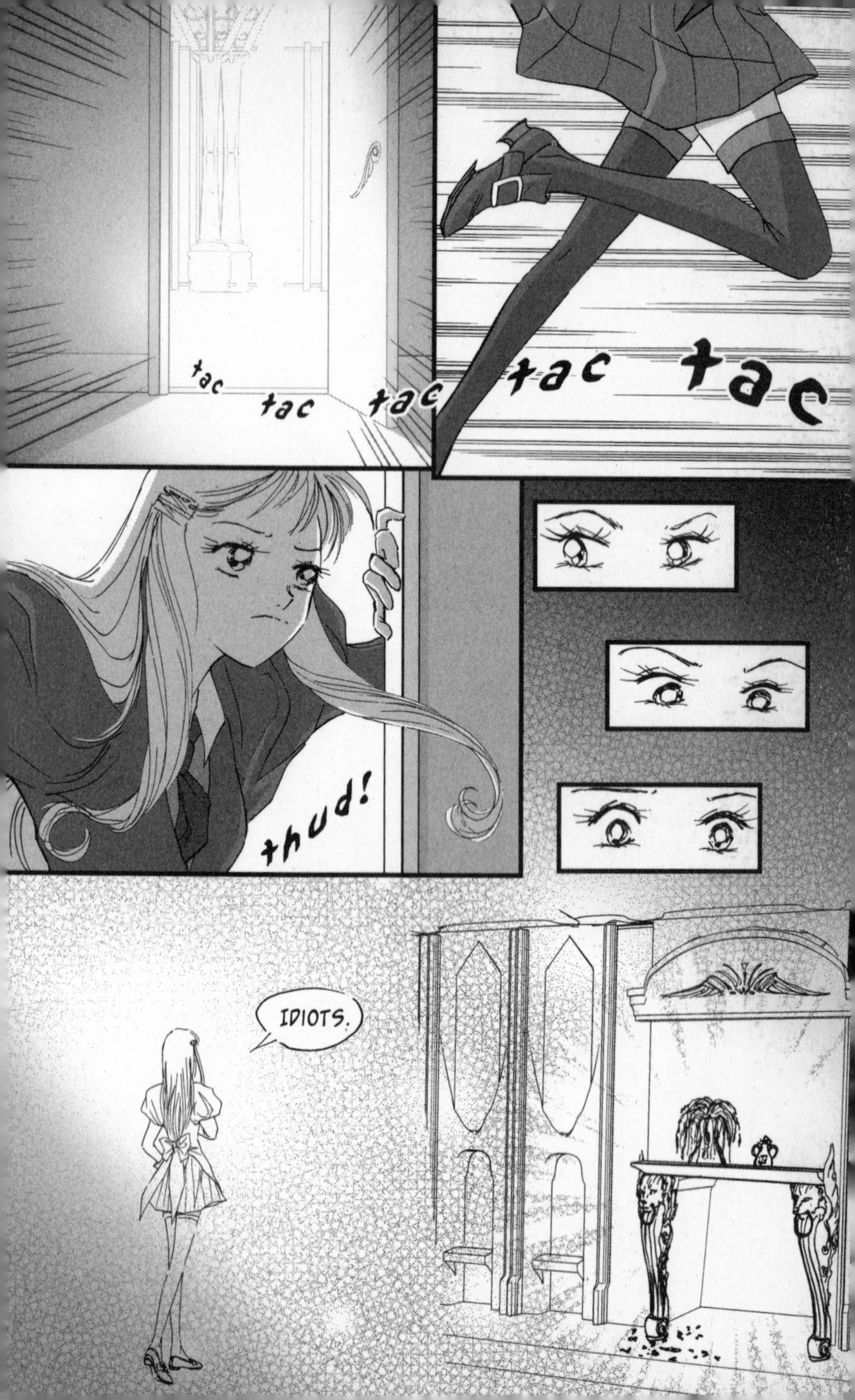
tac
tac
tac
tac
tac
thud!
IDIOTS.

Chapter Three:

What is Outgrabeshness

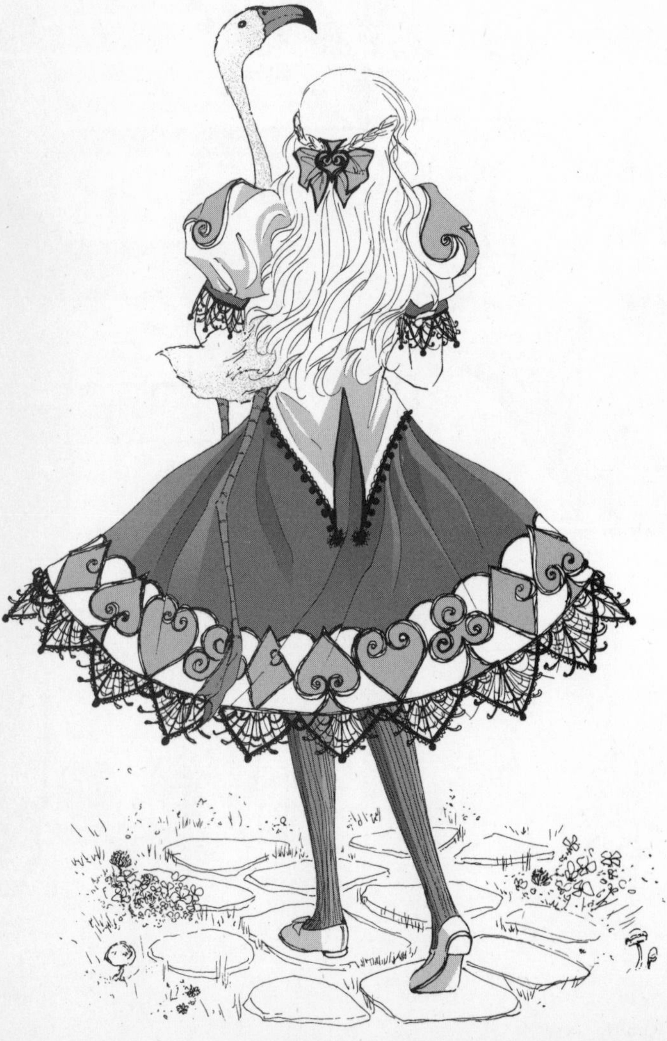

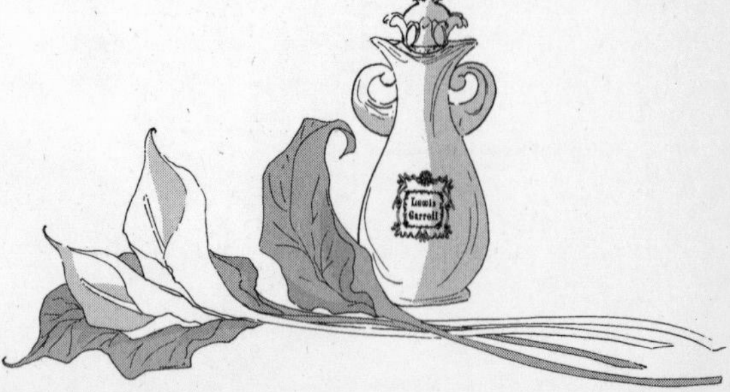
Lewis Carroll

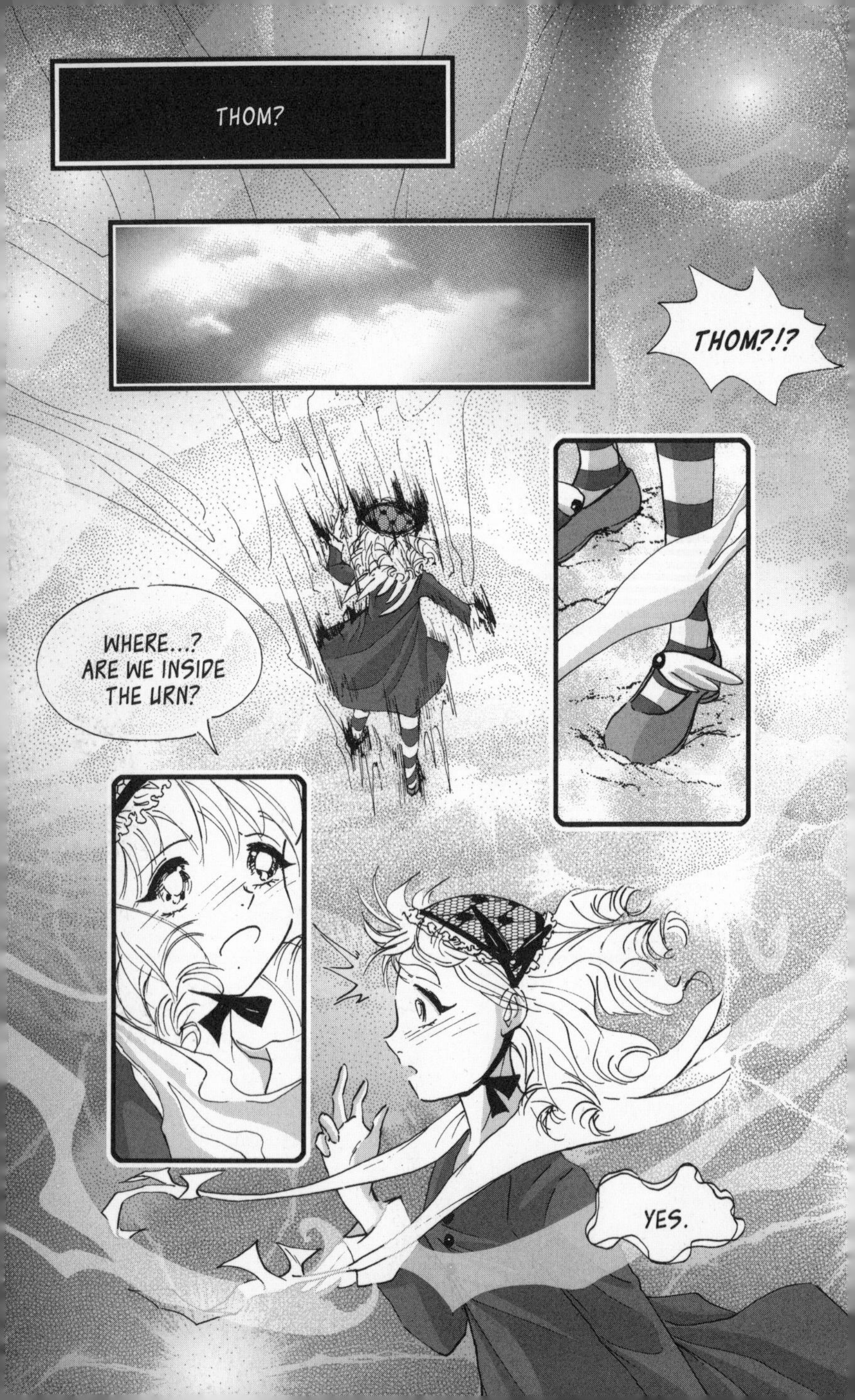
THOM?
THOM?!?
WHERE...? ARE WE INSIDE THE URN?
YES.

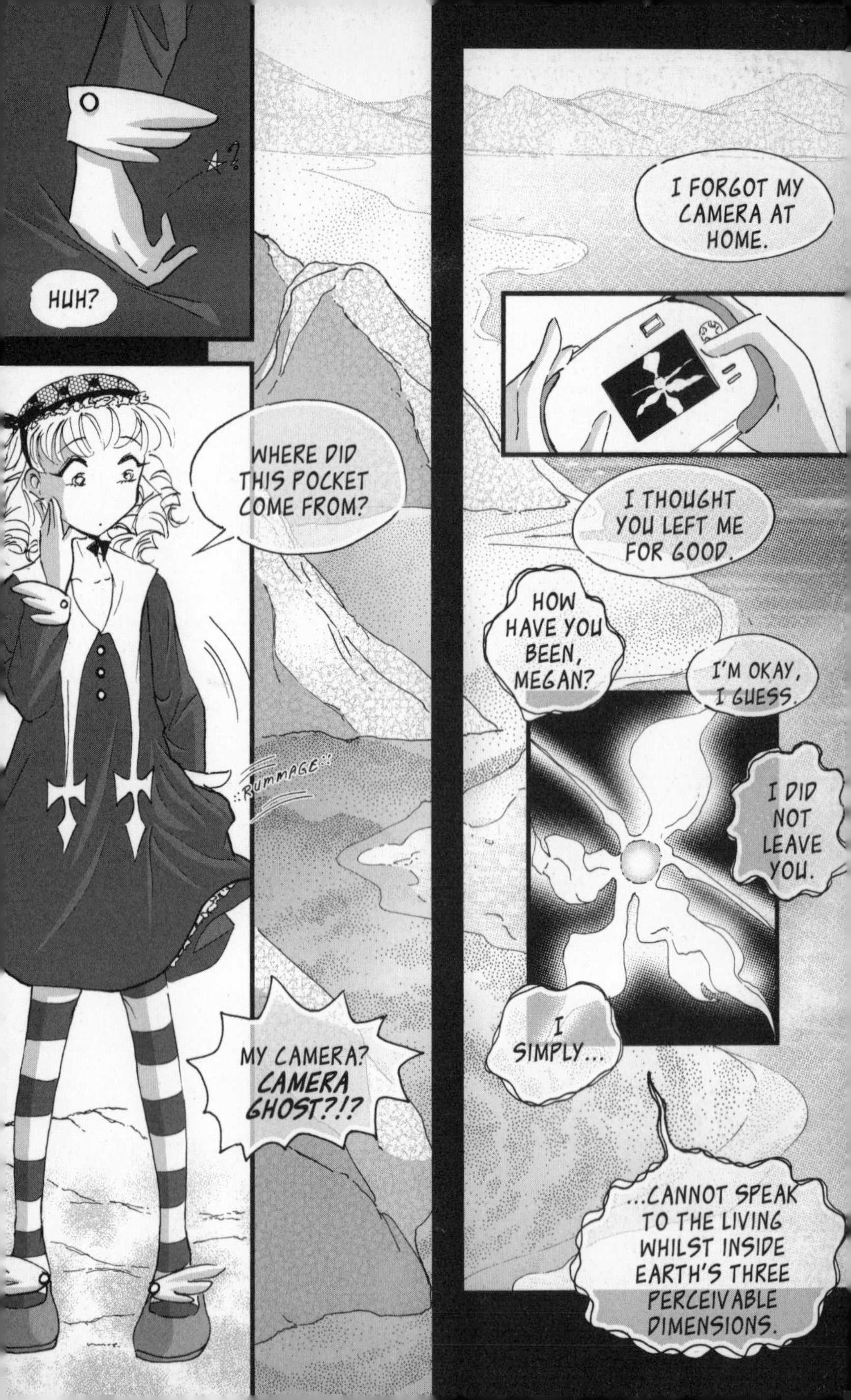
HUH?
WHERE DID THIS POCKET COME FROM?
::RUMMAGE::
MY CAMERA? CAMERA GHOST?!?
I FORGOT MY CAMERA AT HOME.
I THOUGHT YOU LEFT ME FOR GOOD.
HOW HAVE YOU BEEN, MEGAN?
I'M OKAY, I GUESS.
I DID NOT LEAVE YOU.
I SIMPLY...
...CANNOT SPEAK TO THE LIVING WHILST INSIDE EARTH'S THREE PERCEIVABLE DIMENSIONS.

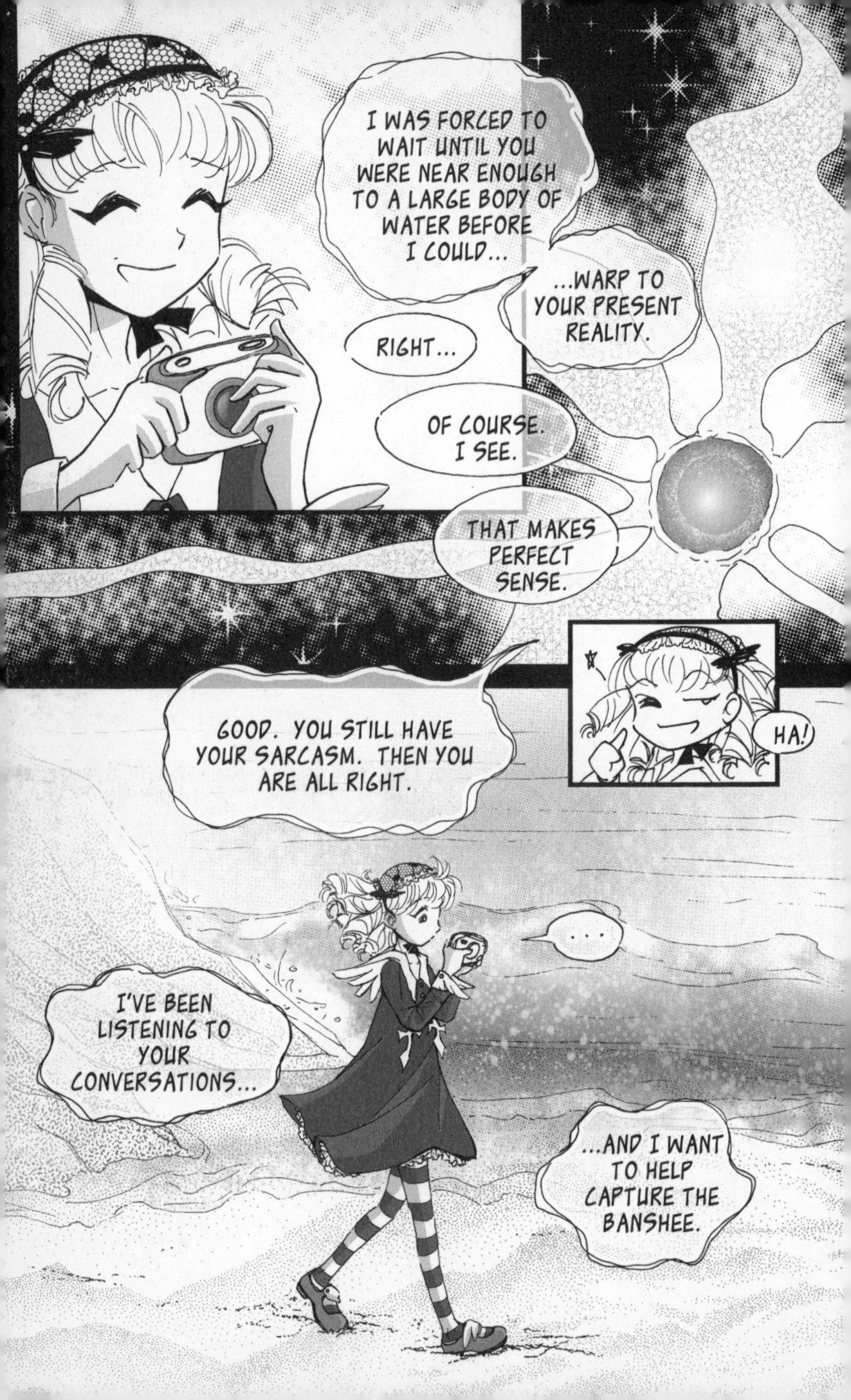
I WAS FORCED TO WAIT UNTIL YOU WERE NEAR ENOUGH TO A LARGE BODY OF WATER BEFORE I COULD...
...WARP TO YOUR PRESENT REALITY.
RIGHT...
OF COURSE. I SEE.
THAT MAKES PERFECT SENSE.
GOOD. YOU STILL HAVE YOUR SARCASM. THEN YOU ARE ALL RIGHT.
HA!
. . .
I'VE BEEN LISTENING TO YOUR CONVERSATIONS...
...AND I WANT TO HELP CAPTURE THE BANSHEE.

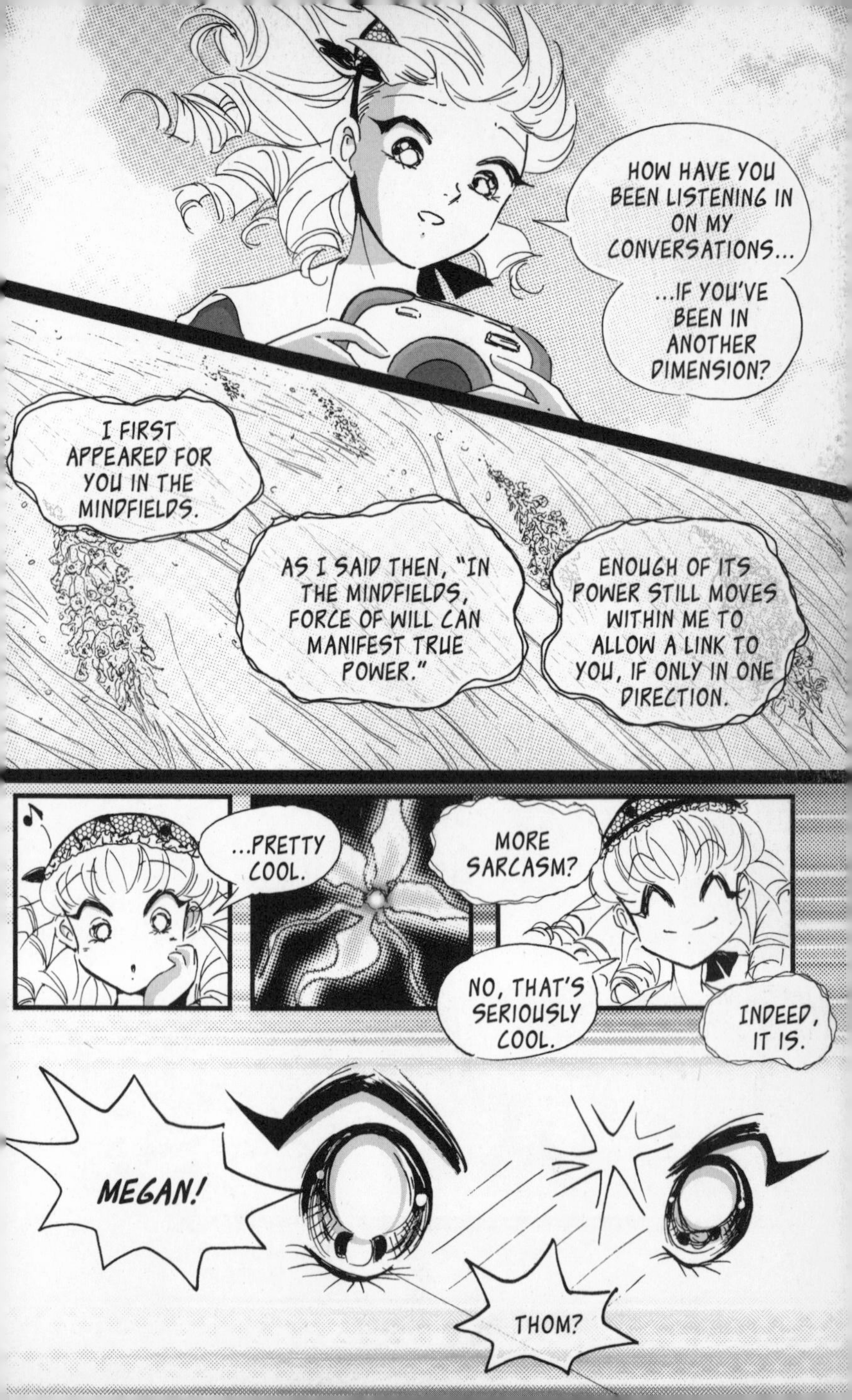
HOW HAVE YOU BEEN LISTENING IN ON MY CONVERSATIONS...
...IF YOU'VE BEEN IN ANOTHER DIMENSION?
I FIRST APPEARED FOR YOU IN THE MINDFIELDS.
AS I SAID THEN, "IN THE MINDFIELDS, FORCE OF WILL CAN MANIFEST TRUE POWER."
ENOUGH OF ITS POWER STILL MOVES WITHIN ME TO ALLOW A LINK TO YOU, IF ONLY IN ONE DIRECTION.
...PRETTY COOL.
MORE SARCASM?
NO, THAT'S SERIOUSLY COOL.
INDEED, IT IS.
MEGAN!
THOM?

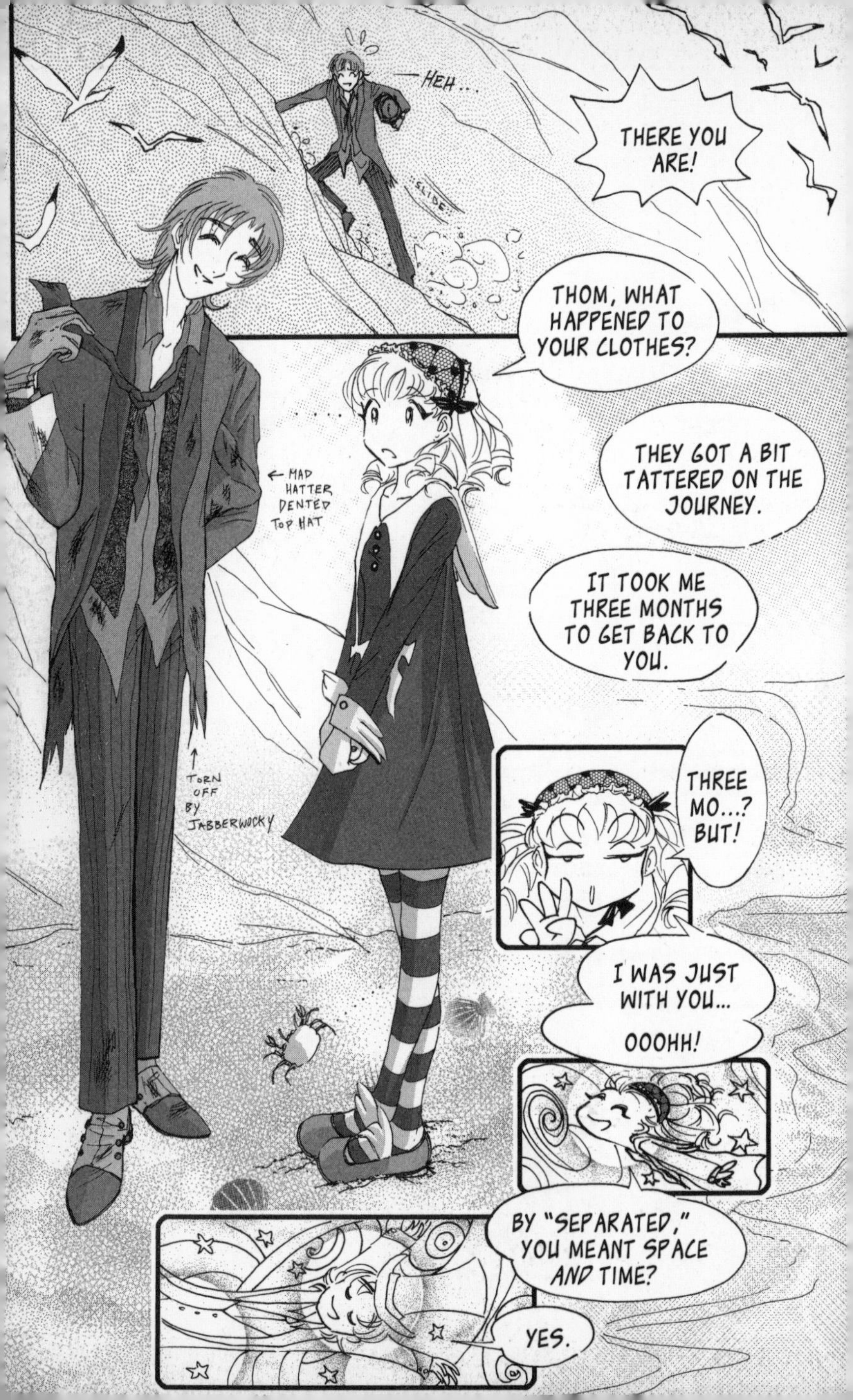
HEH...
THERE YOU ARE!
SLIDE
THOM, WHAT HAPPENED TO YOUR CLOTHES?
...
← MAD HATTER DENTED TOP HAT
↑ TORN OFF BY JABBERWOCKY
THEY GOT A BIT TATTERED ON THE JOURNEY.
IT TOOK ME THREE MONTHS TO GET BACK TO YOU.
THREE MO...? BUT!
I WAS JUST WITH YOU...
OOOHH!
BY "SEPARATED," YOU MEANT SPACE AND TIME?
YES.

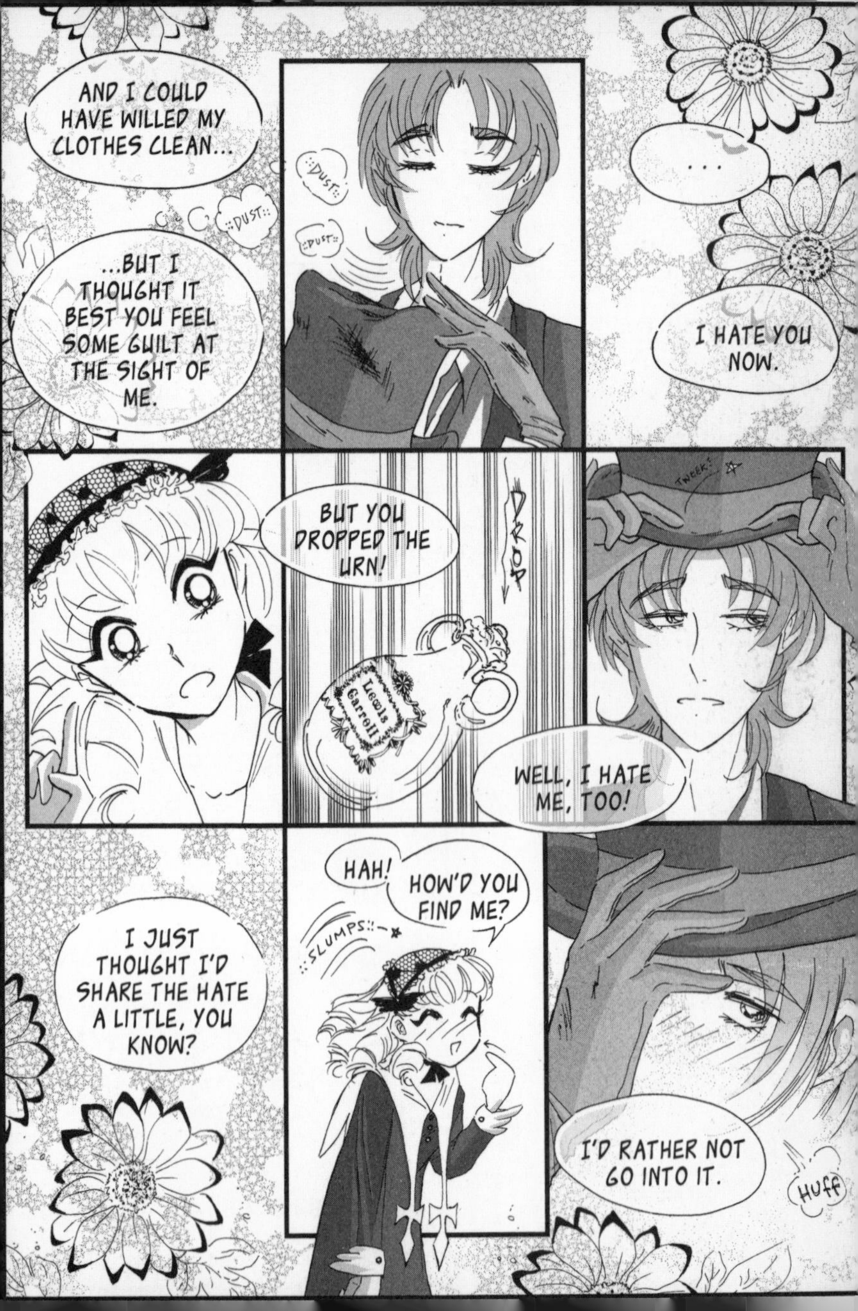
AND I COULD HAVE WILLED MY CLOTHES CLEAN...
::DUST::
...BUT I THOUGHT IT BEST YOU FEEL SOME GUILT AT THE SIGHT OF ME.
::DUST::
::DUST::
...
I HATE YOU NOW.
BUT YOU DROPPED THE URN!
DROP
Lewis Carroll
TWEEK!
WELL, I HATE ME, TOO!
I JUST THOUGHT I'D SHARE THE HATE A LITTLE, YOU KNOW?
HAH!
HOW'D YOU FIND ME?
::SLUMPS::
I'D RATHER NOT GO INTO IT.
HUFF

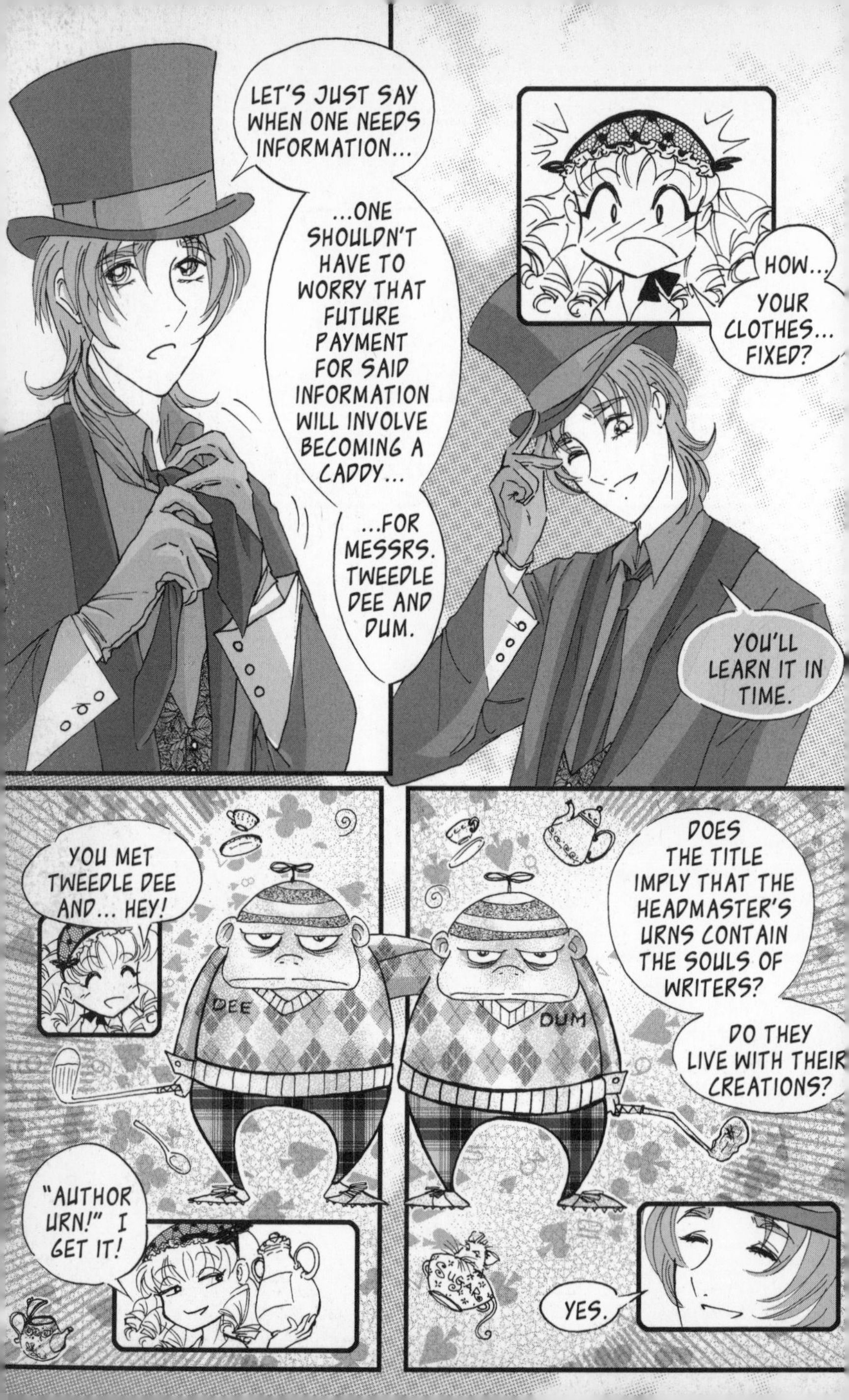
LET'S JUST SAY WHEN ONE NEEDS INFORMATION...
...ONE SHOULDN'T HAVE TO WORRY THAT FUTURE PAYMENT FOR SAID INFORMATION WILL INVOLVE BECOMING A CADDY...
...FOR MESSRS. TWEEDLE DEE AND DUM.
HOW... YOUR CLOTHES... FIXED?
YOU'LL LEARN IT IN TIME.
YOU MET TWEEDLE DEE AND... HEY!
DEE
"AUTHOR URN!" I GET IT!
DUM
DOES THE TITLE IMPLY THAT THE HEADMASTER'S URNS CONTAIN THE SOULS OF WRITERS?
DO THEY LIVE WITH THEIR CREATIONS?
SUGAR
YES.

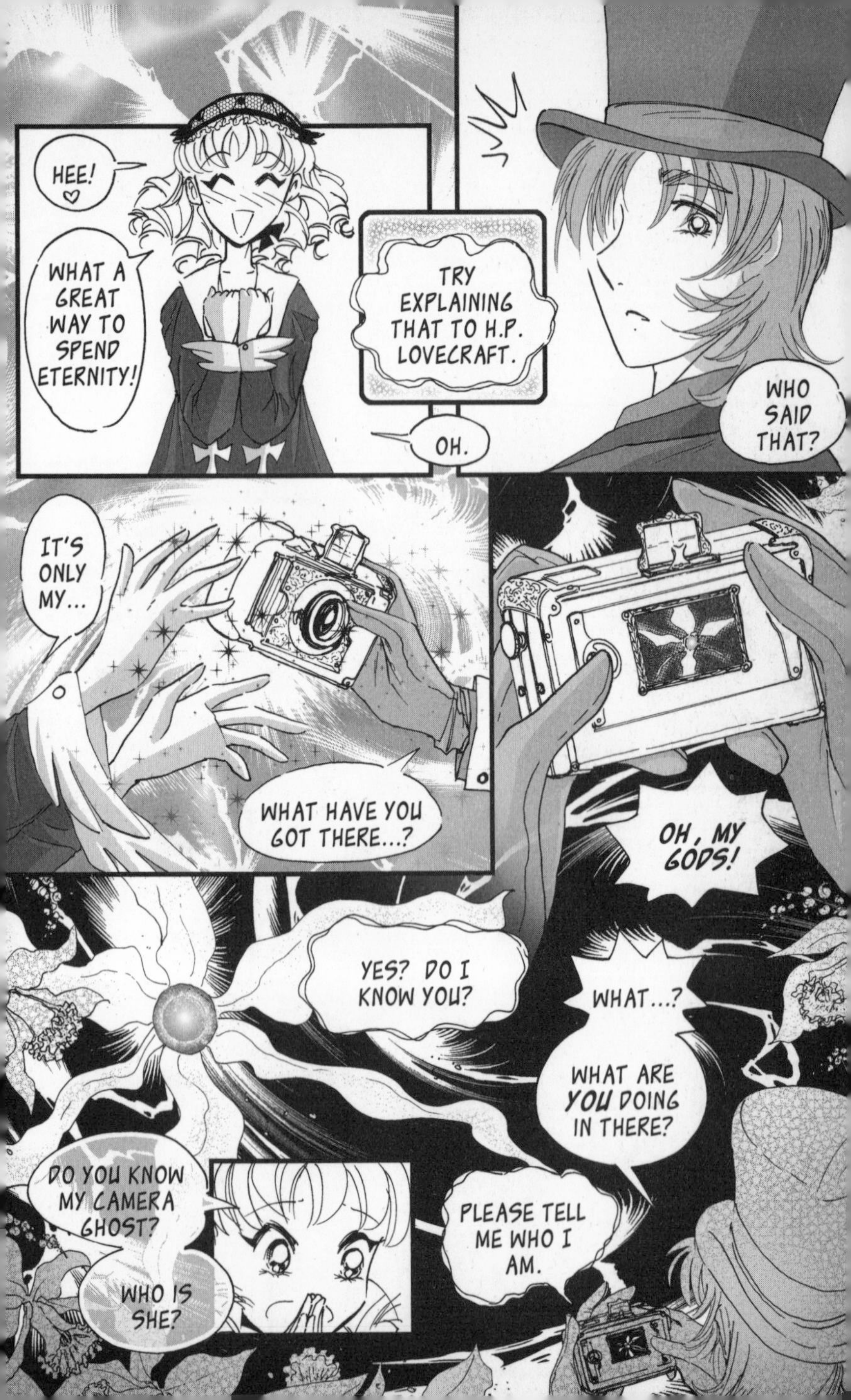
HEE! ♡
WHAT A GREAT WAY TO SPEND ETERNITY!
TRY EXPLAINING THAT TO H.P. LOVECRAFT.
OH.
WHO SAID THAT?
IT'S ONLY MY...
WHAT HAVE YOU GOT THERE...?
OH, MY GODS!
YES? DO I KNOW YOU?
WHAT...?
WHAT ARE YOU DOING IN THERE?
DO YOU KNOW MY CAMERA GHOST?
WHO IS SHE?
PLEASE TELL ME WHO I AM.

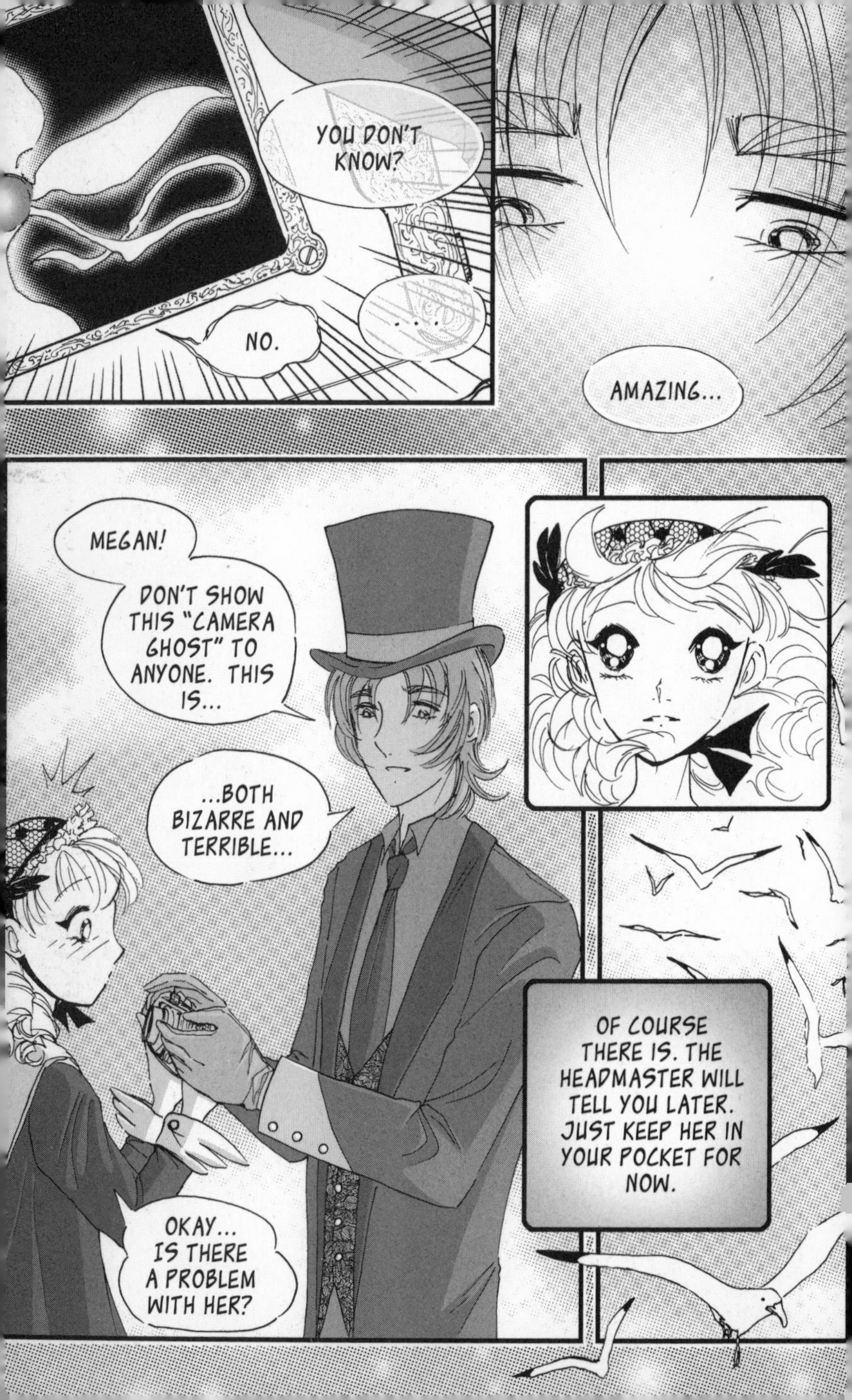
YOU DON'T KNOW?
NO.
...
AMAZING...
MEGAN!
DON'T SHOW THIS "CAMERA GHOST" TO ANYONE. THIS IS...
...BOTH BIZARRE AND TERRIBLE...
OKAY... IS THERE A PROBLEM WITH HER?
OF COURSE THERE IS. THE HEADMASTER WILL TELL YOU LATER. JUST KEEP HER IN YOUR POCKET FOR NOW.

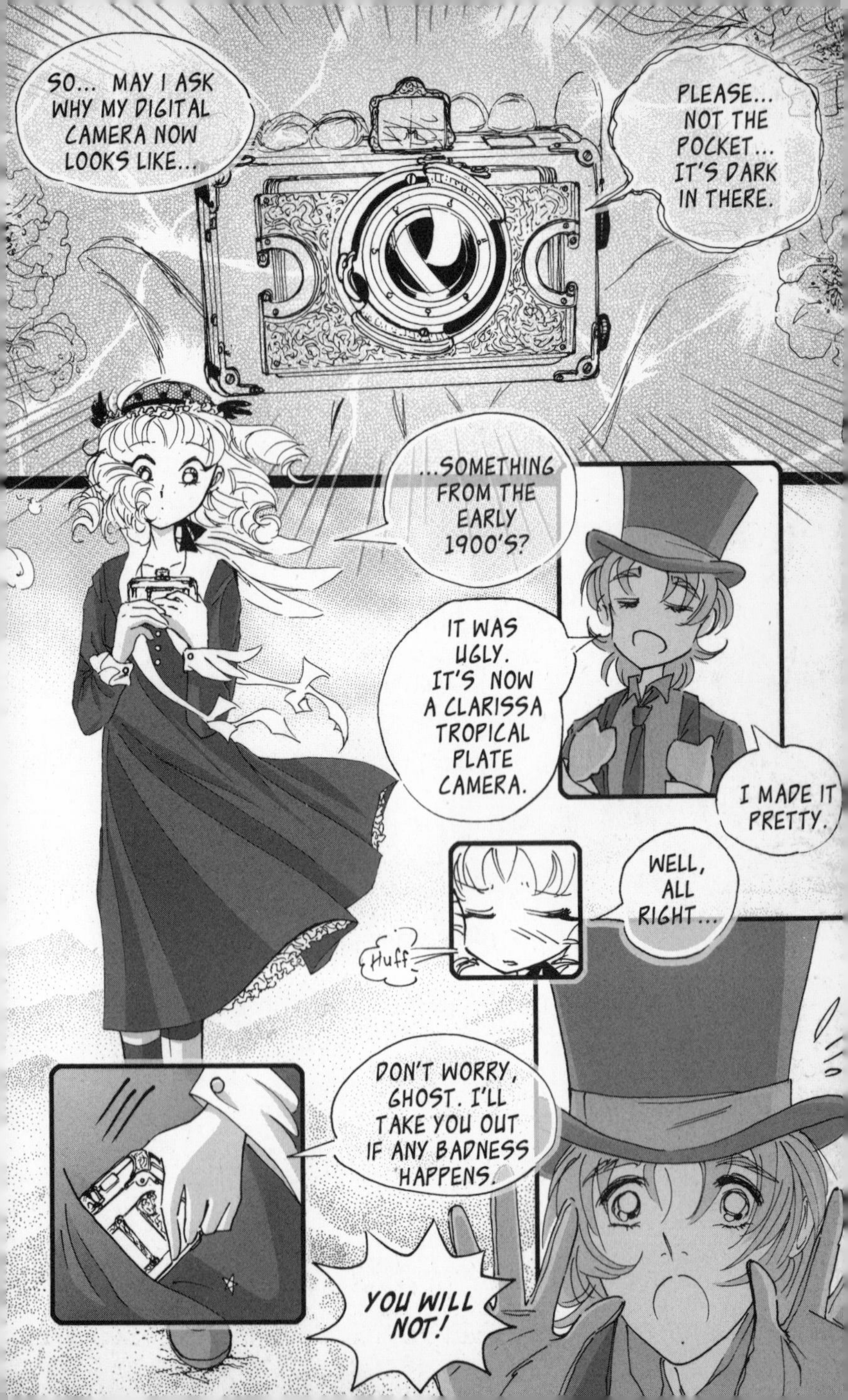
SO... MAY I ASK WHY MY DIGITAL CAMERA NOW LOOKS LIKE...
PLEASE... NOT THE POCKET... IT'S DARK IN THERE.
...SOMETHING FROM THE EARLY 1900'S?
IT WAS UGLY. IT'S NOW A CLARISSA TROPICAL PLATE CAMERA.
I MADE IT PRETTY.
Huff
WELL, ALL RIGHT...
DON'T WORRY, GHOST. I'LL TAKE YOU OUT IF ANY BADNESS HAPPENS.
YOU WILL NOT!

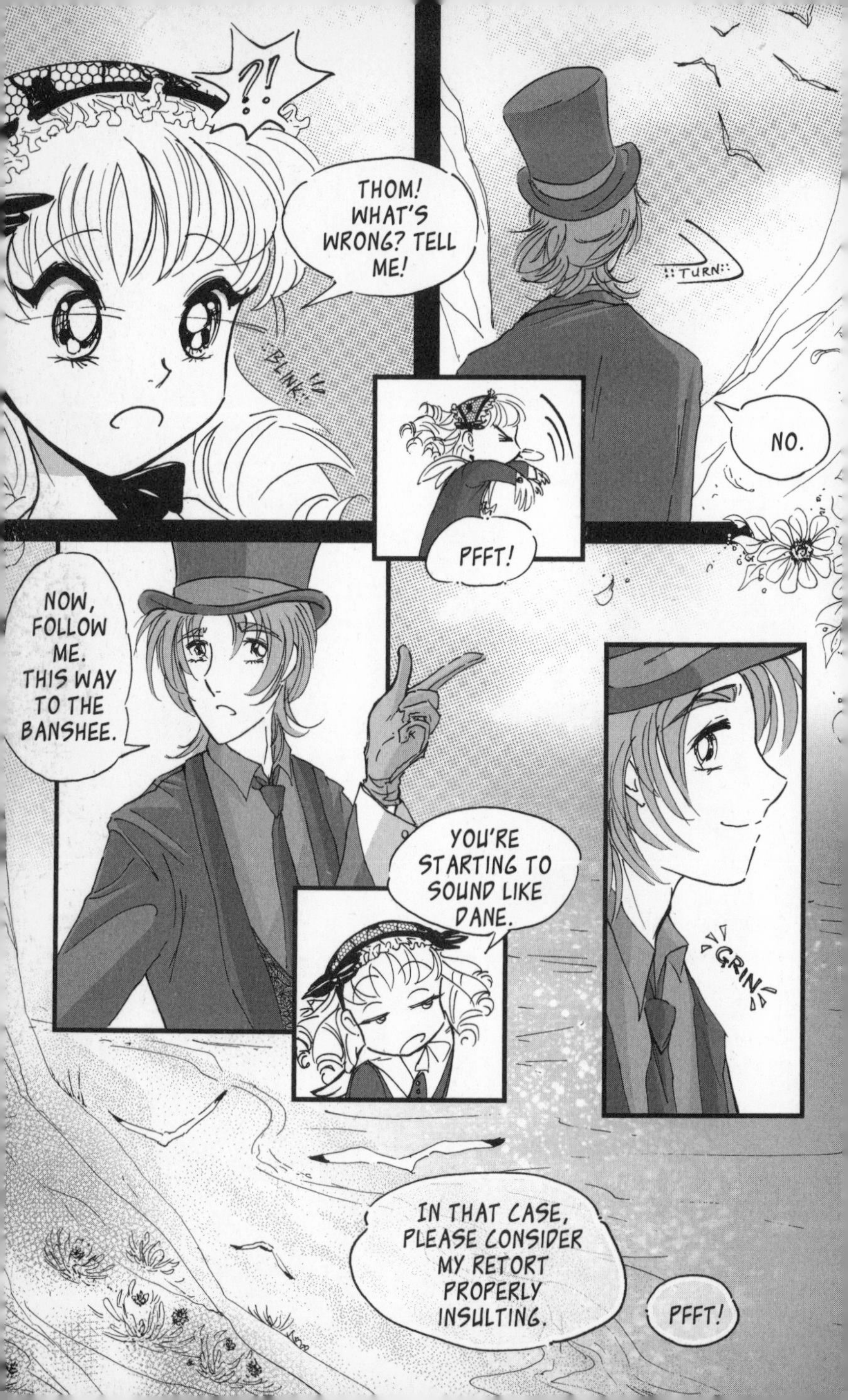
?!
THOM! WHAT'S WRONG? TELL ME!
BLINK
TURN
NO.
PFFT!
NOW, FOLLOW ME. THIS WAY TO THE BANSHEE.
YOU'RE STARTING TO SOUND LIKE DANE.
GRIN
IN THAT CASE, PLEASE CONSIDER MY RETORT PROPERLY INSULTING.
PFFT!

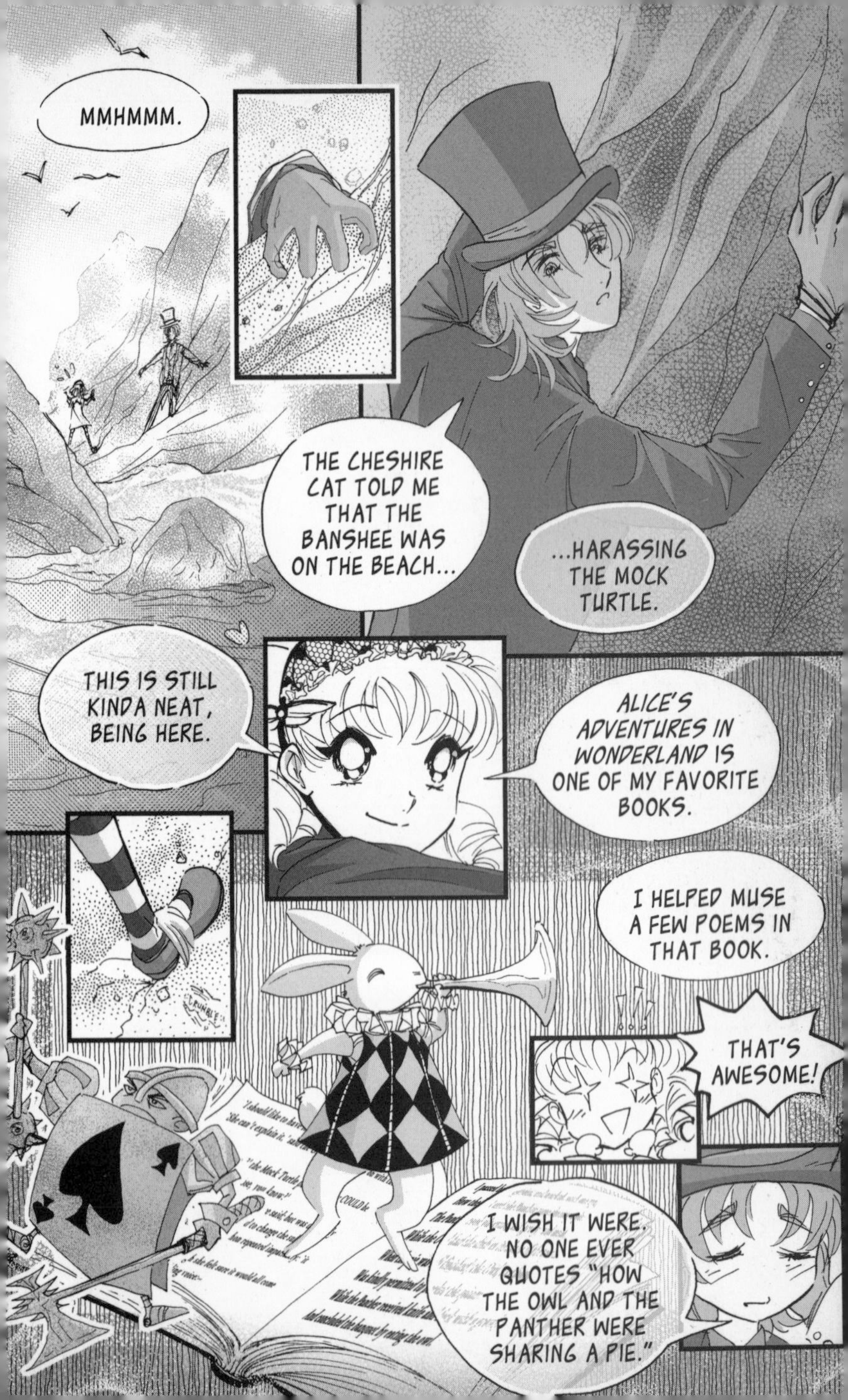
MMHMMM.
THE CHESHIRE CAT TOLD ME THAT THE BANSHEE WAS ON THE BEACH...
...HARASSING THE MOCK TURTLE.
THIS IS STILL KINDA NEAT, BEING HERE.
ALICE'S ADVENTURES IN WONDERLAND IS ONE OF MY FAVORITE BOOKS.
I HELPED MUSE A FEW POEMS IN THAT BOOK.
THAT'S AWESOME!
I WISH IT WERE. NO ONE EVER QUOTES "HOW THE OWL AND THE PANTHER WERE SHARING A PIE."

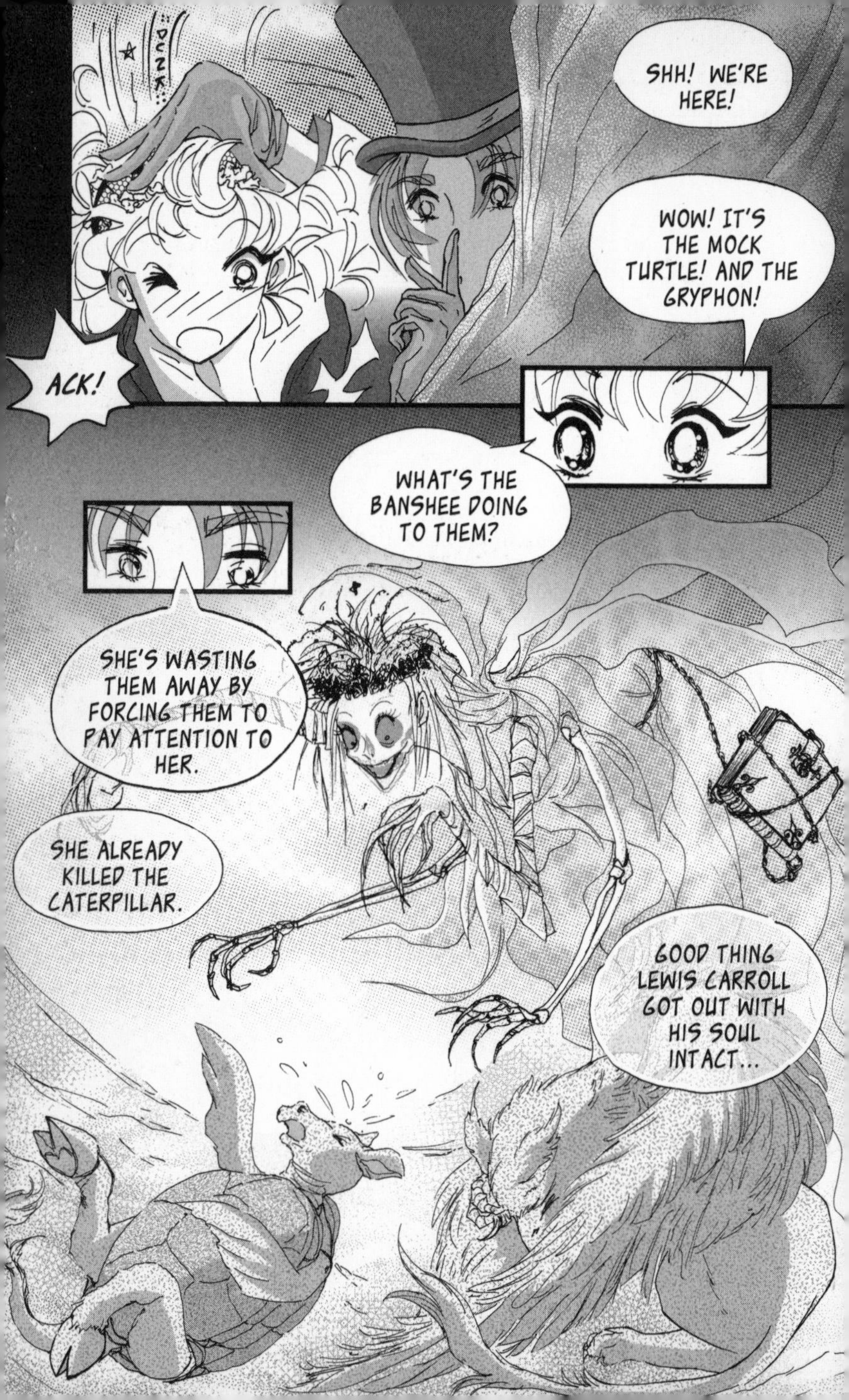
DUNK...!!
ACK!
SHH! WE'RE HERE!
WOW! IT'S THE MOCK TURTLE! AND THE GRYPHON!
WHAT'S THE BANSHEE DOING TO THEM?
SHE'S WASTING THEM AWAY BY FORCING THEM TO PAY ATTENTION TO HER.
SHE ALREADY KILLED THE CATERPILLAR.
GOOD THING LEWIS CARROLL GOT OUT WITH HIS SOUL INTACT...

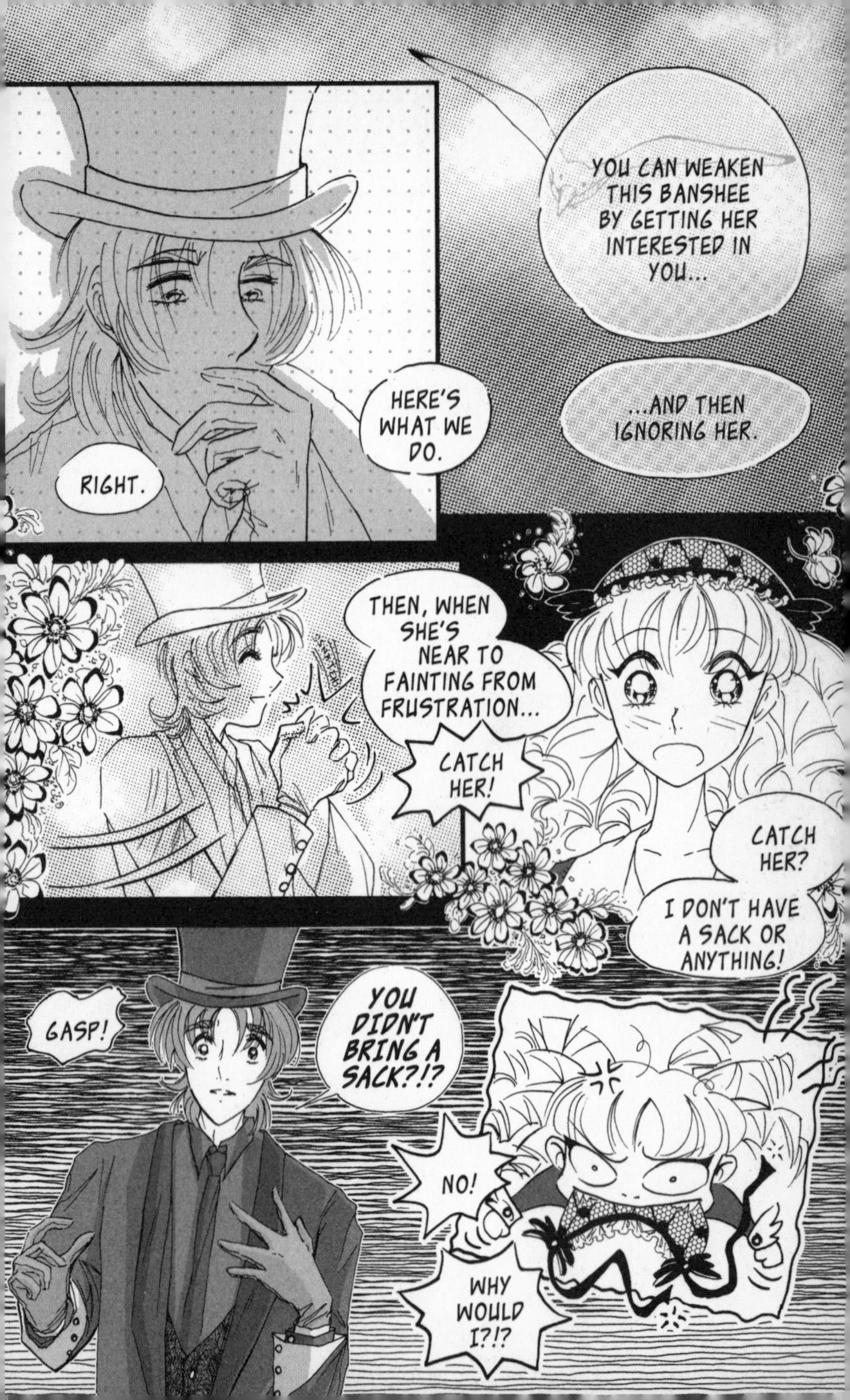
HERE'S WHAT WE DO.
RIGHT.
YOU CAN WEAKEN THIS BANSHEE BY GETTING HER INTERESTED IN YOU...
...AND THEN IGNORING HER.
THEN, WHEN SHE'S NEAR TO FAINTING FROM FRUSTRATION...
CATCH HER!
CATCH HER?
I DON'T HAVE A SACK OR ANYTHING!
GASP!
YOU DIDN'T BRING A SACK?!?
NO!
WHY WOULD I?!?

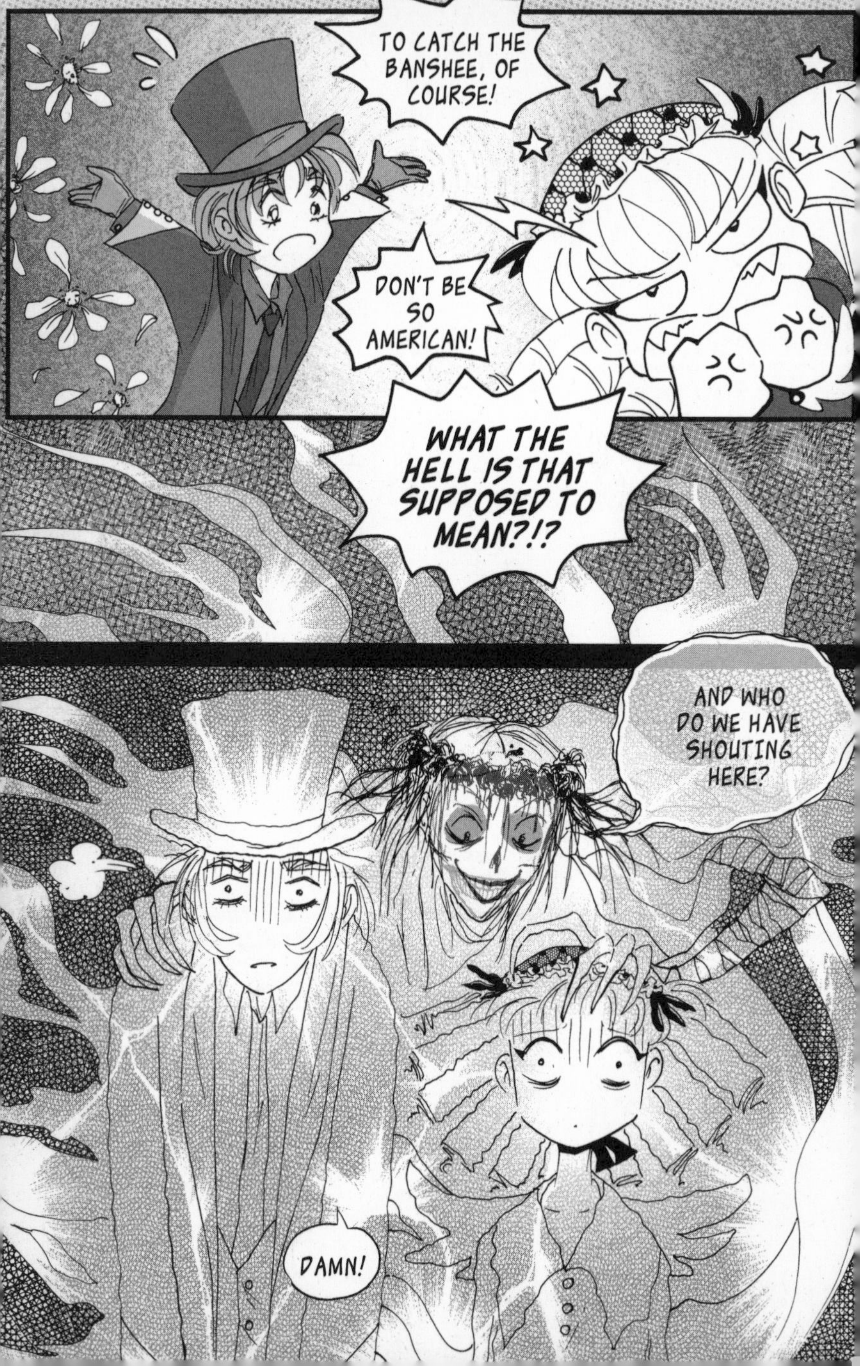
TO CATCH THE BANSHEE, OF COURSE!
DON'T BE SO AMERICAN!
WHAT THE HELL IS THAT SUPPOSED TO MEAN?!?
AND WHO DO WE HAVE SHOUTING HERE?
DAMN!

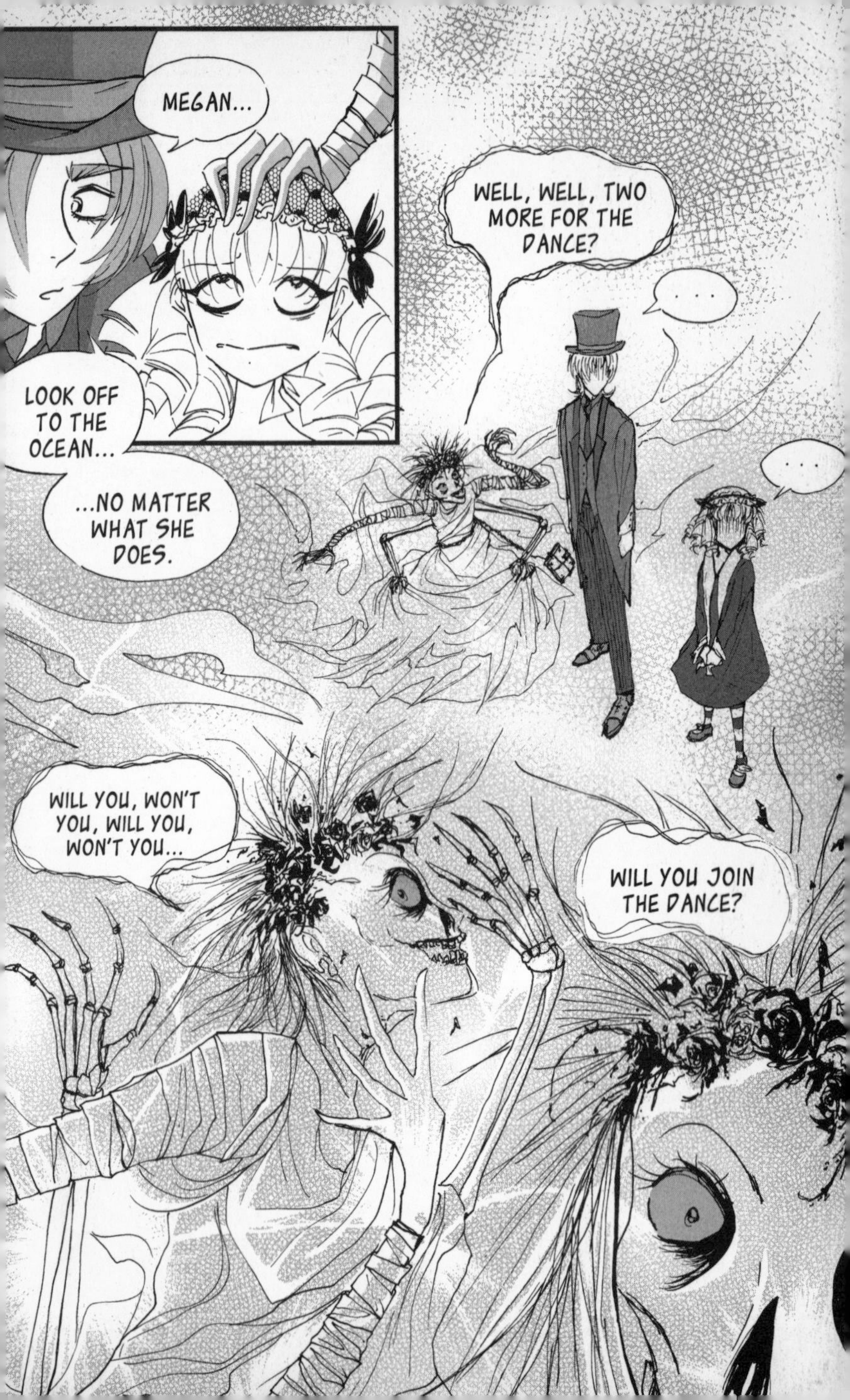
MEGAN...
LOOK OFF TO THE OCEAN...
...NO MATTER WHAT SHE DOES.
WELL, WELL, TWO MORE FOR THE DANCE?
...
...
WILL YOU, WON'T YOU, WILL YOU, WON'T YOU...
WILL YOU JOIN THE DANCE?

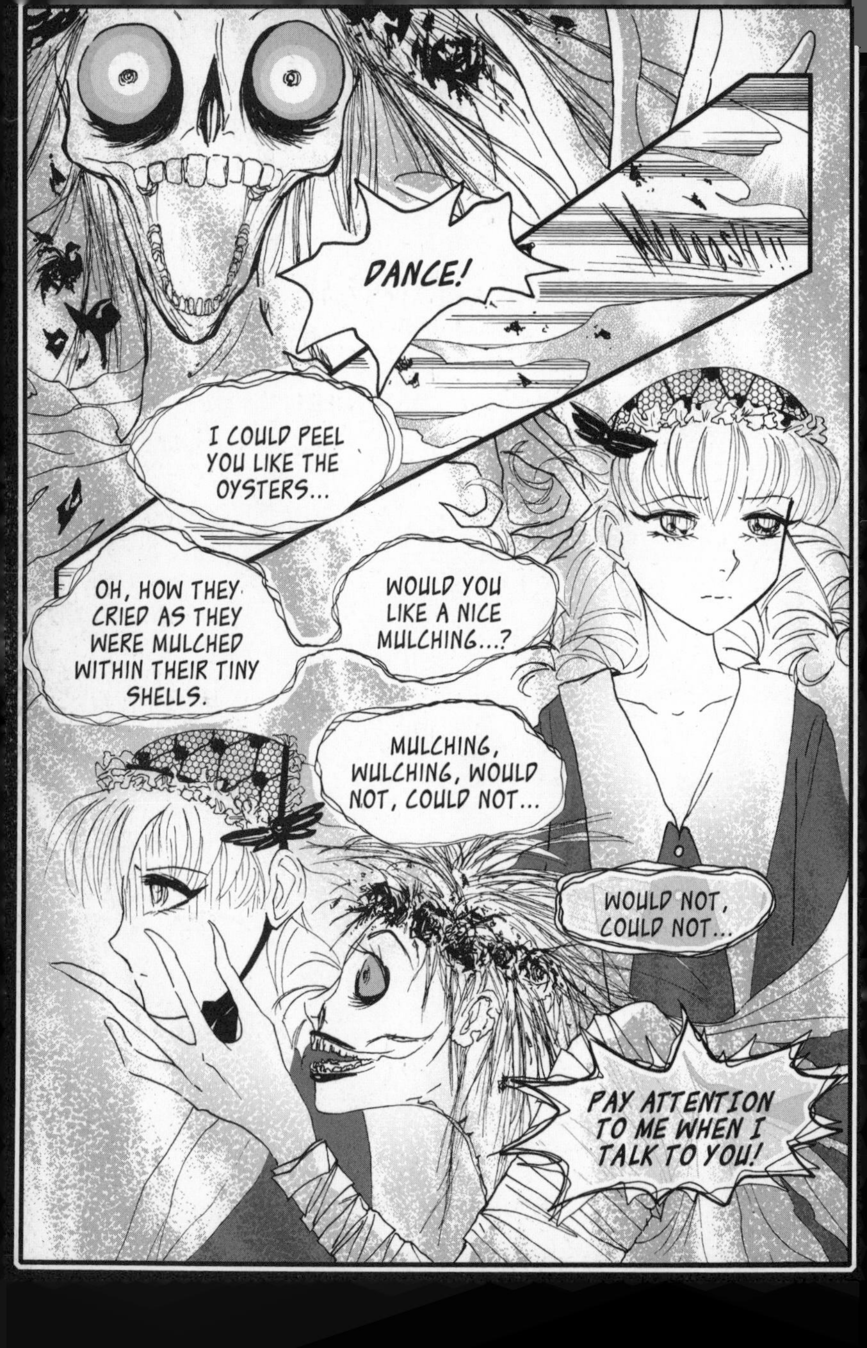
DANCE!
WOOOOSH!!!
I COULD PEEL YOU LIKE THE OYSTERS...
OH, HOW THEY CRIED AS THEY WERE MULCHED WITHIN THEIR TINY SHELLS.
WOULD YOU LIKE A NICE MULCHING...?
MULCHING, WULCHING, WOULD NOT, COULD NOT...
WOULD NOT, COULD NOT...
PAY ATTENTION TO ME WHEN I TALK TO YOU!

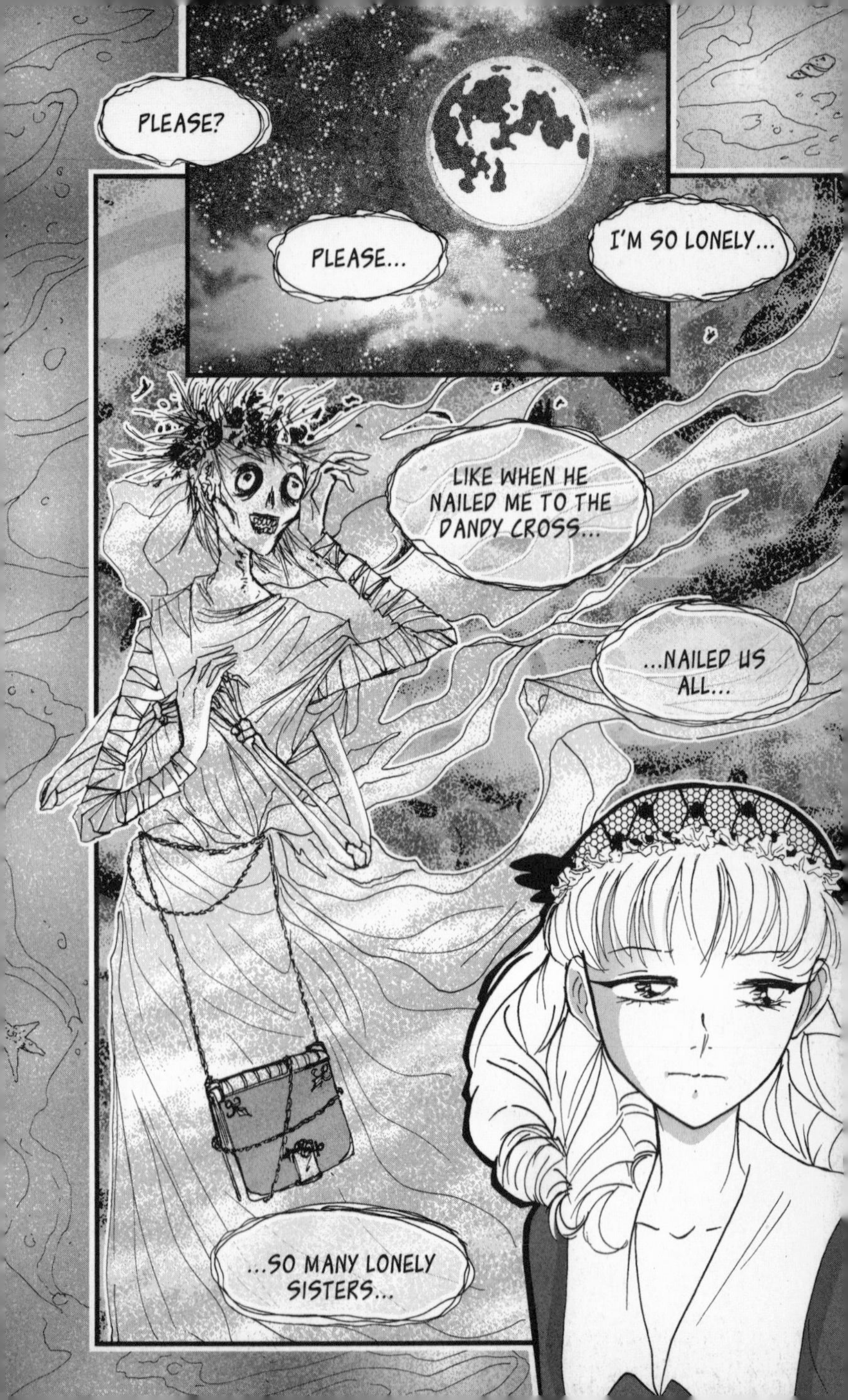
I'M SO LONELY...
PLEASE...
PLEASE?
LIKE WHEN HE NAILED ME TO THE DANDY CROSS...
...NAILED US ALL...
...SO MANY LONELY SISTERS...

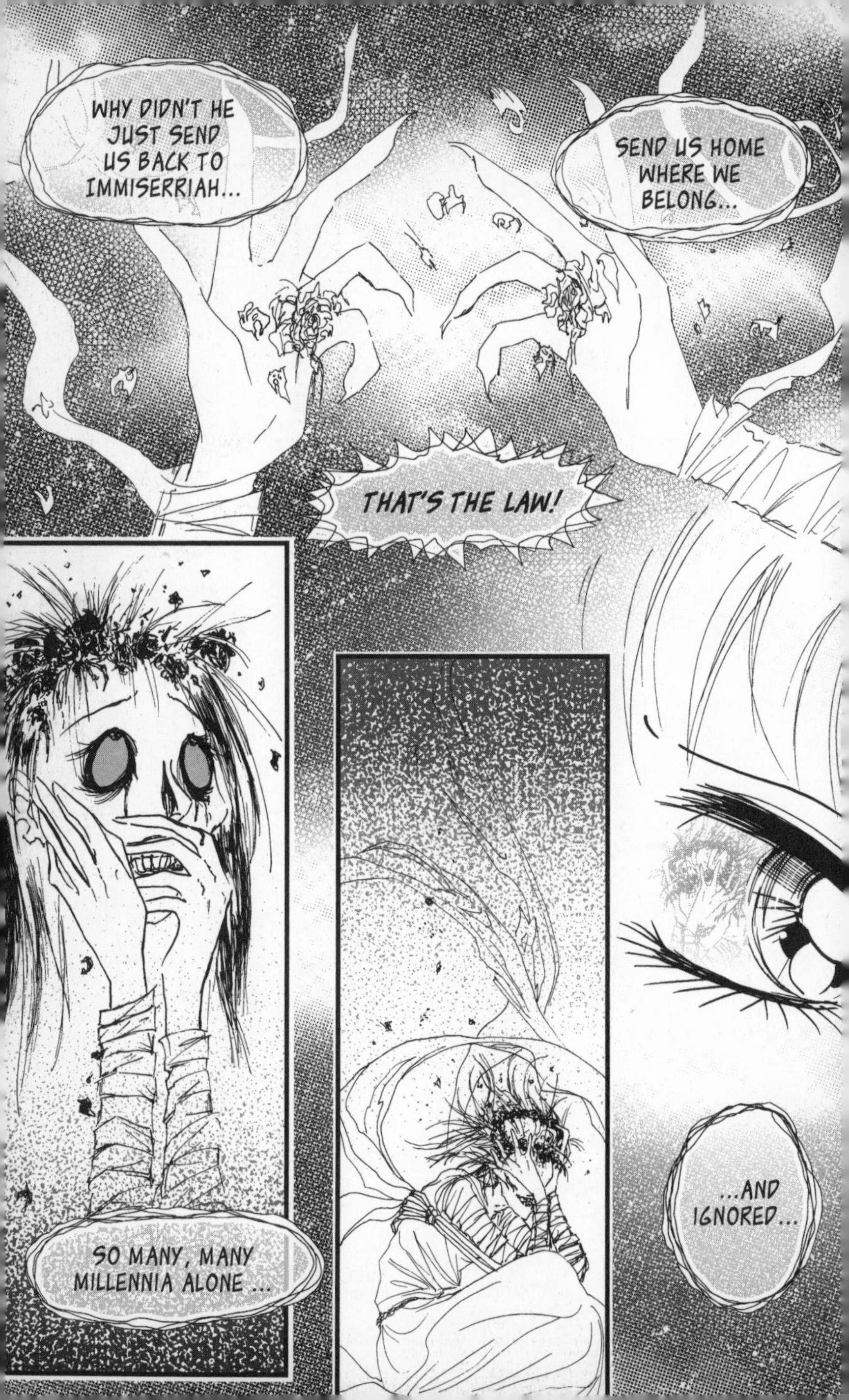
WHY DIDN'T HE JUST SEND US BACK TO IMMISERRIAH...
SEND US HOME WHERE WE BELONG...
THAT'S THE LAW!
SO MANY, MANY MILLENNIA ALONE...
...AND IGNORED...

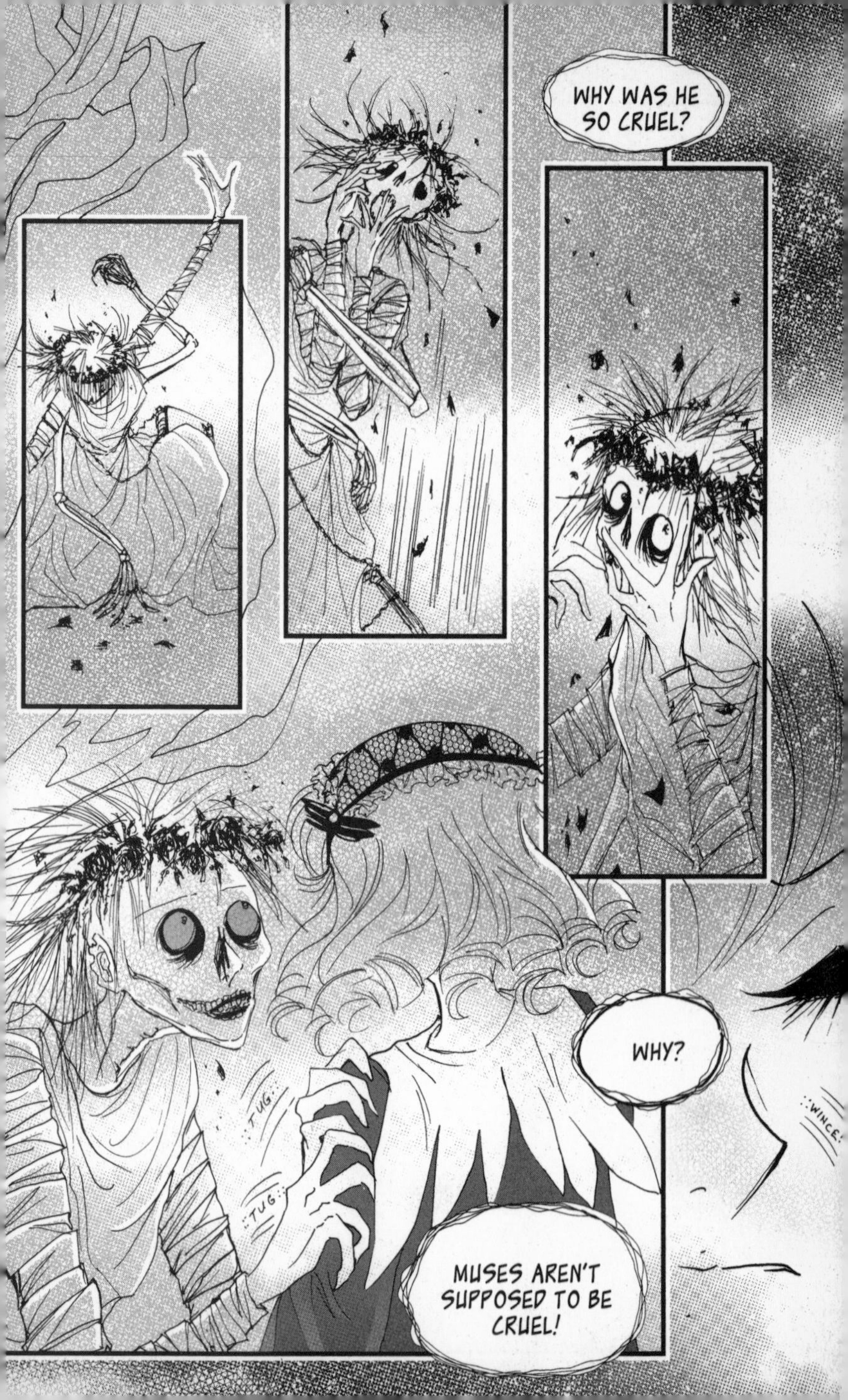
WHY WAS HE SO CRUEL?
::TUG::
::TUG::
WHY?
::WINCE::
MUSES AREN'T SUPPOSED TO BE CRUEL!

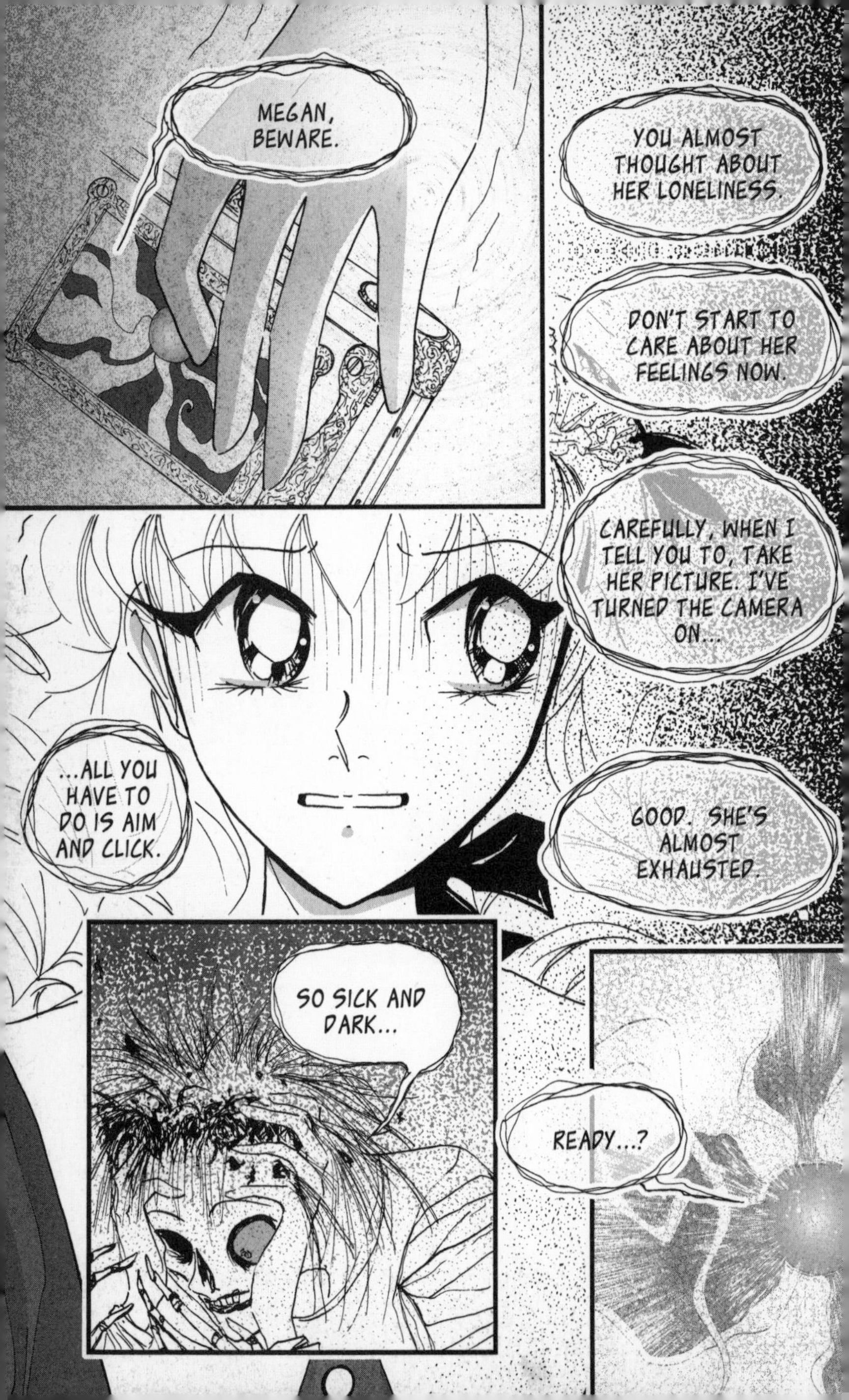
MEGAN, BEWARE.
YOU ALMOST THOUGHT ABOUT HER LONELINESS.
DON'T START TO CARE ABOUT HER FEELINGS NOW.
CAREFULLY, WHEN I TELL YOU TO, TAKE HER PICTURE. I'VE TURNED THE CAMERA ON...
...ALL YOU HAVE TO DO IS AIM AND CLICK.
GOOD. SHE'S ALMOST EXHAUSTED.
SO SICK AND DARK...
READY...?

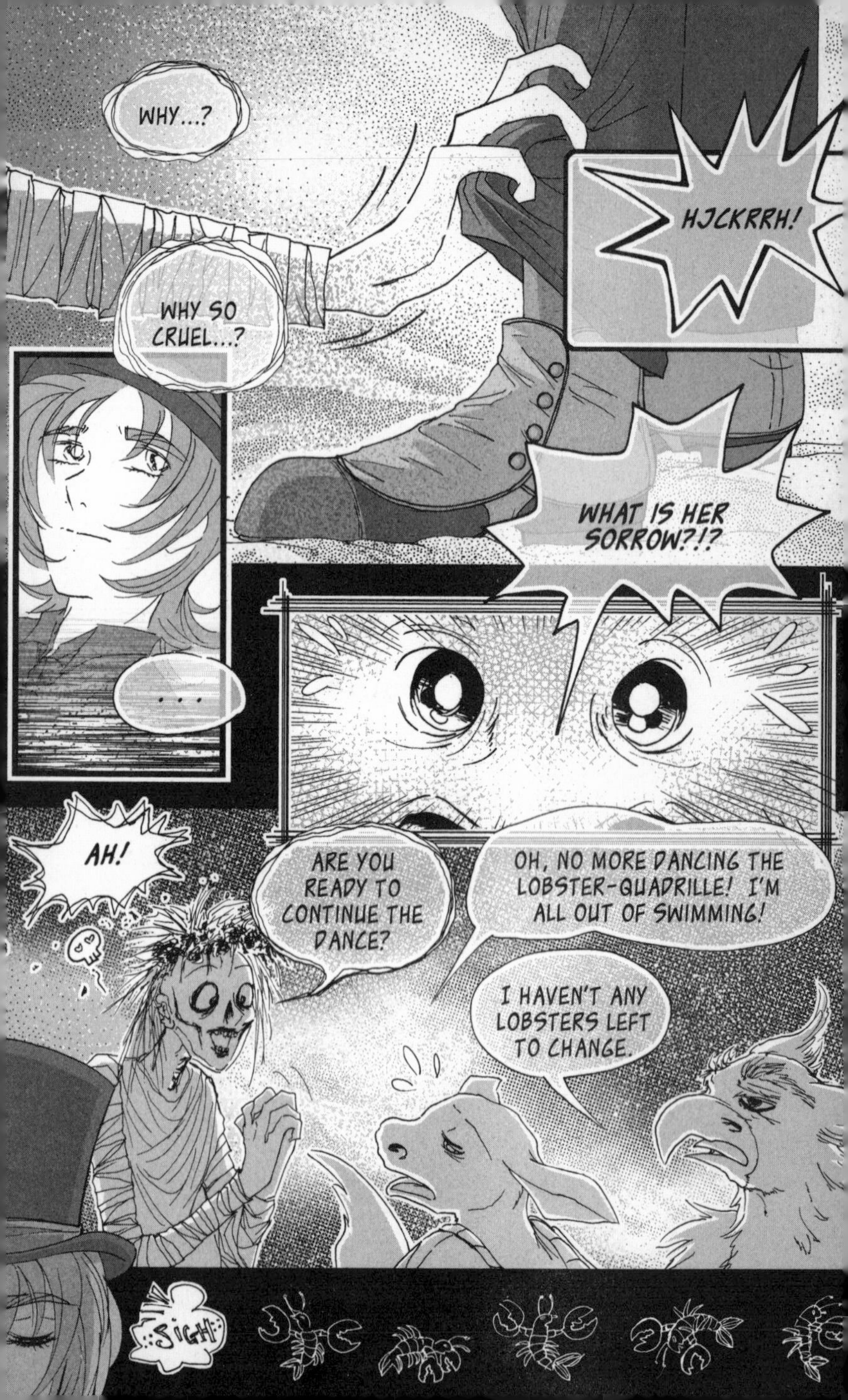
WHY...?
WHY SO CRUEL...?
HJCKRRH!
...
WHAT IS HER SORROW?!?
AH!
ARE YOU READY TO CONTINUE THE DANCE?
OH, NO MORE DANCING THE LOBSTER-QUADRILLE! I'M ALL OUT OF SWIMMING!
I HAVEN'T ANY LOBSTERS LEFT TO CHANGE.
SIGH

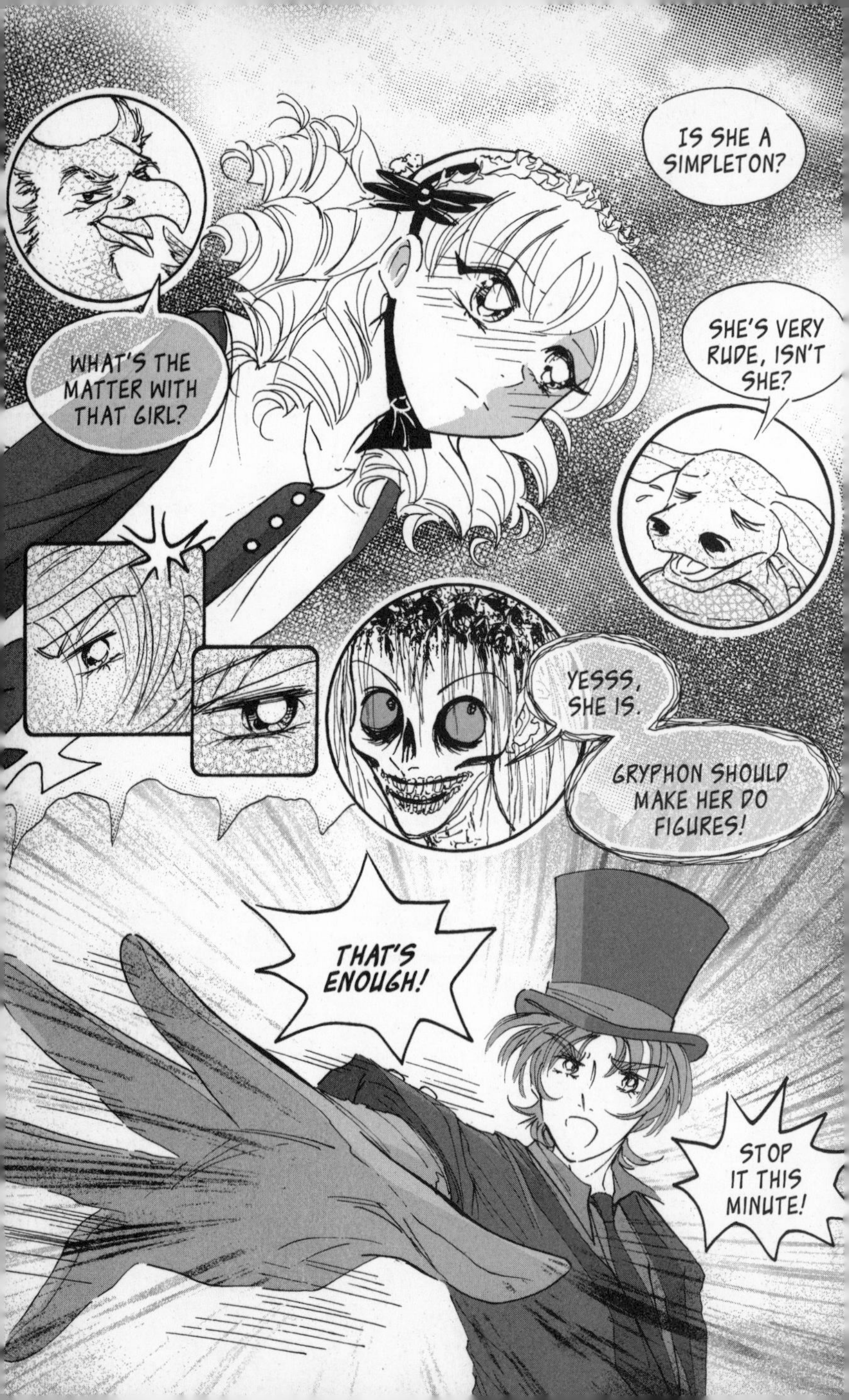
WHAT'S THE MATTER WITH THAT GIRL?
IS SHE A SIMPLETON?
SHE'S VERY RUDE, ISN'T SHE?
YESSS, SHE IS.
GRYPHON SHOULD MAKE HER DO FIGURES!
THAT'S ENOUGH!
STOP IT THIS MINUTE!

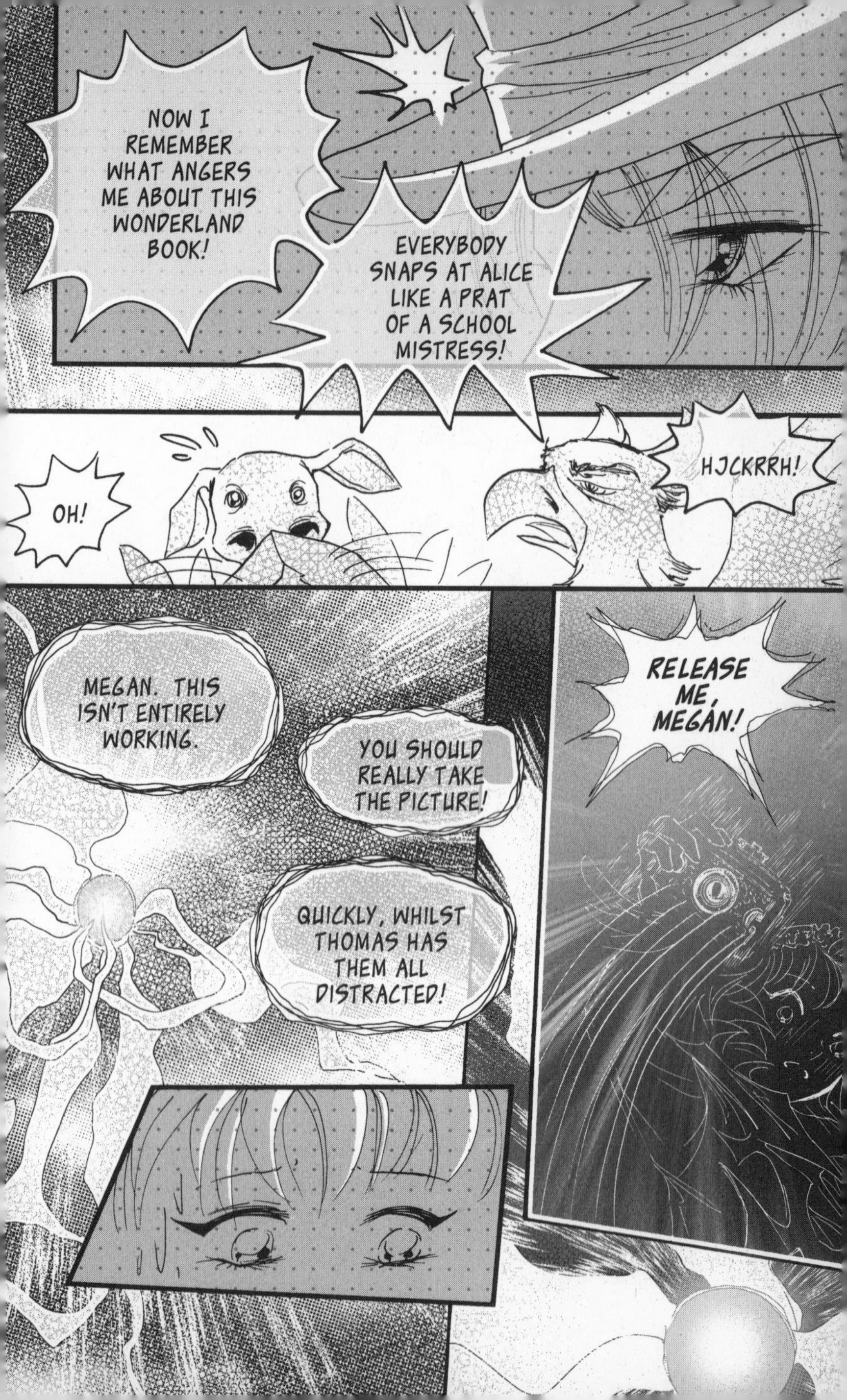
NOW I REMEMBER WHAT ANGERS ME ABOUT THIS WONDERLAND BOOK!
EVERYBODY SNAPS AT ALICE LIKE A PRAT OF A SCHOOL MISTRESS!
OH!
HJCKRRH!
MEGAN. THIS ISN'T ENTIRELY WORKING.
YOU SHOULD REALLY TAKE THE PICTURE!
QUICKLY, WHILST THOMAS HAS THEM ALL DISTRACTED!
RELEASE ME, MEGAN!

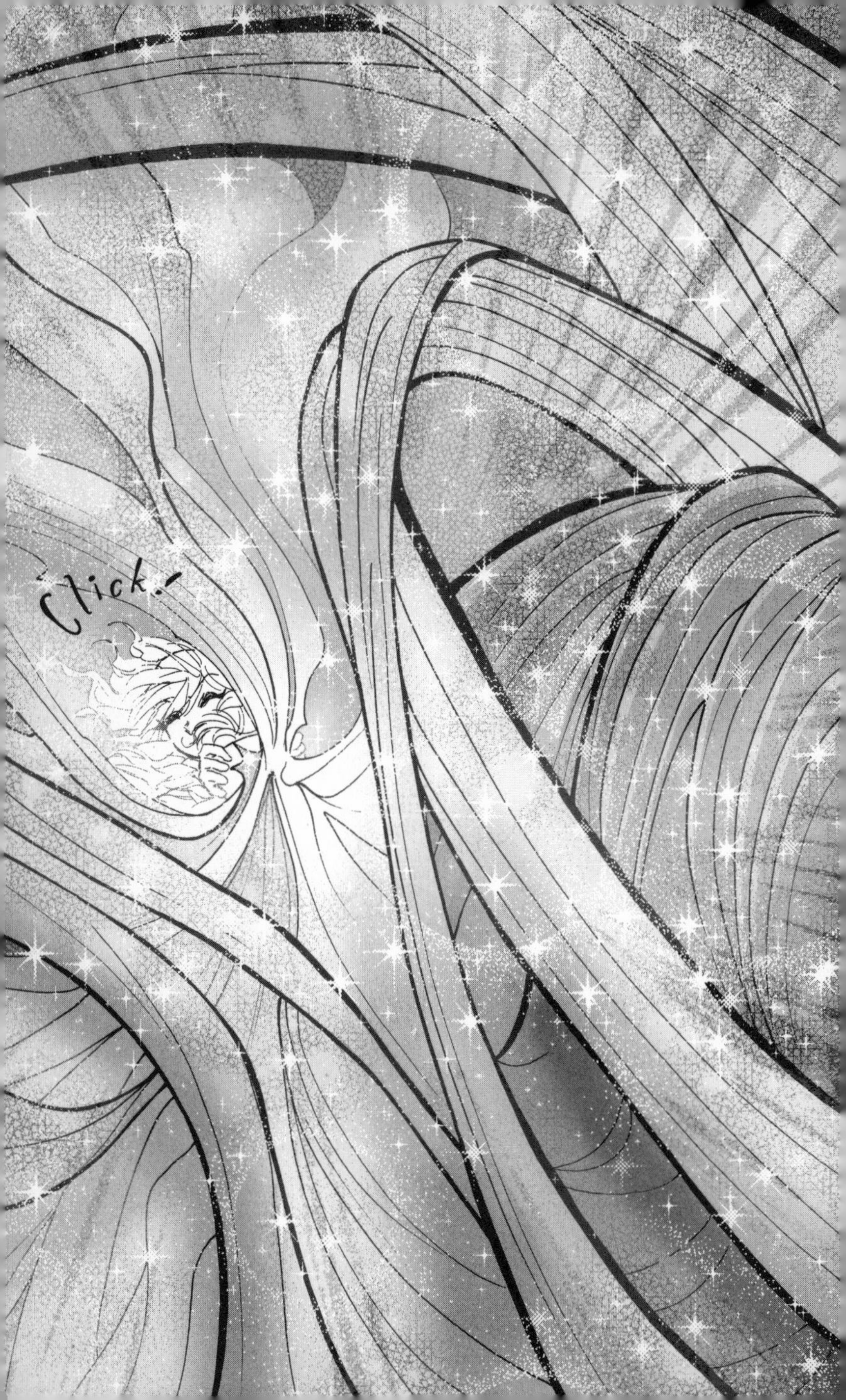
Click!

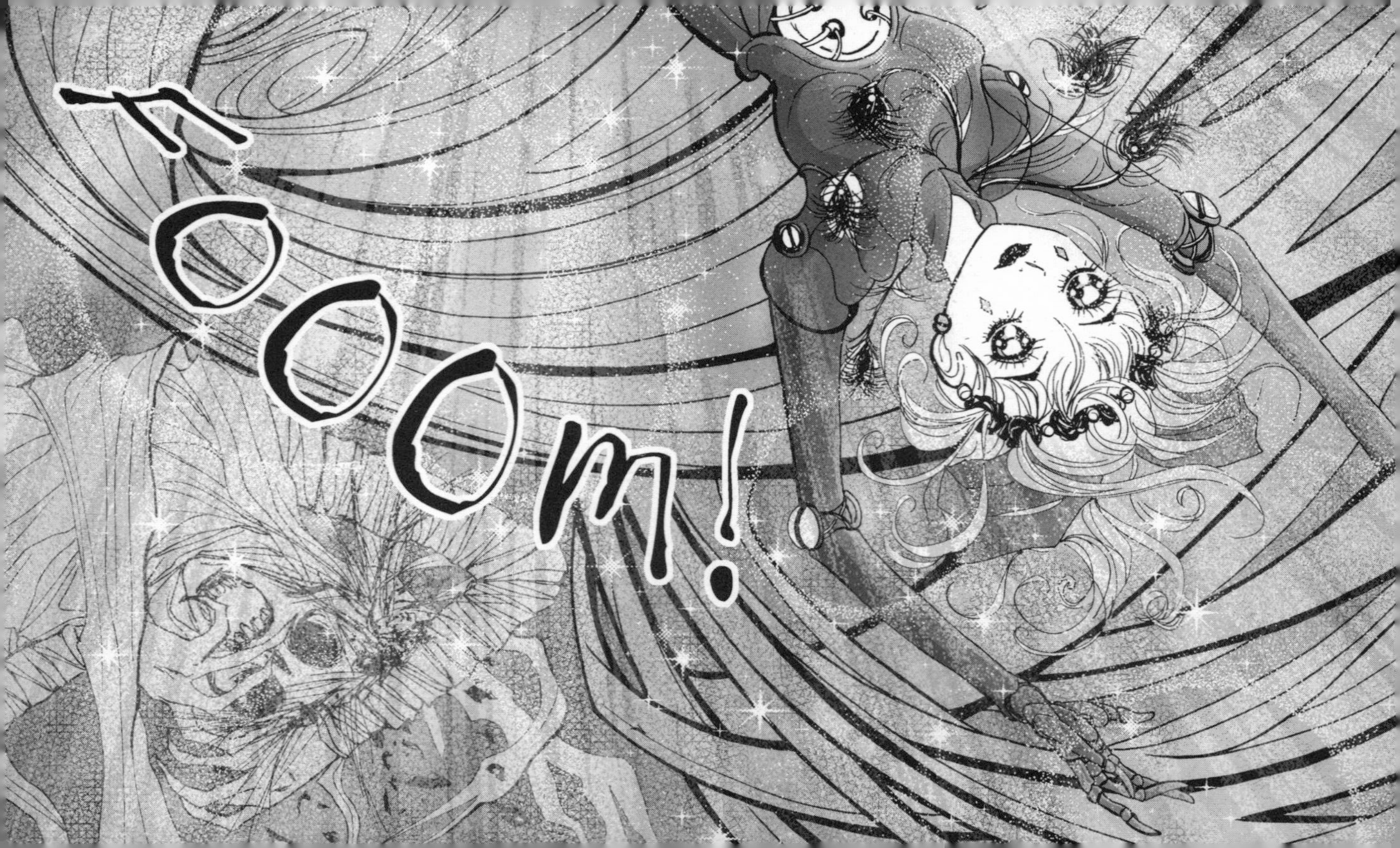
FOOOM!

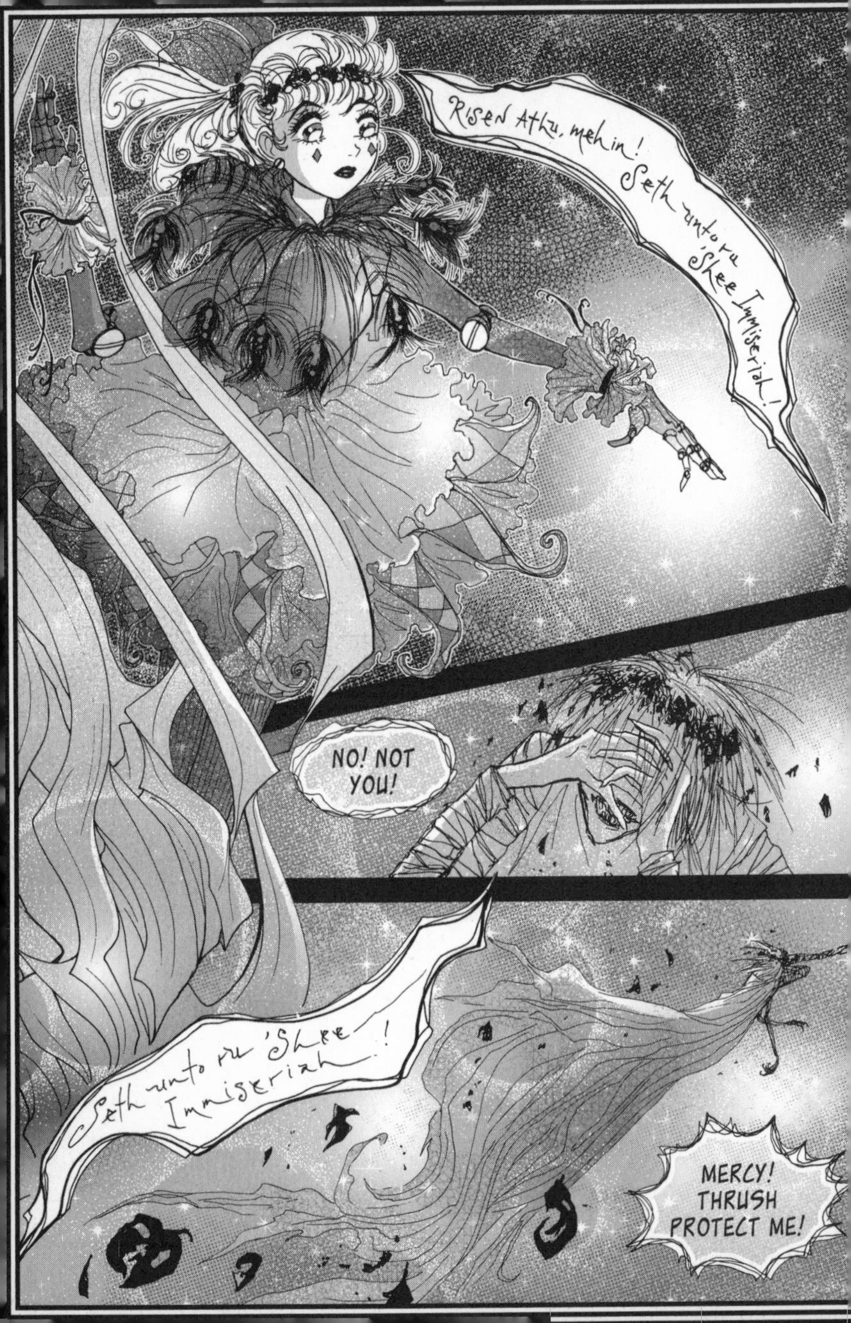
Risen Athu, mehin! Seth untoru 'Shee Immiseriah!
NO! NOT YOU!
Seth untoru 'Shee Immiseriah!
MERCY! THRUSH PROTECT ME!

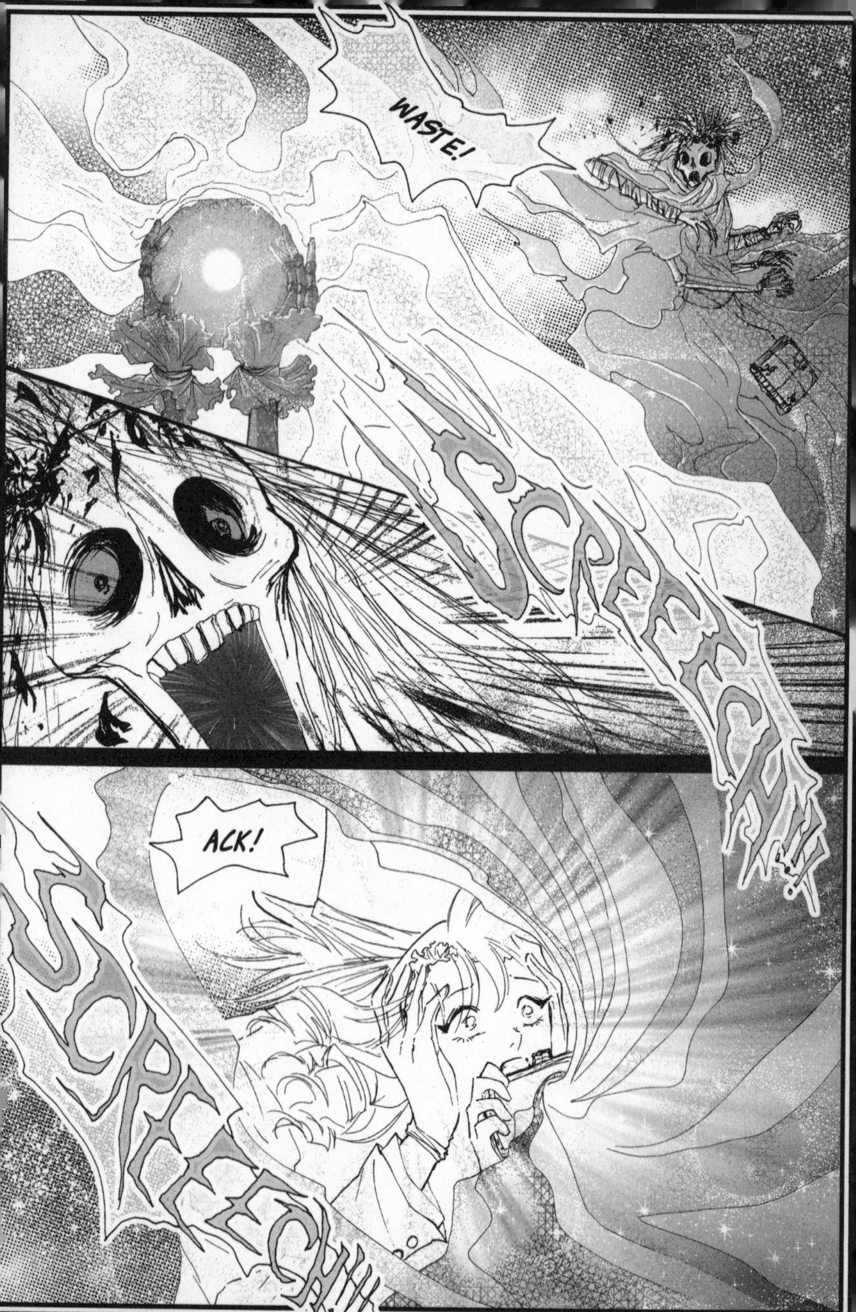
WASTE!
SCREECH!!
ACK!
SCREECH!!!

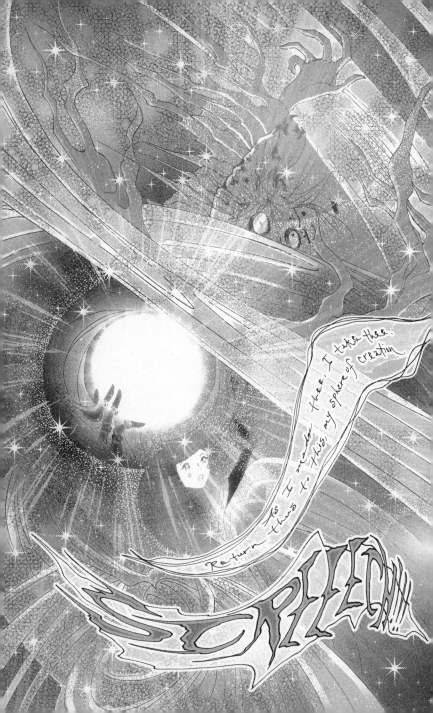

Return thus to thee. I take thee. As I made thee, I take thee. Return thus to this, my sphere of creation.

SCREECH!!!

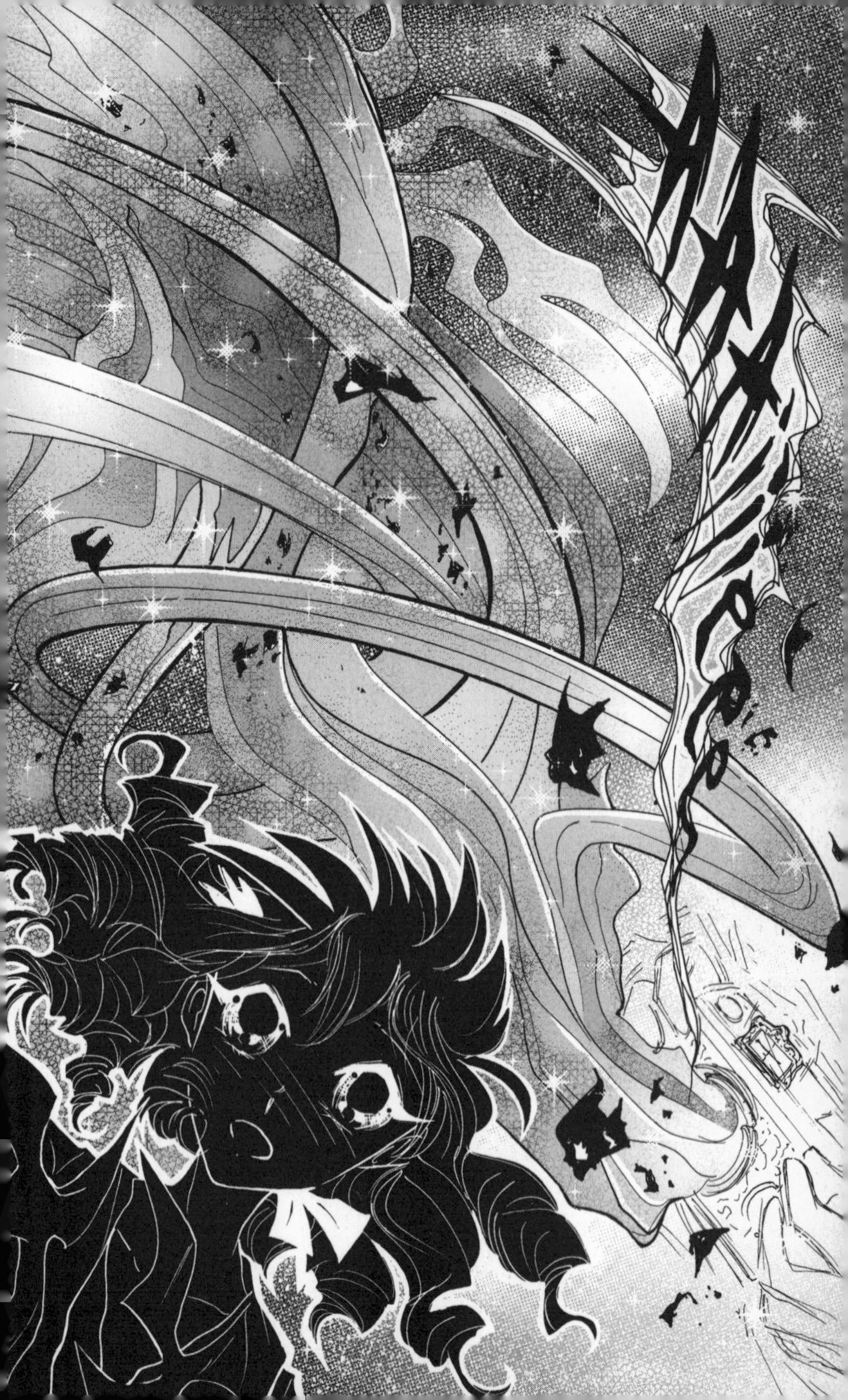

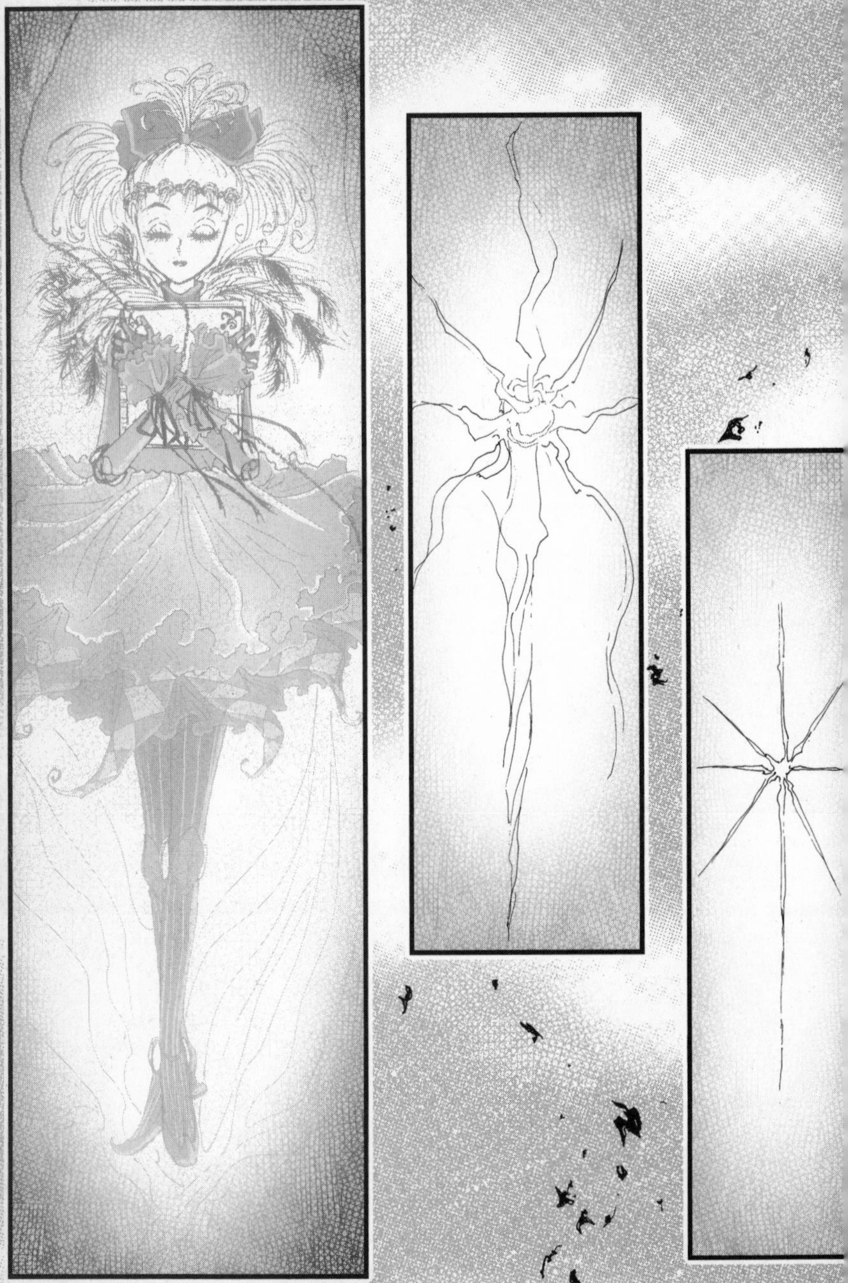

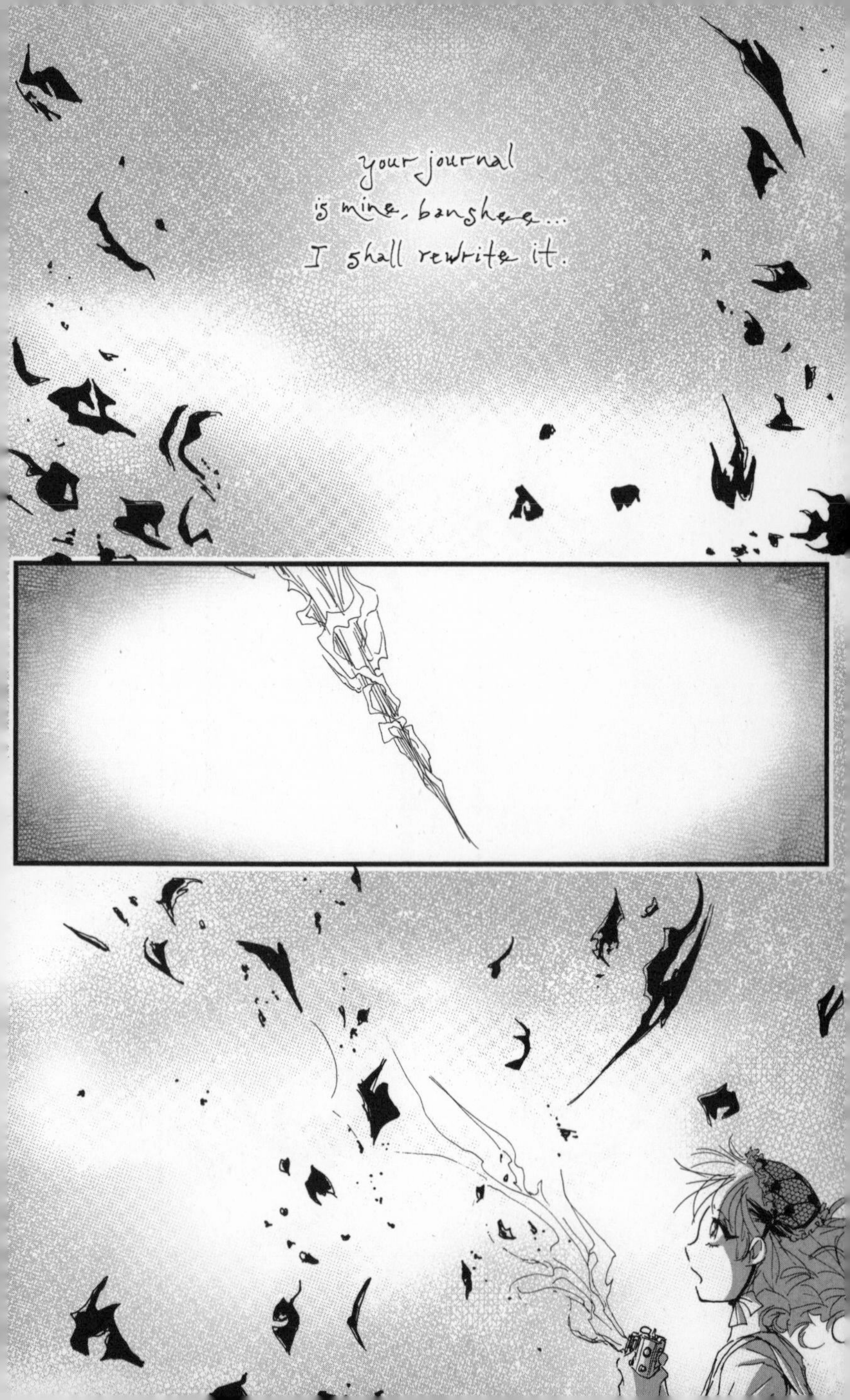
your journal
is mine, banshee...
I shall rewrite it.

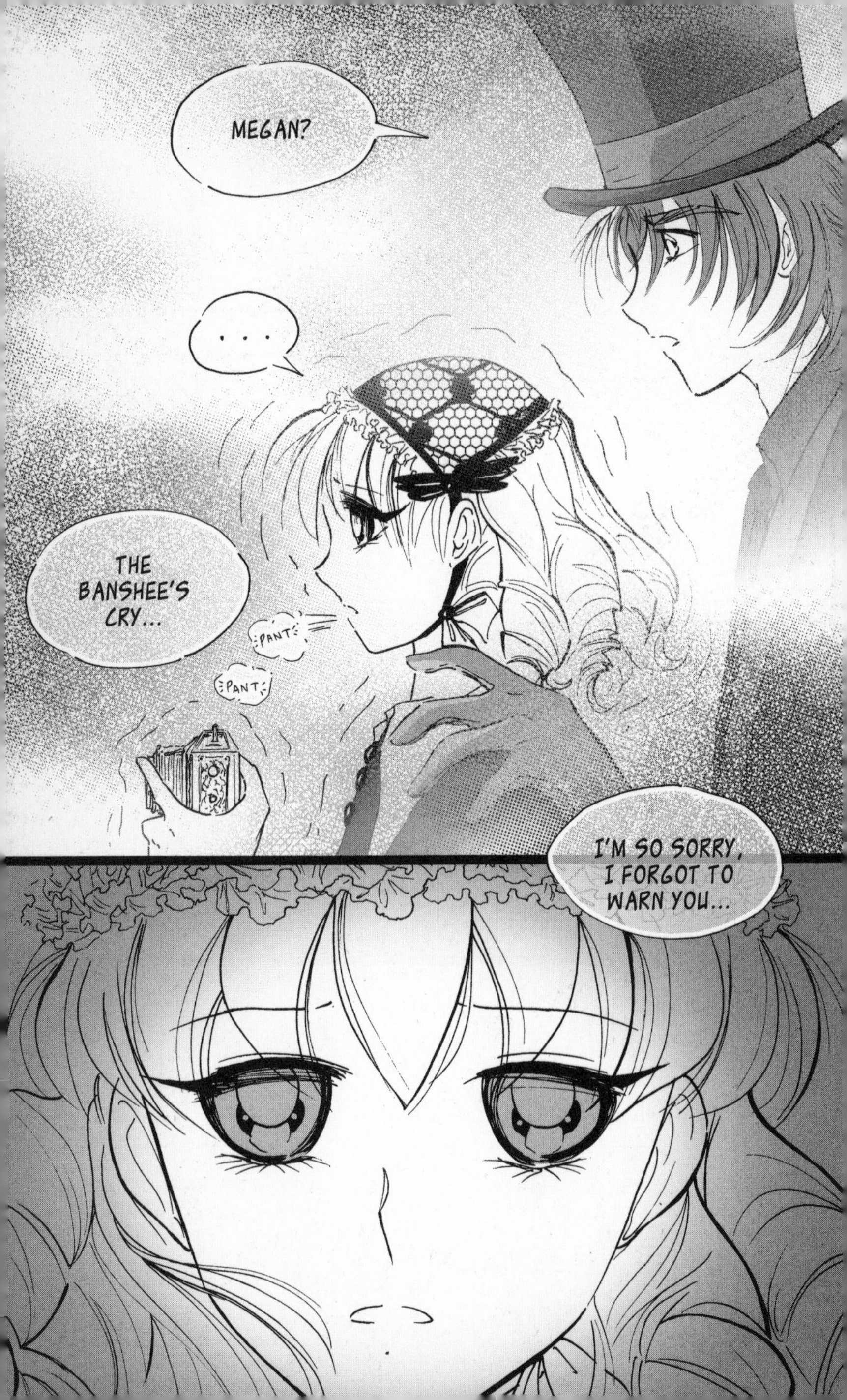
MEGAN?
. . .
THE BANSHEE'S CRY...
PANT
PANT
I'M SO SORRY, I FORGOT TO WARN YOU...

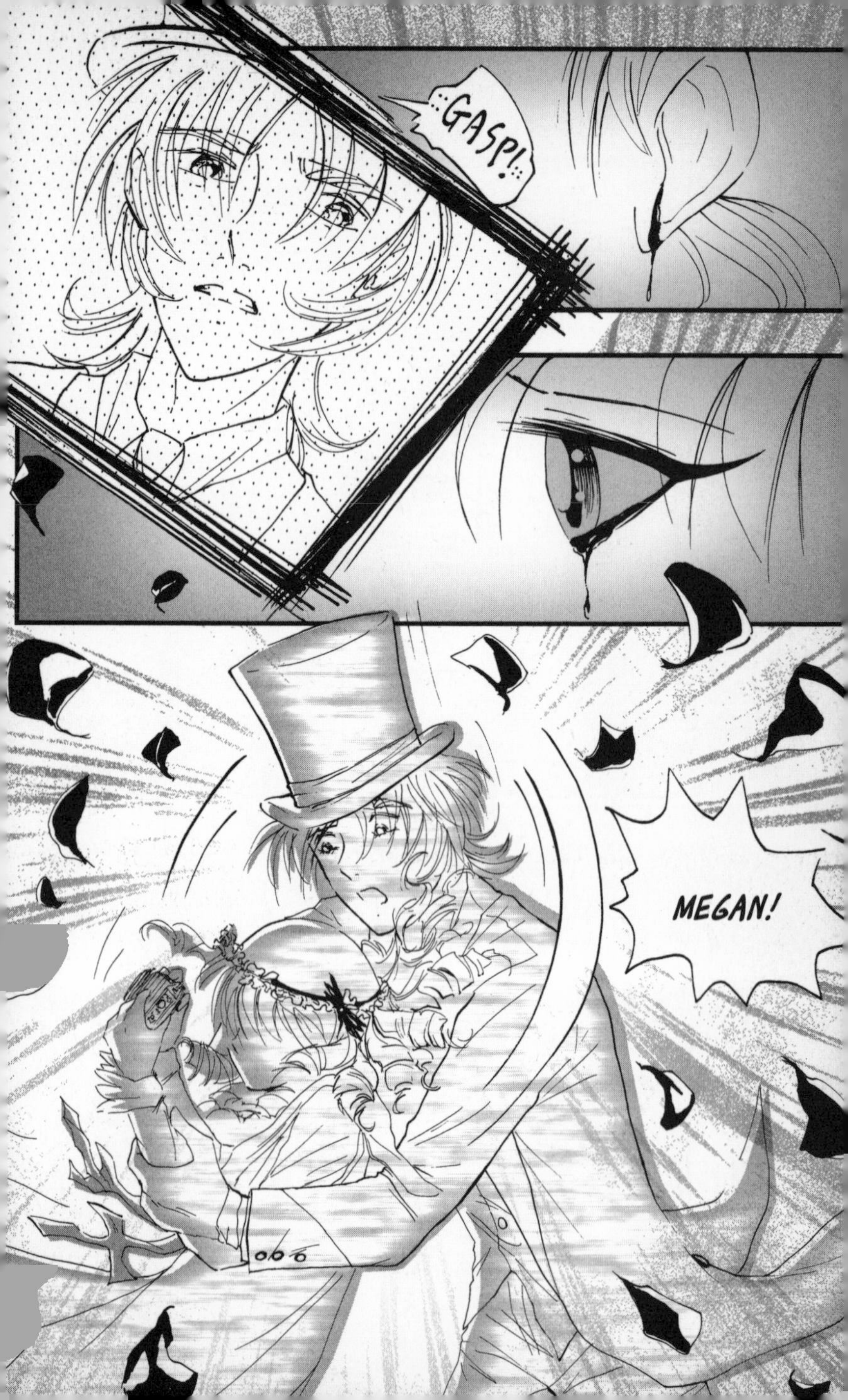

GASP!
MEGAN!

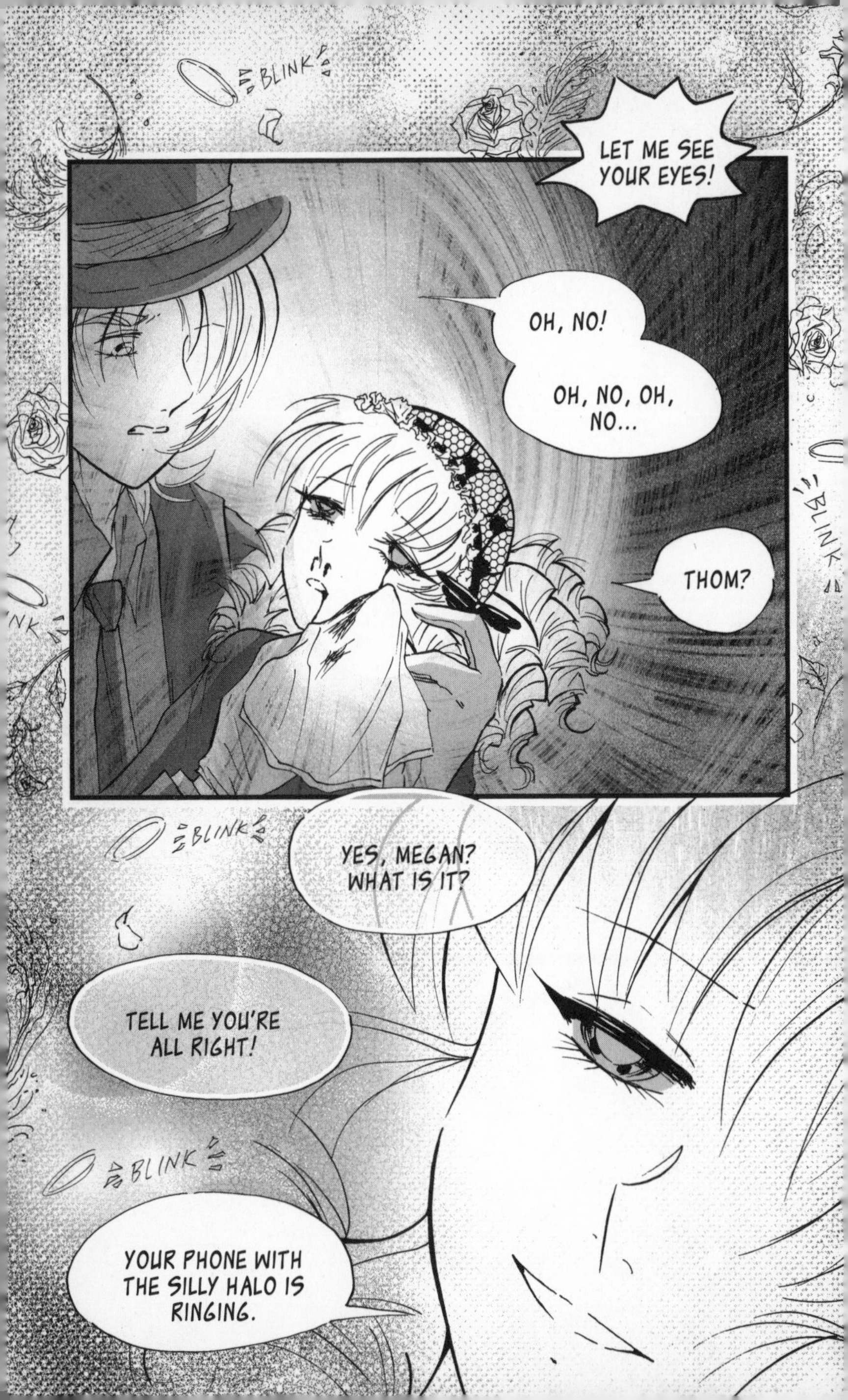
BLINK
LET ME SEE YOUR EYES!
OH, NO!
OH, NO, OH, NO...
BLINK
THOM?
BLINK
YES, MEGAN? WHAT IS IT?
TELL ME YOU'RE ALL RIGHT!
BLINK
YOUR PHONE WITH THE SILLY HALO IS RINGING.

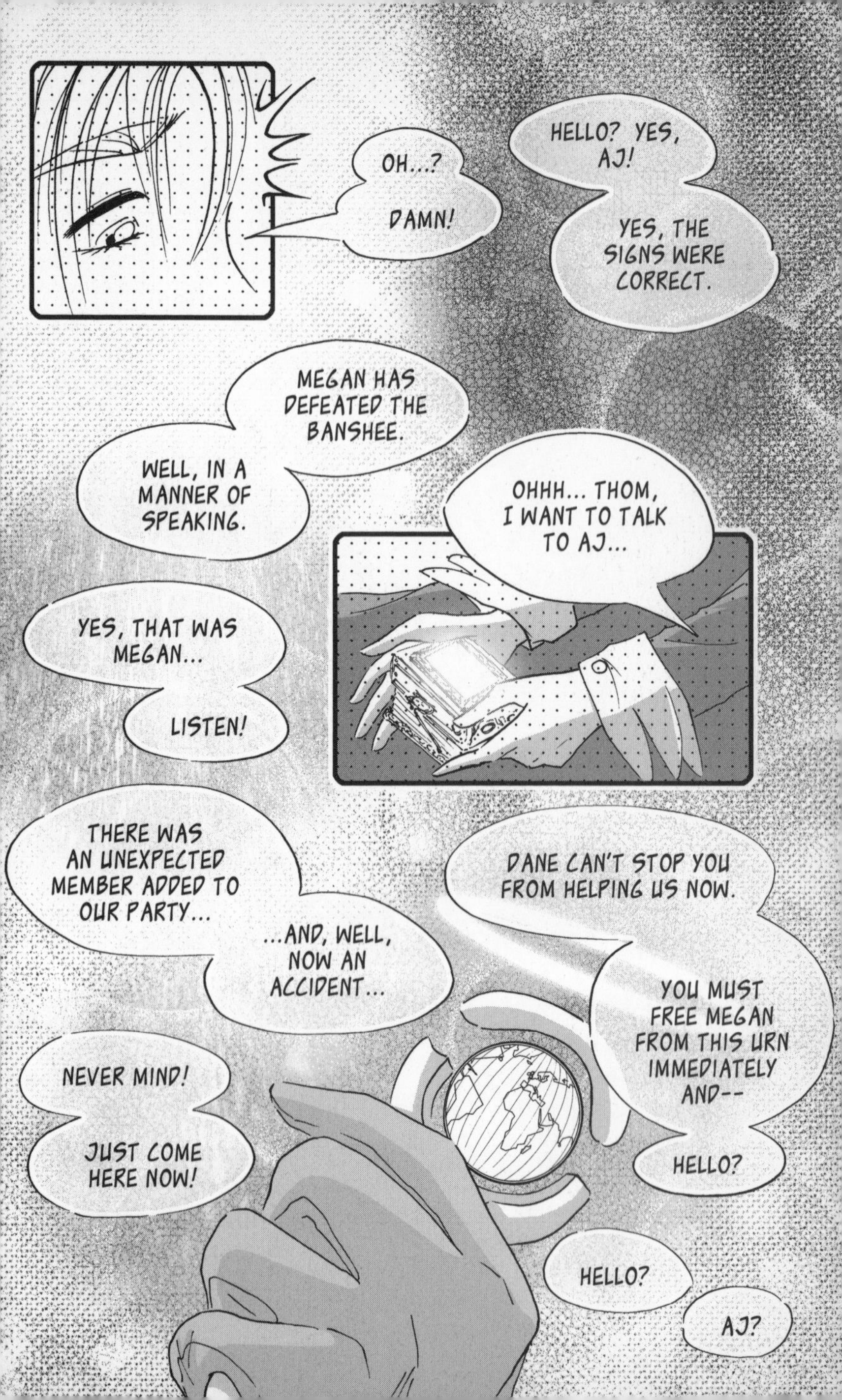
OH...?
DAMN!
HELLO? YES, AJ!
YES, THE SIGNS WERE CORRECT.
MEGAN HAS DEFEATED THE BANSHEE.
WELL, IN A MANNER OF SPEAKING.
OHHH... THOM, I WANT TO TALK TO AJ...
YES, THAT WAS MEGAN...
LISTEN!
THERE WAS AN UNEXPECTED MEMBER ADDED TO OUR PARTY...
...AND, WELL, NOW AN ACCIDENT...
NEVER MIND!
JUST COME HERE NOW!
DANE CAN'T STOP YOU FROM HELPING US NOW.
YOU MUST FREE MEGAN FROM THIS URN IMMEDIATELY AND--
HELLO?
HELLO?
AJ?

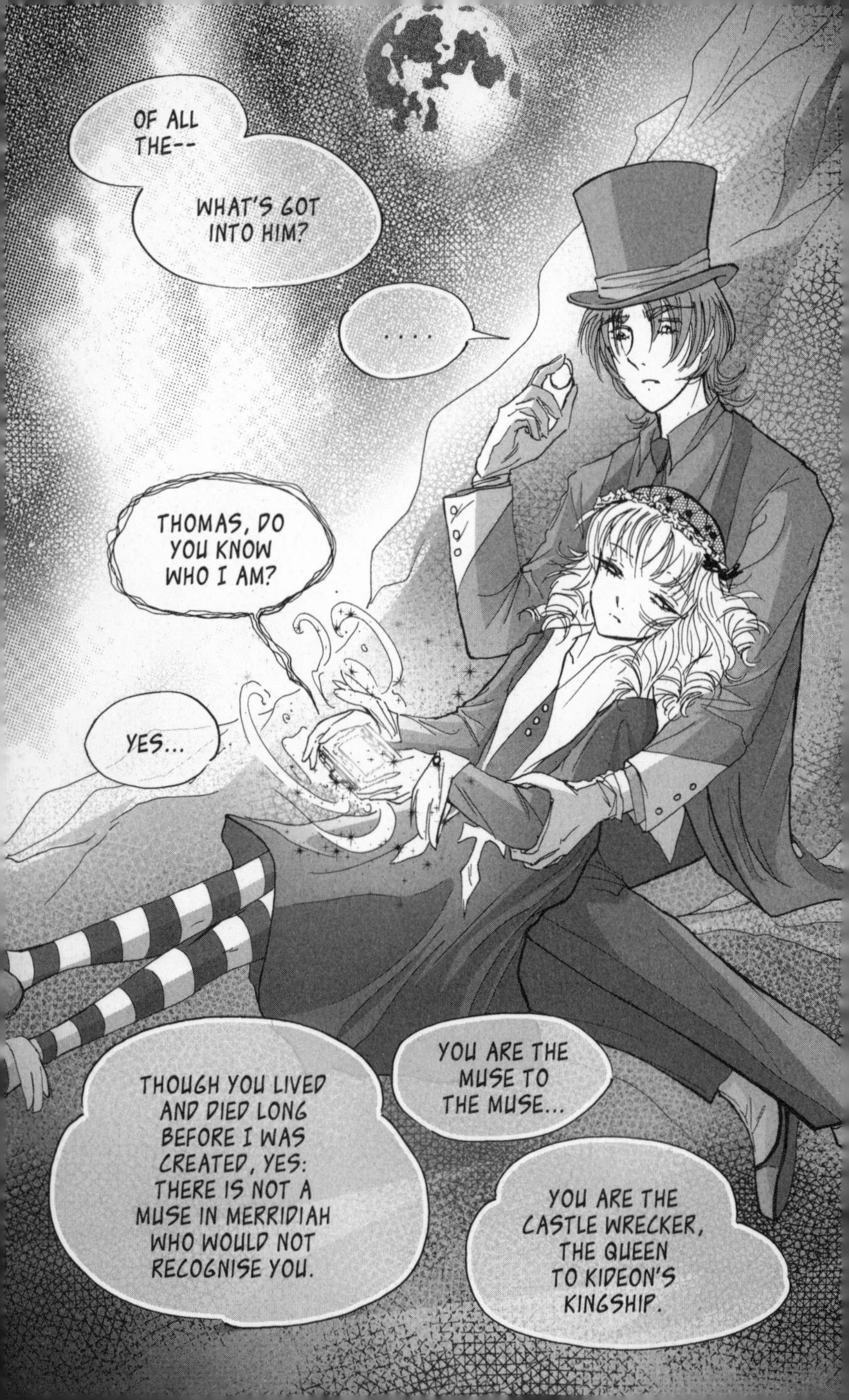
OF ALL THE--
WHAT'S GOT INTO HIM?
....
THOMAS, DO YOU KNOW WHO I AM?
YES...
THOUGH YOU LIVED AND DIED LONG BEFORE I WAS CREATED, YES: THERE IS NOT A MUSE IN MERRIDIAH WHO WOULD NOT RECOGNISE YOU.
YOU ARE THE MUSE TO THE MUSE...
YOU ARE THE CASTLE WRECKER, THE QUEEN TO KIDEON'S KINGSHIP.

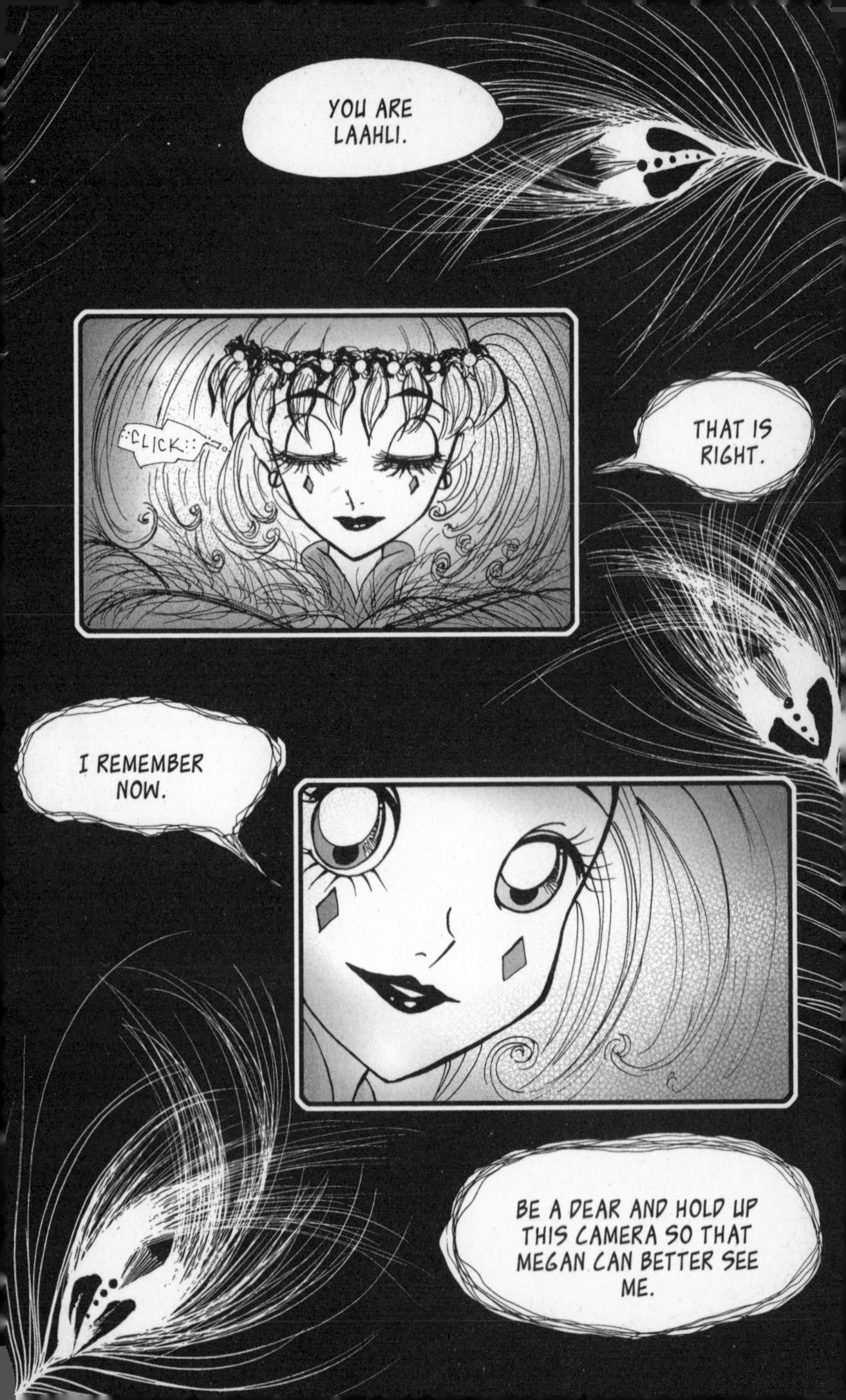
YOU ARE LAAHLI.
THAT IS RIGHT.
CLICK
I REMEMBER NOW.
BE A DEAR AND HOLD UP THIS CAMERA SO THAT MEGAN CAN BETTER SEE ME.

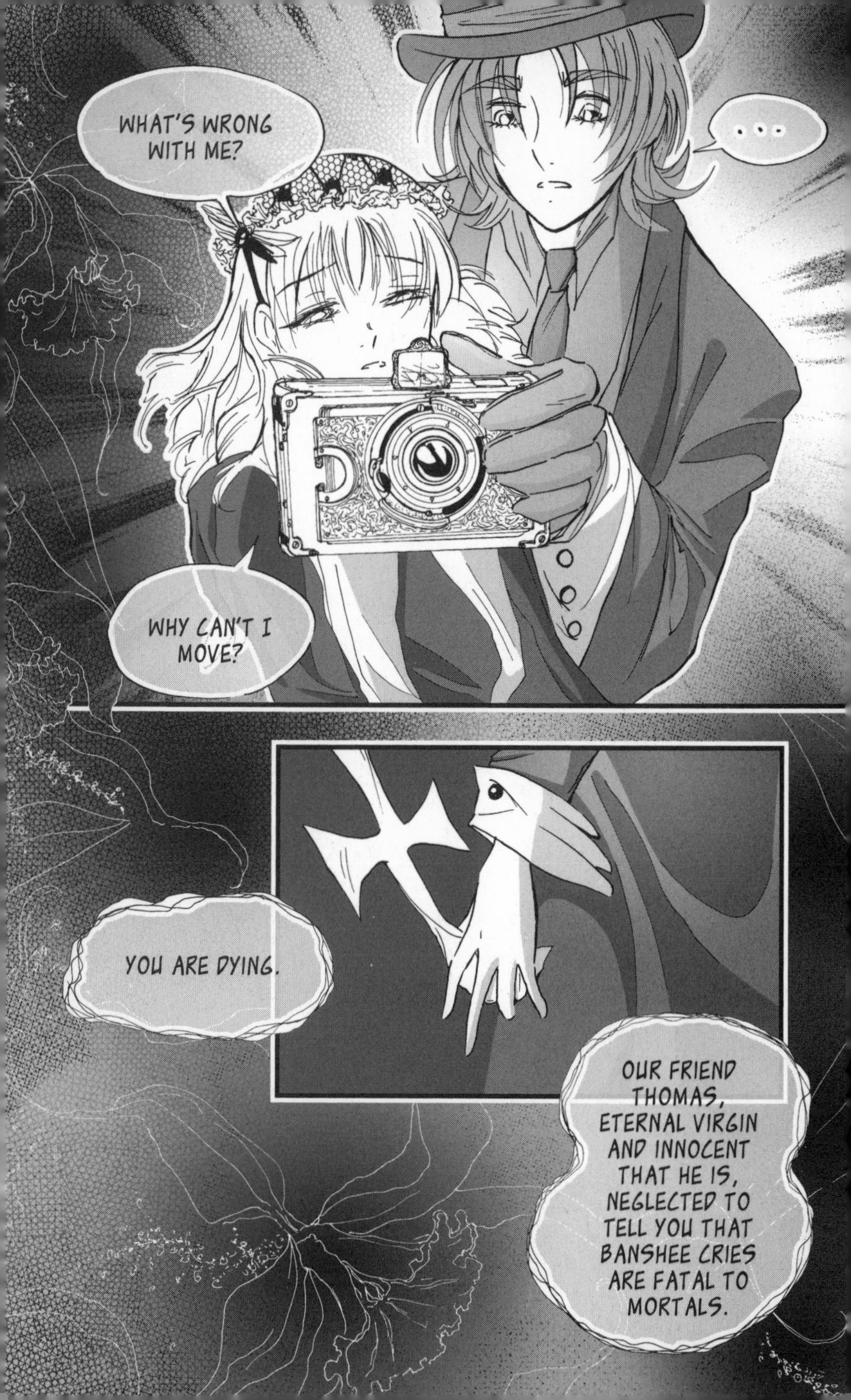
WHAT'S WRONG WITH ME?
...
WHY CAN'T I MOVE?
YOU ARE DYING.
OUR FRIEND THOMAS, ETERNAL VIRGIN AND INNOCENT THAT HE IS, NEGLECTED TO TELL YOU THAT BANSHEE CRIES ARE FATAL TO MORTALS.

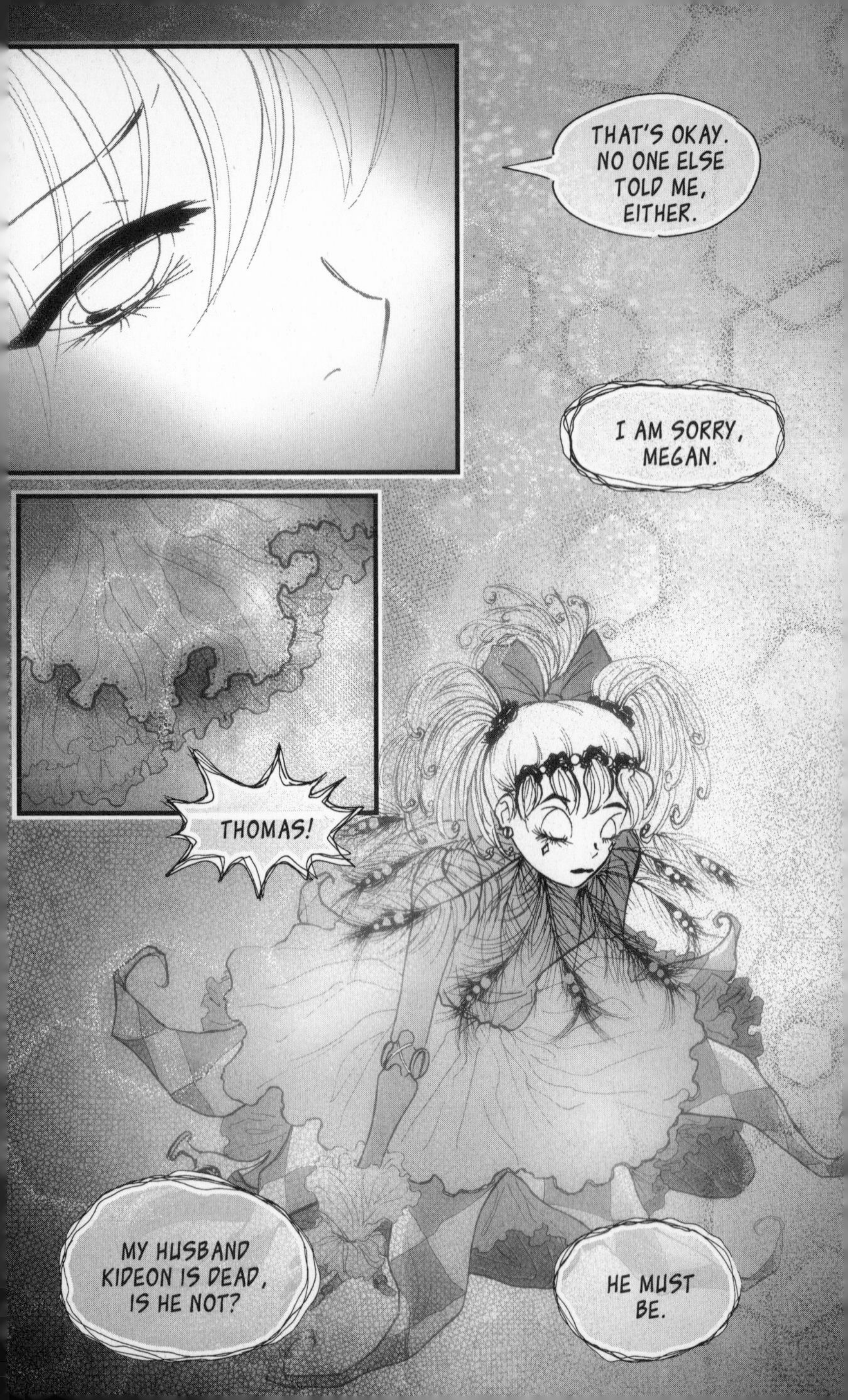
THAT'S OKAY. NO ONE ELSE TOLD ME, EITHER.
I AM SORRY, MEGAN.
THOMAS!
MY HUSBAND KIDEON IS DEAD, IS HE NOT?
HE MUST BE.

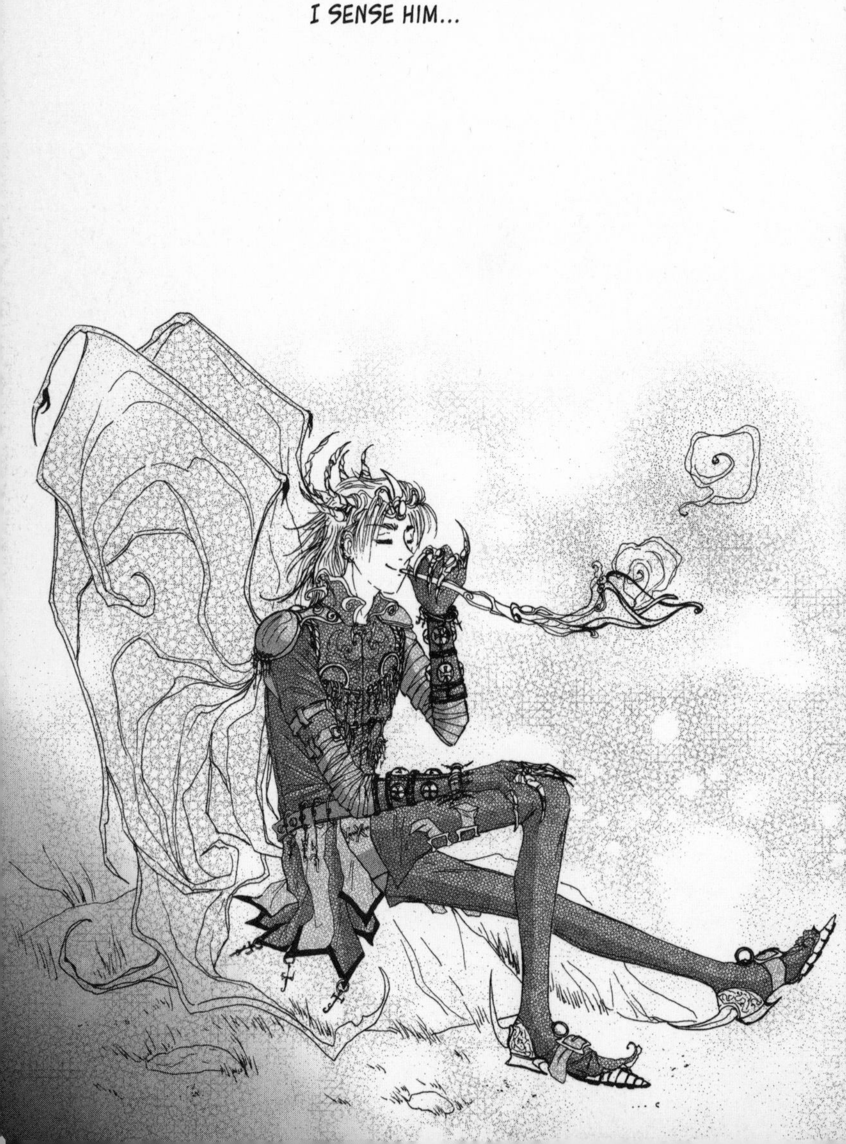
I SENSE HIM...

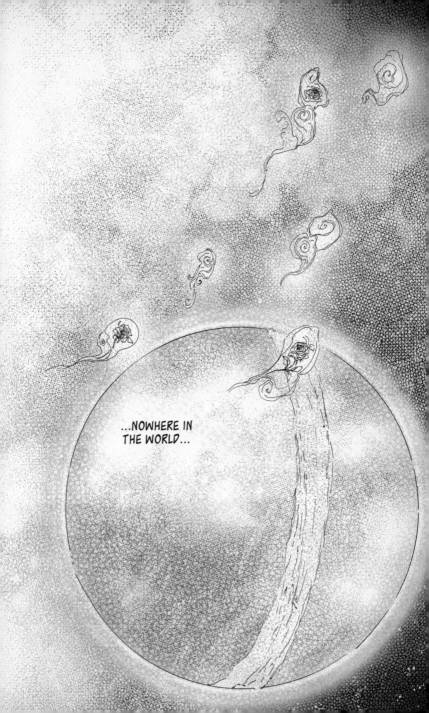

...NOWHERE IN
THE WORLD...

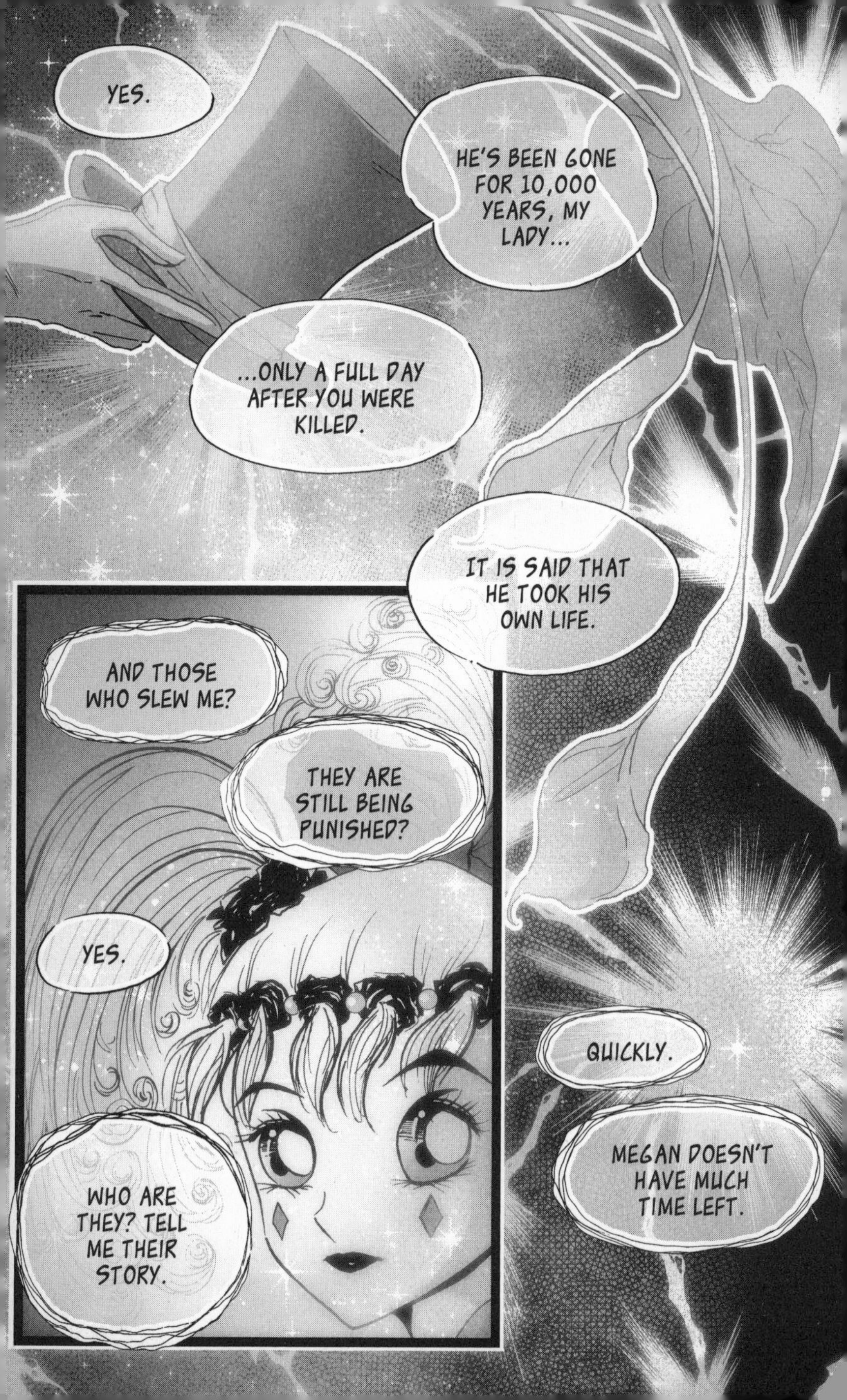
YES.
HE'S BEEN GONE FOR 10,000 YEARS, MY LADY...
...ONLY A FULL DAY AFTER YOU WERE KILLED.
IT IS SAID THAT HE TOOK HIS OWN LIFE.
AND THOSE WHO SLEW ME?
THEY ARE STILL BEING PUNISHED?
YES.
WHO ARE THEY? TELL ME THEIR STORY.
QUICKLY.
MEGAN DOESN'T HAVE MUCH TIME LEFT.

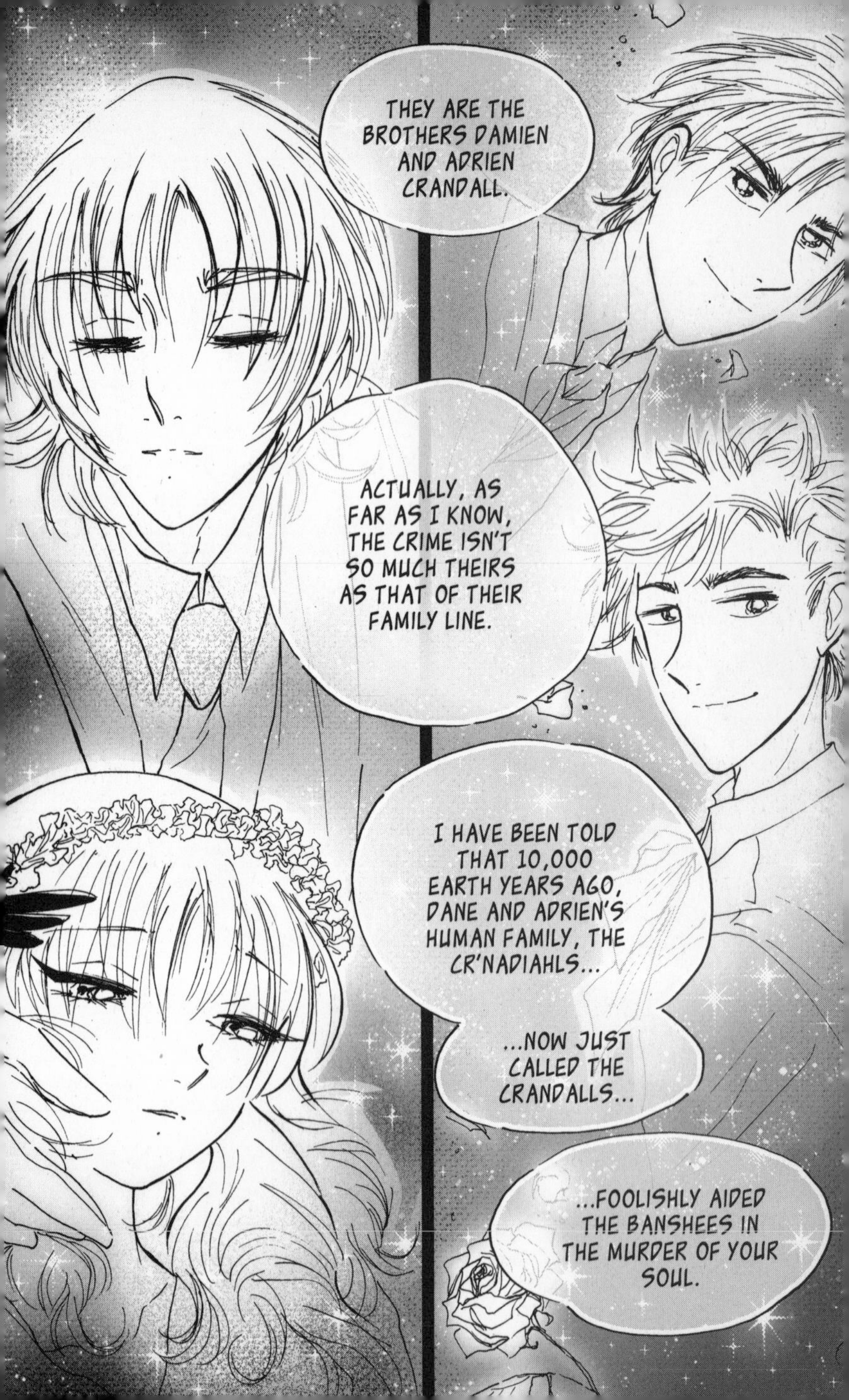
THEY ARE THE BROTHERS DAMIEN AND ADRIEN CRANDALL.
ACTUALLY, AS FAR AS I KNOW, THE CRIME ISN'T SO MUCH THEIRS AS THAT OF THEIR FAMILY LINE.
I HAVE BEEN TOLD THAT 10,000 EARTH YEARS AGO, DANE AND ADRIEN'S HUMAN FAMILY, THE CR'NADIAHLS...
...NOW JUST CALLED THE CRANDALLS...
...FOOLISHLY AIDED THE BANSHEES IN THE MURDER OF YOUR SOUL.

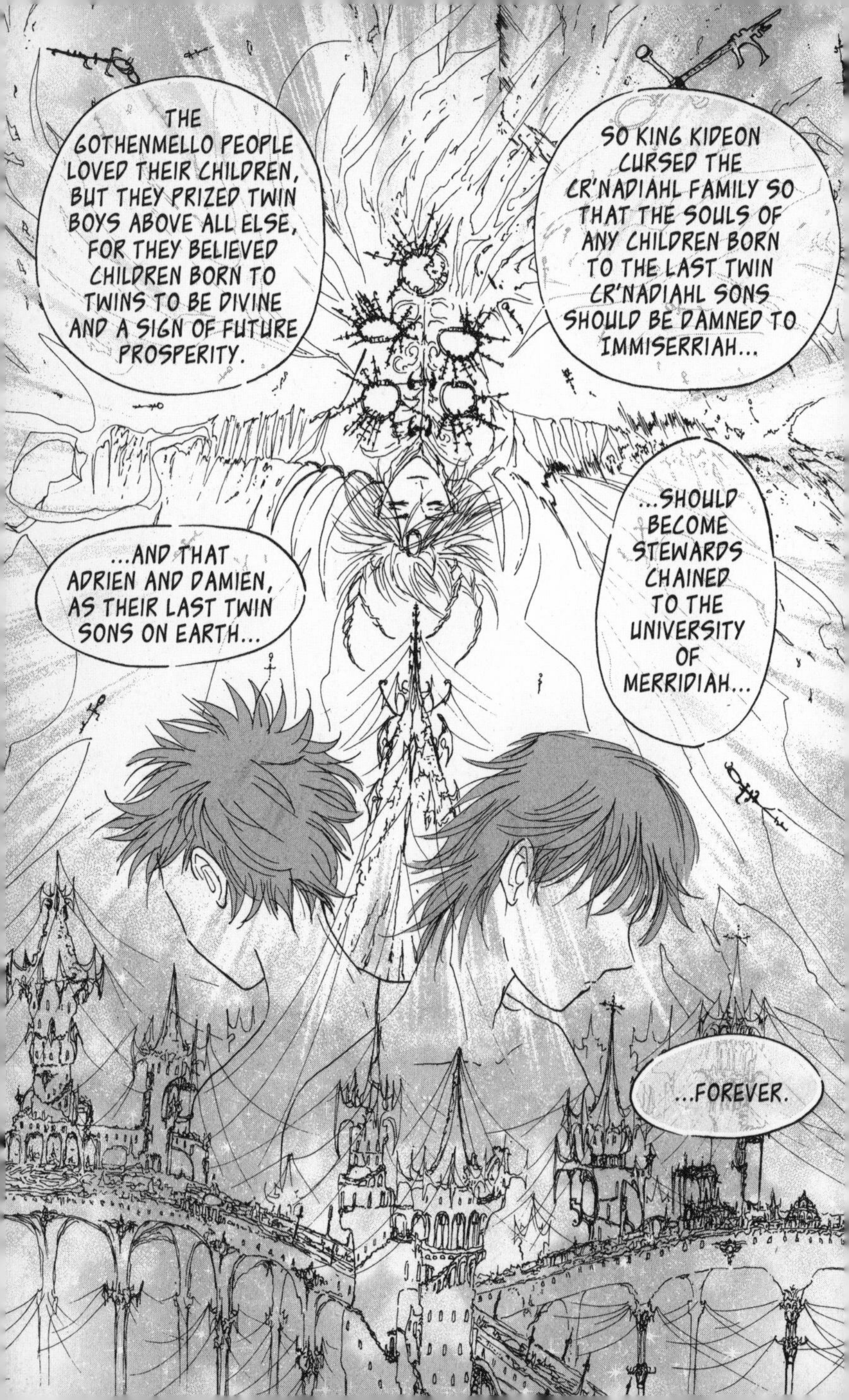
THE GOTHENMELLO PEOPLE LOVED THEIR CHILDREN, BUT THEY PRIZED TWIN BOYS ABOVE ALL ELSE, FOR THEY BELIEVED CHILDREN BORN TO TWINS TO BE DIVINE AND A SIGN OF FUTURE PROSPERITY.
SO KING KIDEON CURSED THE CR'NADIAHL FAMILY SO THAT THE SOULS OF ANY CHILDREN BORN TO THE LAST TWIN CR'NADIAHL SONS SHOULD BE DAMNED TO IMMISERRIAH...
...AND THAT ADRIEN AND DAMIEN, AS THEIR LAST TWIN SONS ON EARTH...
...SHOULD BECOME STEWARDS CHAINED TO THE UNIVERSITY OF MERRIDIAH...
...FOREVER.

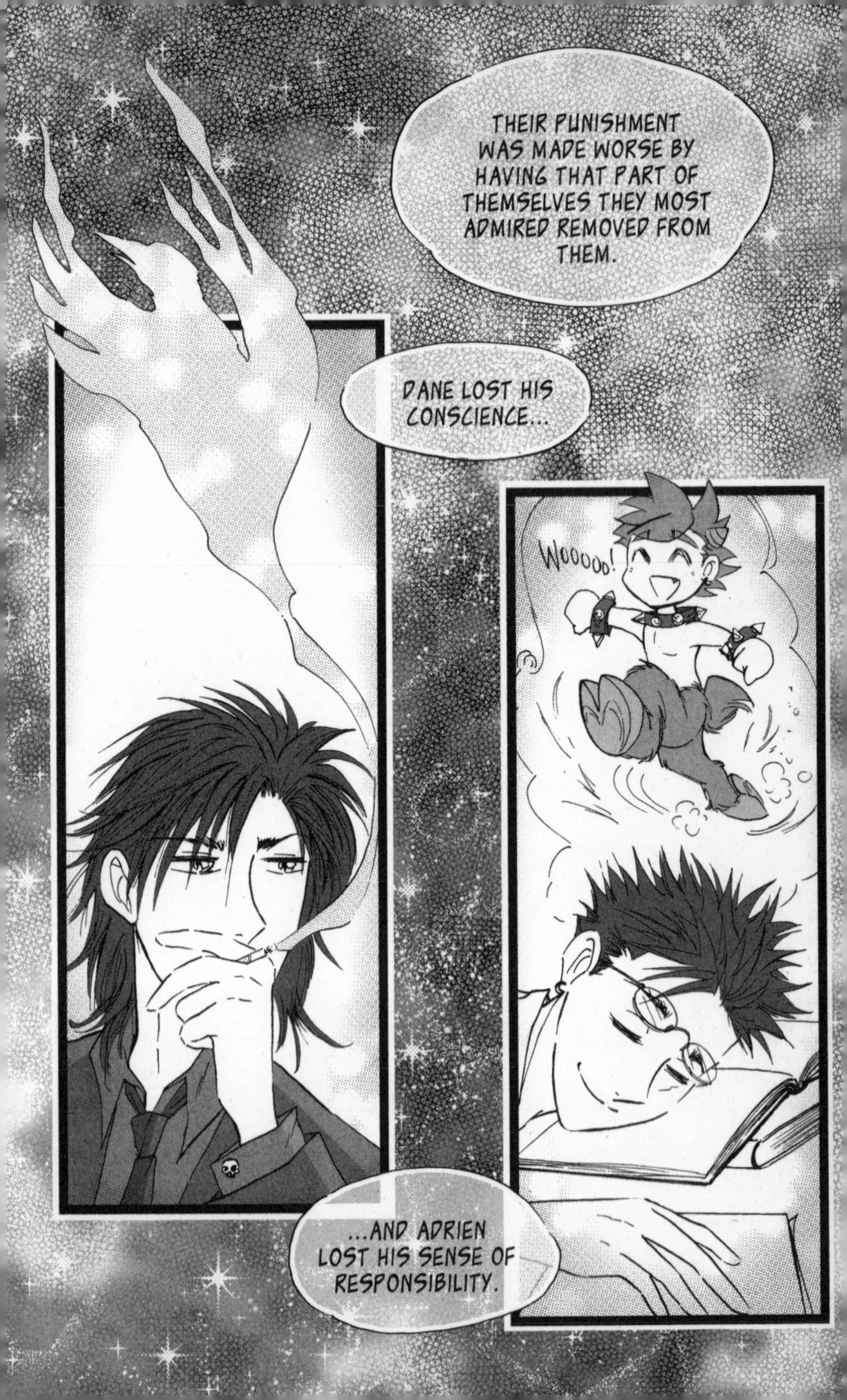
THEIR PUNISHMENT WAS MADE WORSE BY HAVING THAT PART OF THEMSELVES THEY MOST ADMIRED REMOVED FROM THEM.
DANE LOST HIS CONSCIENCE...
WOOOOO!
...AND ADRIEN LOST HIS SENSE OF RESPONSIBILITY.

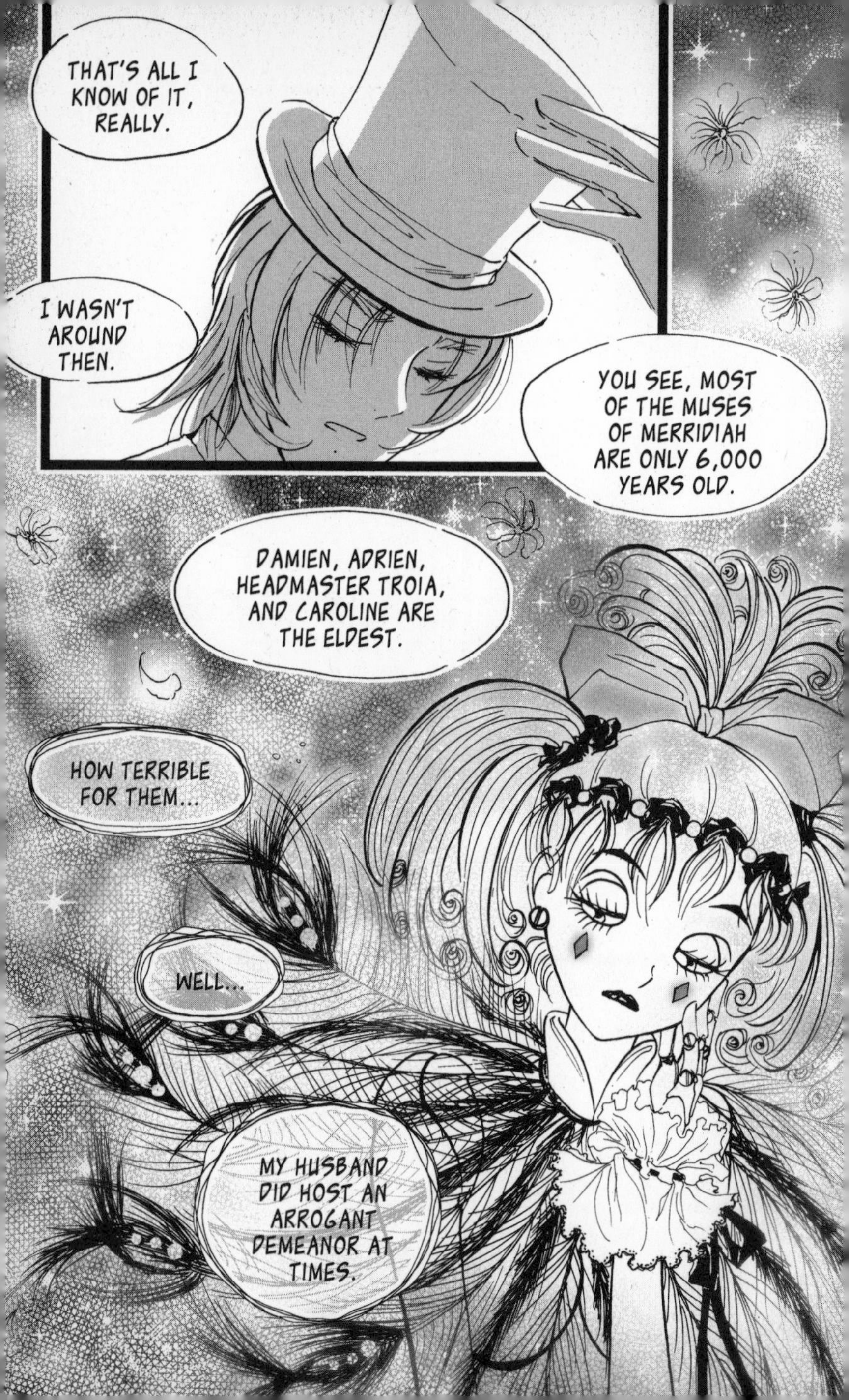
THAT'S ALL I KNOW OF IT, REALLY.
I WASN'T AROUND THEN.
YOU SEE, MOST OF THE MUSES OF MERRIDIAH ARE ONLY 6,000 YEARS OLD.
DAMIEN, ADRIEN, HEADMASTER TROIA, AND CAROLINE ARE THE ELDEST.
HOW TERRIBLE FOR THEM...
WELL...
MY HUSBAND DID HOST AN ARROGANT DEMEANOR AT TIMES.

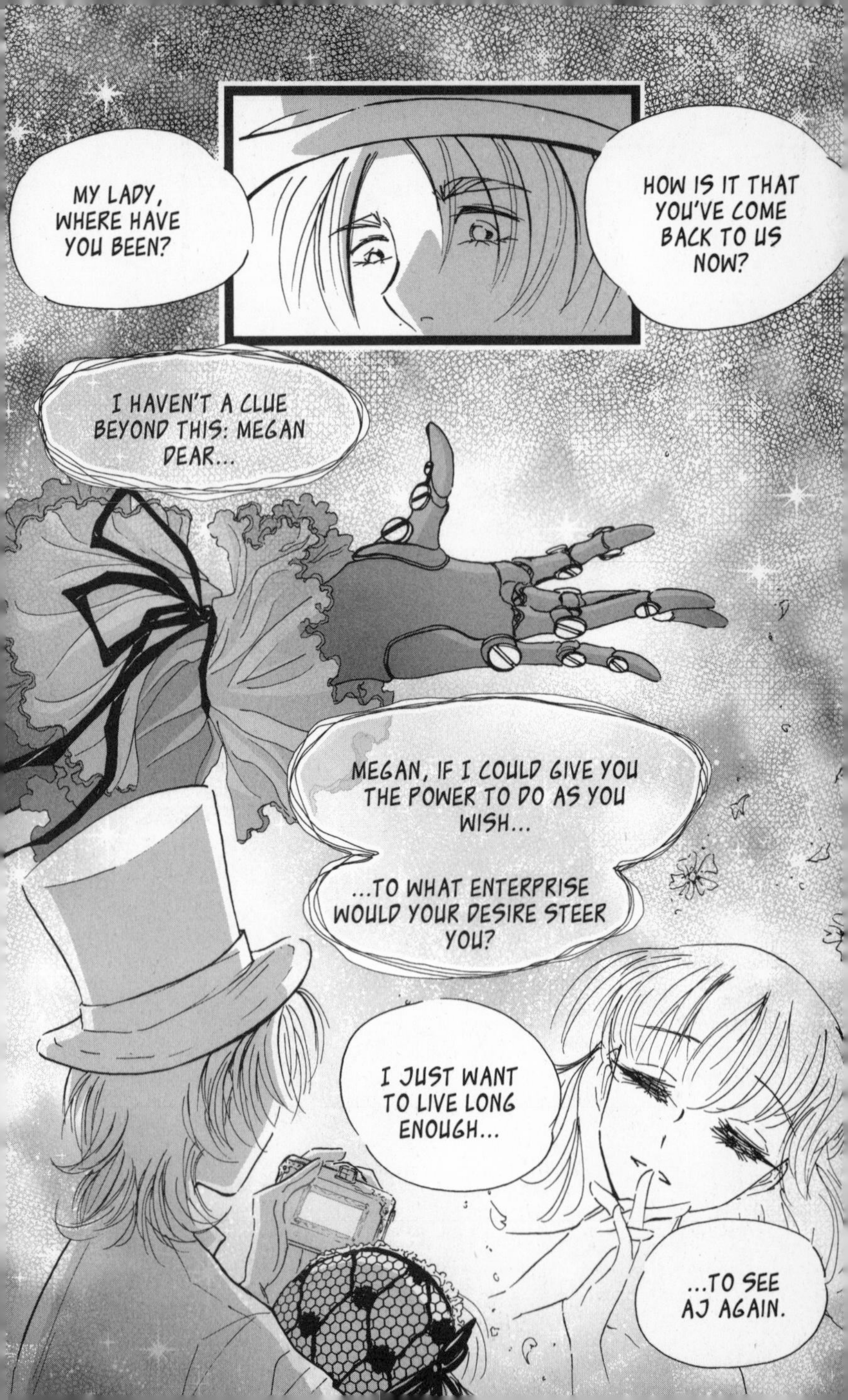
MY LADY, WHERE HAVE YOU BEEN?
HOW IS IT THAT YOU'VE COME BACK TO US NOW?
I HAVEN'T A CLUE BEYOND THIS: MEGAN DEAR...
MEGAN, IF I COULD GIVE YOU THE POWER TO DO AS YOU WISH...
...TO WHAT ENTERPRISE WOULD YOUR DESIRE STEER YOU?
I JUST WANT TO LIVE LONG ENOUGH...
...TO SEE AJ AGAIN.

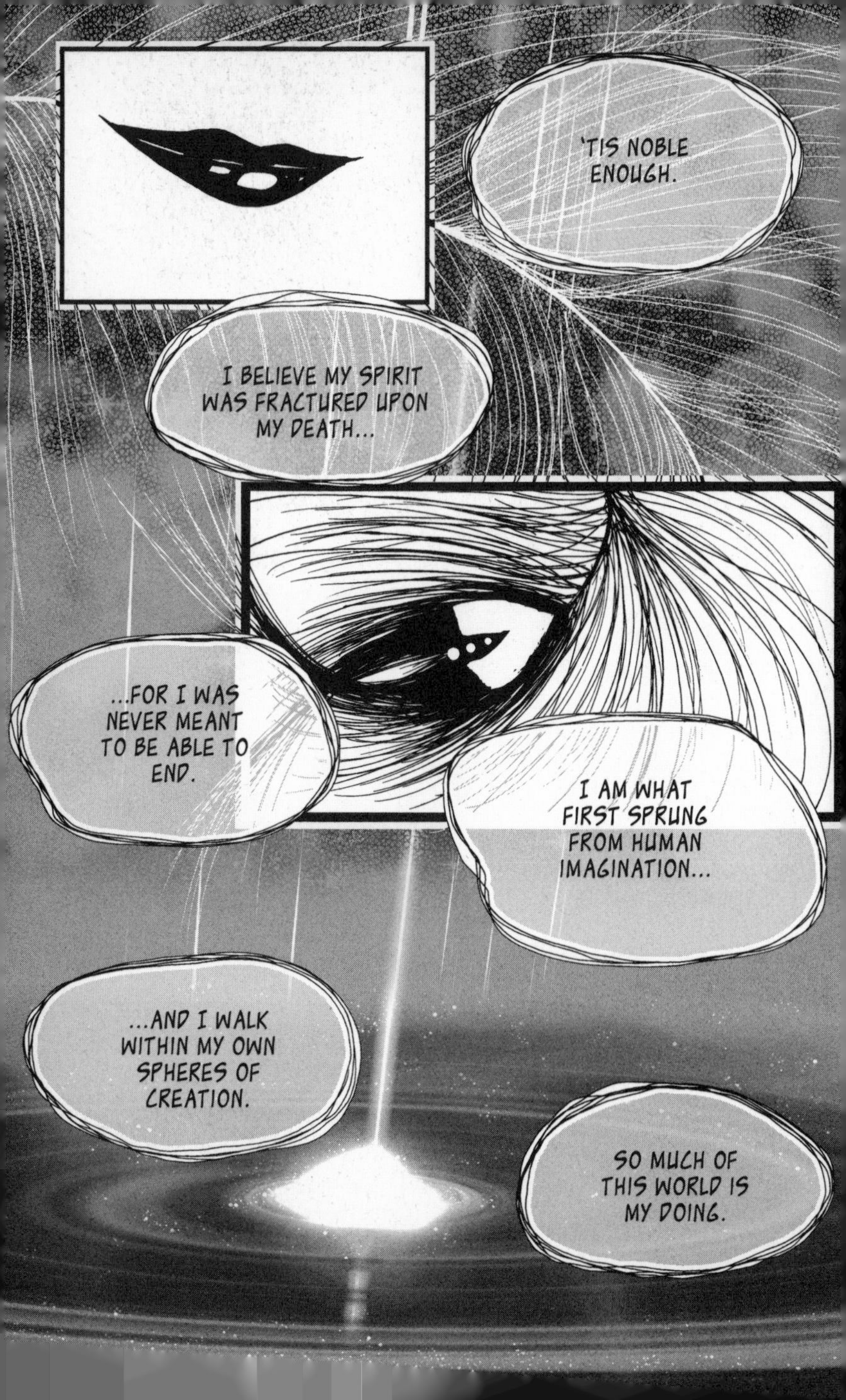
'TIS NOBLE ENOUGH.
I BELIEVE MY SPIRIT WAS FRACTURED UPON MY DEATH...
...FOR I WAS NEVER MEANT TO BE ABLE TO END.
I AM WHAT FIRST SPRUNG FROM HUMAN IMAGINATION...
...AND I WALK WITHIN MY OWN SPHERES OF CREATION.
SO MUCH OF THIS WORLD IS MY DOING.

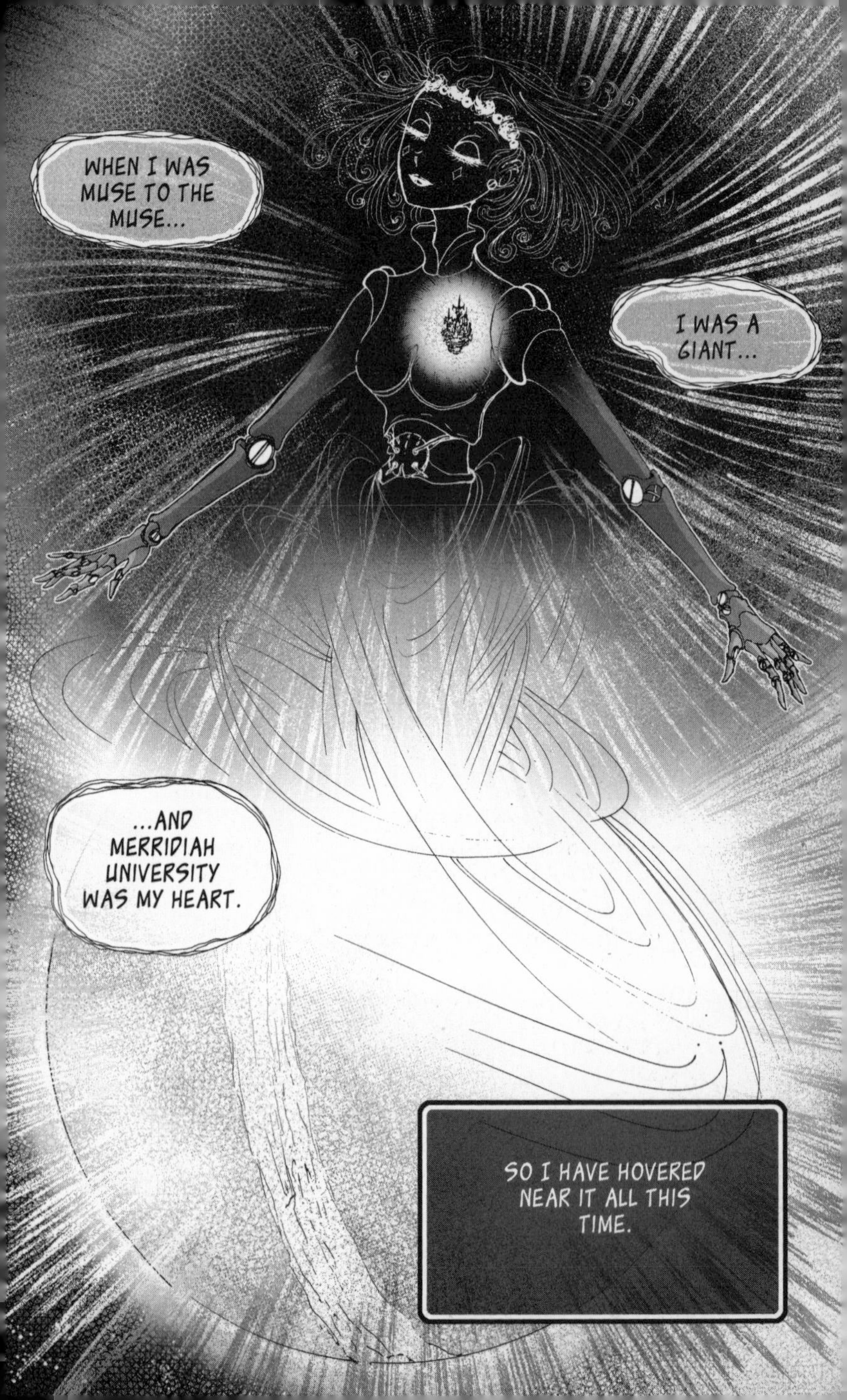

WHEN I WAS MUSE TO THE MUSE...
I WAS A GIANT...
...AND MERRIDIAH UNIVERSITY WAS MY HEART.
SO I HAVE HOVERED NEAR IT ALL THIS TIME.

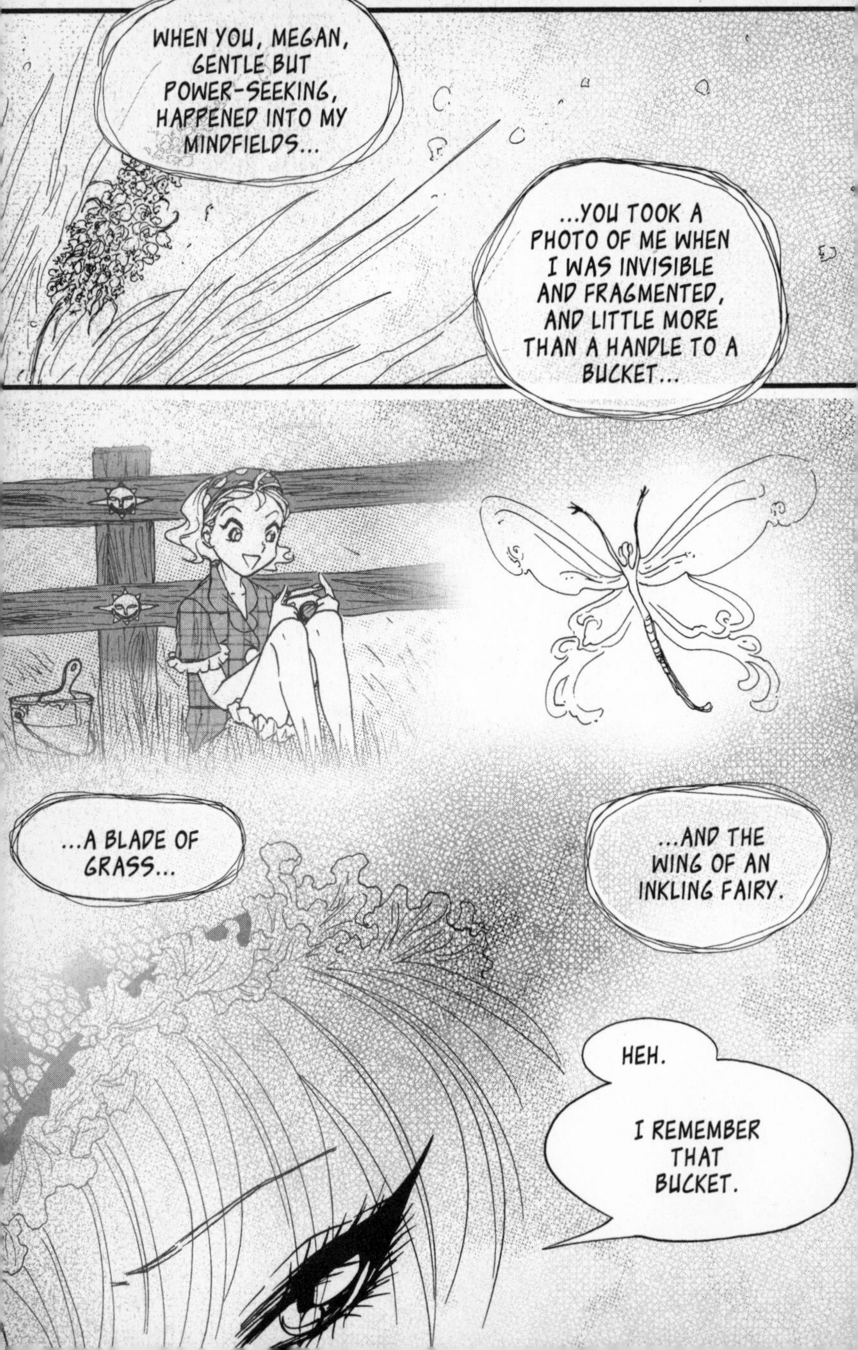
WHEN YOU, MEGAN, GENTLE BUT POWER-SEEKING, HAPPENED INTO MY MINDFIELDS...
...YOU TOOK A PHOTO OF ME WHEN I WAS INVISIBLE AND FRAGMENTED, AND LITTLE MORE THAN A HANDLE TO A BUCKET...
...A BLADE OF GRASS...
...AND THE WING OF AN INKLING FAIRY.
HEH.
I REMEMBER THAT BUCKET.

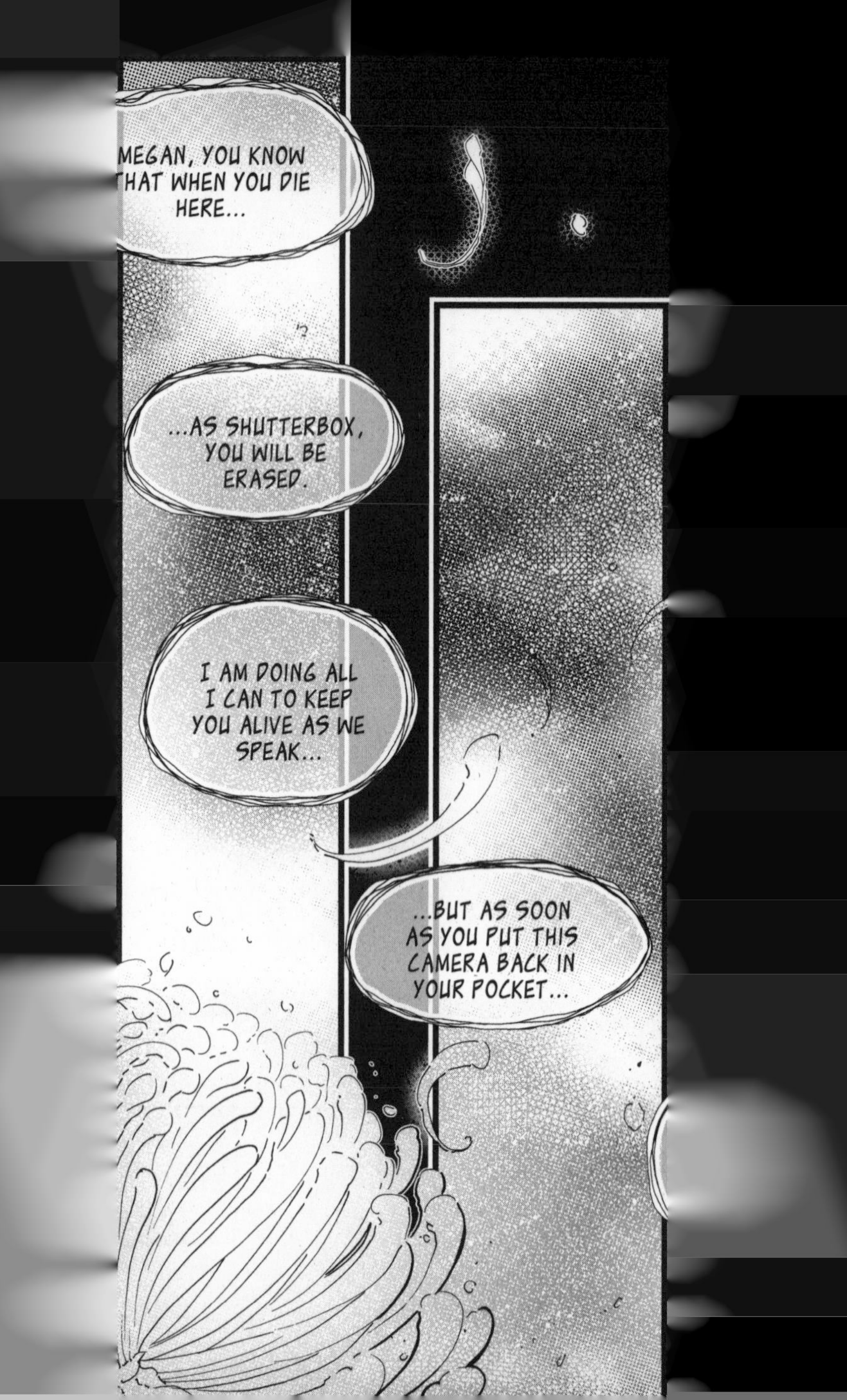
MEGAN, YOU KNOW THAT WHEN YOU DIE HERE...
...AS SHUTTERBOX, YOU WILL BE ERASED.
I AM DOING ALL I CAN TO KEEP YOU ALIVE AS WE SPEAK...
...BUT AS SOON AS YOU PUT THIS CAMERA BACK IN YOUR POCKET...

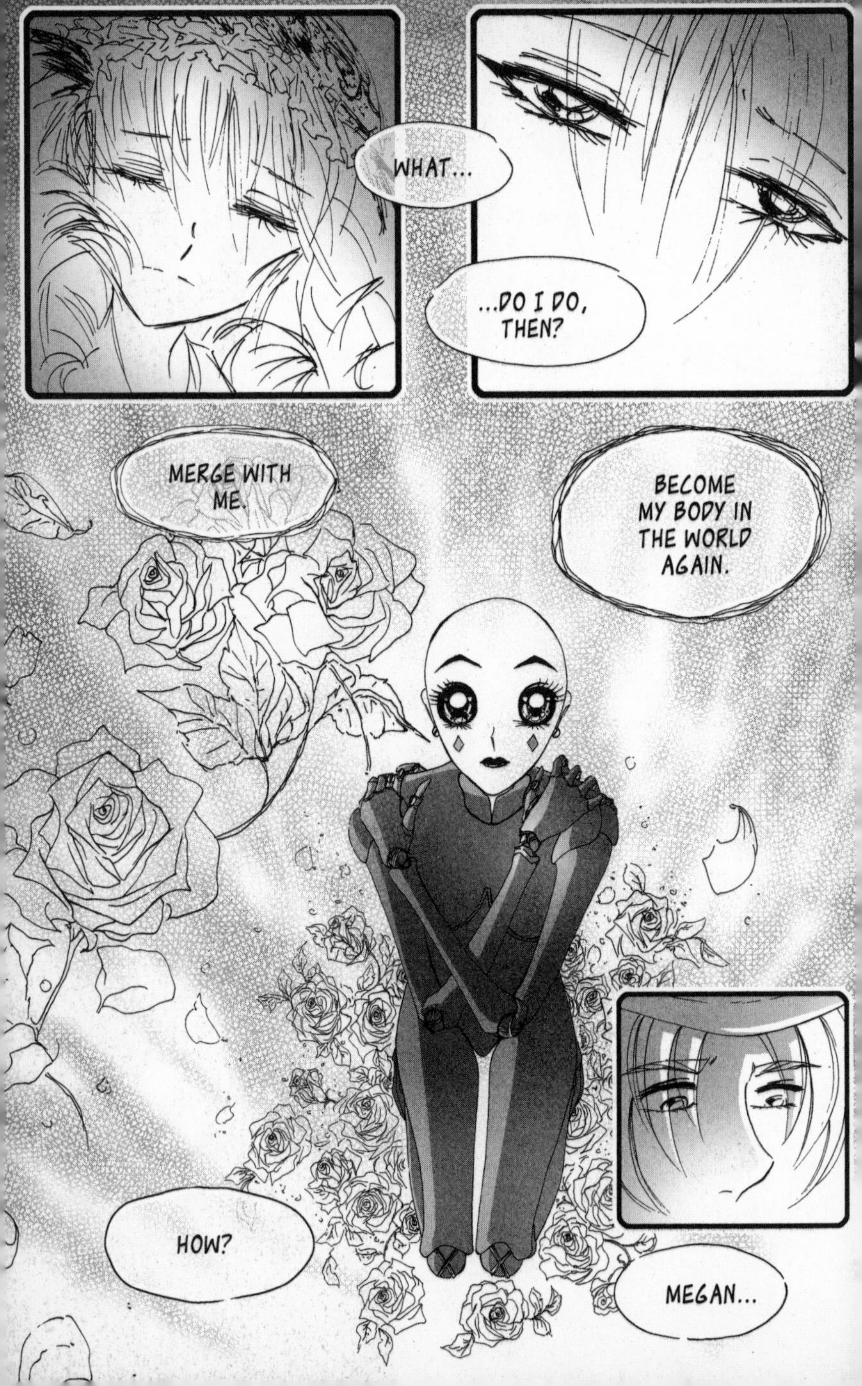
WHAT...
...DO I DO, THEN?
MERGE WITH ME.
BECOME MY BODY IN THE WORLD AGAIN.
HOW?
MEGAN...

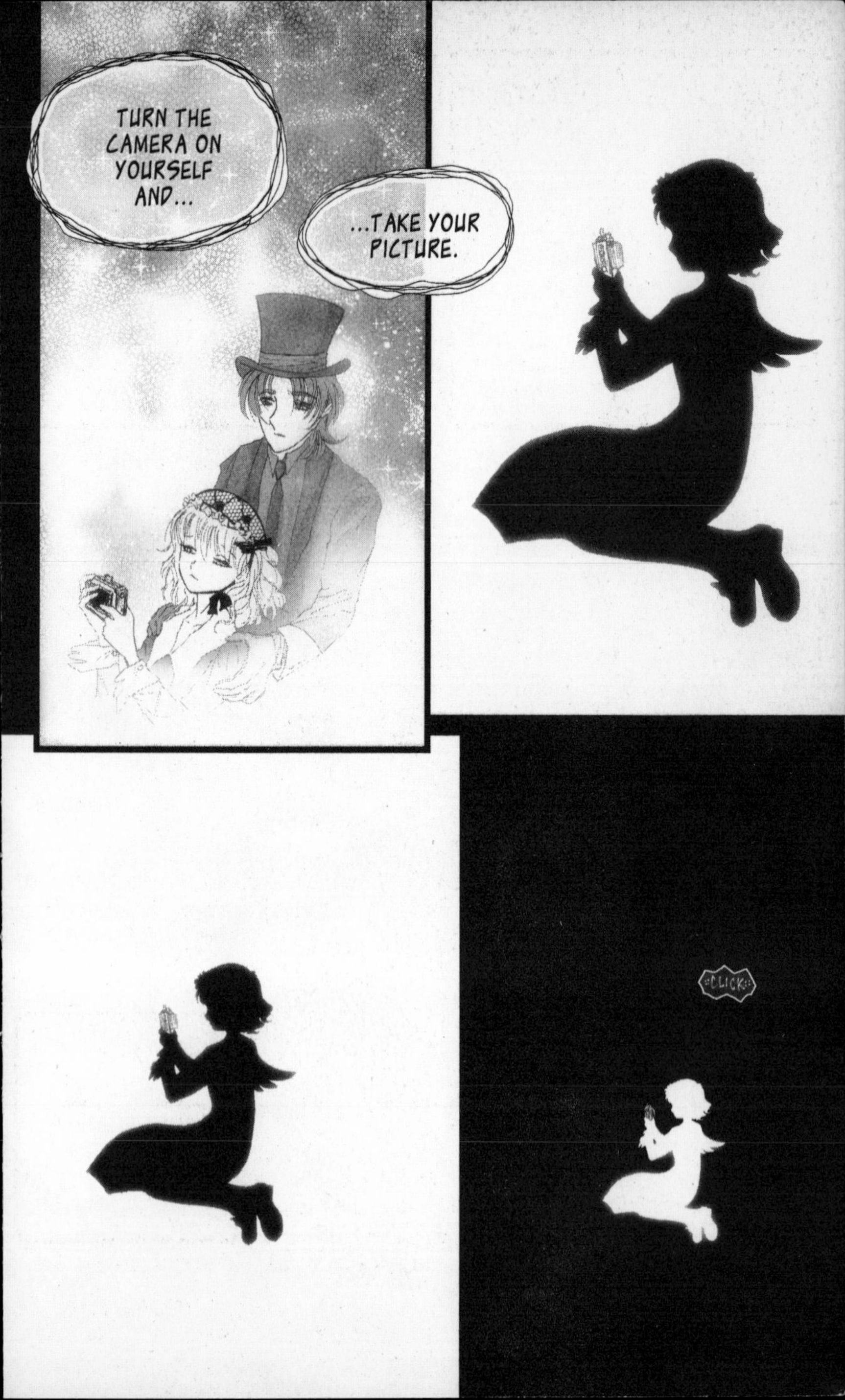
TURN THE CAMERA ON YOURSELF AND...
...TAKE YOUR PICTURE.
CLICK

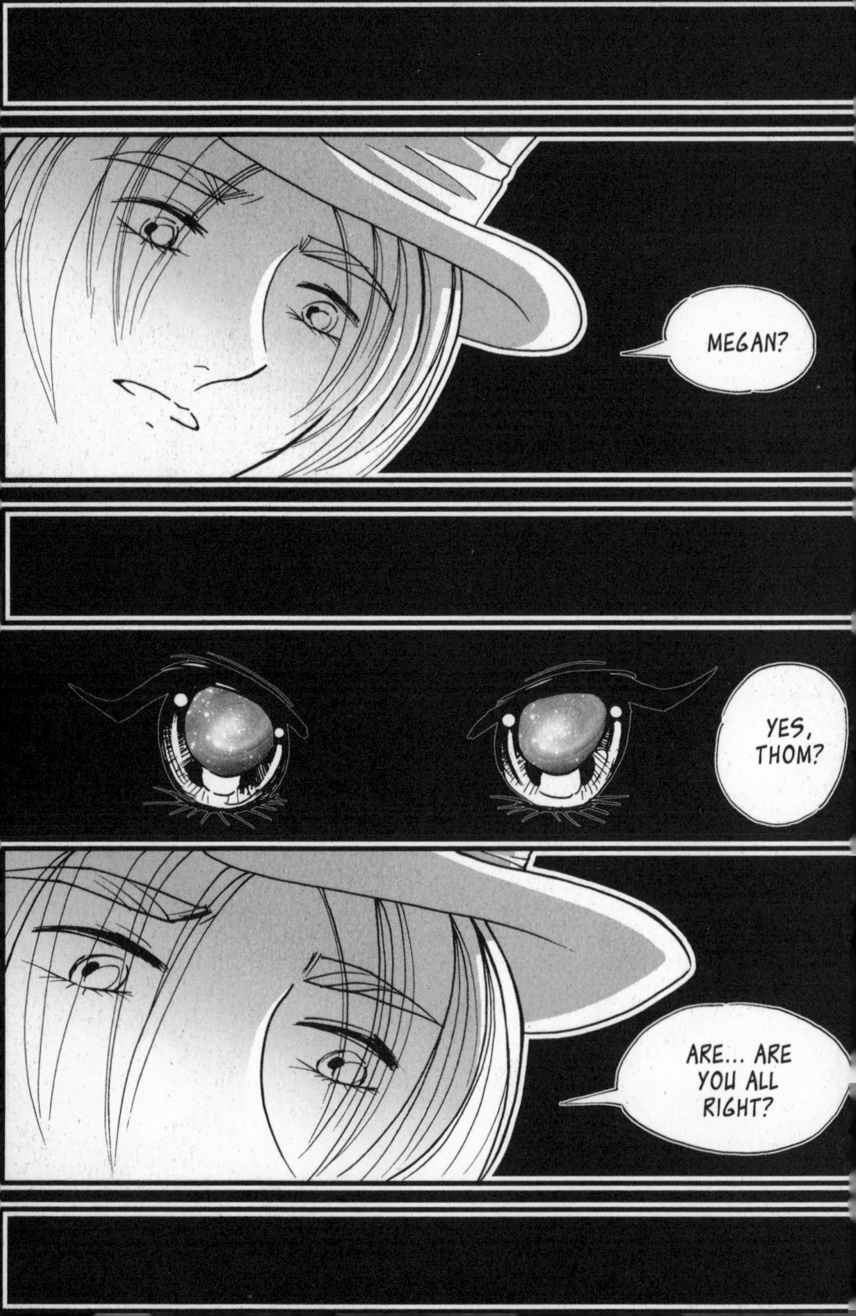
MEGAN?
YES, THOM?
ARE... ARE YOU ALL RIGHT?

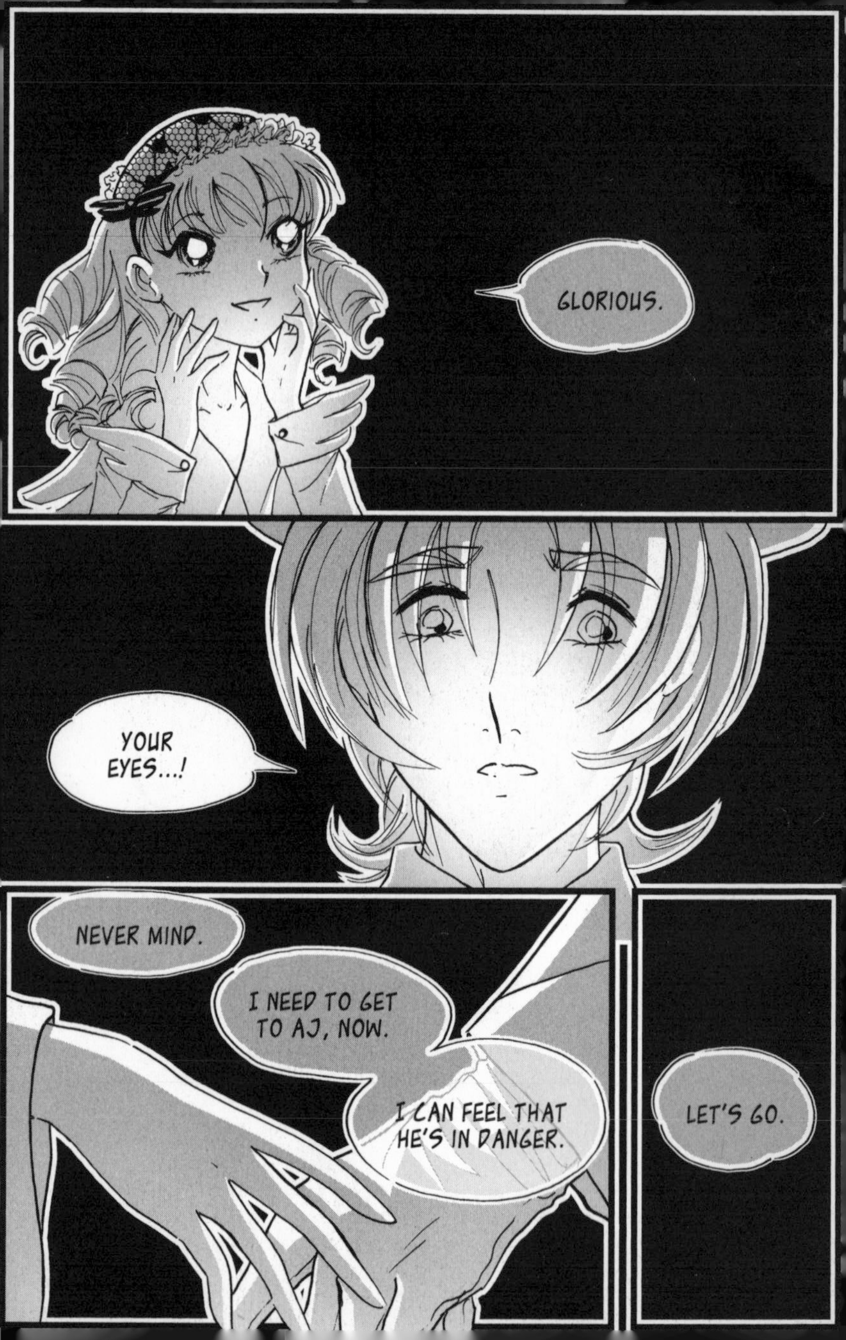
GLORIOUS.
YOUR EYES...!
NEVER MIND.
I NEED TO GET TO AJ, NOW.
I CAN FEEL THAT HE'S IN DANGER.
LET'S GO.

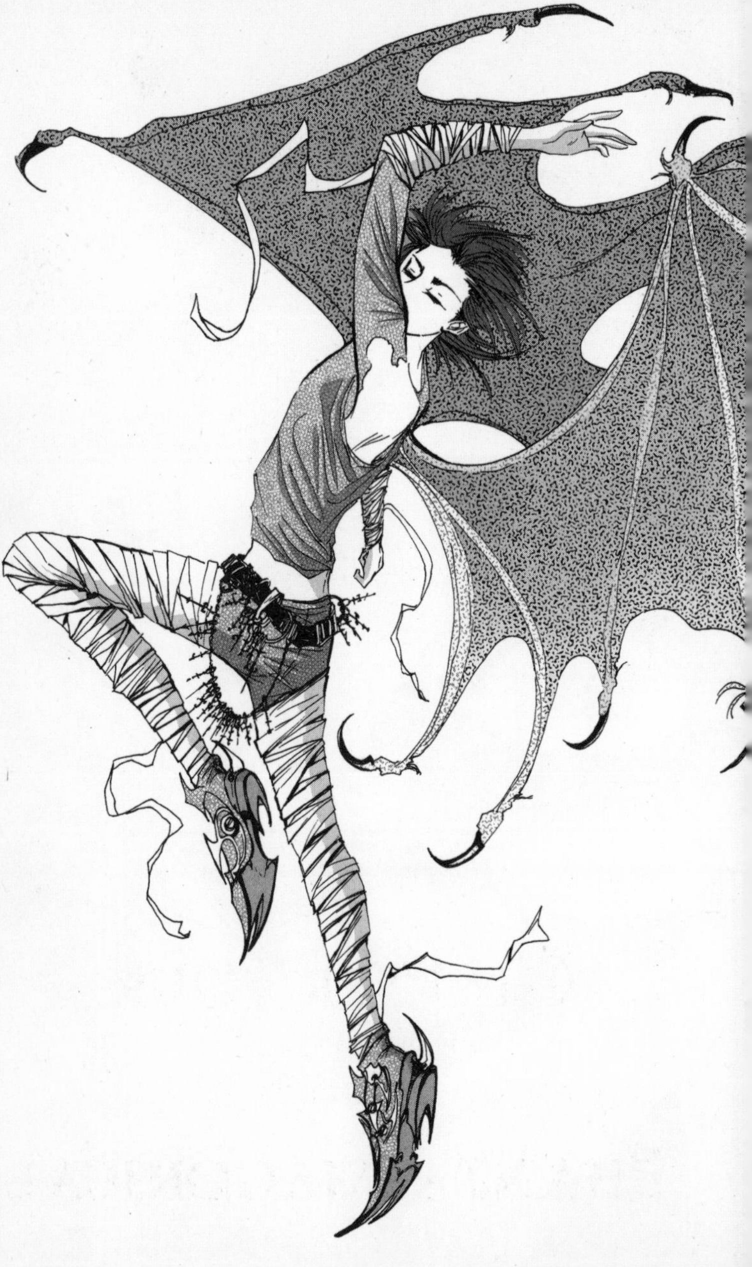

CHAPTER FOUR:

WHAT IS

PHANTASMAGORICAL

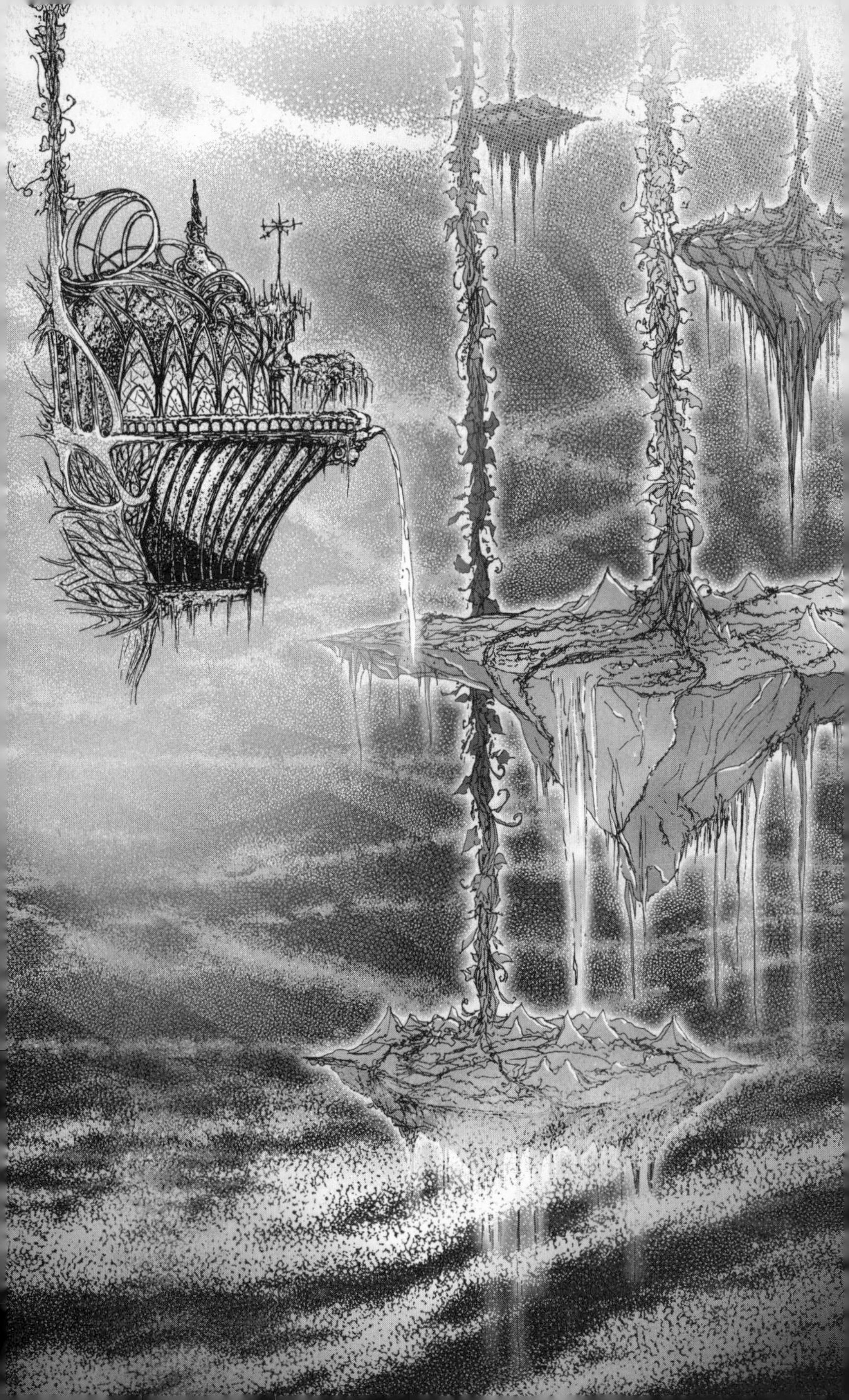

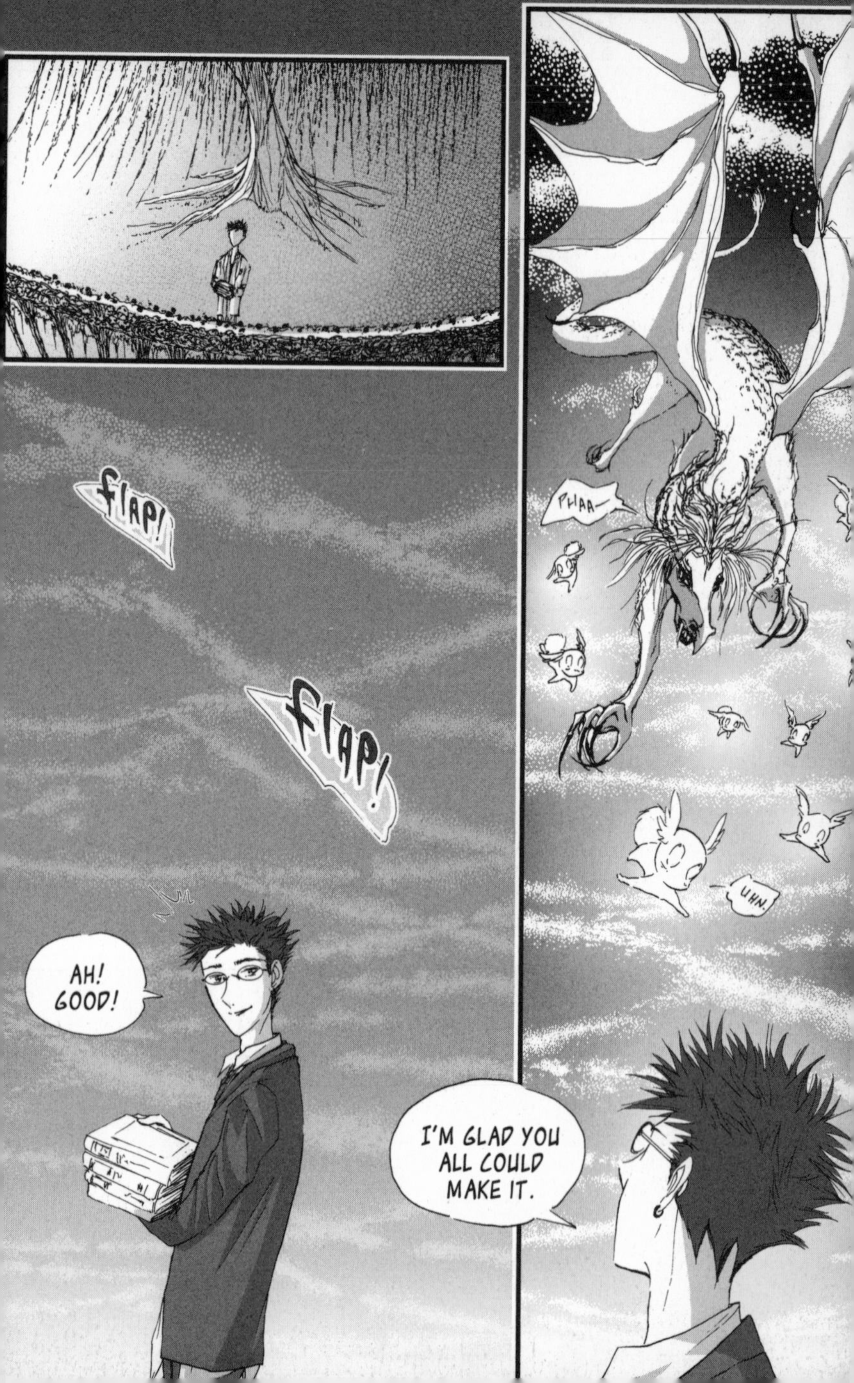
FLAP!
FLAP!
AH! GOOD!
PHAA—
UHN.
I'M GLAD YOU ALL COULD MAKE IT.

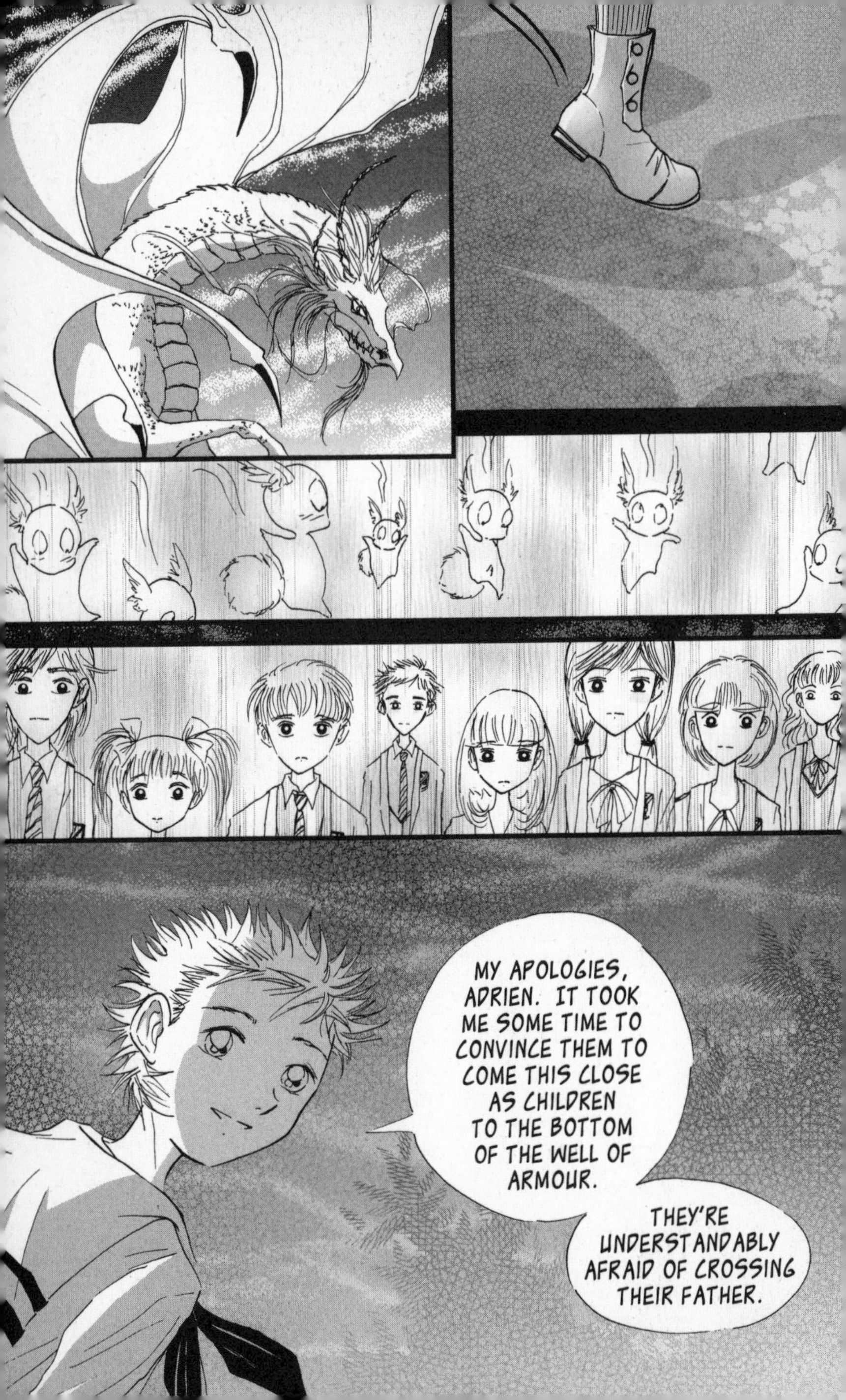
MY APOLOGIES, ADRIEN. IT TOOK ME SOME TIME TO CONVINCE THEM TO COME THIS CLOSE AS CHILDREN TO THE BOTTOM OF THE WELL OF ARMOUR.
THEY'RE UNDERSTANDABLY AFRAID OF CROSSING THEIR FATHER.

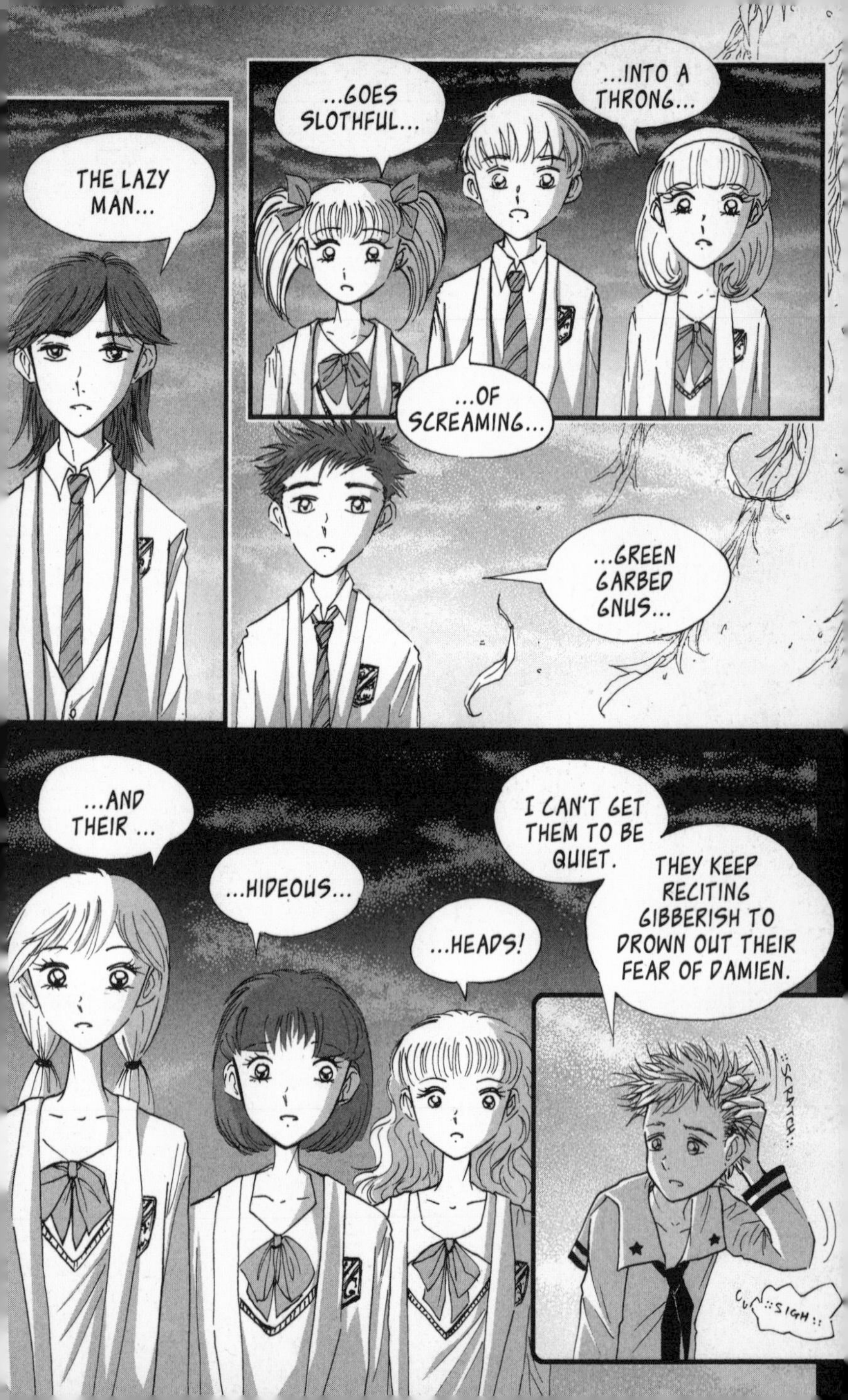
THE LAZY MAN...
...GOES SLOTHFUL...
...INTO A THRONG...
...OF SCREAMING...
...GREEN GARBED GNUS...
...AND THEIR ...
...HIDEOUS...
...HEADS!
I CAN'T GET THEM TO BE QUIET.
THEY KEEP RECITING GIBBERISH TO DROWN OUT THEIR FEAR OF DAMIEN.
::SCRATCH::
::SIGH::

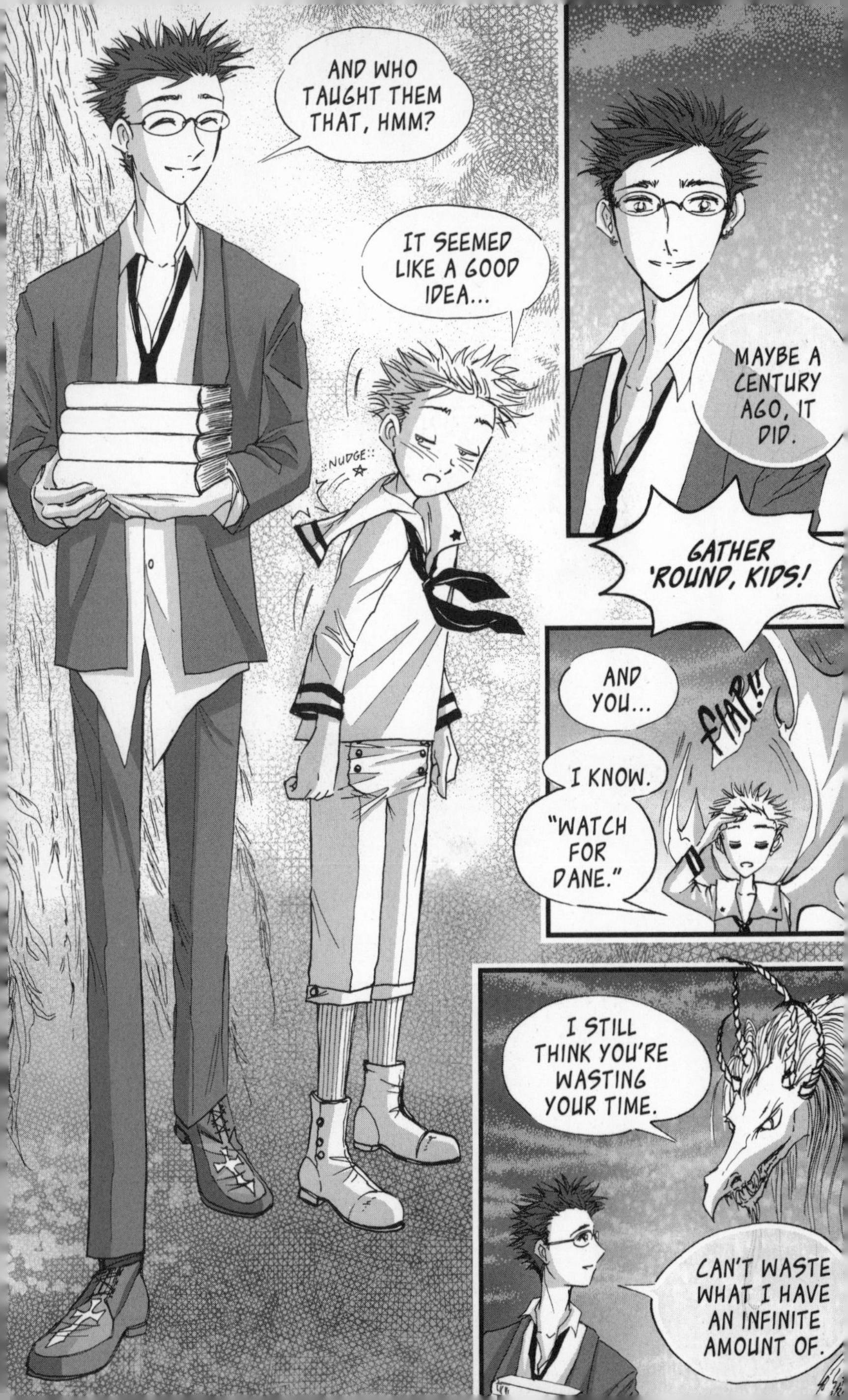
AND WHO TAUGHT THEM THAT, HMM?
IT SEEMED LIKE A GOOD IDEA...
::NUDGE::
MAYBE A CENTURY AGO, IT DID.
GATHER 'ROUND, KIDS!
AND YOU...
FLAP!!
I KNOW.
"WATCH FOR DANE."
I STILL THINK YOU'RE WASTING YOUR TIME.
CAN'T WASTE WHAT I HAVE AN INFINITE AMOUNT OF.

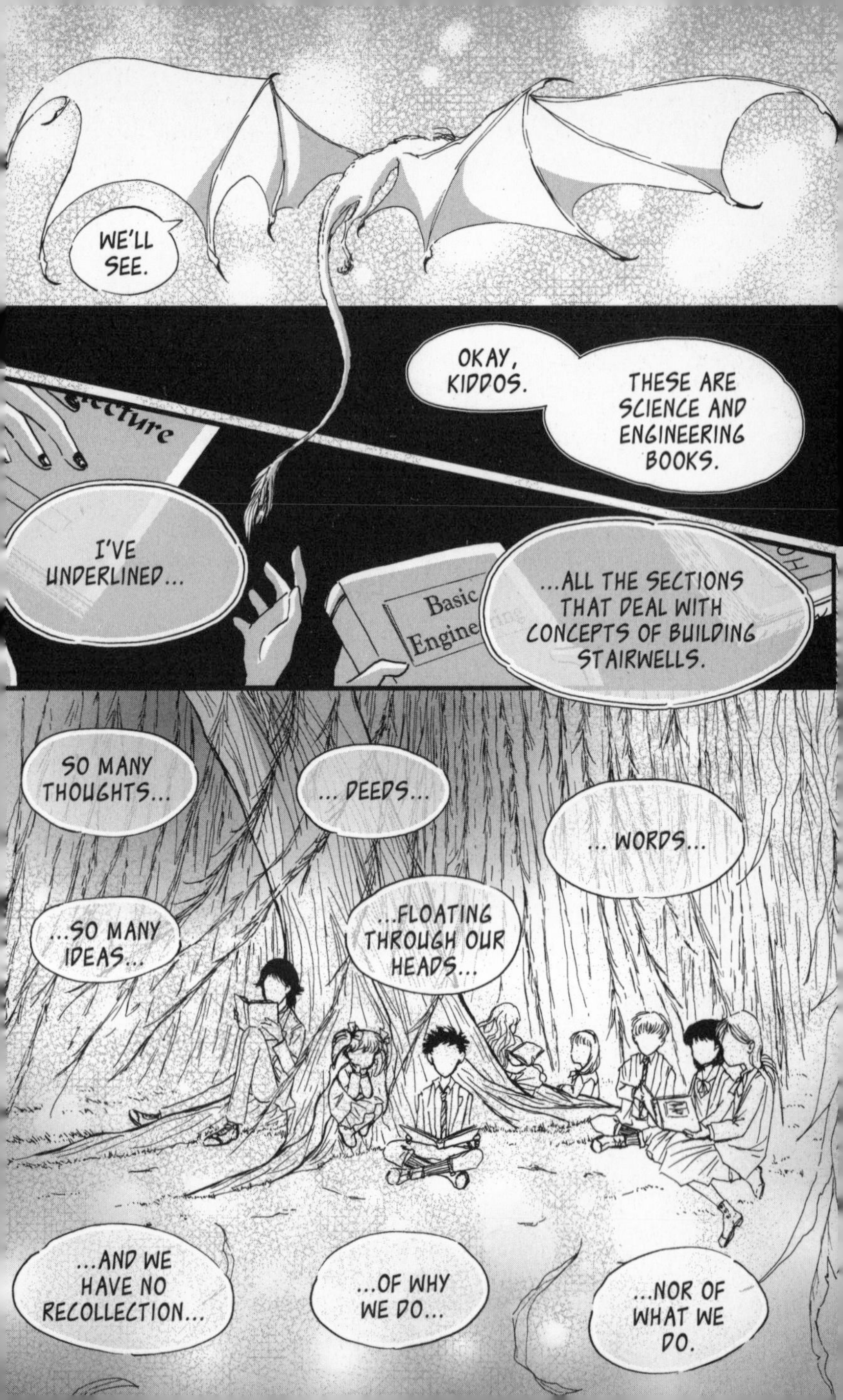
WE'LL SEE.
OKAY, KIDDOS.
THESE ARE SCIENCE AND ENGINEERING BOOKS.
I'VE UNDERLINED...
...ALL THE SECTIONS THAT DEAL WITH CONCEPTS OF BUILDING STAIRWELLS.
SO MANY THOUGHTS...
...DEEDS...
...WORDS...
...SO MANY IDEAS...
...FLOATING THROUGH OUR HEADS...
...AND WE HAVE NO RECOLLECTION...
...OF WHY WE DO...
...NOR OF WHAT WE DO.

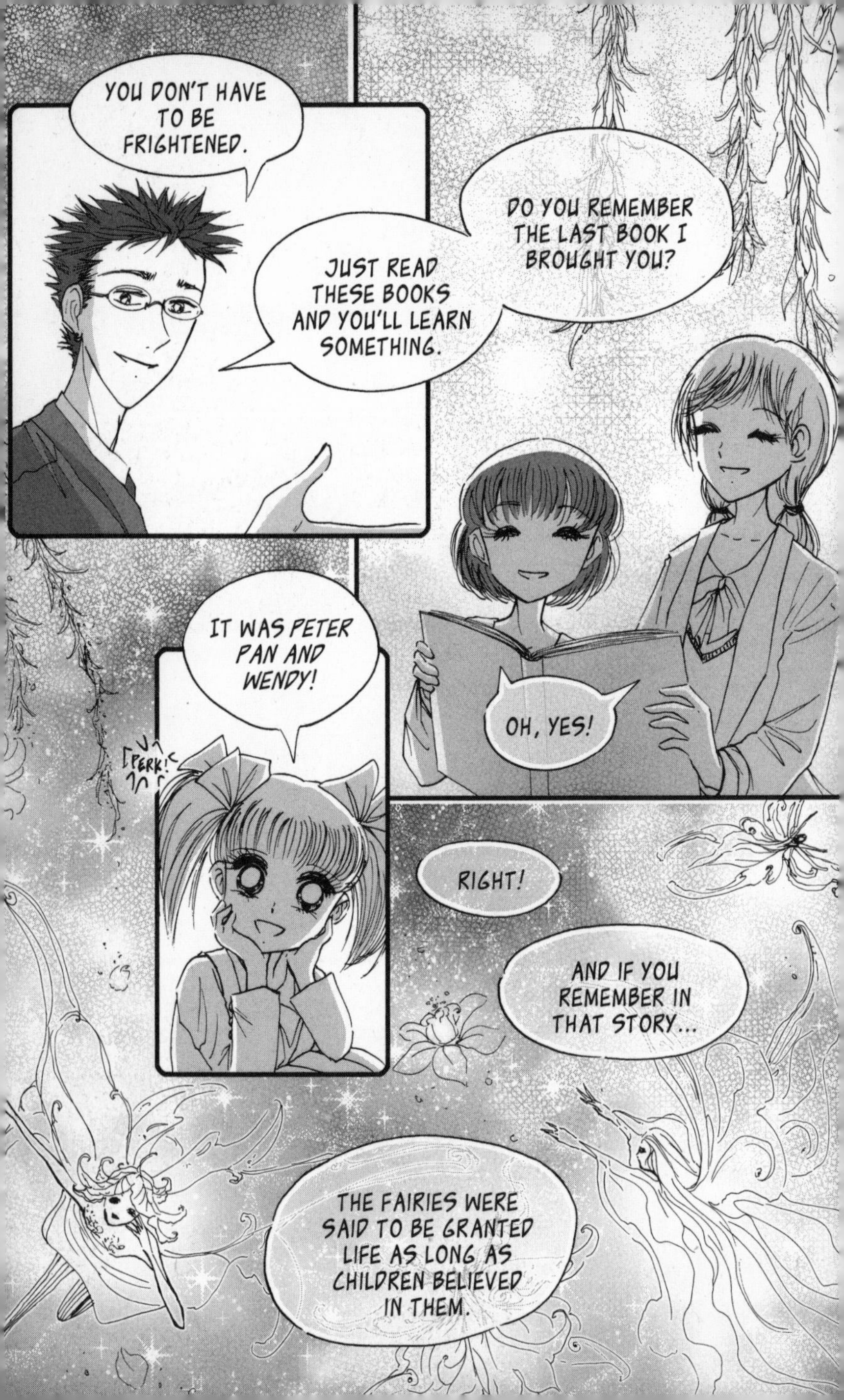
YOU DON'T HAVE TO BE FRIGHTENED.
JUST READ THESE BOOKS AND YOU'LL LEARN SOMETHING.
DO YOU REMEMBER THE LAST BOOK I BROUGHT YOU?
OH, YES!
IT WAS PETER PAN AND WENDY!
PERK!
RIGHT!
AND IF YOU REMEMBER IN THAT STORY...
THE FAIRIES WERE SAID TO BE GRANTED LIFE AS LONG AS CHILDREN BELIEVED IN THEM.

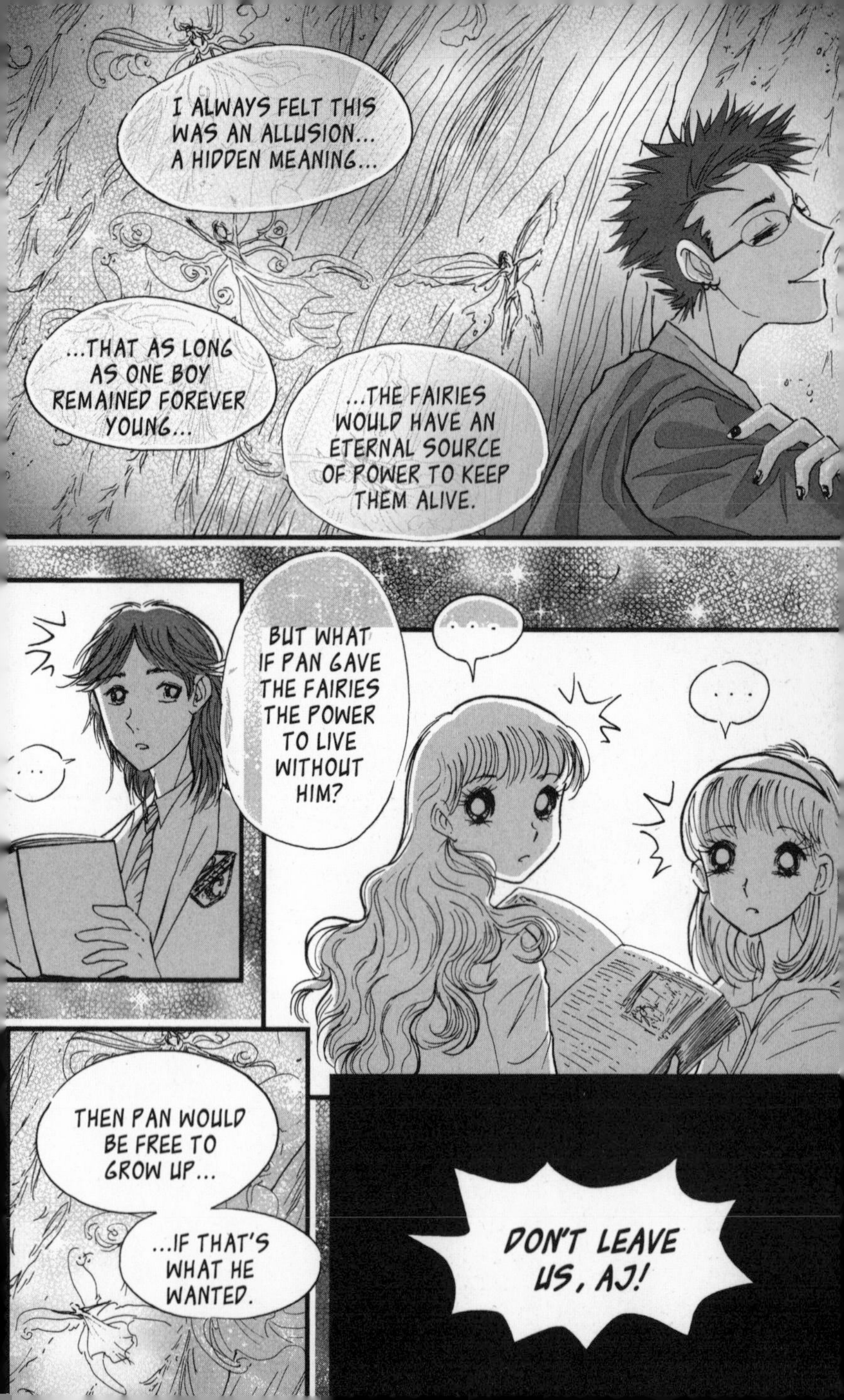
I ALWAYS FELT THIS WAS AN ALLUSION... A HIDDEN MEANING...
...THAT AS LONG AS ONE BOY REMAINED FOREVER YOUNG...
...THE FAIRIES WOULD HAVE AN ETERNAL SOURCE OF POWER TO KEEP THEM ALIVE.
. . .
BUT WHAT IF PAN GAVE THE FAIRIES THE POWER TO LIVE WITHOUT HIM?
. . .
. . .
THEN PAN WOULD BE FREE TO GROW UP...
...IF THAT'S WHAT HE WANTED.
DON'T LEAVE US, AJ!

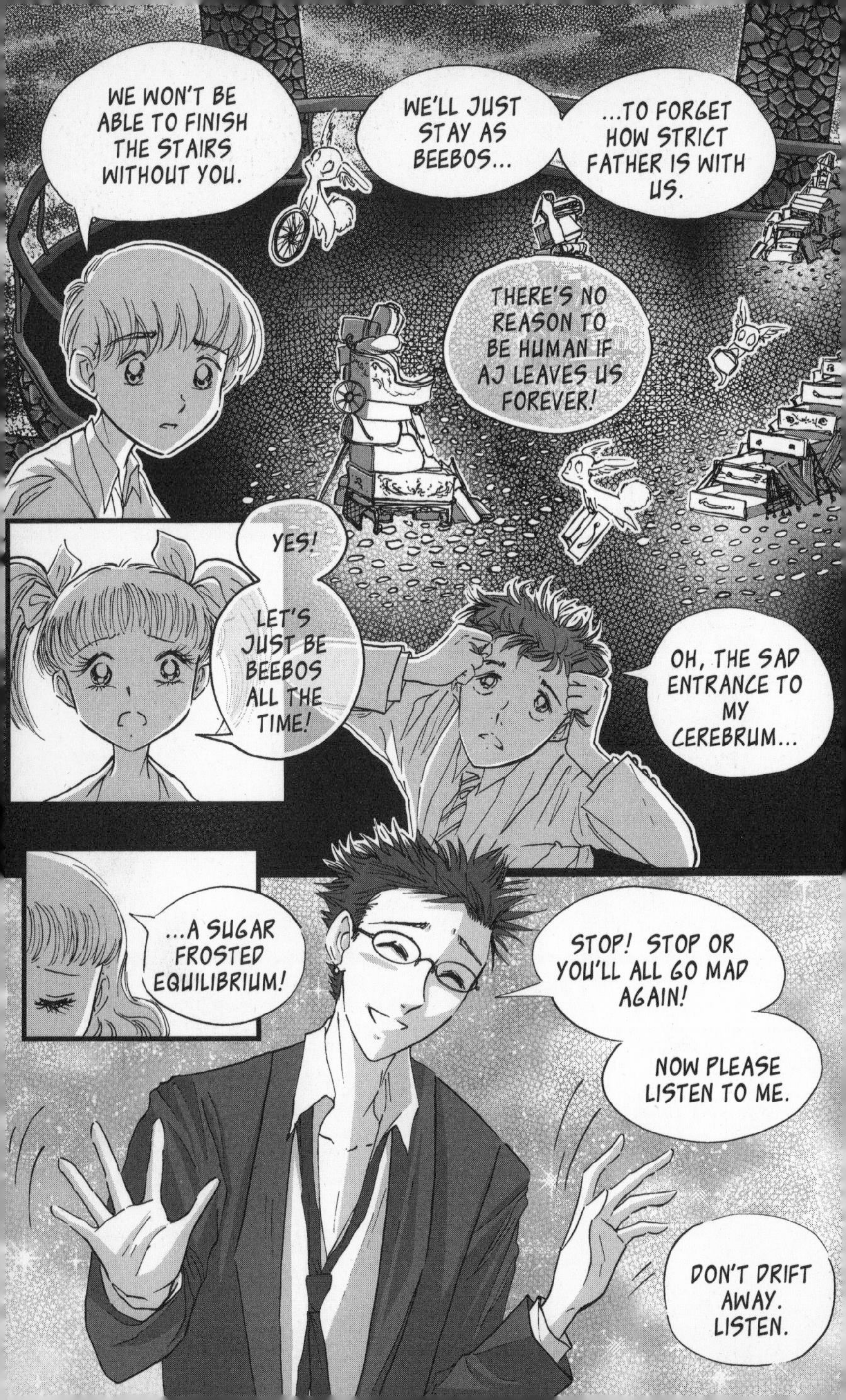
WE WON'T BE ABLE TO FINISH THE STAIRS WITHOUT YOU.
WE'LL JUST STAY AS BEEBOS...
...TO FORGET HOW STRICT FATHER IS WITH US.
THERE'S NO REASON TO BE HUMAN IF AJ LEAVES US FOREVER!
YES!
LET'S JUST BE BEEBOS ALL THE TIME!
OH, THE SAD ENTRANCE TO MY CEREBRUM...
...A SUGAR FROSTED EQUILIBRIUM!
STOP! STOP OR YOU'LL ALL GO MAD AGAIN!
NOW PLEASE LISTEN TO ME.
DON'T DRIFT AWAY. LISTEN.

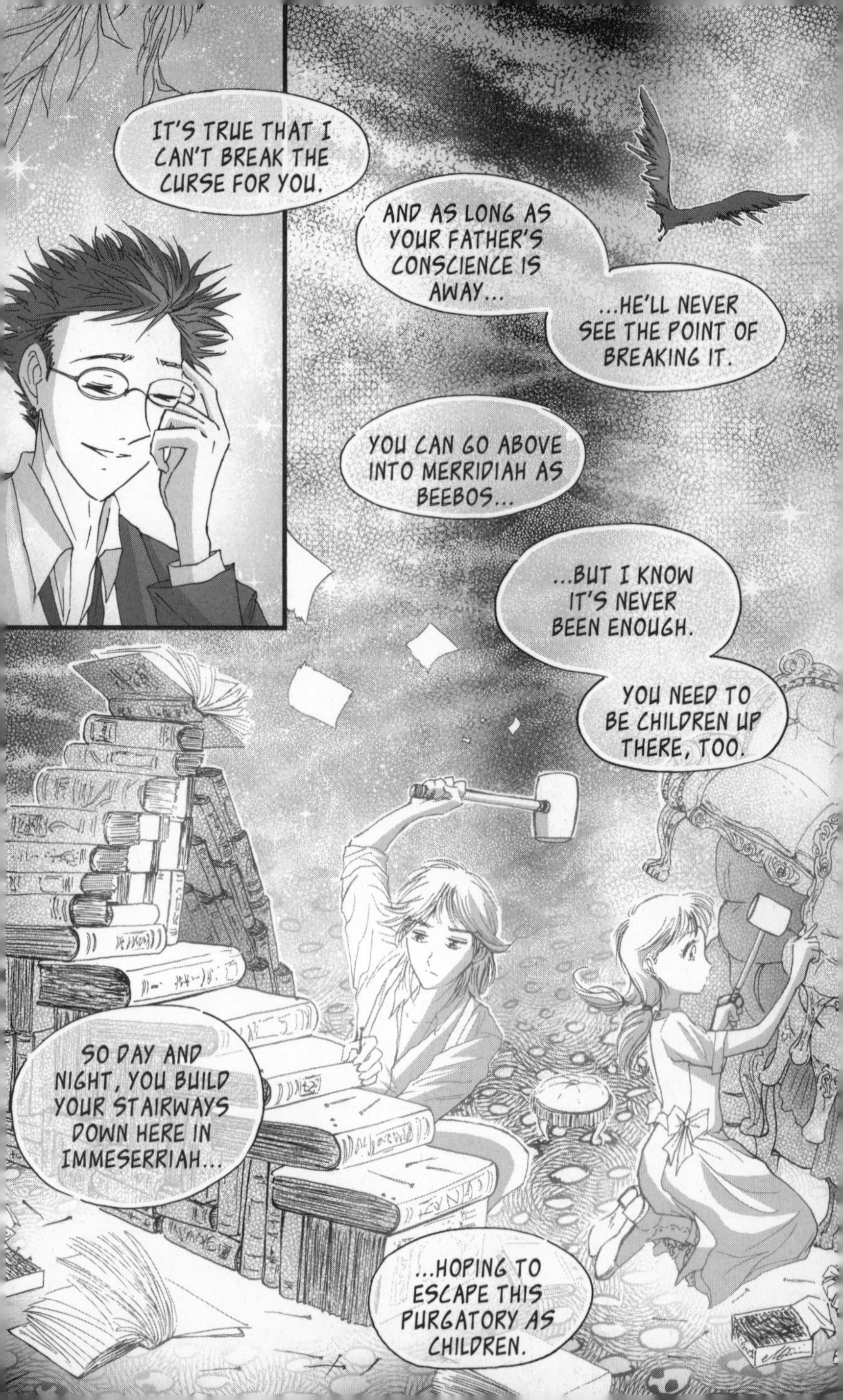
IT'S TRUE THAT I CAN'T BREAK THE CURSE FOR YOU.
AND AS LONG AS YOUR FATHER'S CONSCIENCE IS AWAY...
...HE'LL NEVER SEE THE POINT OF BREAKING IT.
YOU CAN GO ABOVE INTO MERRIDIAH AS BEEBOS...
...BUT I KNOW IT'S NEVER BEEN ENOUGH.
YOU NEED TO BE CHILDREN UP THERE, TOO.
SO DAY AND NIGHT, YOU BUILD YOUR STAIRWAYS DOWN HERE IN IMMESERRIAH...
...HOPING TO ESCAPE THIS PURGATORY AS CHILDREN.

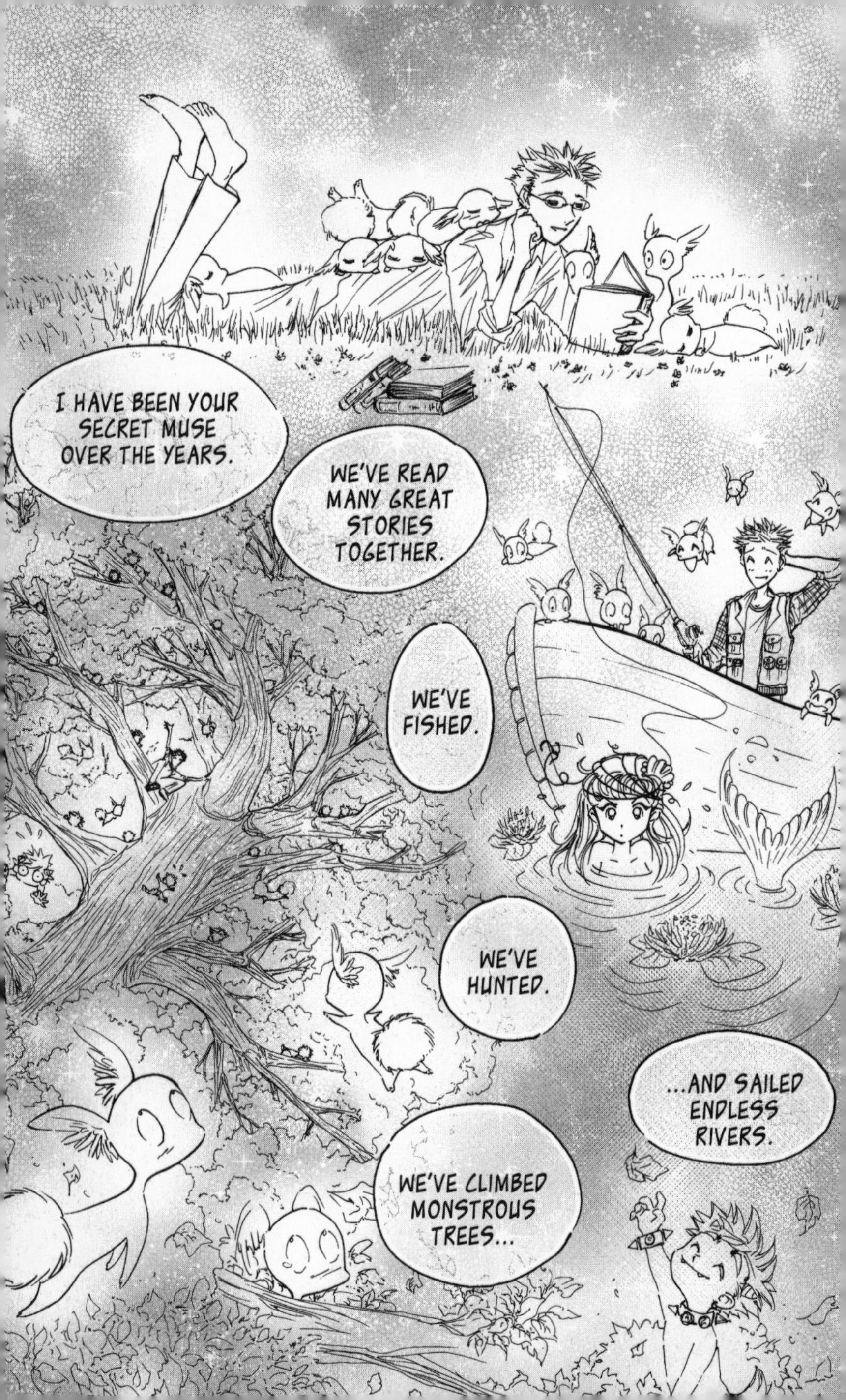

I HAVE BEEN YOUR SECRET MUSE OVER THE YEARS.
WE'VE READ MANY GREAT STORIES TOGETHER.
WE'VE FISHED.
WE'VE HUNTED.
WE'VE CLIMBED MONSTROUS TREES...
...AND SAILED ENDLESS RIVERS.

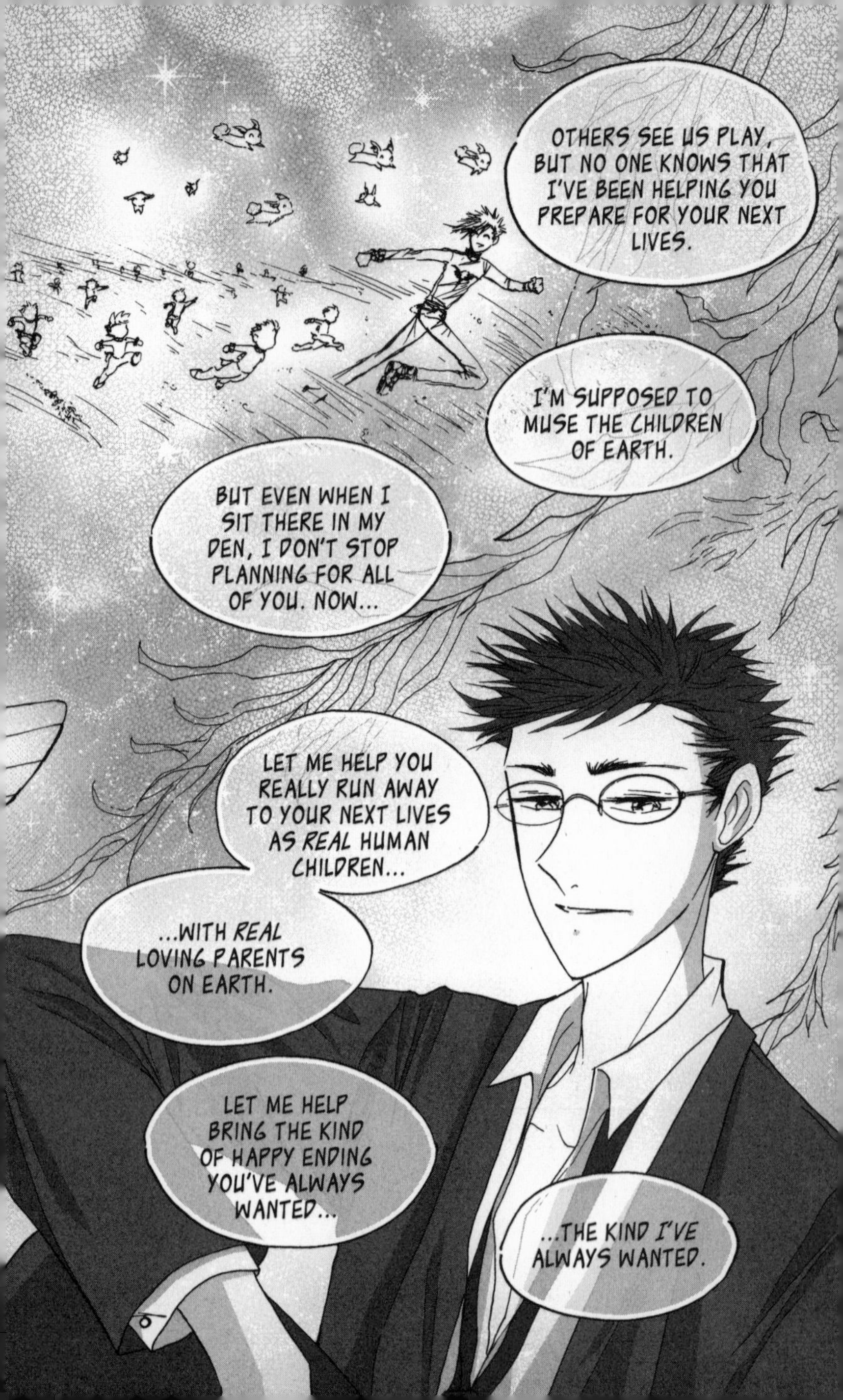
OTHERS SEE US PLAY, BUT NO ONE KNOWS THAT I'VE BEEN HELPING YOU PREPARE FOR YOUR NEXT LIVES.
I'M SUPPOSED TO MUSE THE CHILDREN OF EARTH.
BUT EVEN WHEN I SIT THERE IN MY DEN, I DON'T STOP PLANNING FOR ALL OF YOU. NOW...
LET ME HELP YOU REALLY RUN AWAY TO YOUR NEXT LIVES AS *REAL* HUMAN CHILDREN...
...WITH *REAL* LOVING PARENTS ON EARTH.
LET ME HELP BRING THE KIND OF HAPPY ENDING YOU'VE ALWAYS WANTED...
...THE KIND *I'VE* ALWAYS WANTED.

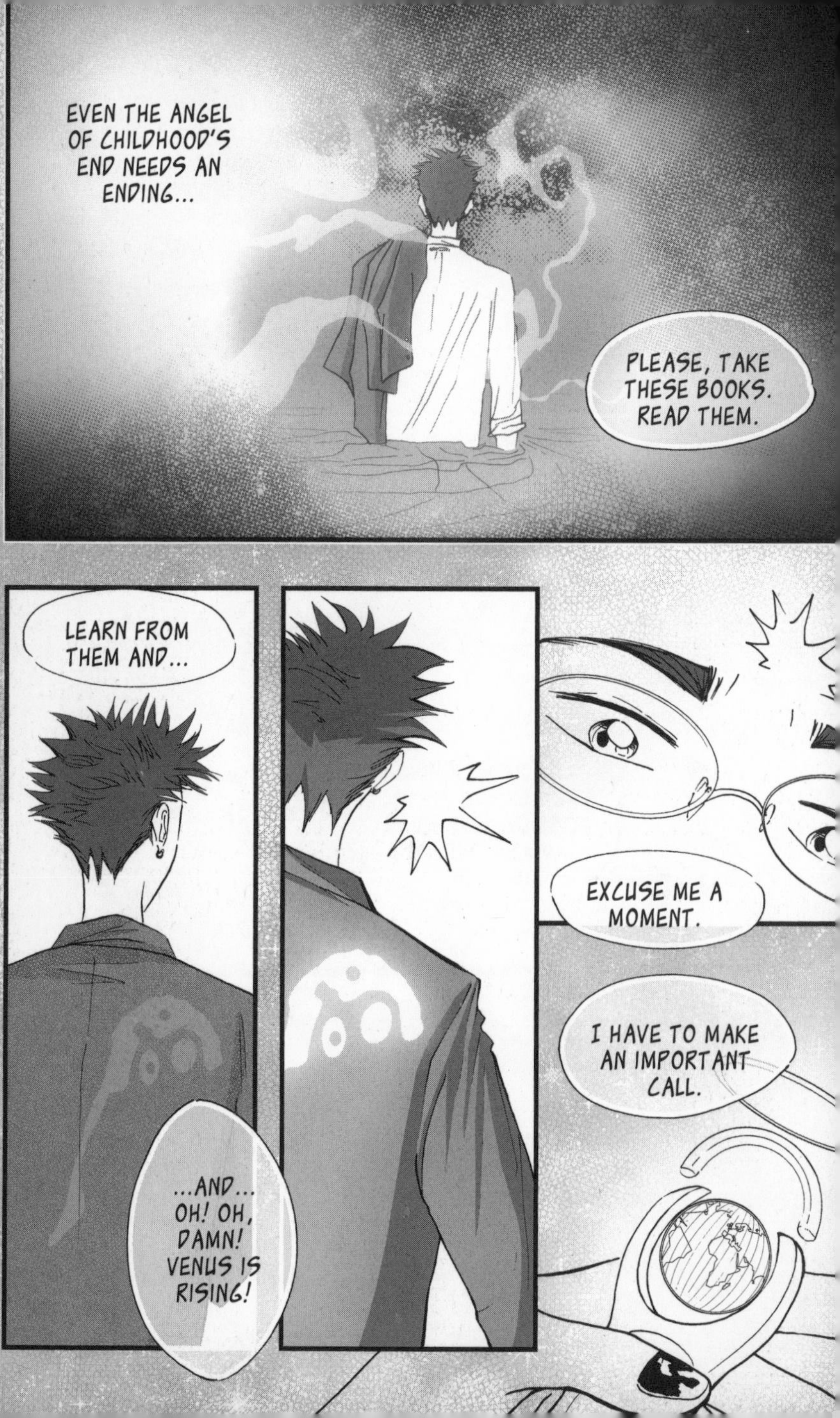
EVEN THE ANGEL OF CHILDHOOD'S END NEEDS AN ENDING...
PLEASE, TAKE THESE BOOKS. READ THEM.
LEARN FROM THEM AND...
...AND... OH! OH, DAMN! VENUS IS RISING!
EXCUSE ME A MOMENT.
I HAVE TO MAKE AN IMPORTANT CALL.

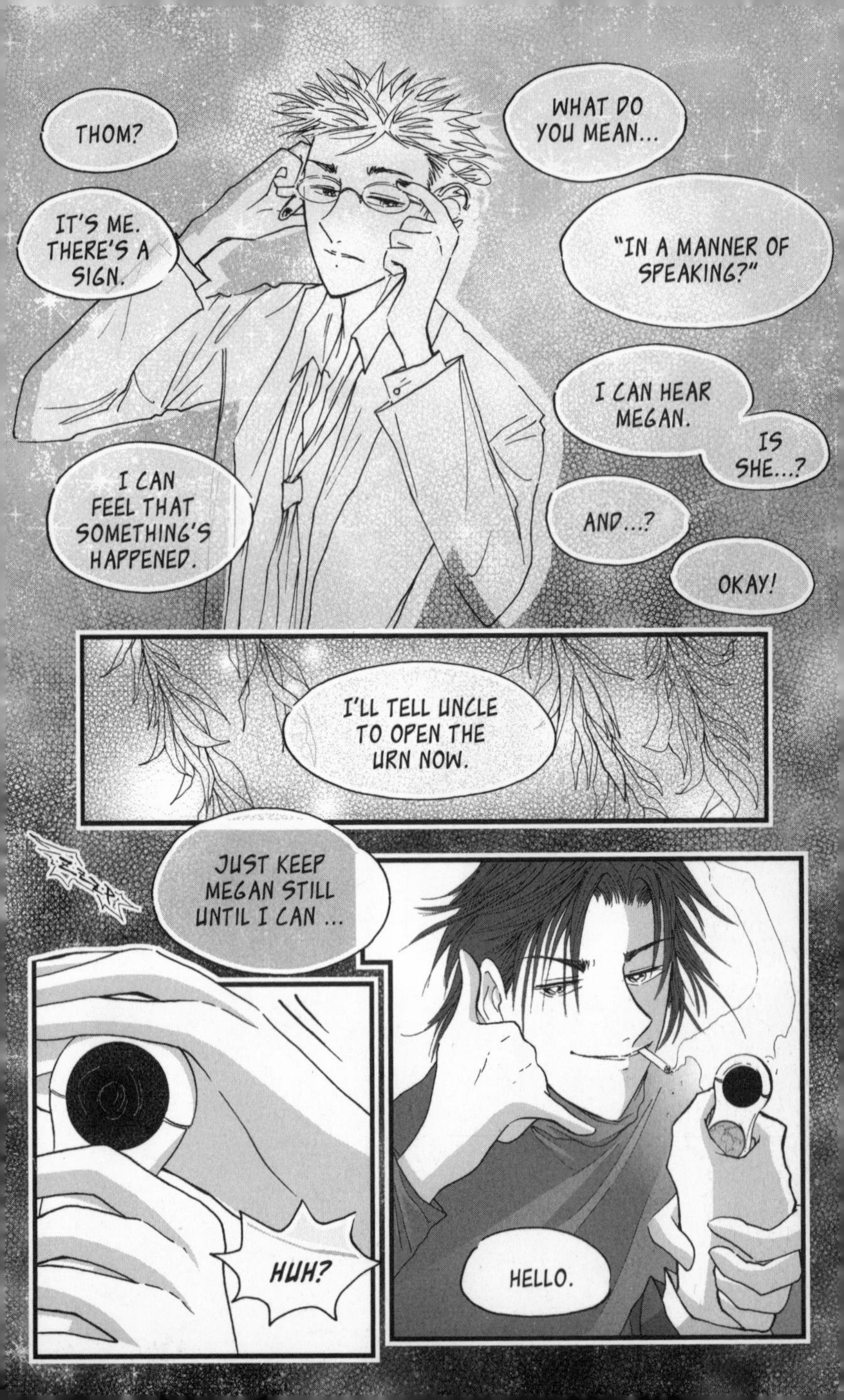
THOM?
WHAT DO YOU MEAN...
IT'S ME. THERE'S A SIGN.
"IN A MANNER OF SPEAKING?"
I CAN HEAR MEGAN.
IS SHE...?
I CAN FEEL THAT SOMETHING'S HAPPENED.
AND...?
OKAY!
I'LL TELL UNCLE TO OPEN THE URN NOW.
JUST KEEP MEGAN STILL UNTIL I CAN ...
HUH?
HELLO.

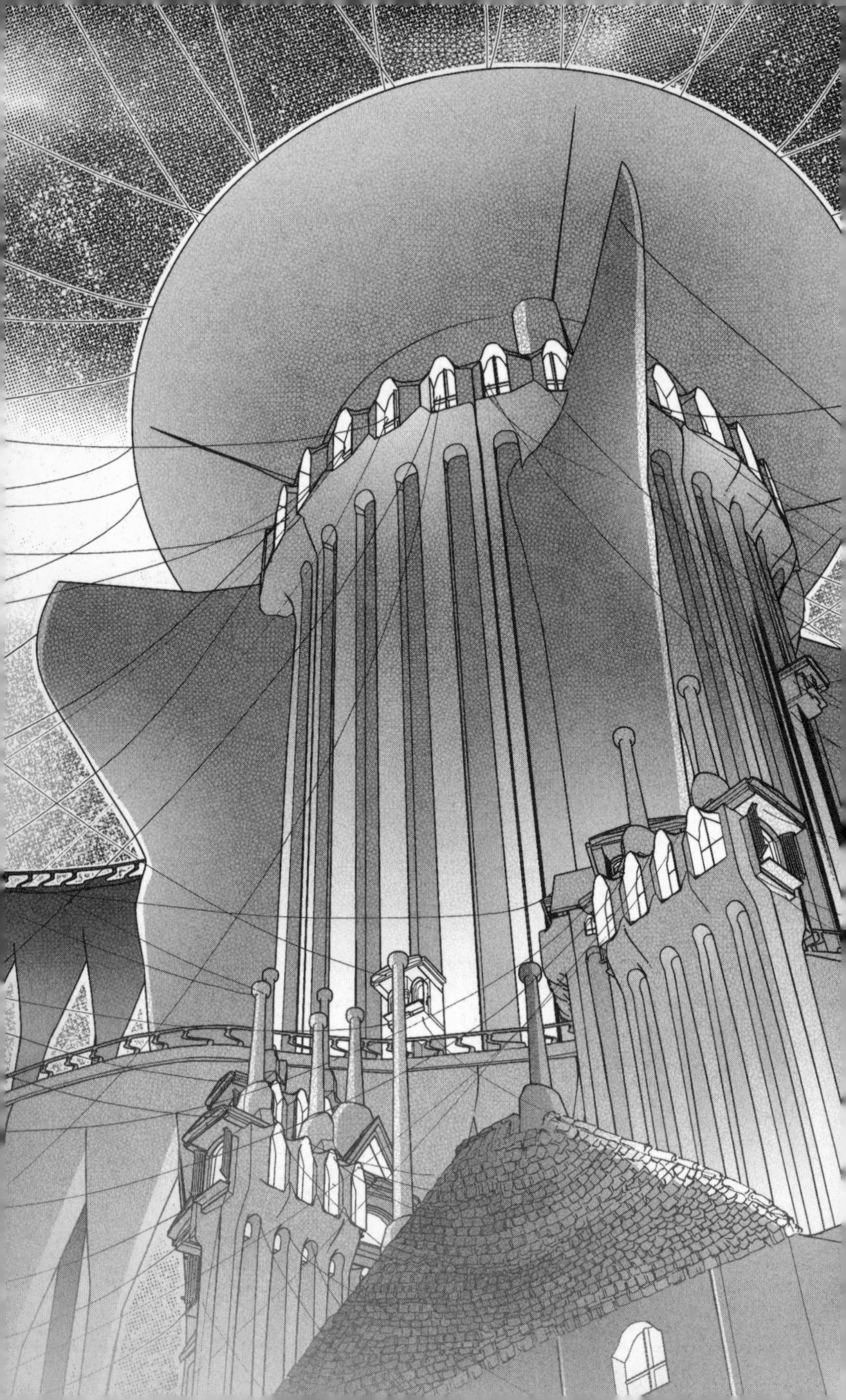

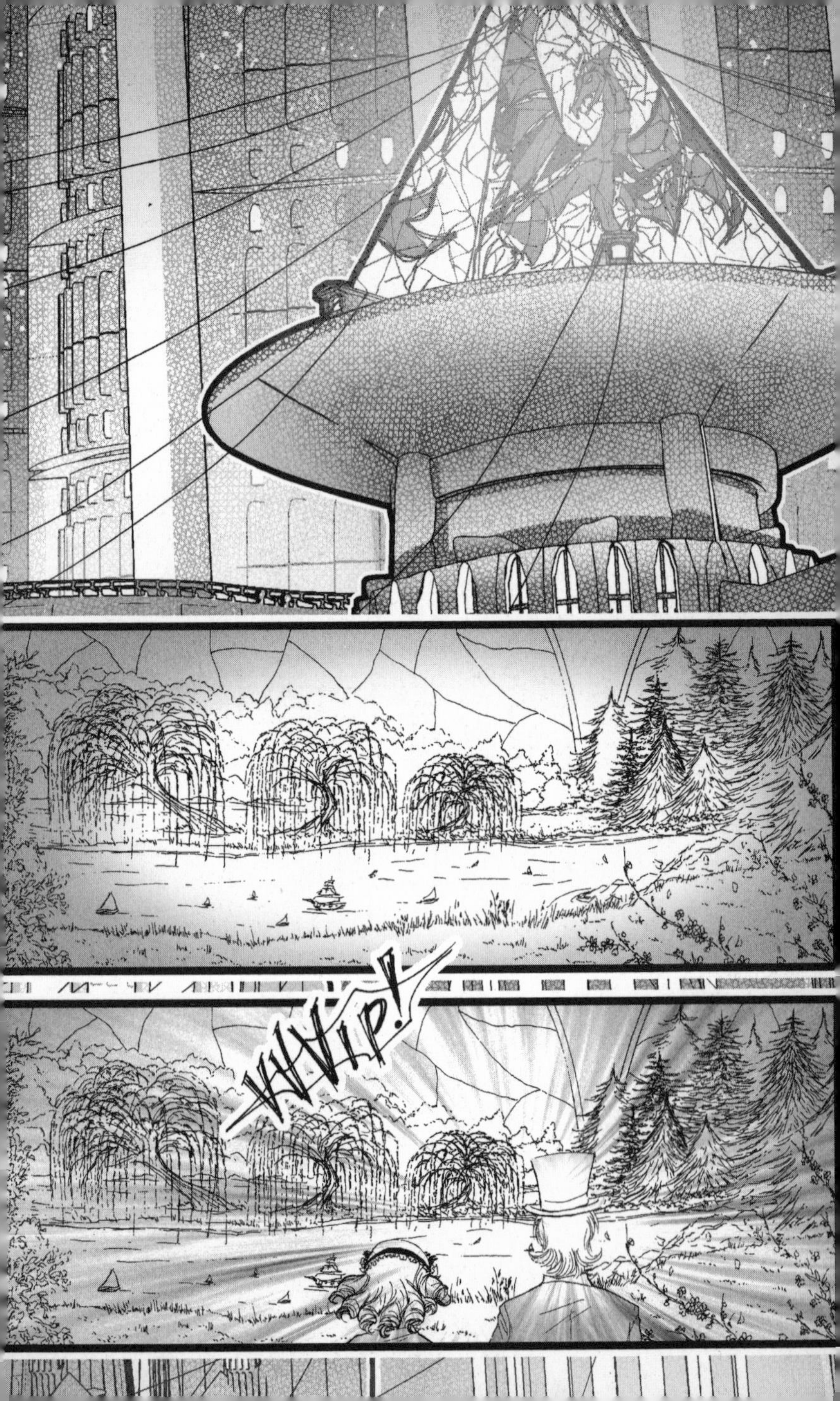
VVVIP!

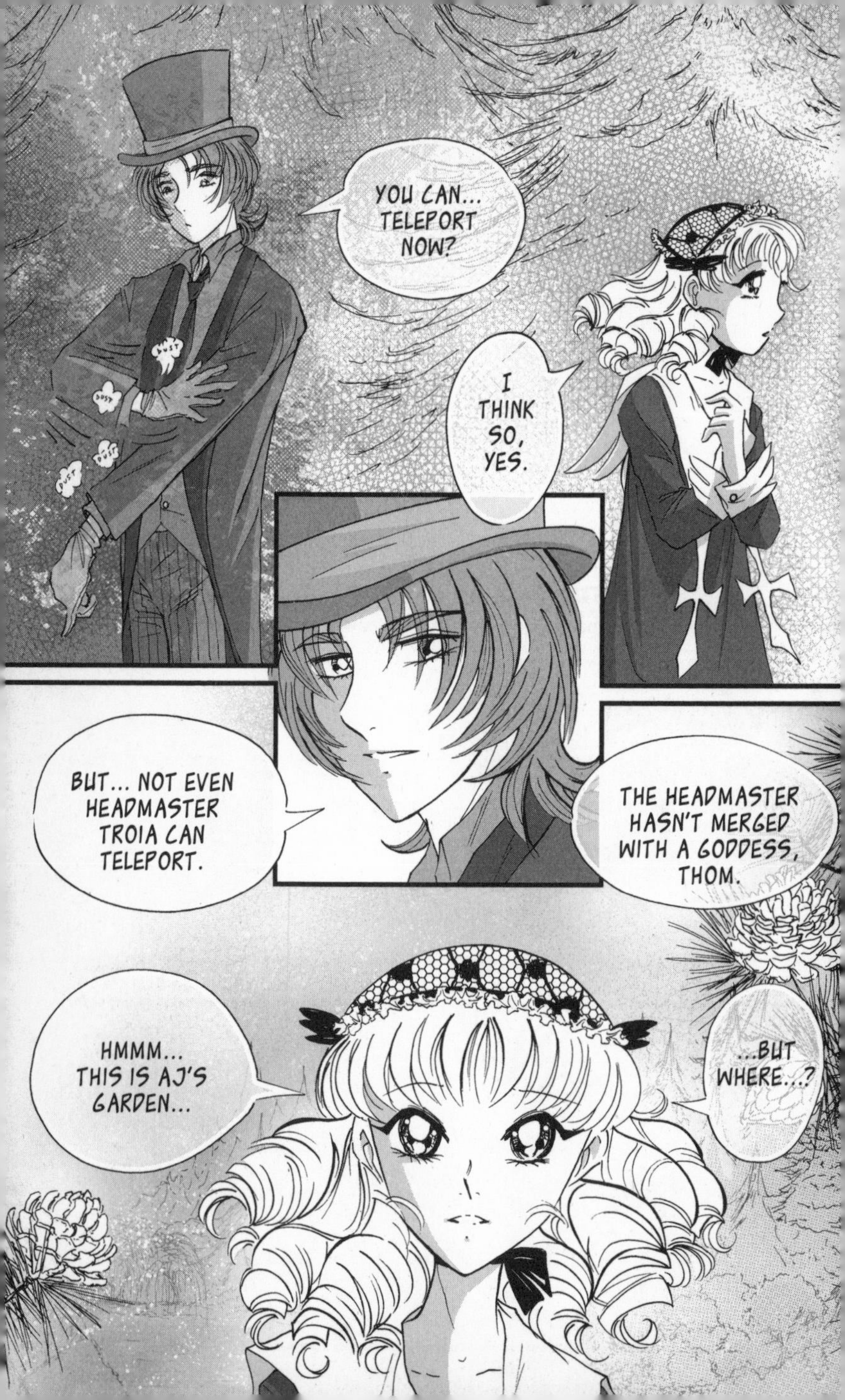
YOU CAN... TELEPORT NOW?
I THINK SO, YES.
BUT... NOT EVEN HEADMASTER TROIA CAN TELEPORT.
THE HEADMASTER HASN'T MERGED WITH A GODDESS, THOM.
HMMM... THIS IS AJ'S GARDEN...
...BUT WHERE...?

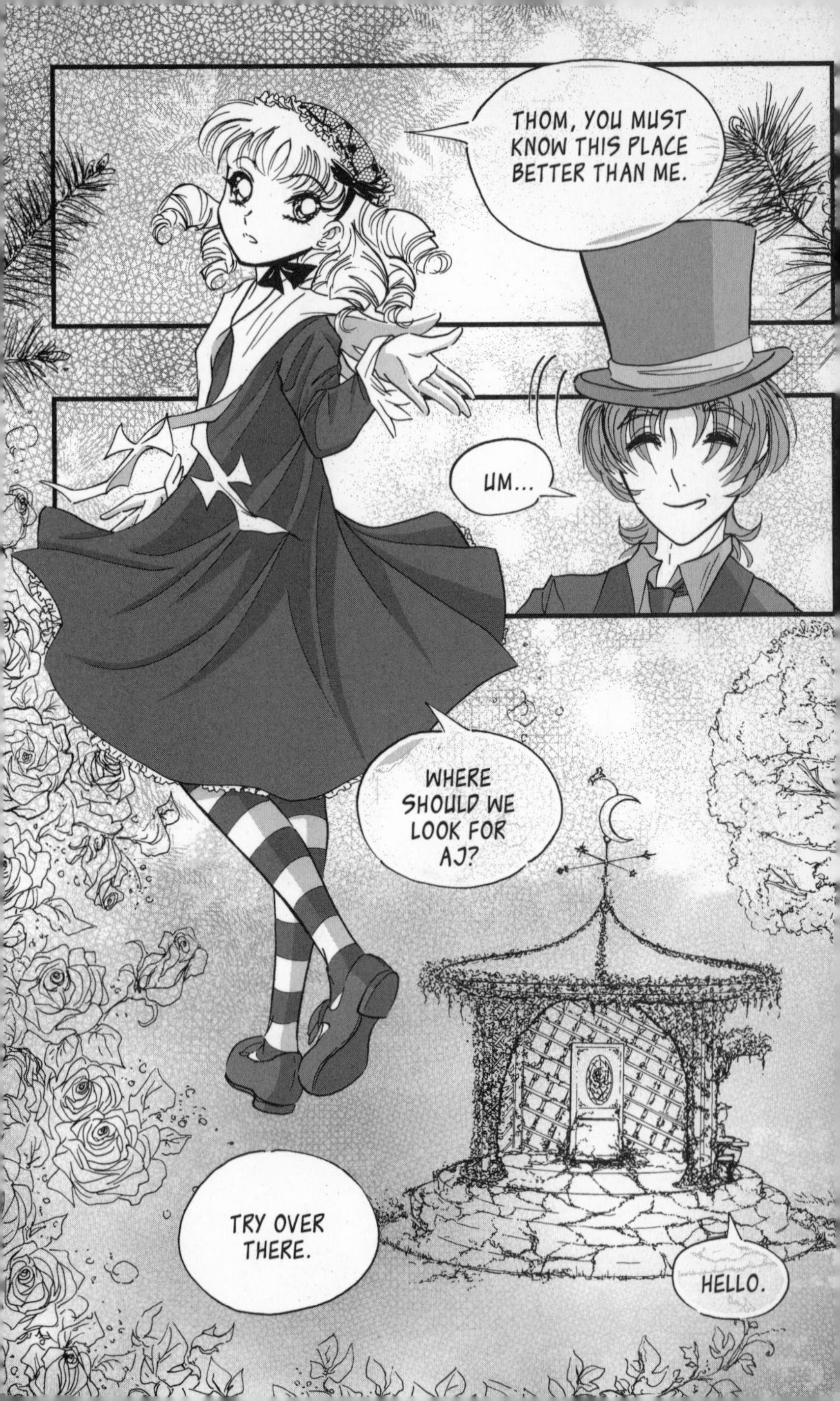
THOM, YOU MUST KNOW THIS PLACE BETTER THAN ME.
UM...
WHERE SHOULD WE LOOK FOR AJ?
TRY OVER THERE.
HELLO.

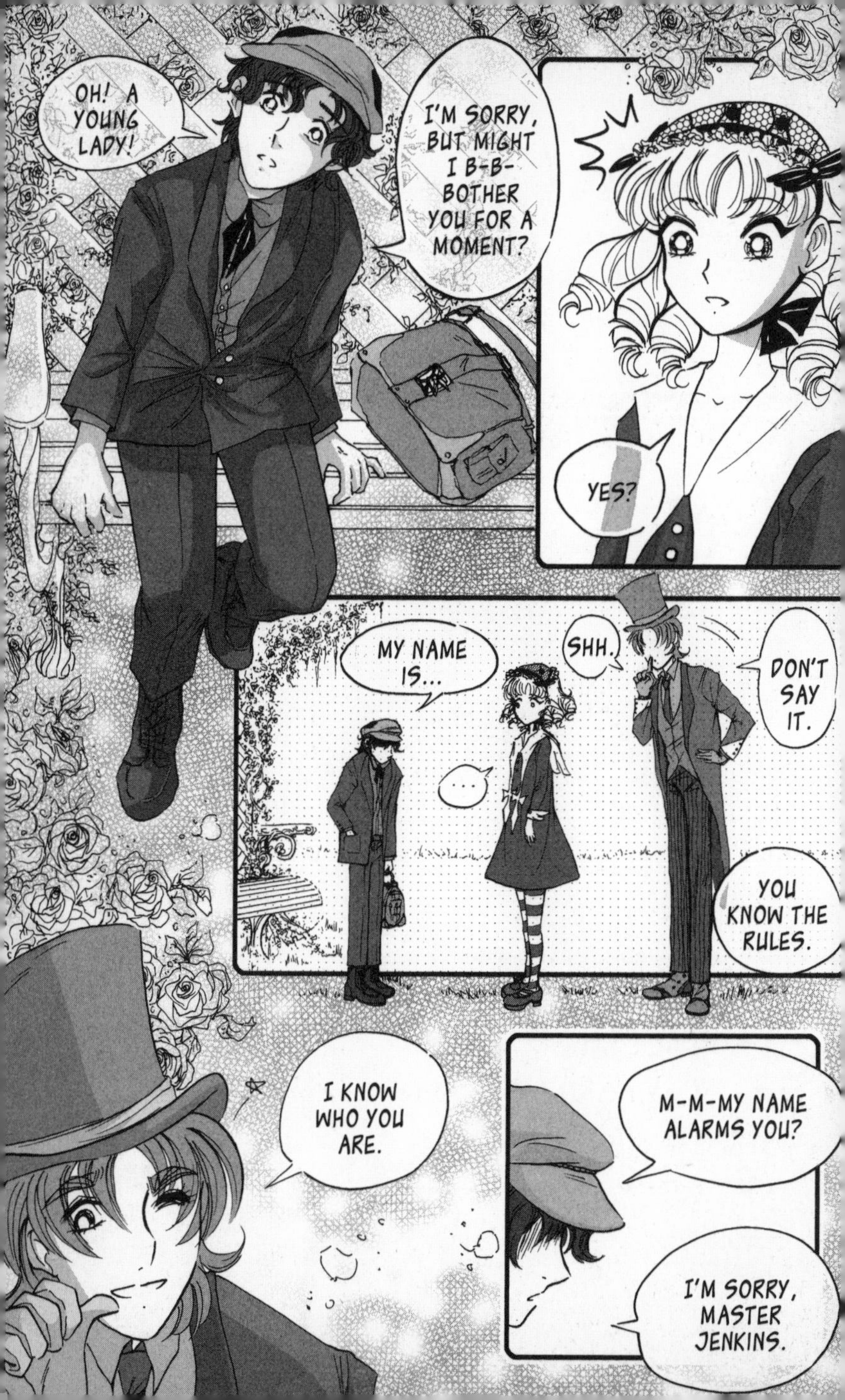
OH! A YOUNG LADY!
I'M SORRY, BUT MIGHT I B-B-BOTHER YOU FOR A MOMENT?
YES?
MY NAME IS...
...
SHH.
DON'T SAY IT.
YOU KNOW THE RULES.
I KNOW WHO YOU ARE.
M-M-MY NAME ALARMS YOU?
I'M SORRY, MASTER JENKINS.

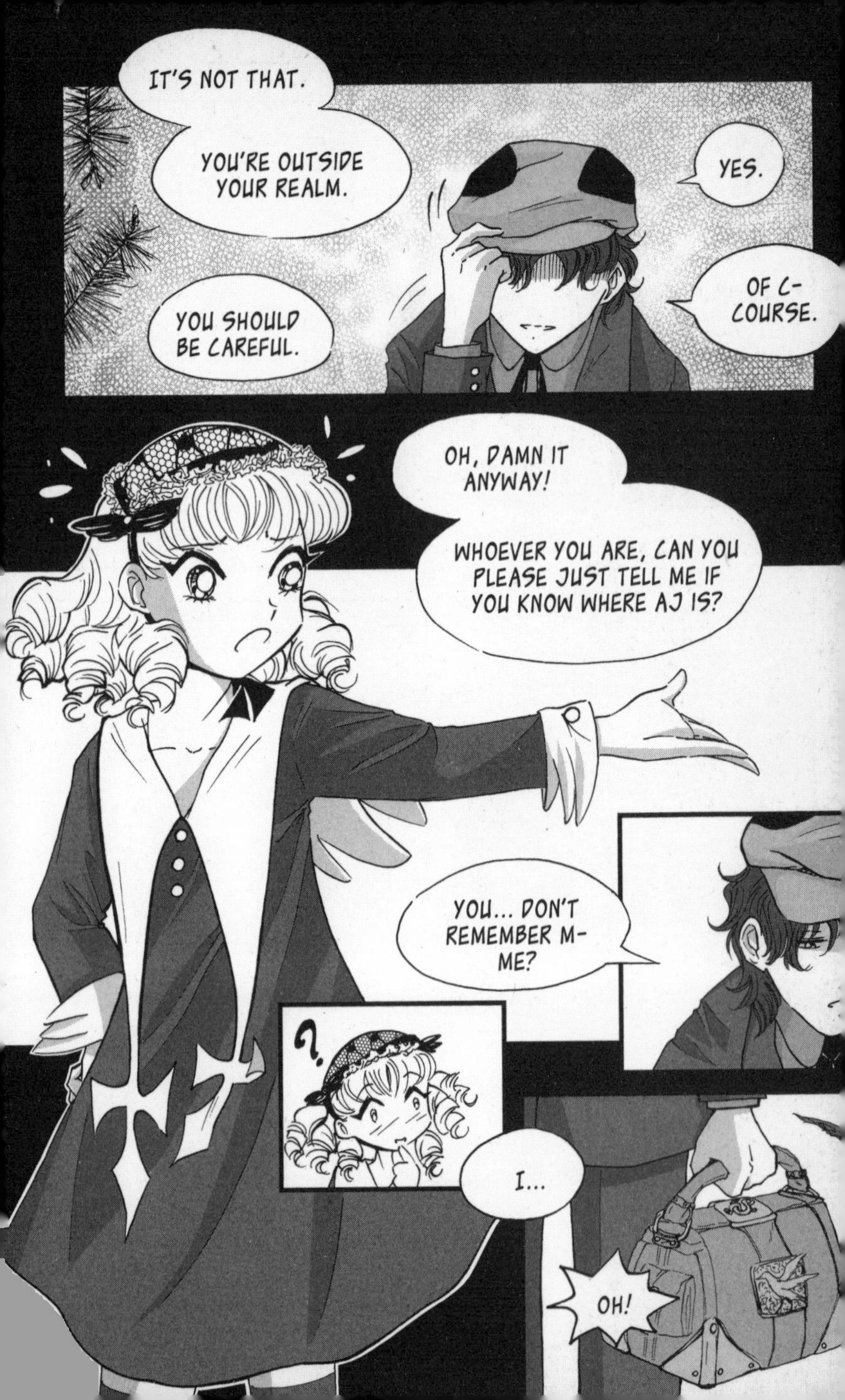
IT'S NOT THAT.
YOU'RE OUTSIDE YOUR REALM.
YOU SHOULD BE CAREFUL.
YES.
OF C-COURSE.
OH, DAMN IT ANYWAY!
WHOEVER YOU ARE, CAN YOU PLEASE JUST TELL ME IF YOU KNOW WHERE AJ IS?
YOU... DON'T REMEMBER M-ME?
I...
OH!

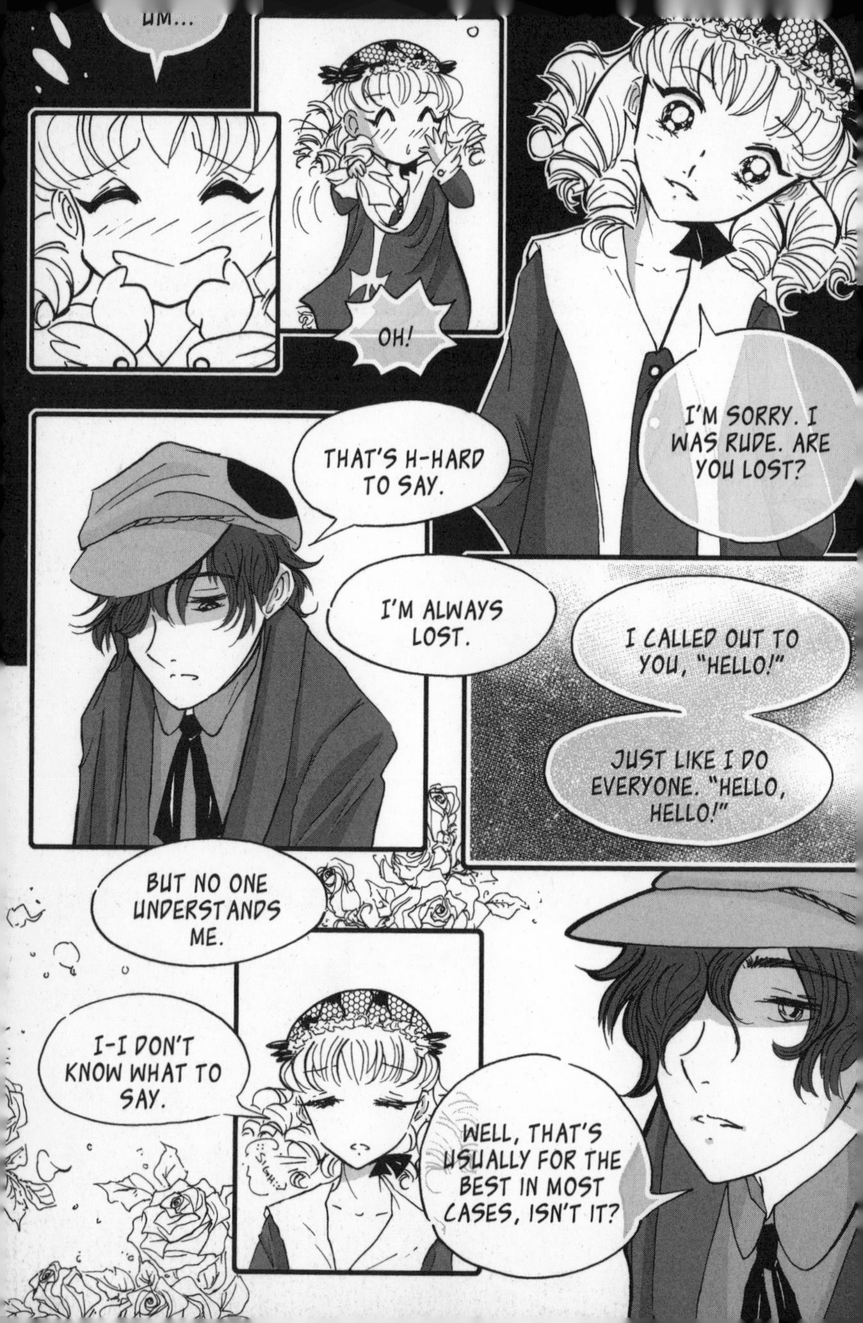
UM...
OH!
I'M SORRY. I WAS RUDE. ARE YOU LOST?
THAT'S H-HARD TO SAY.
I'M ALWAYS LOST.
I CALLED OUT TO YOU, "HELLO!"
JUST LIKE I DO EVERYONE. "HELLO, HELLO!"
BUT NO ONE UNDERSTANDS ME.
I-I DON'T KNOW WHAT TO SAY.
WELL, THAT'S USUALLY FOR THE BEST IN MOST CASES, ISN'T IT?

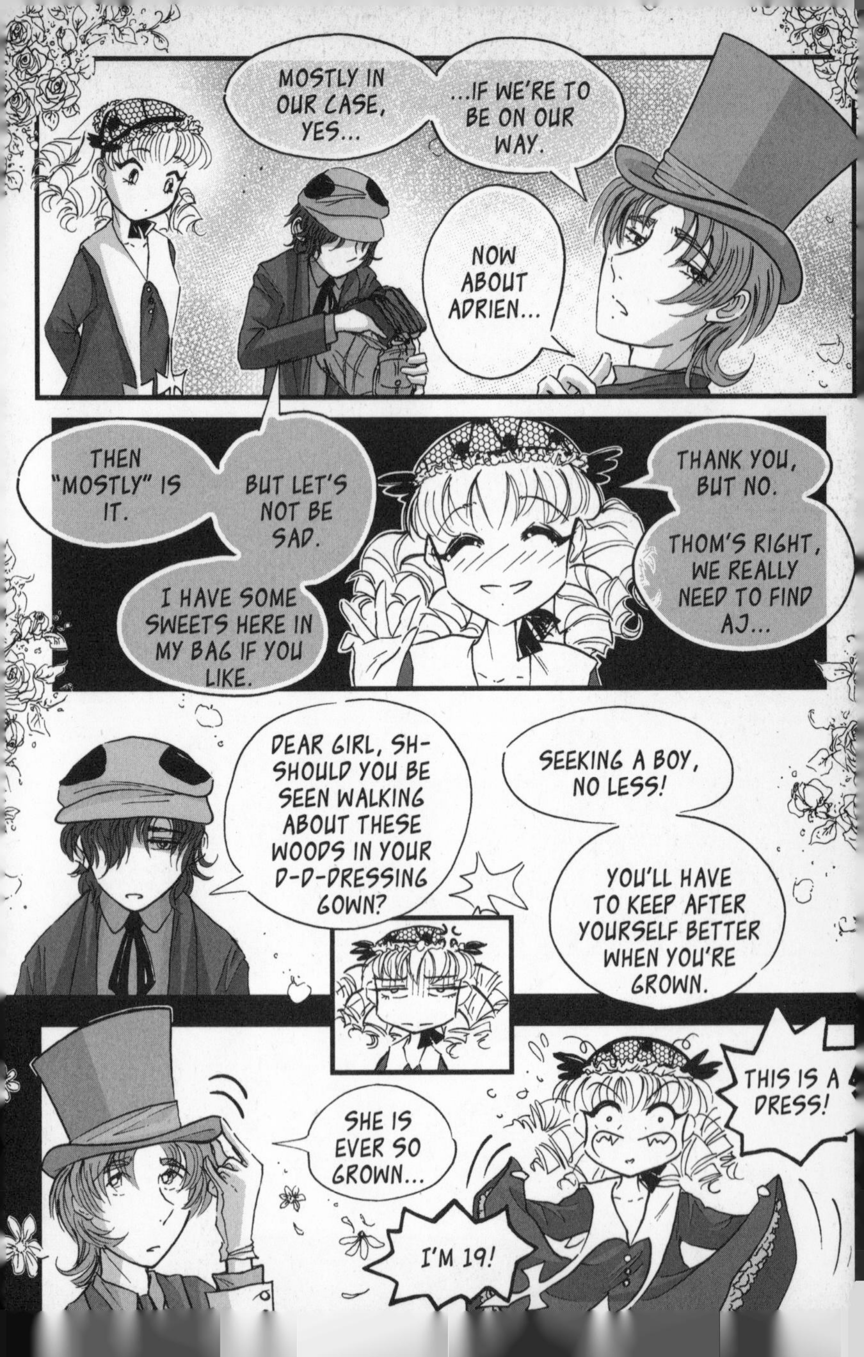
MOSTLY IN OUR CASE, YES...
...IF WE'RE TO BE ON OUR WAY.
NOW ABOUT ADRIEN...
THEN "MOSTLY" IS IT.
BUT LET'S NOT BE SAD.
I HAVE SOME SWEETS HERE IN MY BAG IF YOU LIKE.
THANK YOU, BUT NO.
THOM'S RIGHT, WE REALLY NEED TO FIND AJ...
DEAR GIRL, SH-SHOULD YOU BE SEEN WALKING ABOUT THESE WOODS IN YOUR D-D-DRESSING GOWN?
SEEKING A BOY, NO LESS!
YOU'LL HAVE TO KEEP AFTER YOURSELF BETTER WHEN YOU'RE GROWN.
SHE IS EVER SO GROWN...
THIS IS A DRESS!
I'M 19!

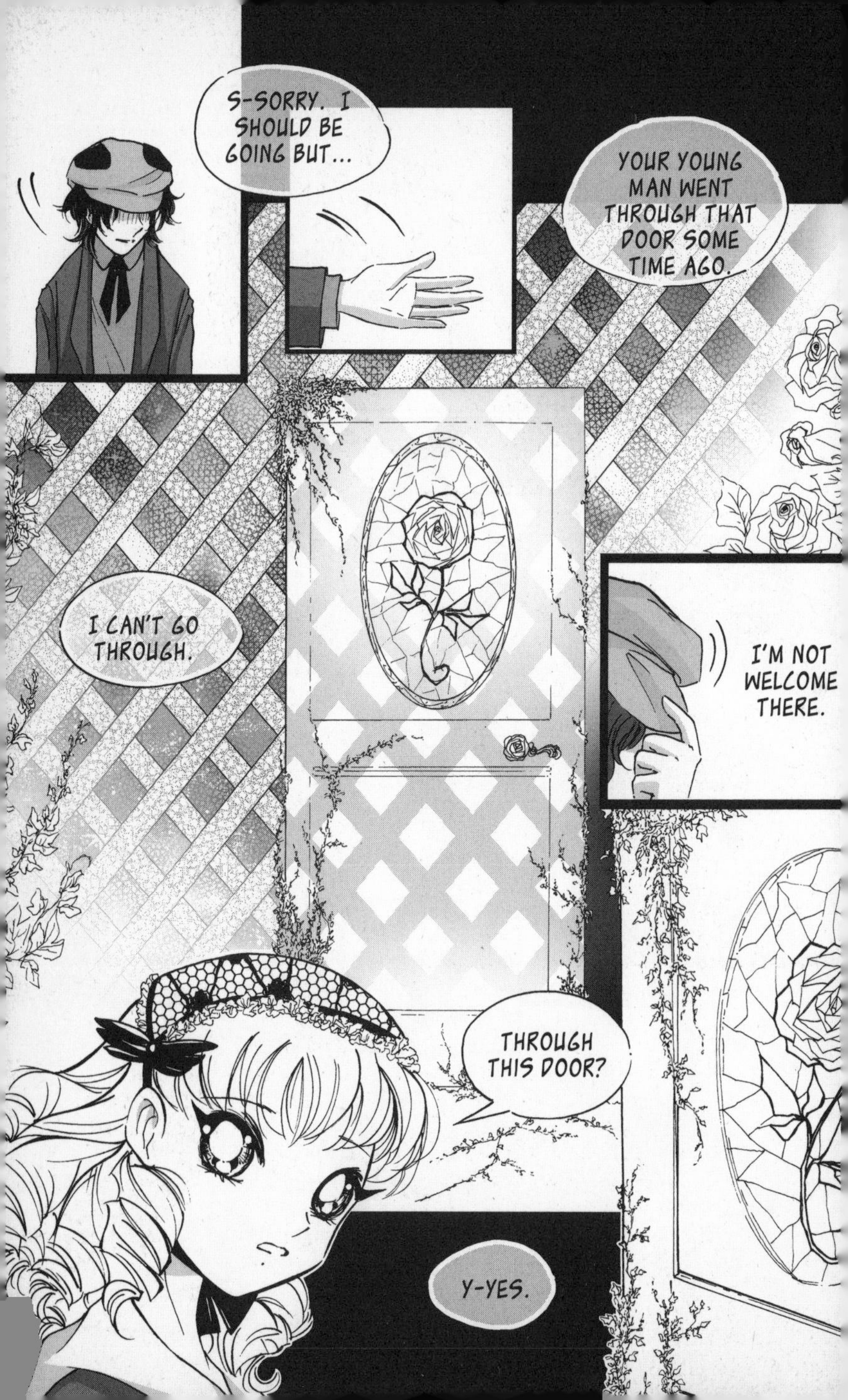
S-SORRY. I SHOULD BE GOING BUT...
YOUR YOUNG MAN WENT THROUGH THAT DOOR SOME TIME AGO.
I CAN'T GO THROUGH.
I'M NOT WELCOME THERE.
THROUGH THIS DOOR?
Y-YES.

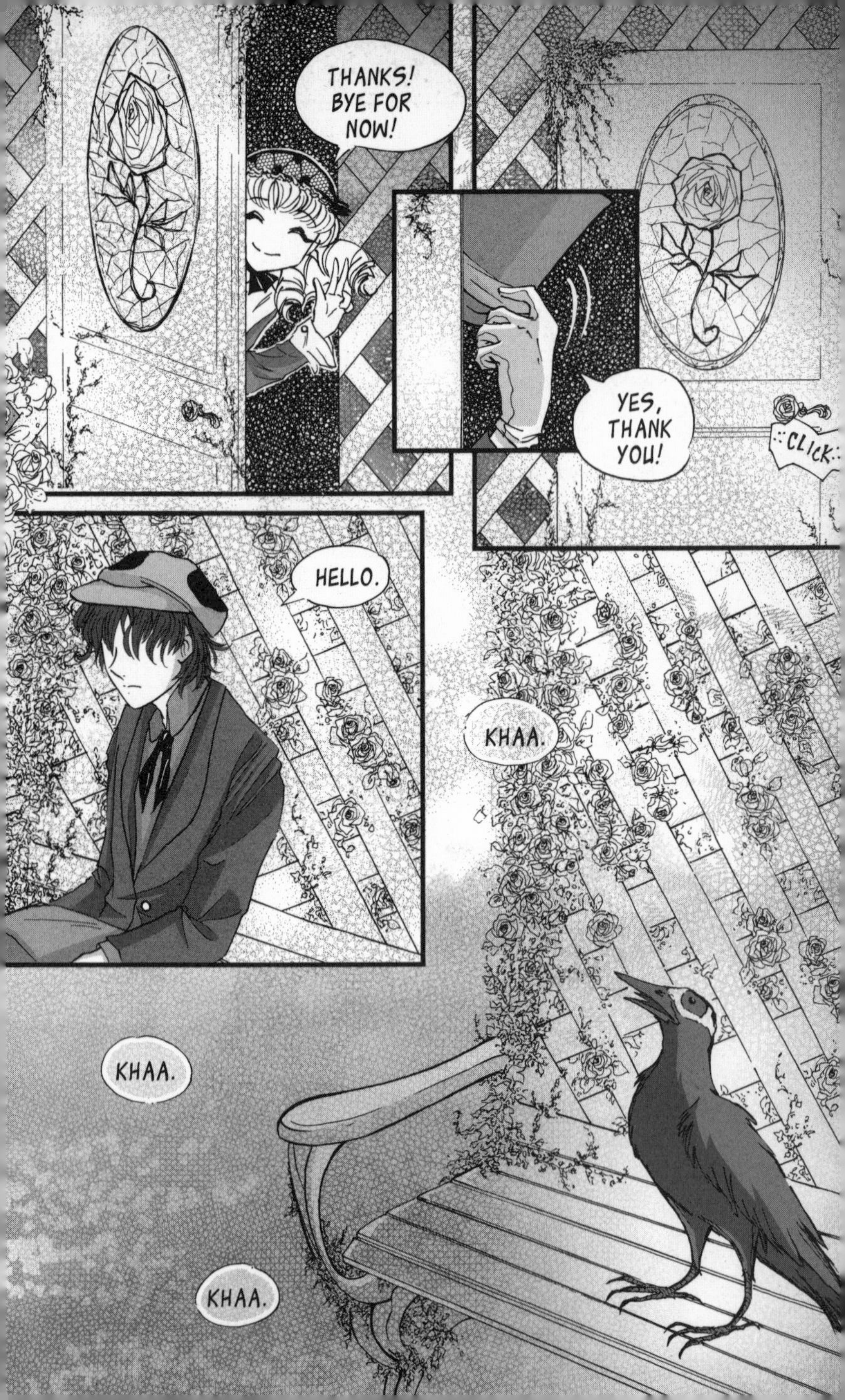
THANKS! BYE FOR NOW!
YES, THANK YOU!
CLICK
HELLO.
KHAA.
KHAA.
KHAA.

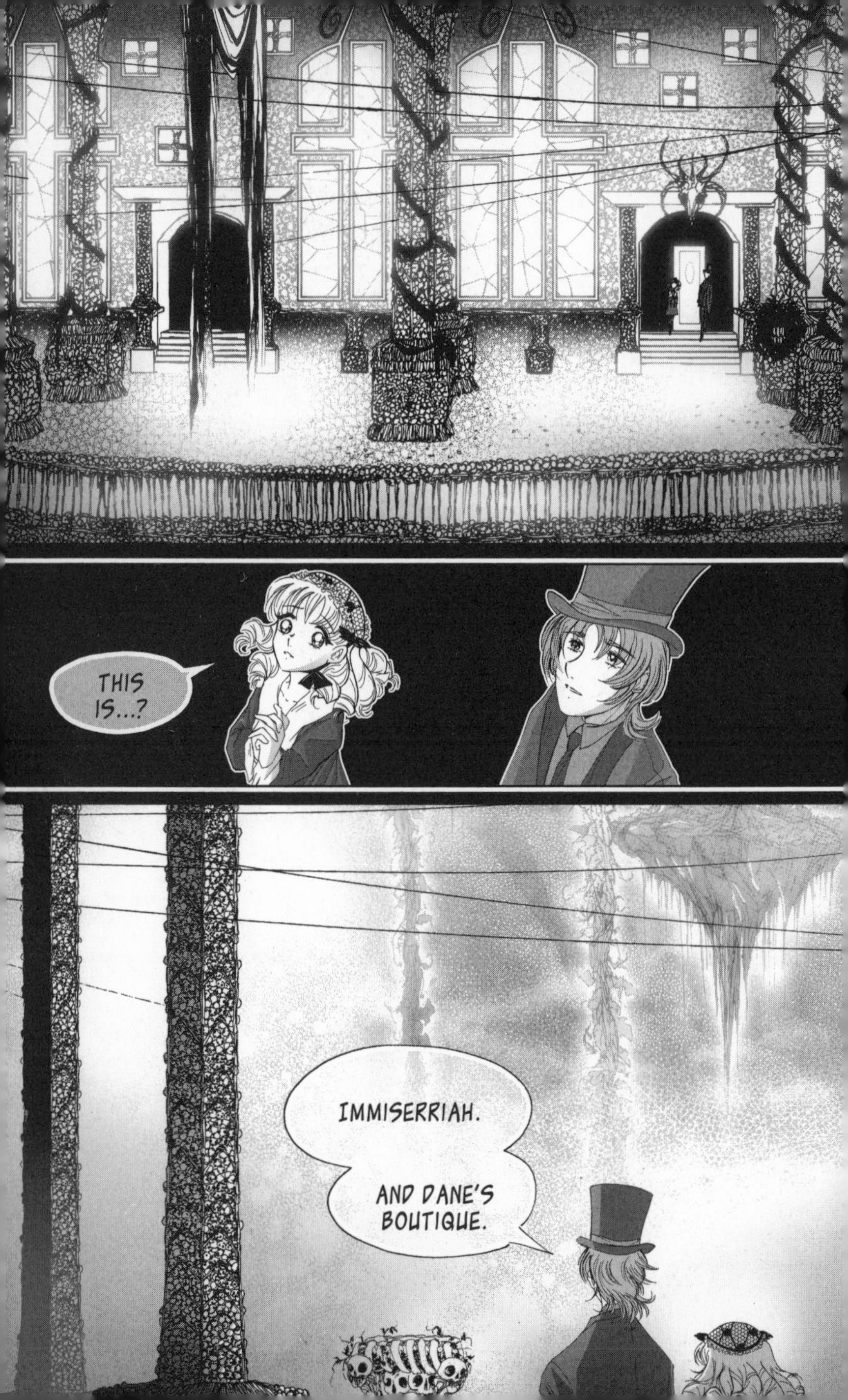
THIS IS...?
IMMISERRIAH.
AND DANE'S BOUTIQUE.

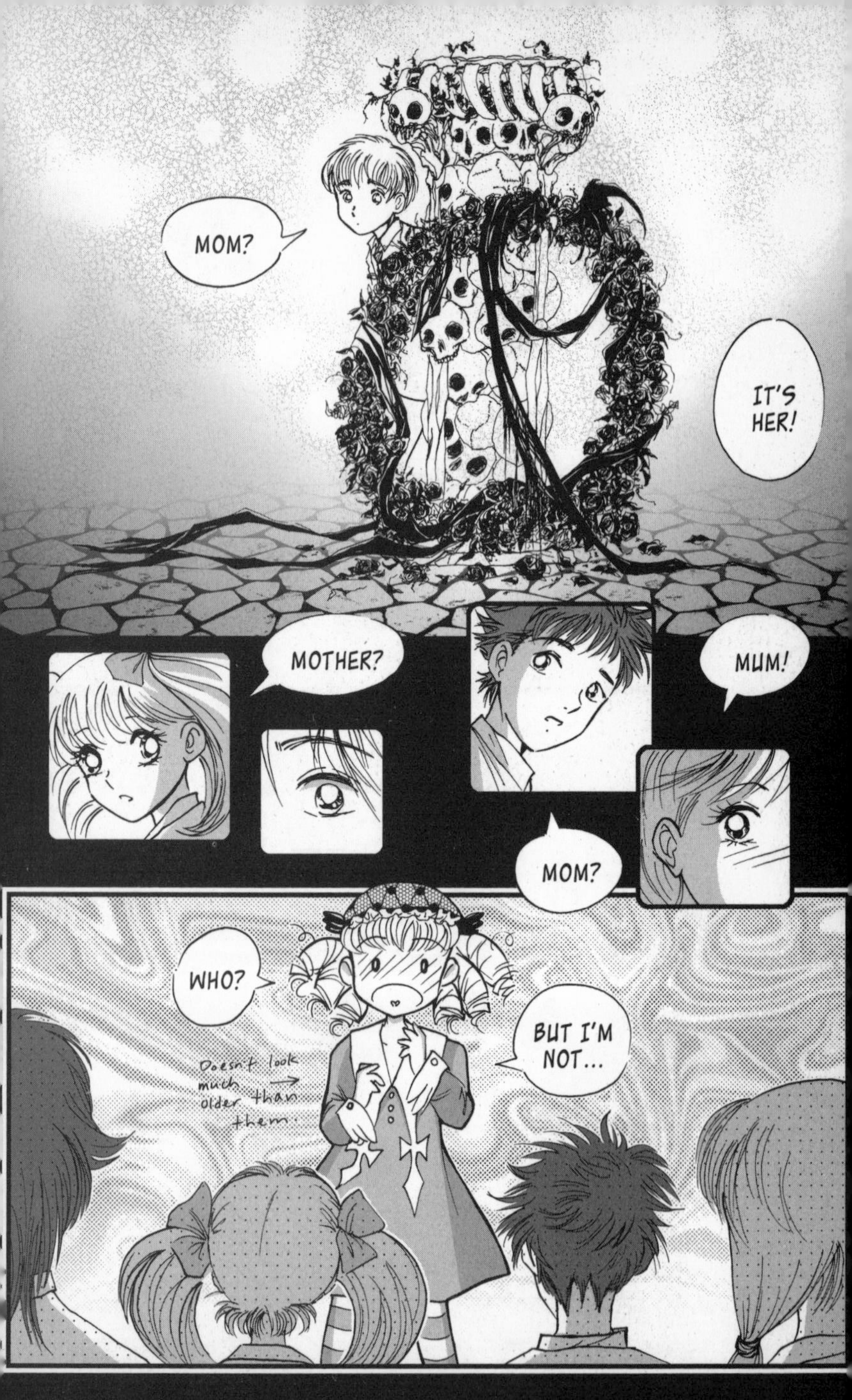
MOM?
IT'S HER!
MOTHER?
MUM!
MOM?
WHO?
BUT I'M NOT...
Doesn't look much older than them.

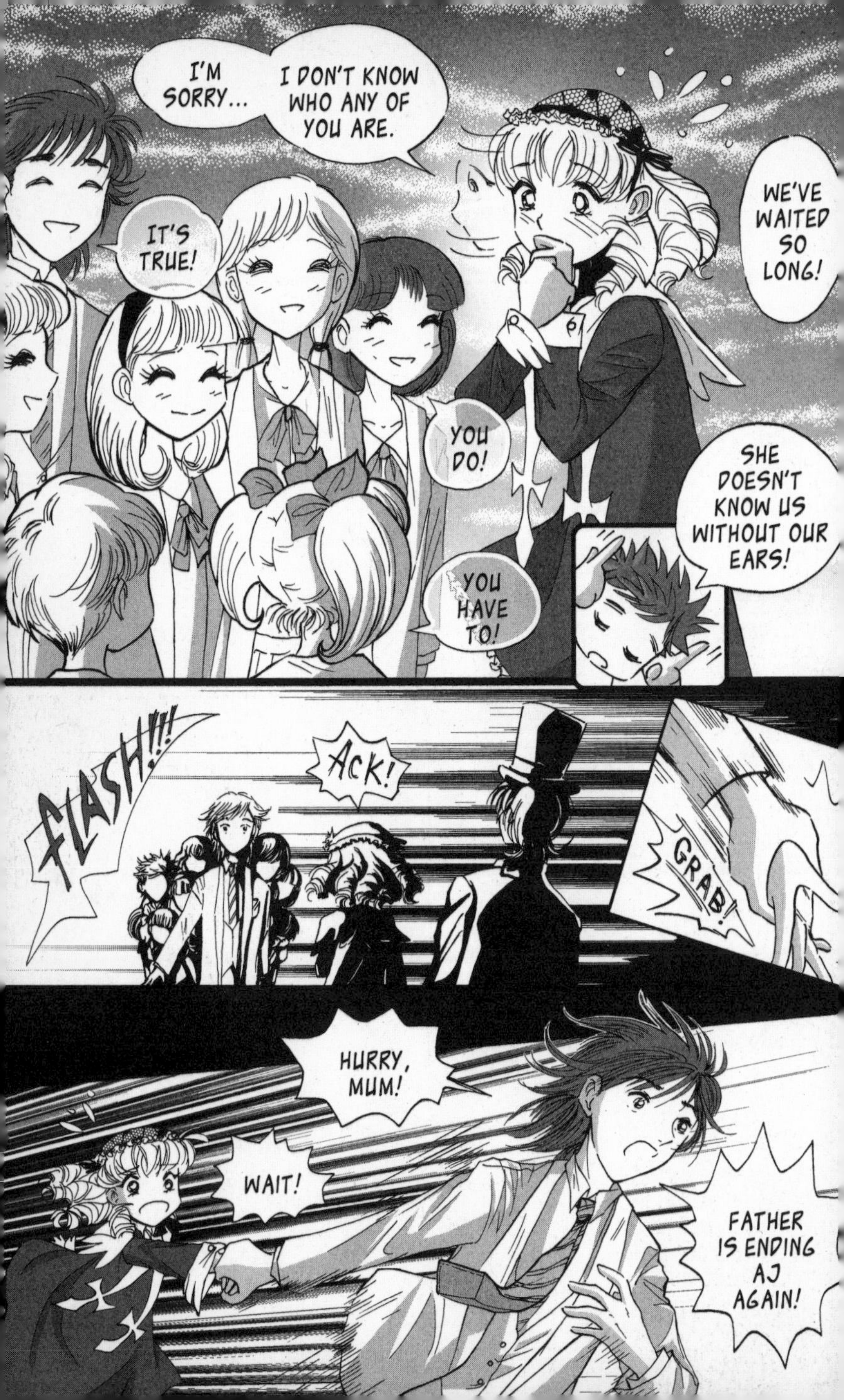
I'M SORRY...
I DON'T KNOW WHO ANY OF YOU ARE.
IT'S TRUE!
YOU DO!
YOU HAVE TO!
WE'VE WAITED SO LONG!
SHE DOESN'T KNOW US WITHOUT OUR EARS!
FLASH!!!
ACK!
GRAB!
HURRY, MUM!
WAIT!
FATHER IS ENDING AJ AGAIN!

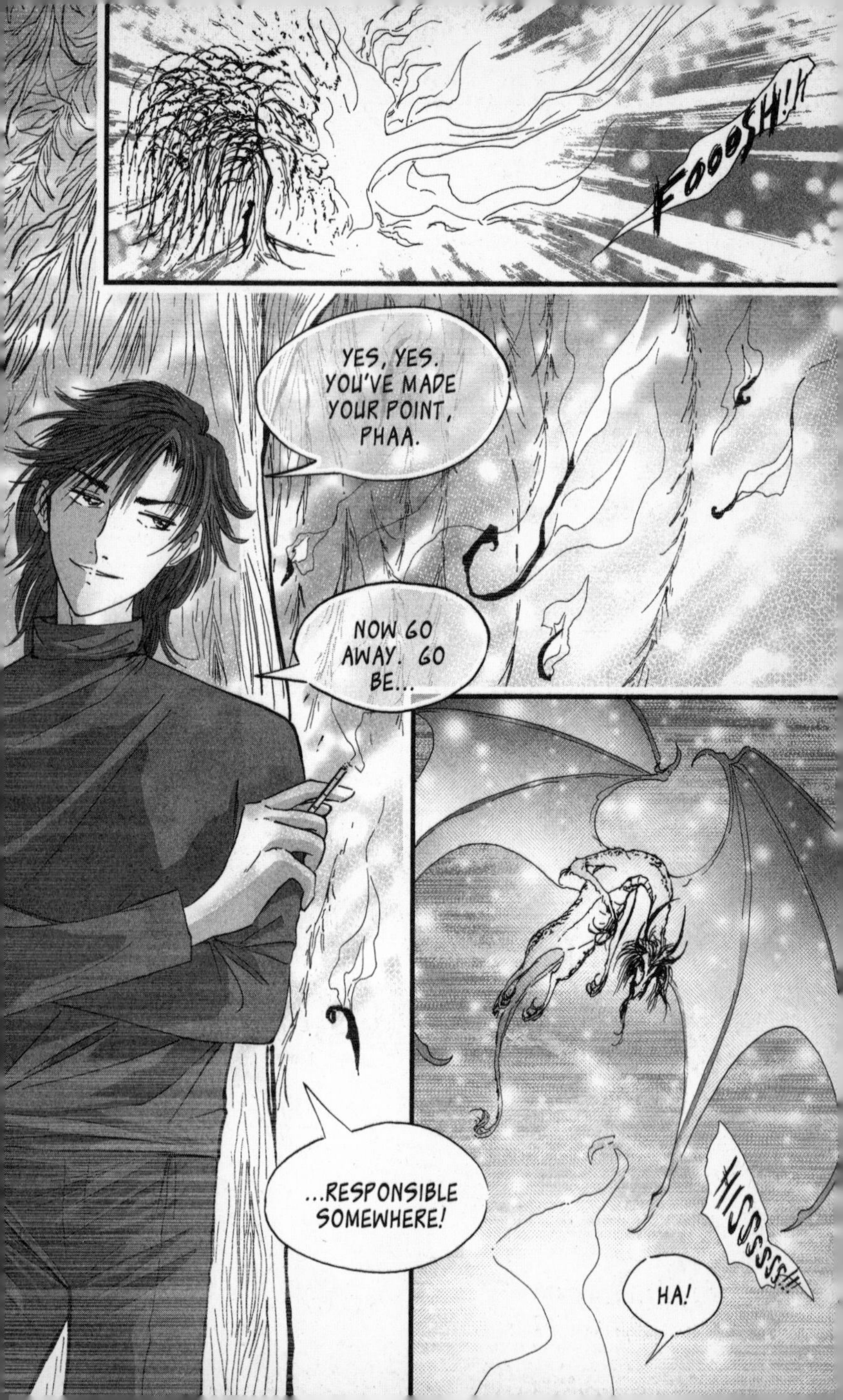
FOOOSH!!
YES, YES. YOU'VE MADE YOUR POINT, PHAA.
NOW GO AWAY. GO BE...
...RESPONSIBLE SOMEWHERE!
HISSSSSS!!
HA!

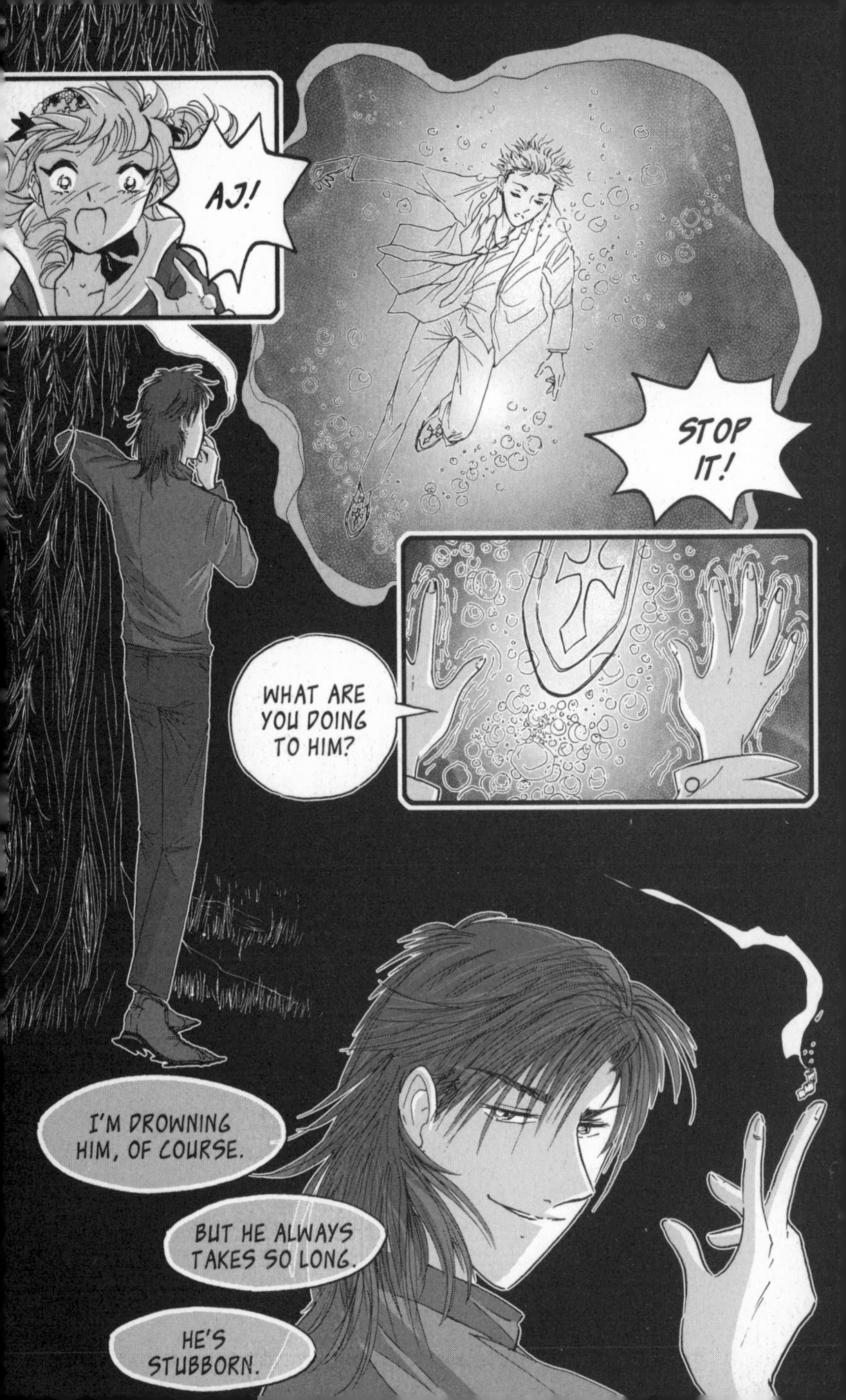
AJ!
STOP IT!
WHAT ARE YOU DOING TO HIM?
I'M DROWNING HIM, OF COURSE.
BUT HE ALWAYS TAKES SO LONG.
HE'S STUBBORN.

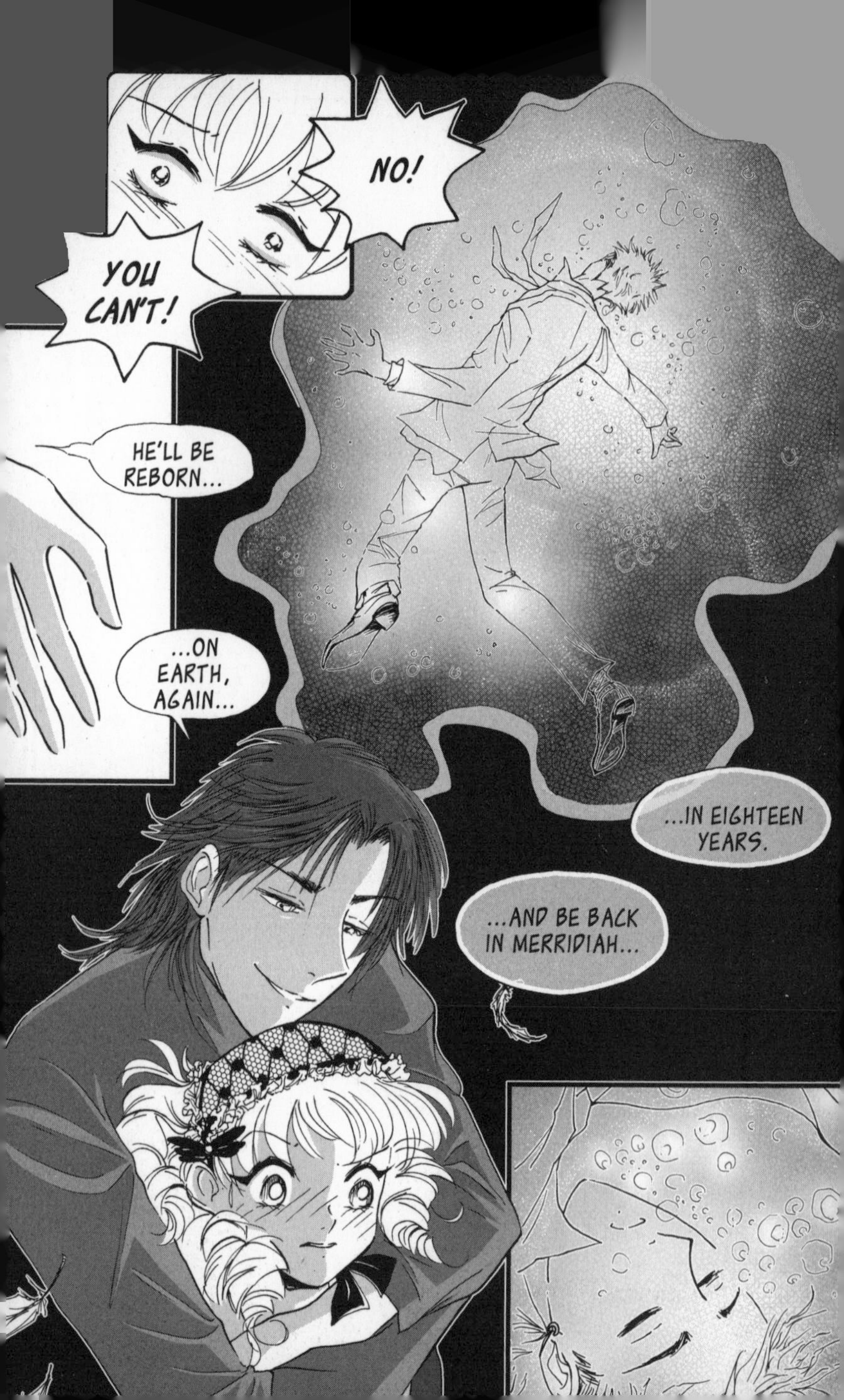
NO!
YOU CAN'T!
HE'LL BE REBORN...
...ON EARTH, AGAIN...
...IN EIGHTEEN YEARS.
...AND BE BACK IN MERRIDIAH...

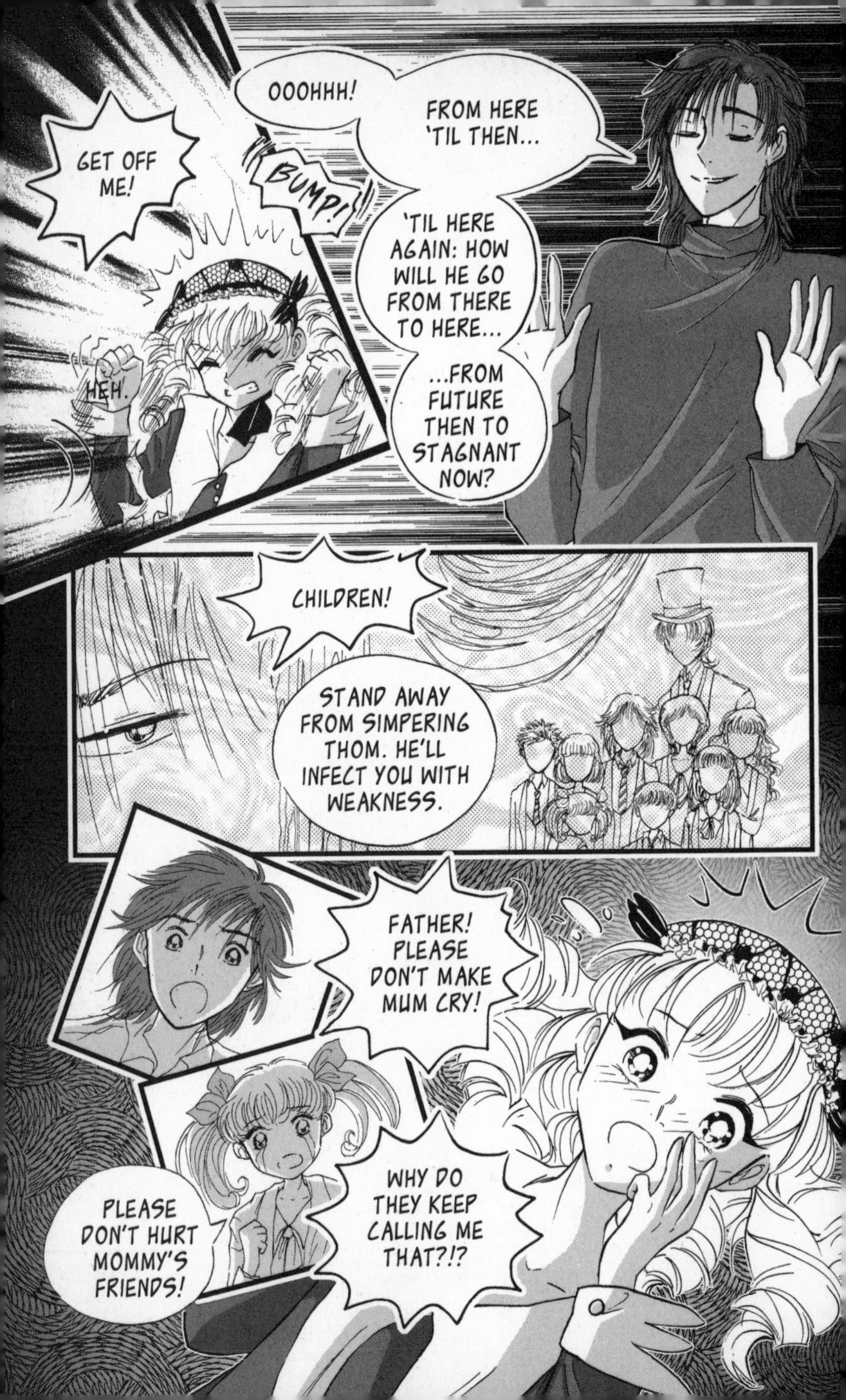
GET OFF ME!
BUMP!
HEH.
OOOHHH!
FROM HERE 'TIL THEN...
'TIL HERE AGAIN: HOW WILL HE GO FROM THERE TO HERE...
...FROM FUTURE THEN TO STAGNANT NOW?
CHILDREN!
STAND AWAY FROM SIMPERING THOM. HE'LL INFECT YOU WITH WEAKNESS.
FATHER! PLEASE DON'T MAKE MUM CRY!
PLEASE DON'T HURT MOMMY'S FRIENDS!
WHY DO THEY KEEP CALLING ME THAT?!?

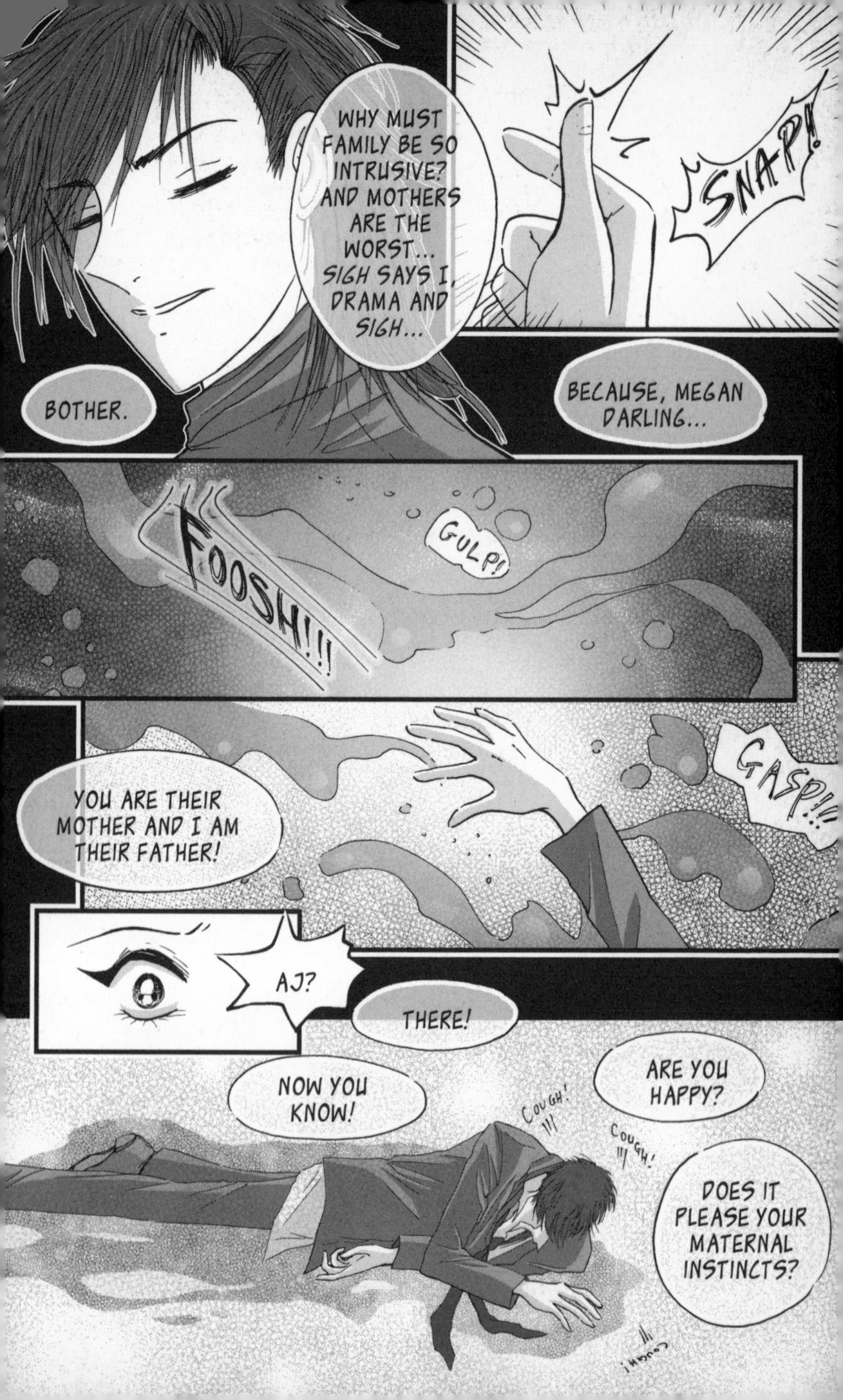
WHY MUST FAMILY BE SO INTRUSIVE? AND MOTHERS ARE THE WORST... SIGH SAYS I, DRAMA AND SIGH...
BOTHER.
SNAP!
BECAUSE, MEGAN DARLING...
FOOSH!!!
GULP!
YOU ARE THEIR MOTHER AND I AM THEIR FATHER!
GASP!!!
AJ?
THERE!
NOW YOU KNOW!
ARE YOU HAPPY?
COUGH!
COUGH!
DOES IT PLEASE YOUR MATERNAL INSTINCTS?
COUGH!

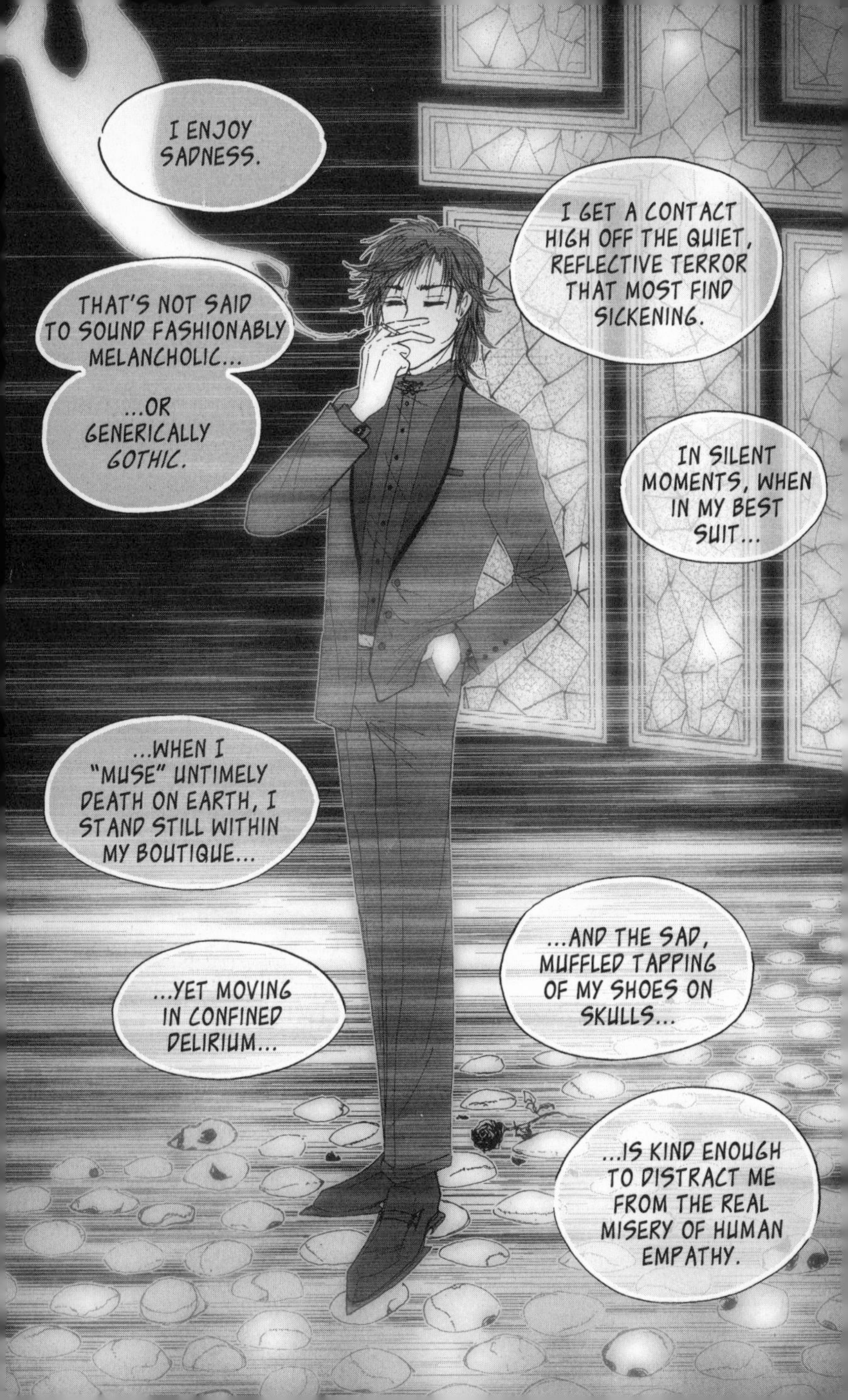
I ENJOY SADNESS.
THAT'S NOT SAID TO SOUND FASHIONABLY MELANCHOLIC...
...OR GENERICALLY GOTHIC.
I GET A CONTACT HIGH OFF THE QUIET, REFLECTIVE TERROR THAT MOST FIND SICKENING.
IN SILENT MOMENTS, WHEN IN MY BEST SUIT...
...WHEN I "MUSE" UNTIMELY DEATH ON EARTH, I STAND STILL WITHIN MY BOUTIQUE...
...YET MOVING IN CONFINED DELIRIUM...
...AND THE SAD, MUFFLED TAPPING OF MY SHOES ON SKULLS...
...IS KIND ENOUGH TO DISTRACT ME FROM THE REAL MISERY OF HUMAN EMPATHY.

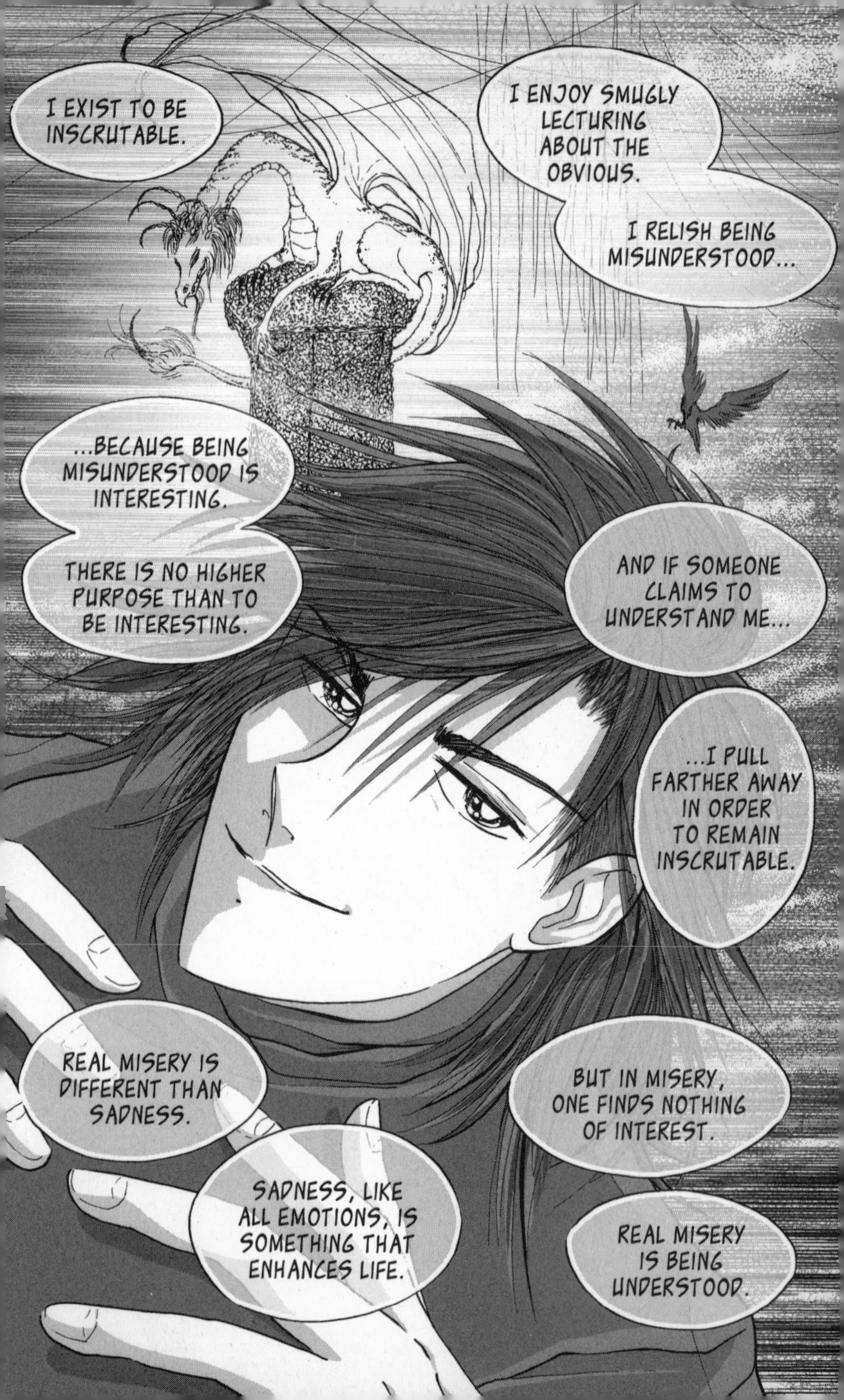
I EXIST TO BE INSCRUTABLE.
I ENJOY SMUGLY LECTURING ABOUT THE OBVIOUS.
I RELISH BEING MISUNDERSTOOD...
...BECAUSE BEING MISUNDERSTOOD IS INTERESTING.
THERE IS NO HIGHER PURPOSE THAN TO BE INTERESTING.
AND IF SOMEONE CLAIMS TO UNDERSTAND ME...
...I PULL FARTHER AWAY IN ORDER TO REMAIN INSCRUTABLE.
REAL MISERY IS DIFFERENT THAN SADNESS.
SADNESS, LIKE ALL EMOTIONS, IS SOMETHING THAT ENHANCES LIFE.
BUT IN MISERY, ONE FINDS NOTHING OF INTEREST.
REAL MISERY IS BEING UNDERSTOOD.

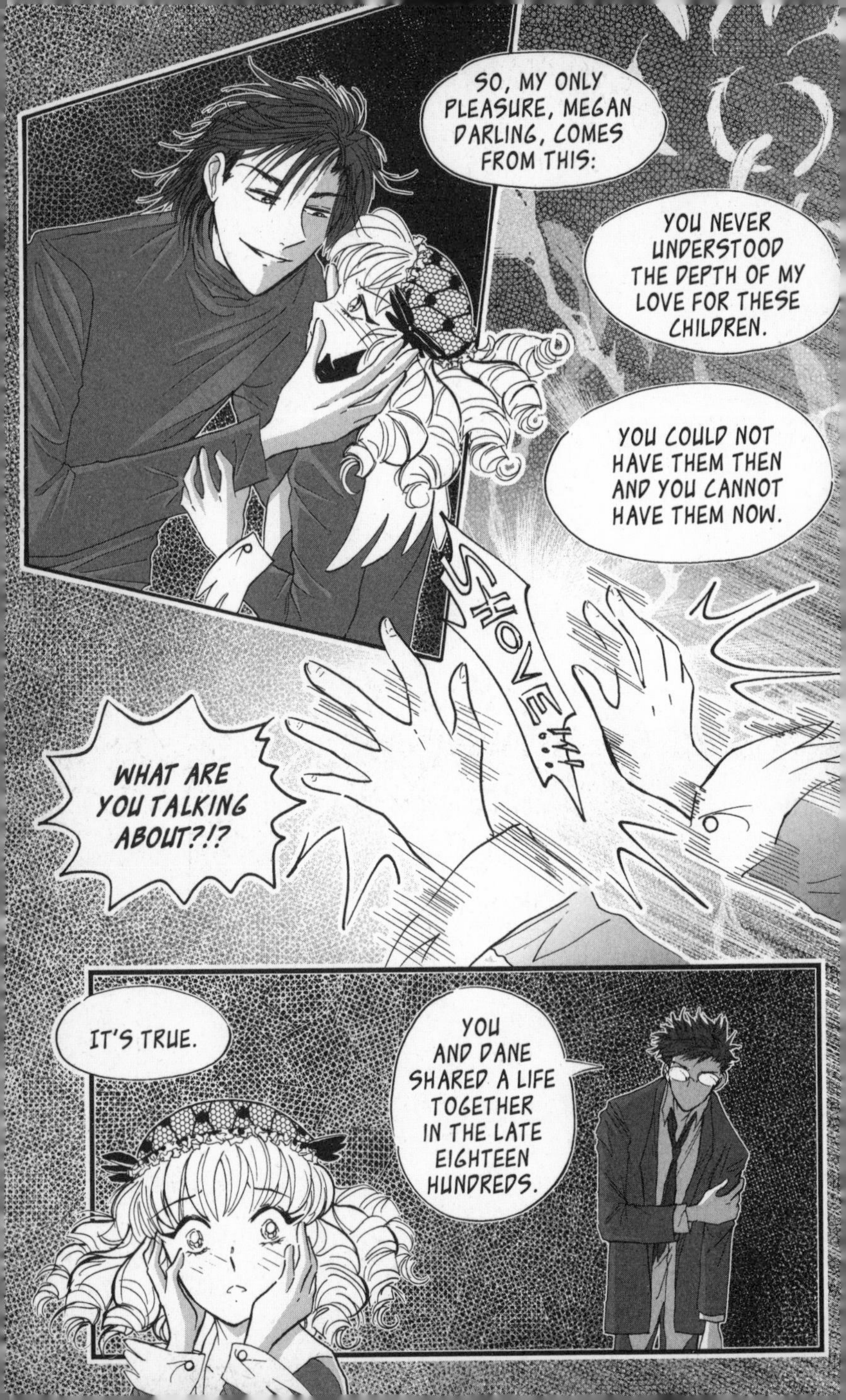
SO, MY ONLY PLEASURE, MEGAN DARLING, COMES FROM THIS:
YOU NEVER UNDERSTOOD THE DEPTH OF MY LOVE FOR THESE CHILDREN.
YOU COULD NOT HAVE THEM THEN AND YOU CANNOT HAVE THEM NOW.
WHAT ARE YOU TALKING ABOUT?!?
SHOVE!!!
IT'S TRUE.
YOU AND DANE SHARED A LIFE TOGETHER IN THE LATE EIGHTEEN HUNDREDS.

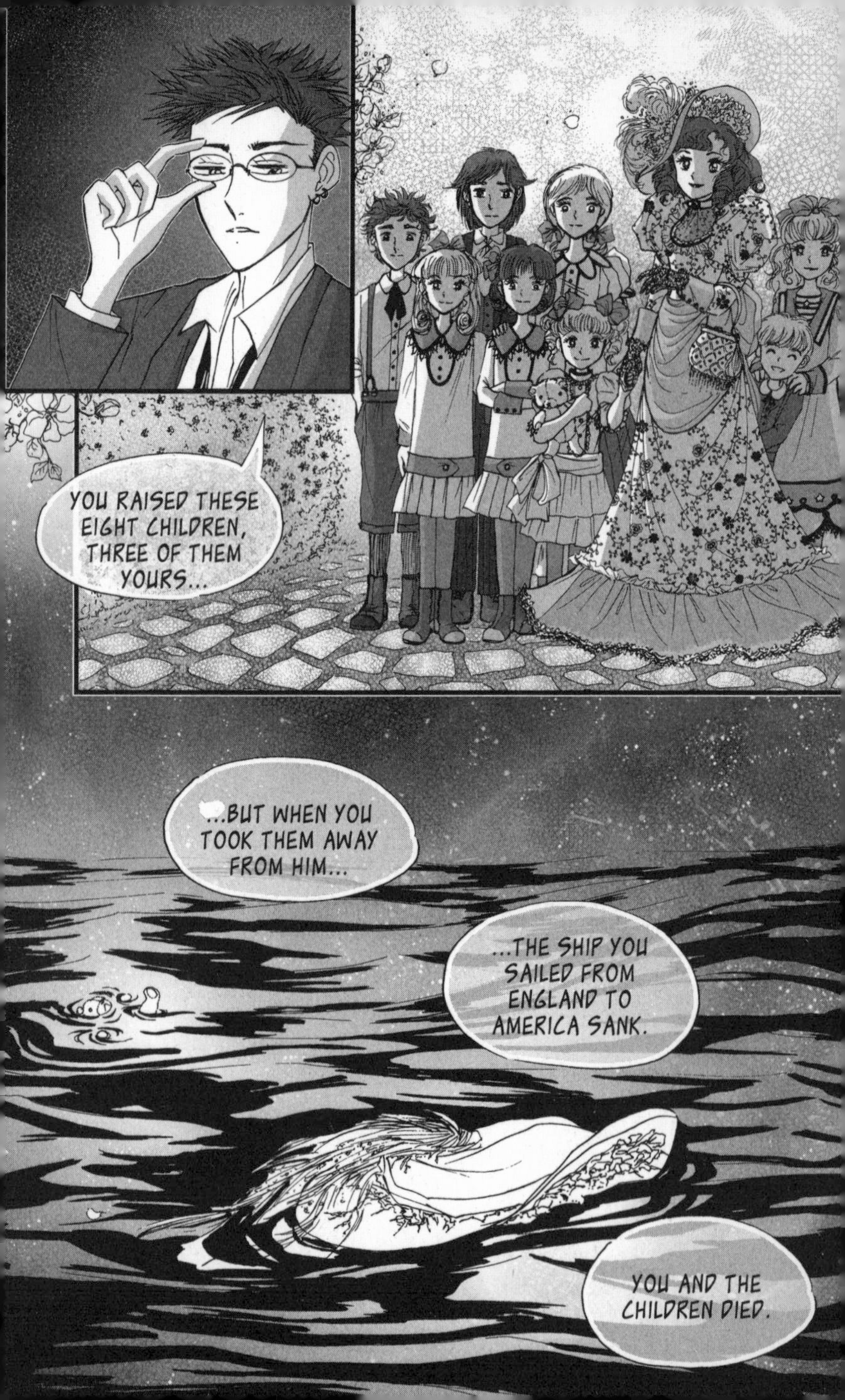
YOU RAISED THESE EIGHT CHILDREN, THREE OF THEM YOURS...
...BUT WHEN YOU TOOK THEM AWAY FROM HIM...
...THE SHIP YOU SAILED FROM ENGLAND TO AMERICA SANK.
YOU AND THE CHILDREN DIED.

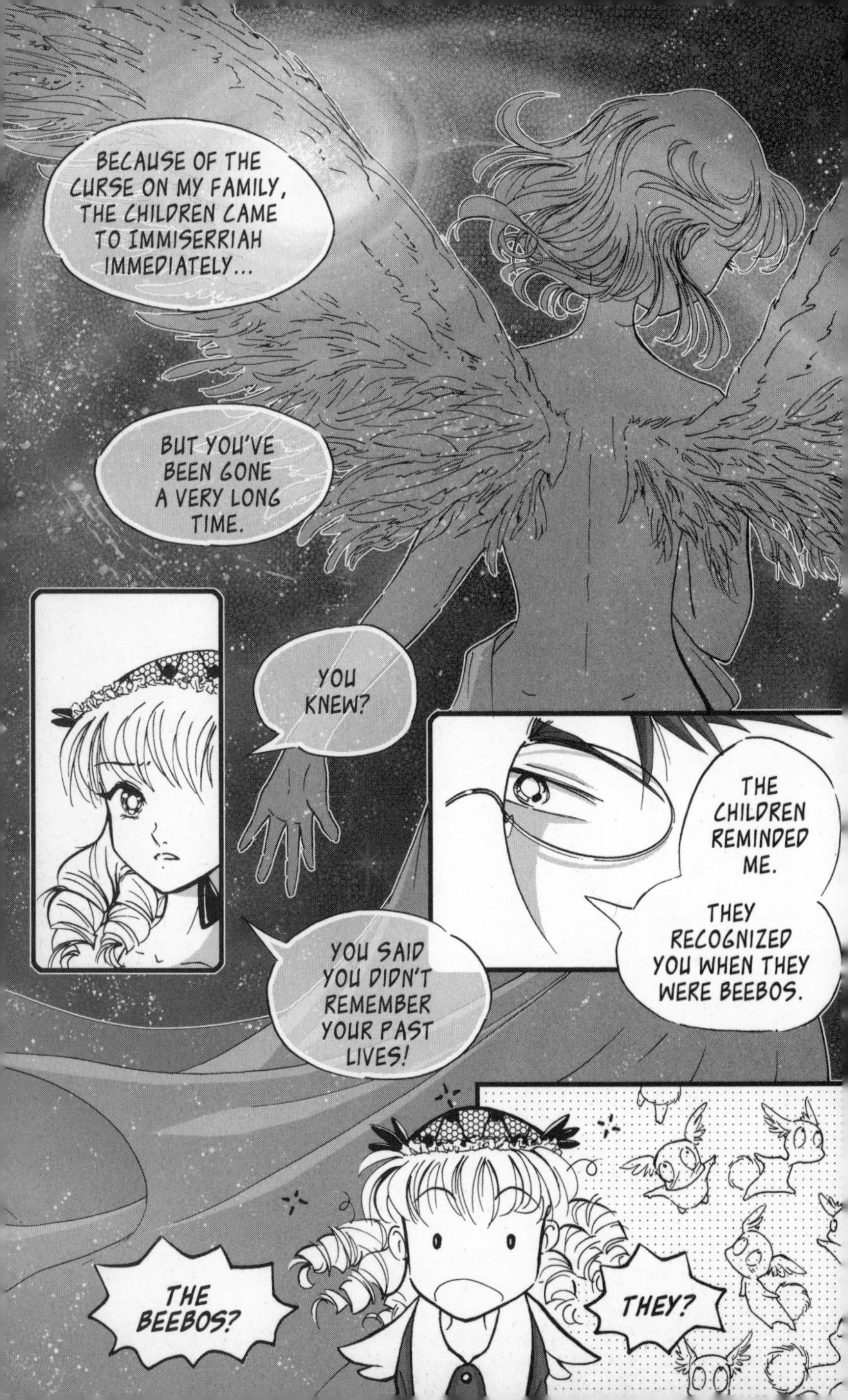
BECAUSE OF THE CURSE ON MY FAMILY, THE CHILDREN CAME TO IMMISERRIAH IMMEDIATELY...
BUT YOU'VE BEEN GONE A VERY LONG TIME.
YOU KNEW?
YOU SAID YOU DIDN'T REMEMBER YOUR PAST LIVES!
THE CHILDREN REMINDED ME.
THEY RECOGNIZED YOU WHEN THEY WERE BEEBOS.
THE BEEBOS?
THEY?

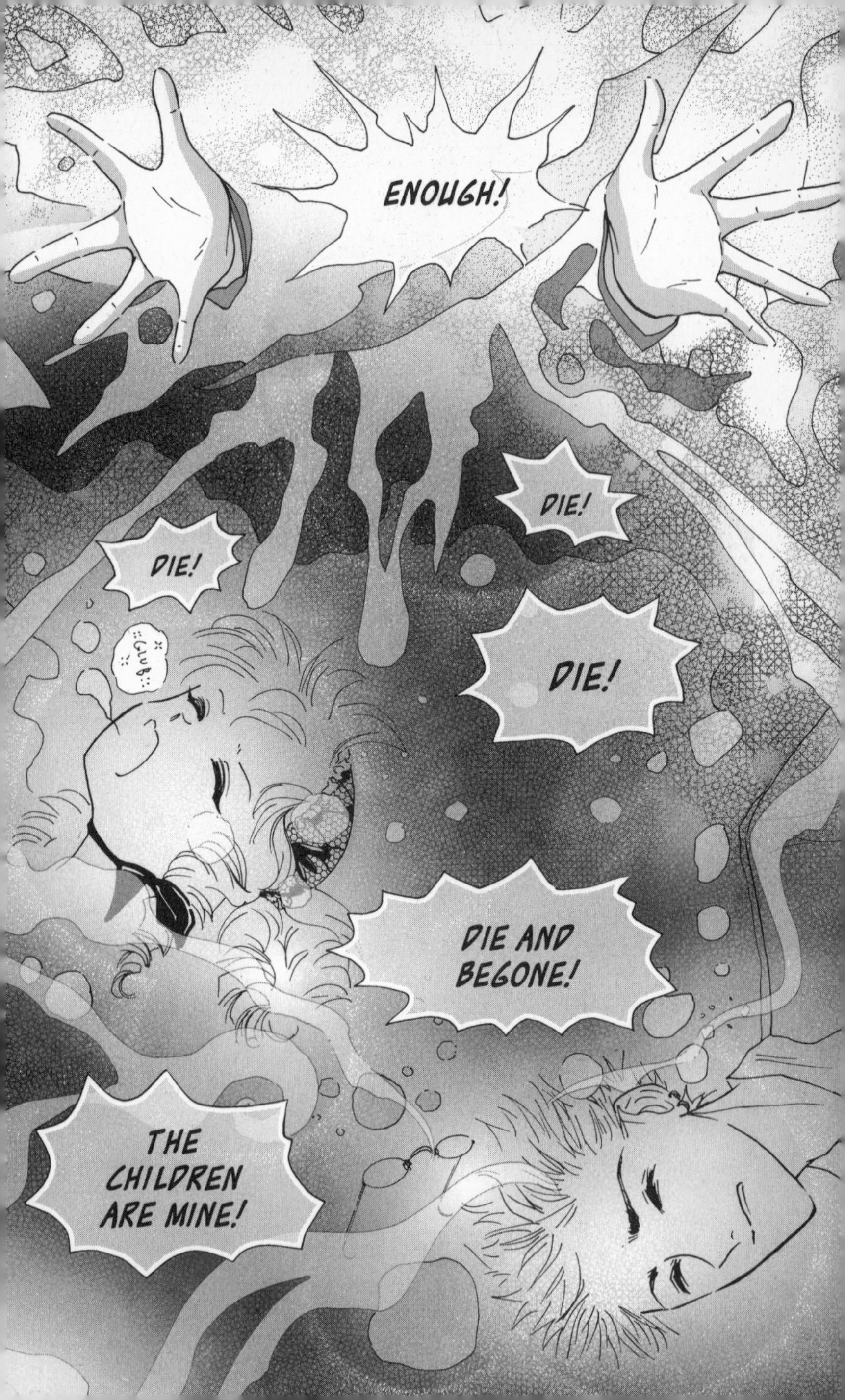
ENOUGH!
DIE!
DIE!
::GLUB::
DIE!
DIE AND BEGONE!
THE CHILDREN ARE MINE!

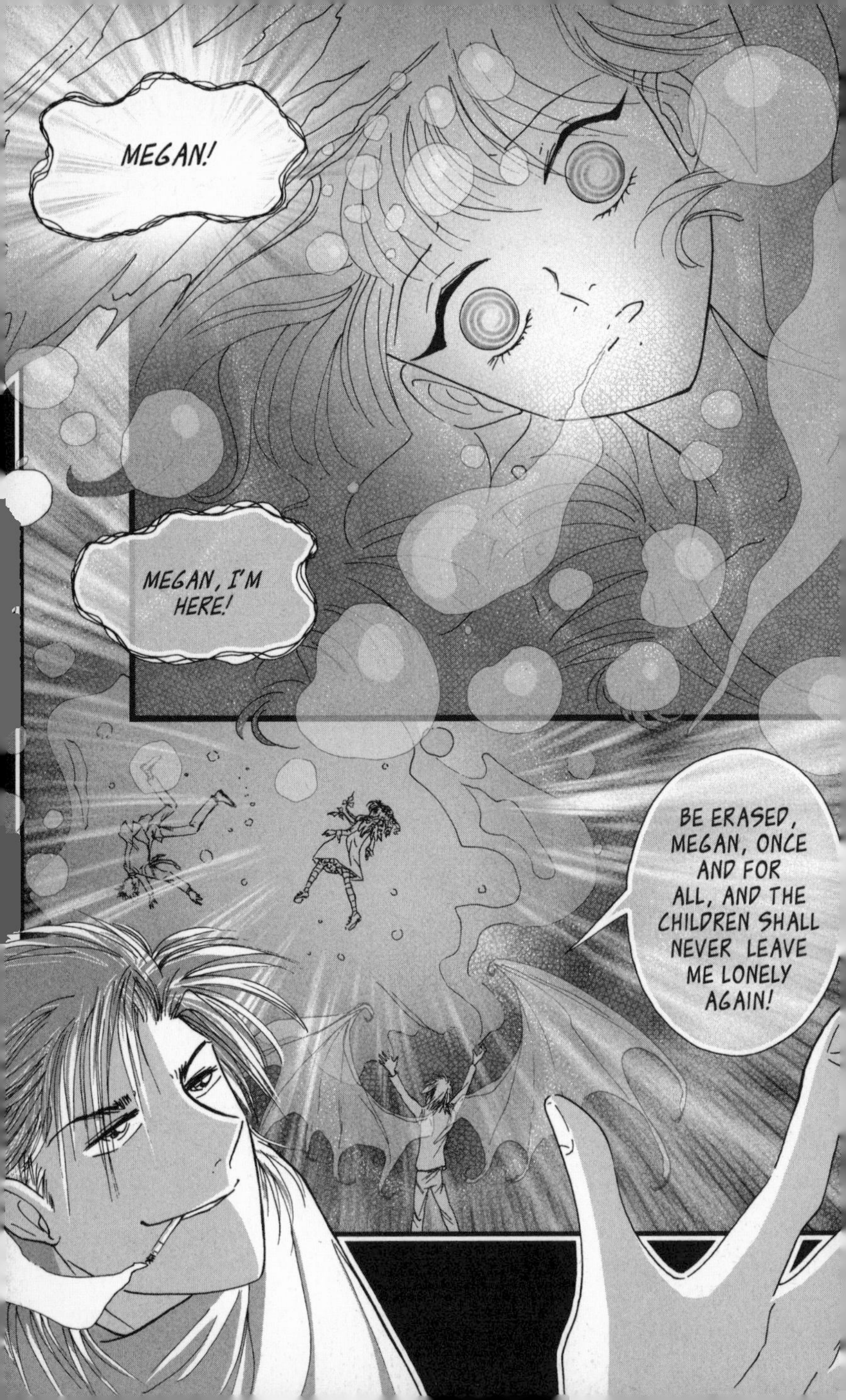
MEGAN!
MEGAN, I'M HERE!
BE ERASED, MEGAN, ONCE AND FOR ALL, AND THE CHILDREN SHALL NEVER LEAVE ME LONELY AGAIN!

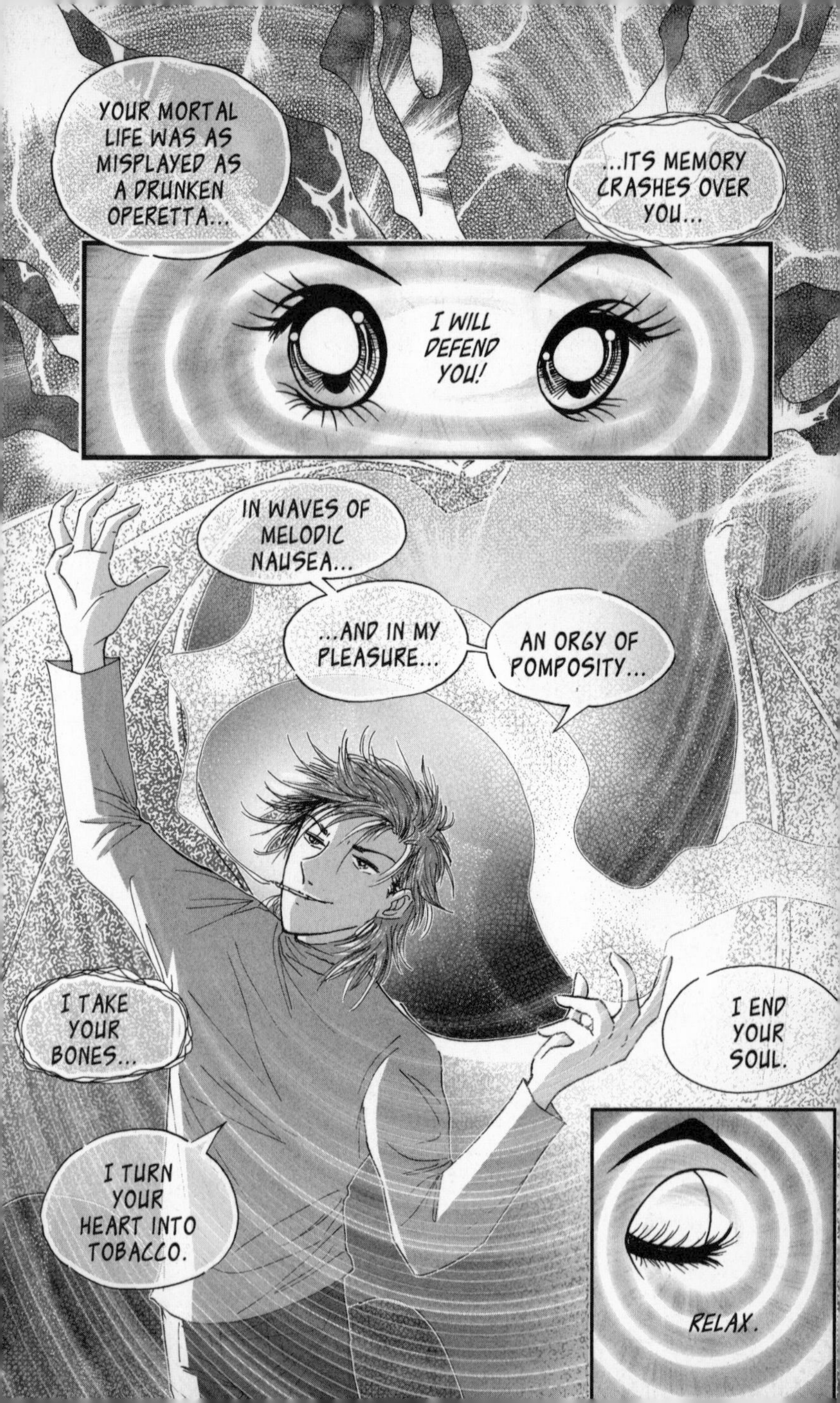
YOUR MORTAL LIFE WAS AS MISPLAYED AS A DRUNKEN OPERETTA...
...ITS MEMORY CRASHES OVER YOU...
I WILL DEFEND YOU!
IN WAVES OF MELODIC NAUSEA...
...AND IN MY PLEASURE...
AN ORGY OF POMPOSITY...
I TAKE YOUR BONES...
I END YOUR SOUL.
I TURN YOUR HEART INTO TOBACCO.
RELAX.

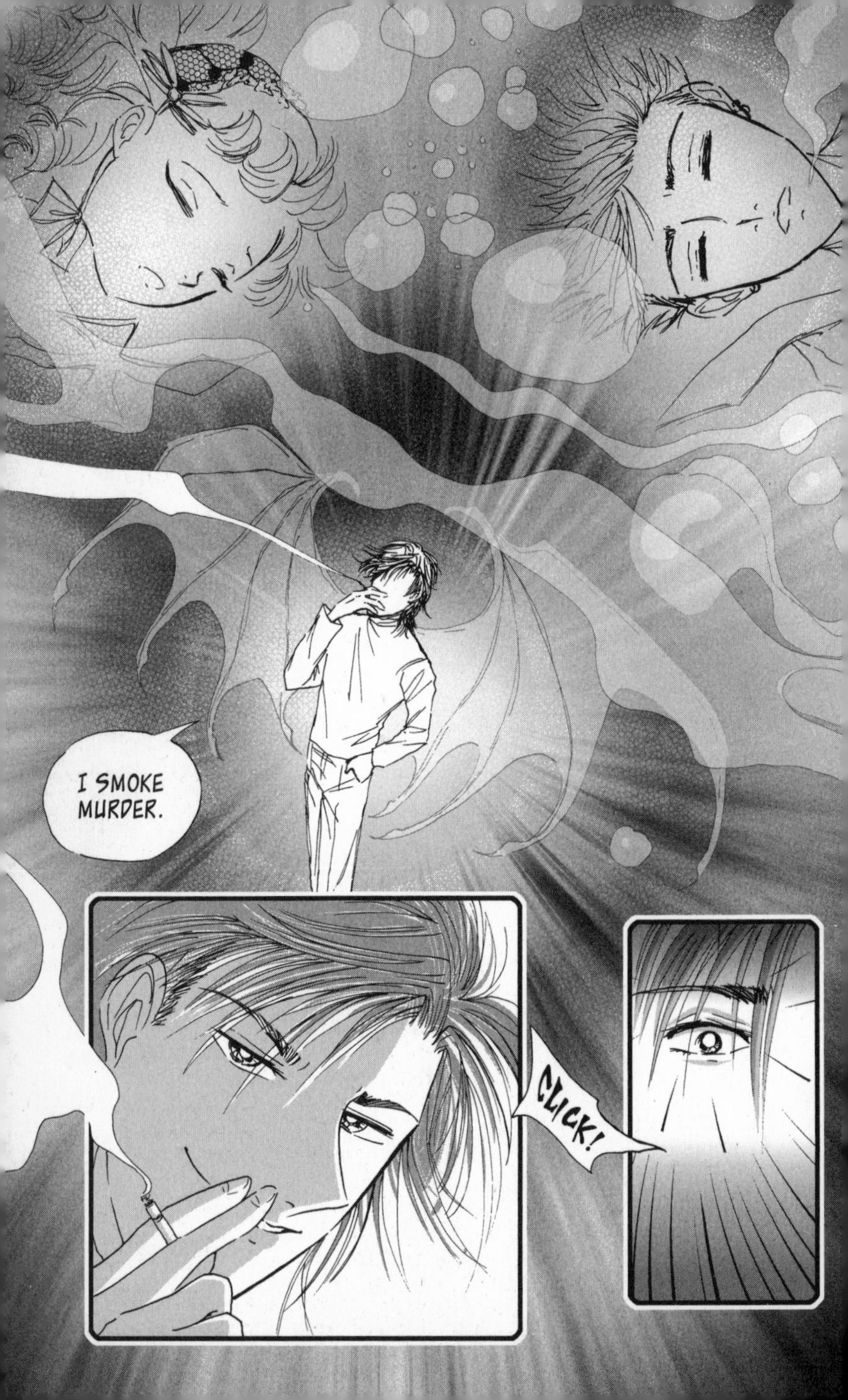
I SMOKE MURDER.
CLICK!

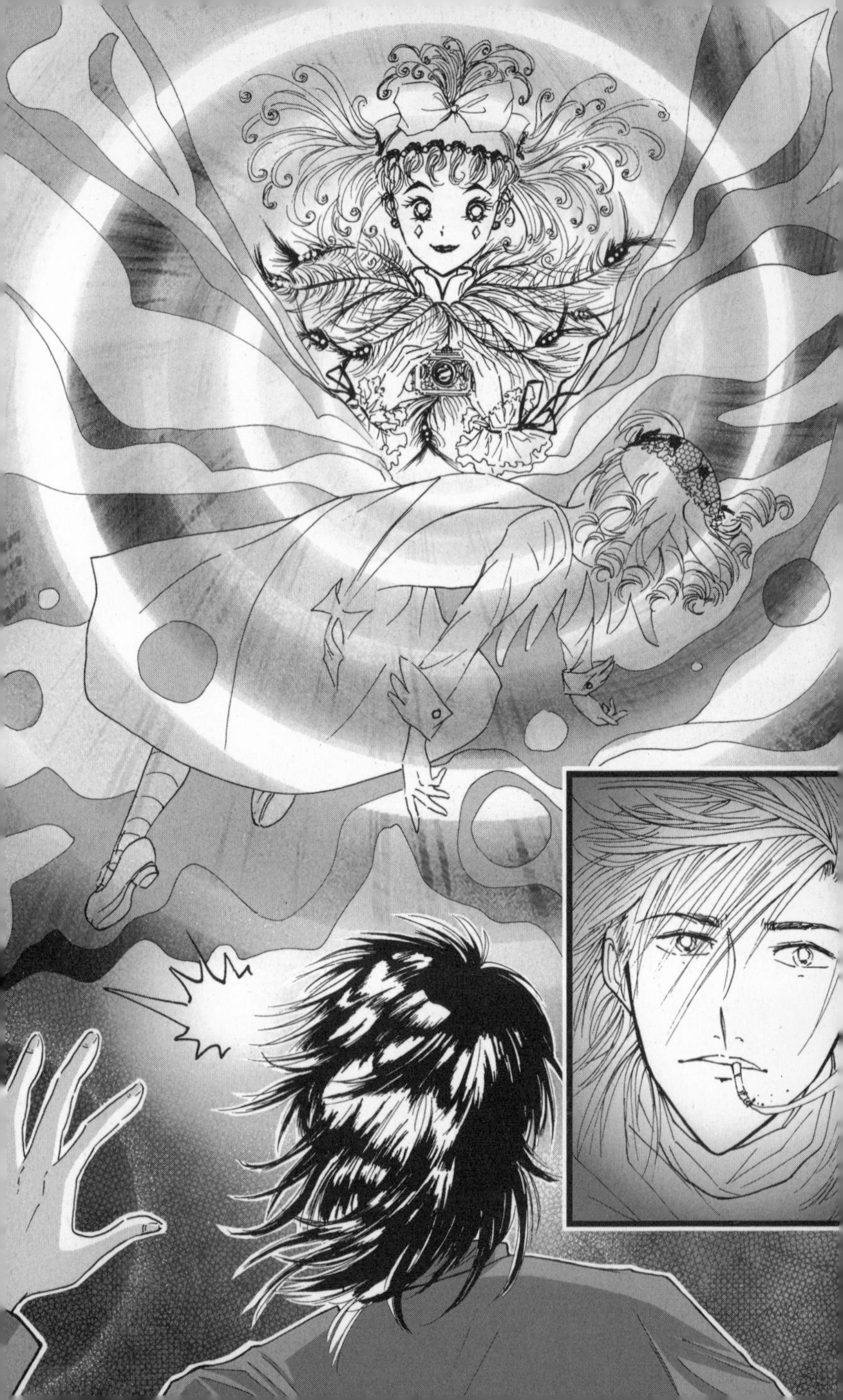

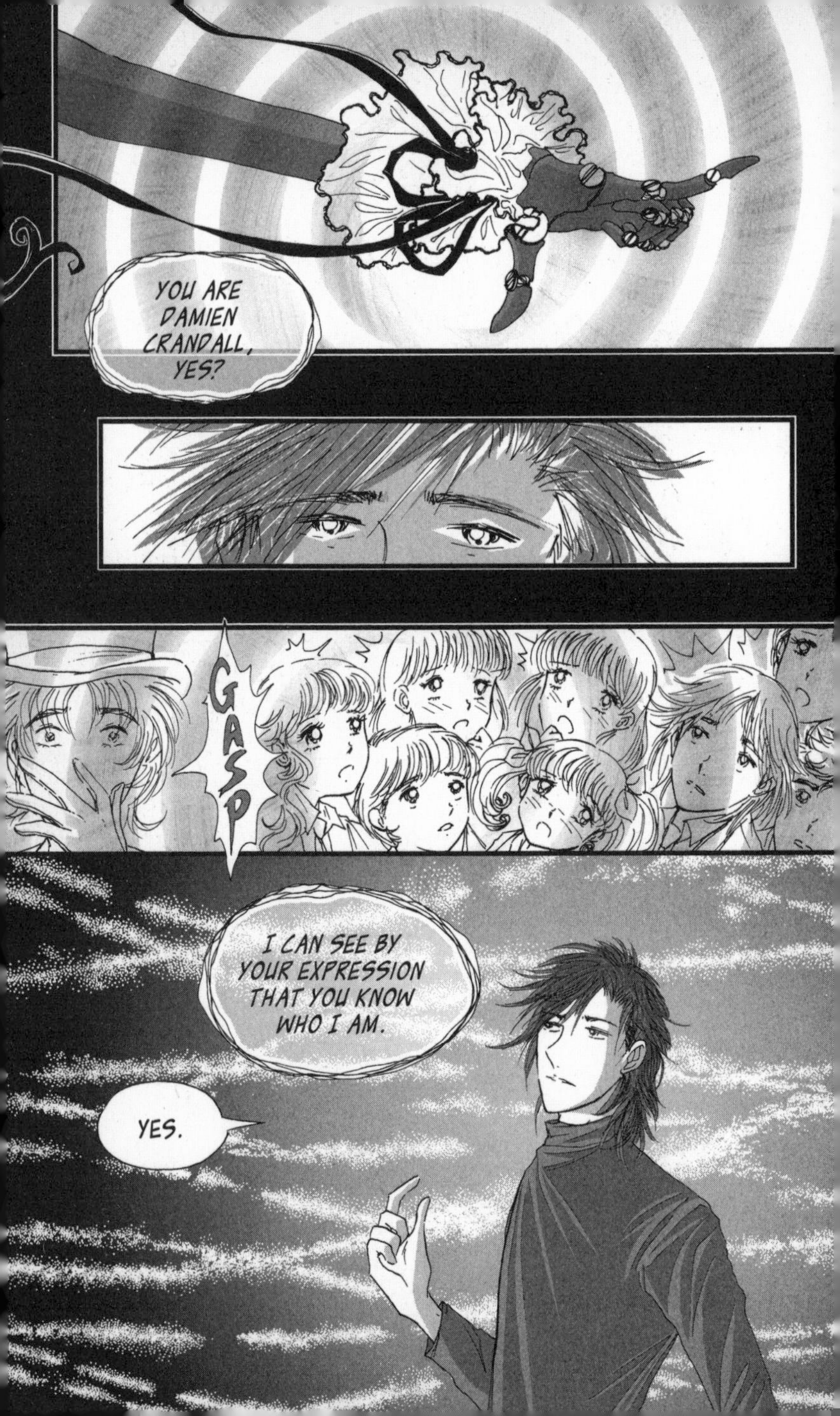
YOU ARE DAMIEN CRANDALL, YES?
GASP
I CAN SEE BY YOUR EXPRESSION THAT YOU KNOW WHO I AM.
YES.

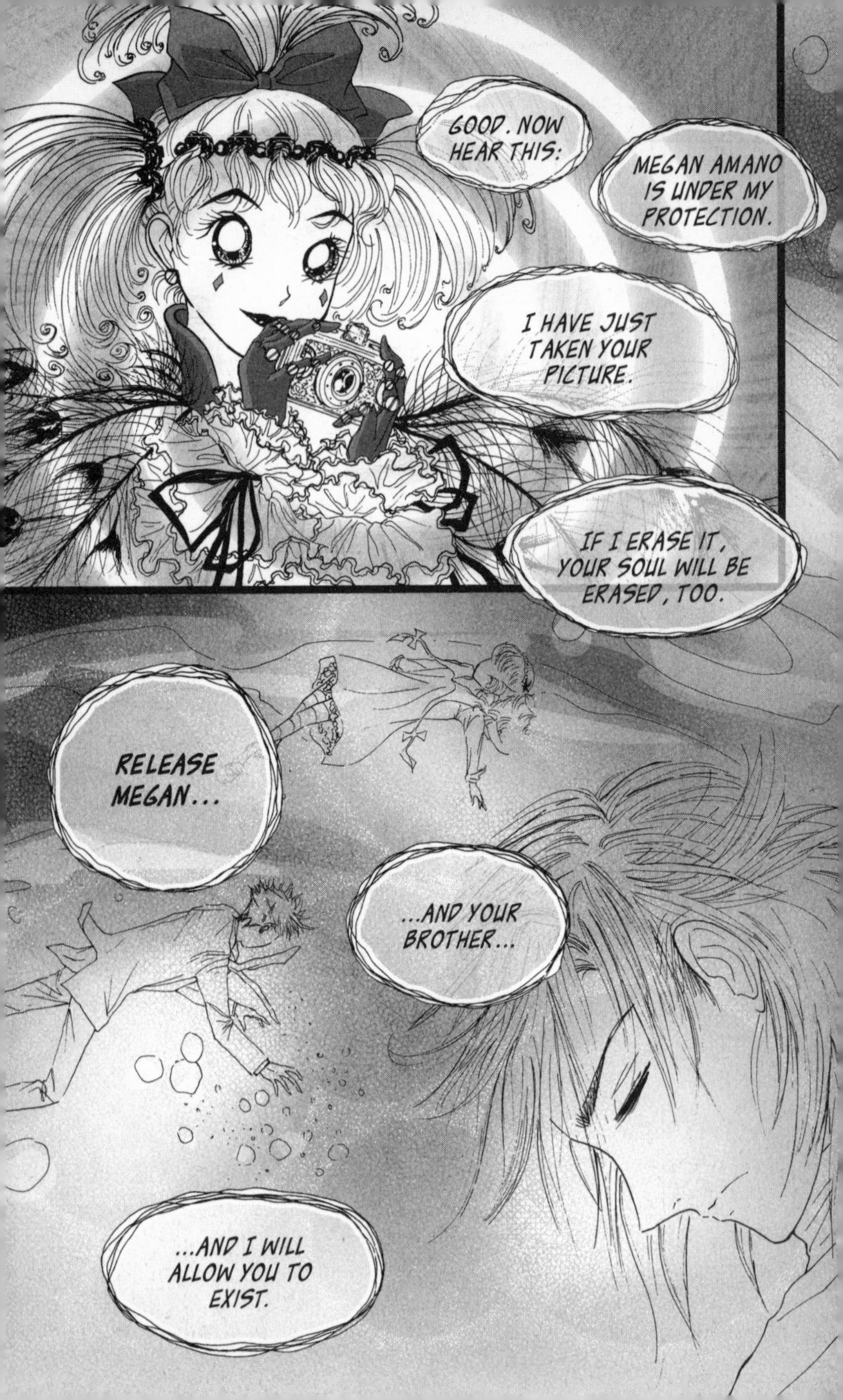
GOOD. NOW HEAR THIS:
MEGAN AMANO IS UNDER MY PROTECTION.
I HAVE JUST TAKEN YOUR PICTURE.
IF I ERASE IT, YOUR SOUL WILL BE ERASED, TOO.
RELEASE MEGAN...
...AND YOUR BROTHER...
...AND I WILL ALLOW YOU TO EXIST.

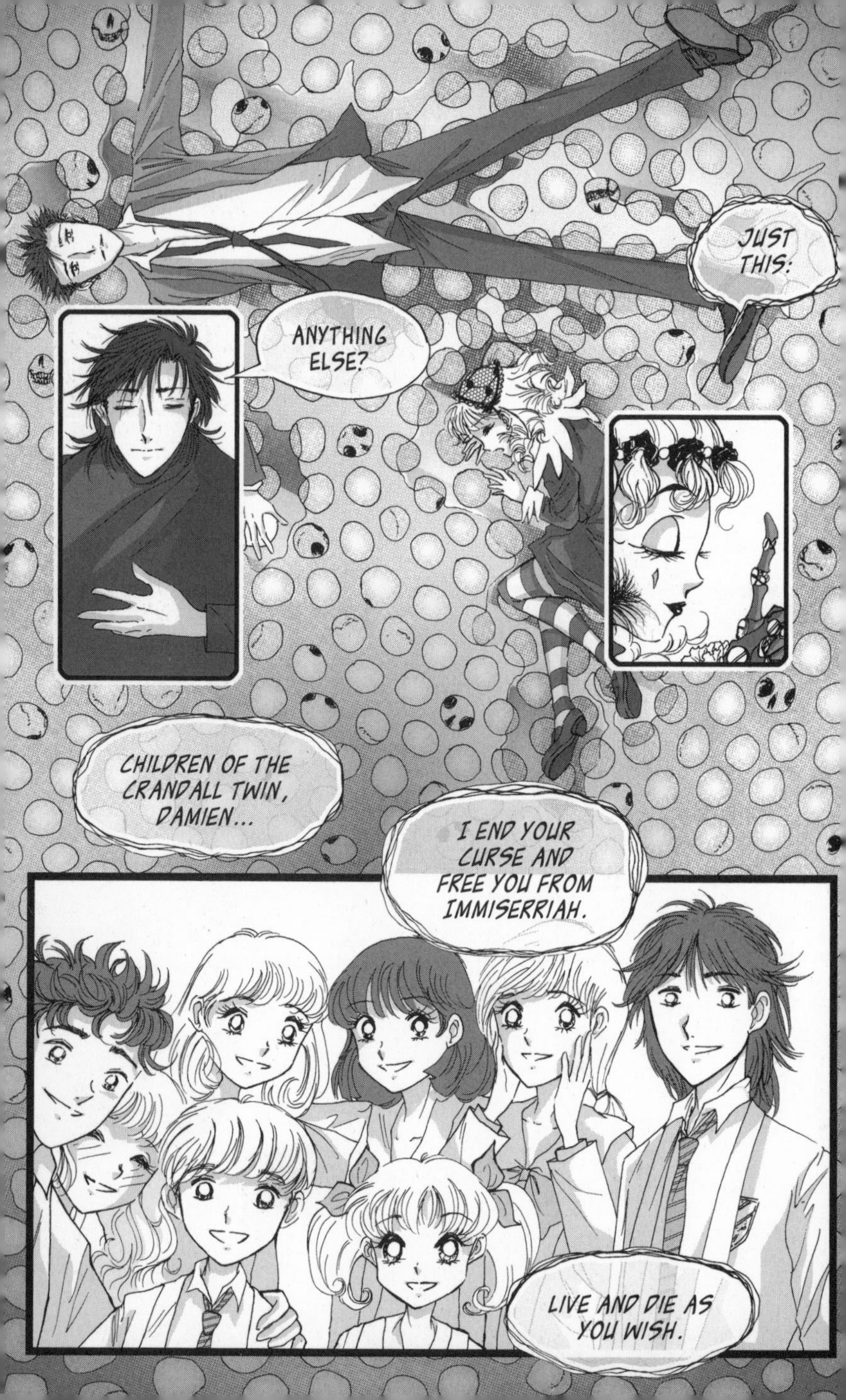
ANYTHING ELSE?
JUST THIS:
CHILDREN OF THE CRANDALL TWIN, DAMIEN...
I END YOUR CURSE AND FREE YOU FROM IMMISERRIAH.
LIVE AND DIE AS YOU WISH.

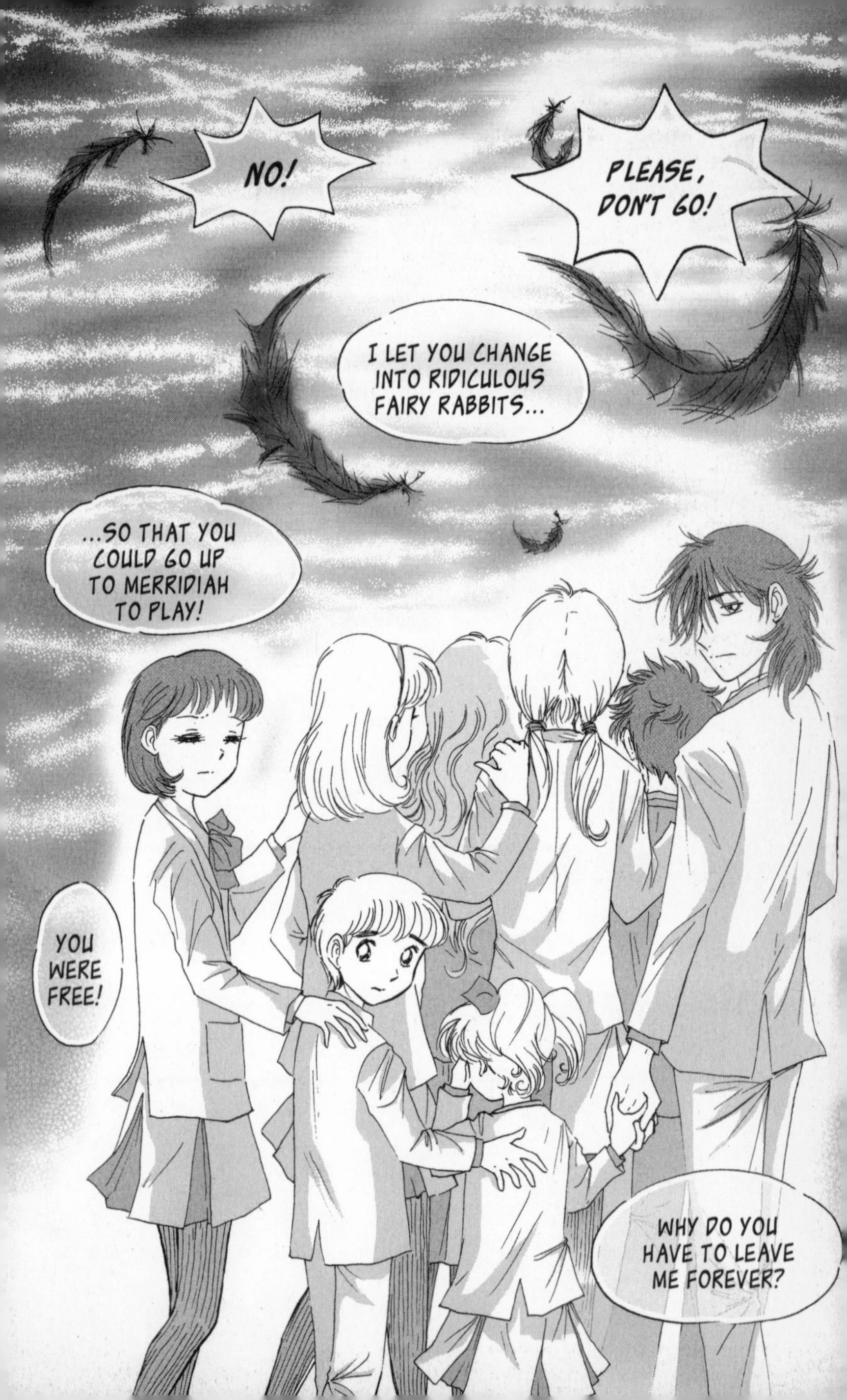
NO!
PLEASE, DON'T GO!
I LET YOU CHANGE INTO RIDICULOUS FAIRY RABBITS...
...SO THAT YOU COULD GO UP TO MERRIDIAH TO PLAY!
YOU WERE FREE!
WHY DO YOU HAVE TO LEAVE ME FOREVER?

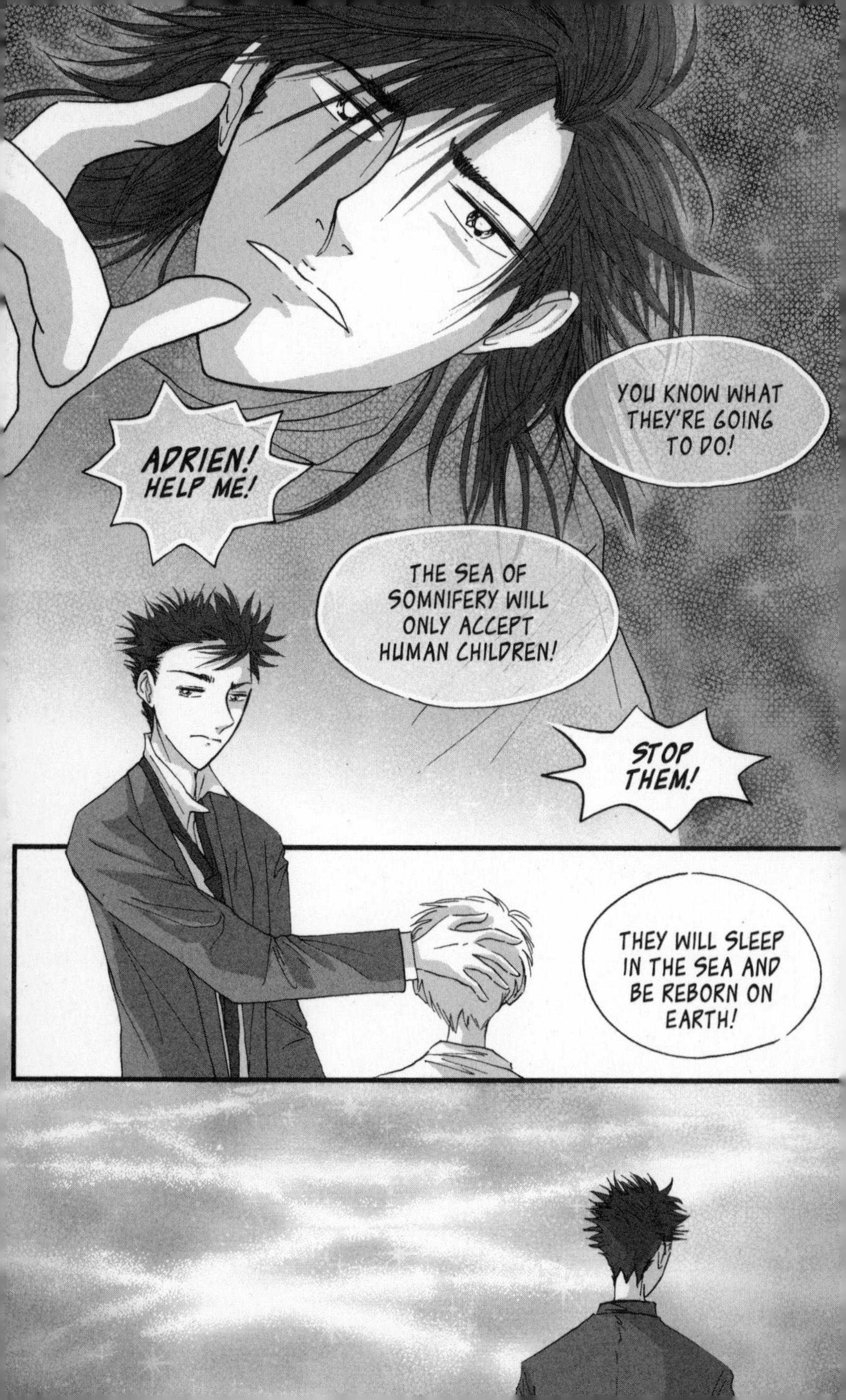
ADRIEN! HELP ME!
YOU KNOW WHAT THEY'RE GOING TO DO!
THE SEA OF SOMNIFERY WILL ONLY ACCEPT HUMAN CHILDREN!
STOP THEM!
THEY WILL SLEEP IN THE SEA AND BE REBORN ON EARTH!

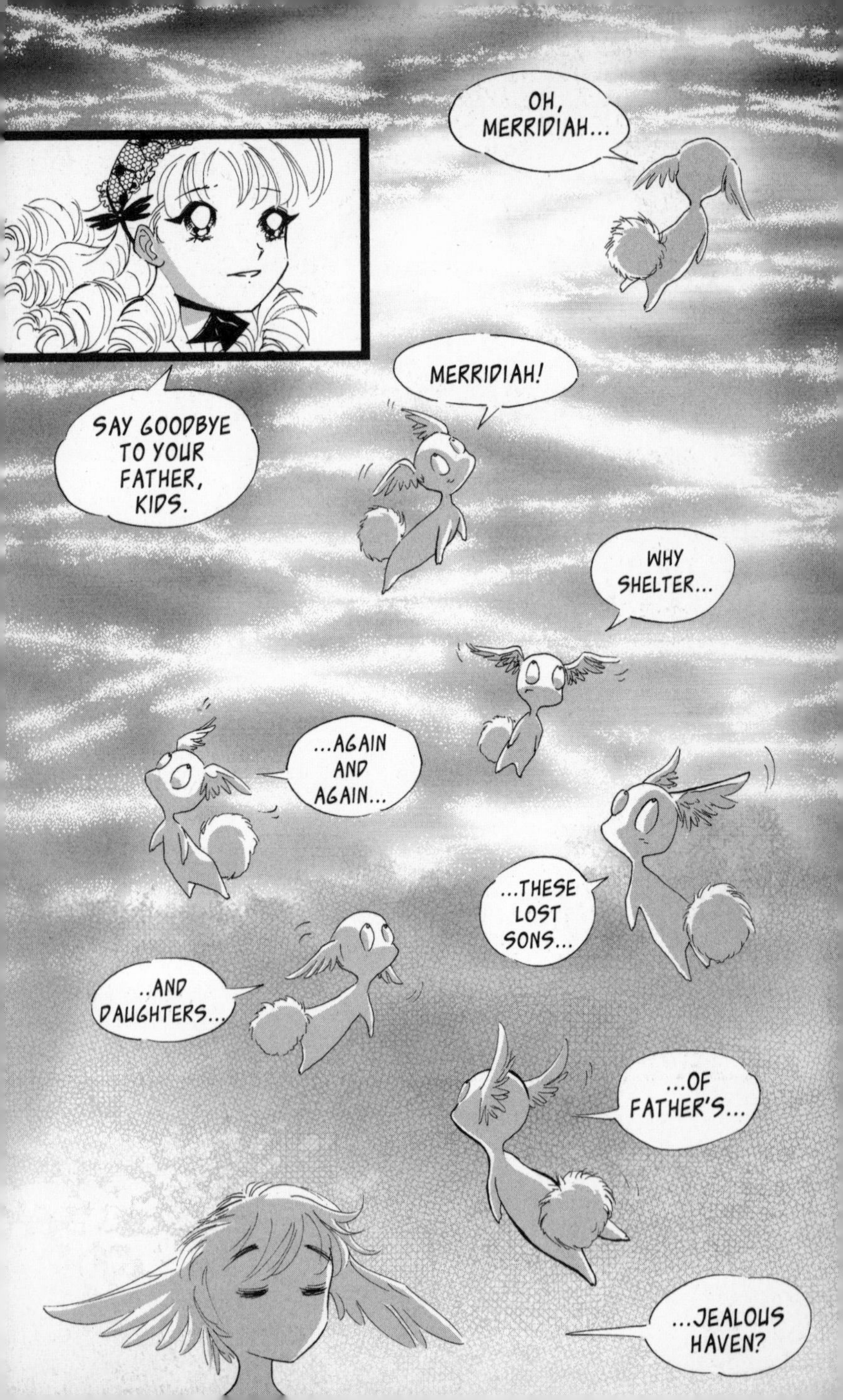
OH, MERRIDIAH...
SAY GOODBYE TO YOUR FATHER, KIDS.
MERRIDIAH!
WHY SHELTER...
...AGAIN AND AGAIN...
...THESE LOST SONS...
..AND DAUGHTERS...
...OF FATHER'S...
...JEALOUS HAVEN?

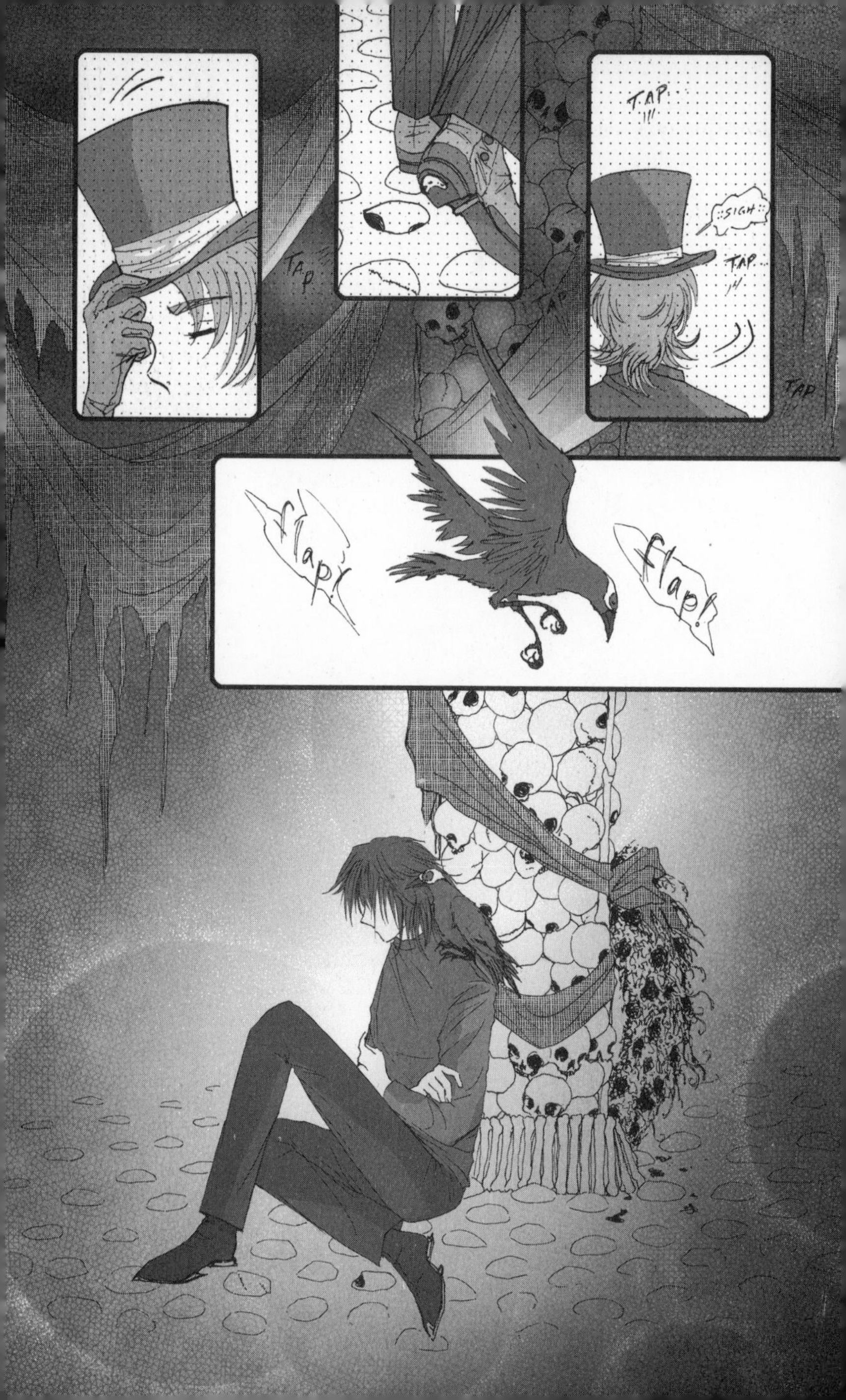
TAP
TAP
TAP
::SIGH::
TAP
TAP
flap!
flap!

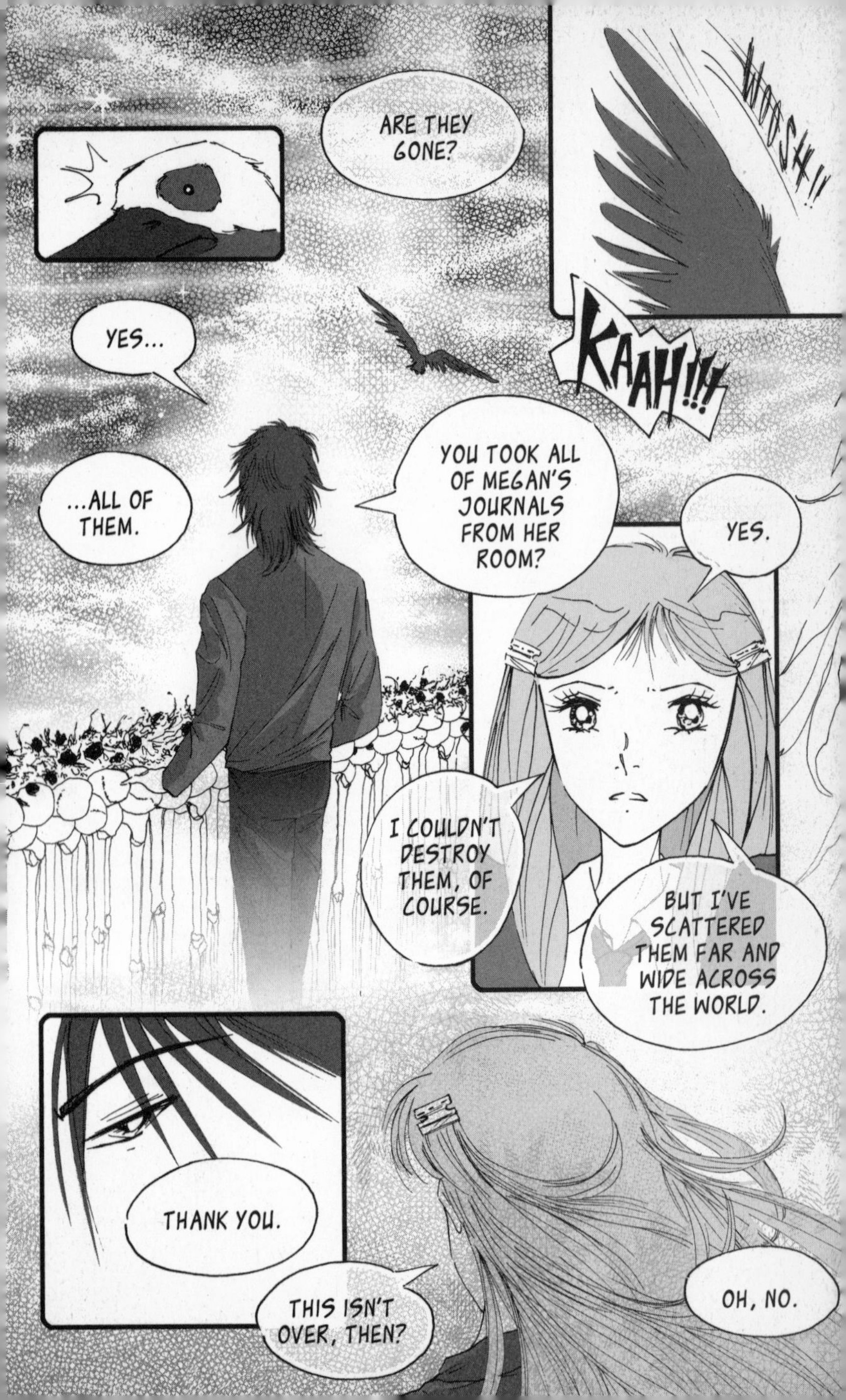
ARE THEY GONE?
WOOSH!!
KAAH!!!
YES...
...ALL OF THEM.
YOU TOOK ALL OF MEGAN'S JOURNALS FROM HER ROOM?
YES.
I COULDN'T DESTROY THEM, OF COURSE.
BUT I'VE SCATTERED THEM FAR AND WIDE ACROSS THE WORLD.
THANK YOU.
THIS ISN'T OVER, THEN?
OH, NO.

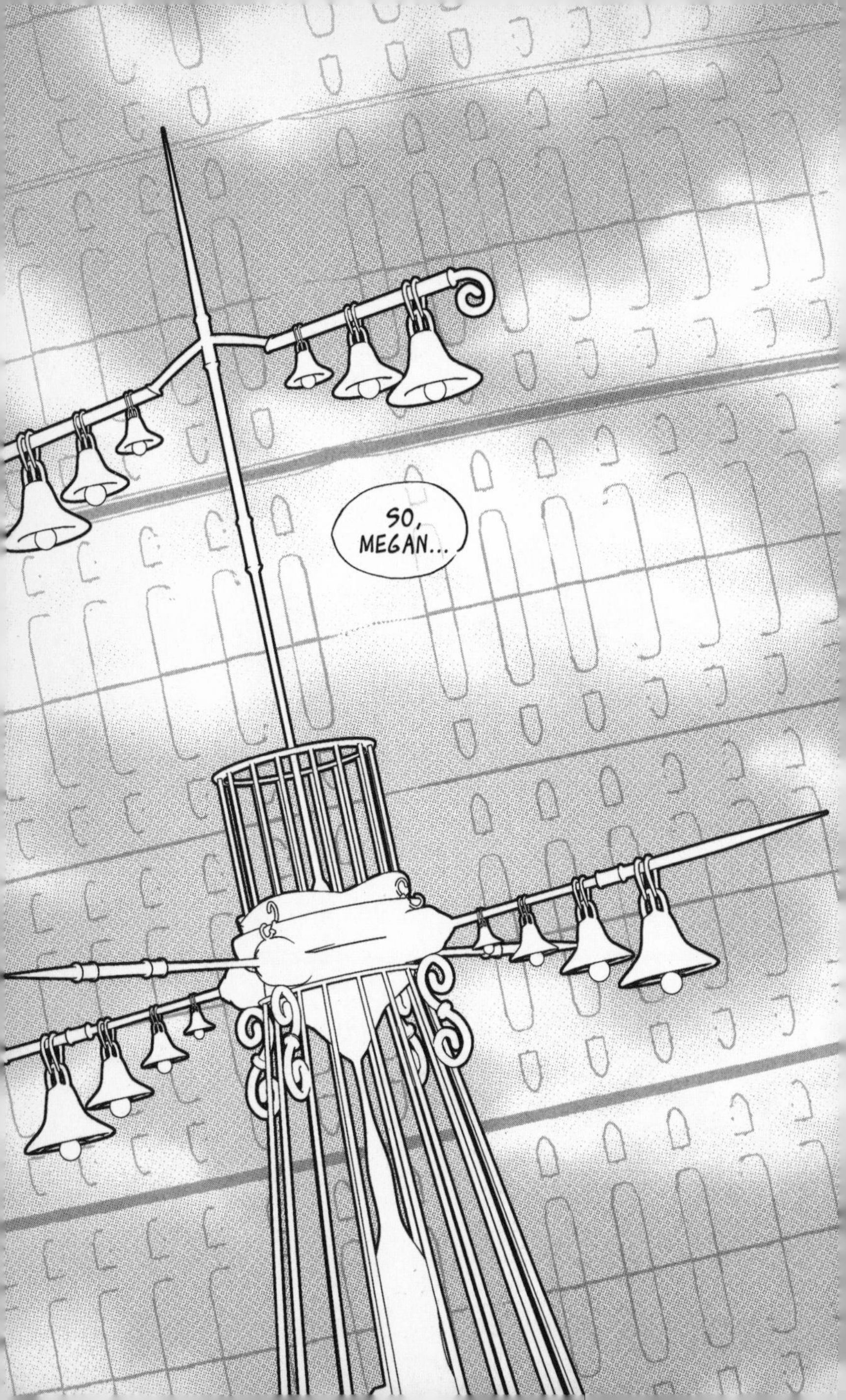
SO, MEGAN...

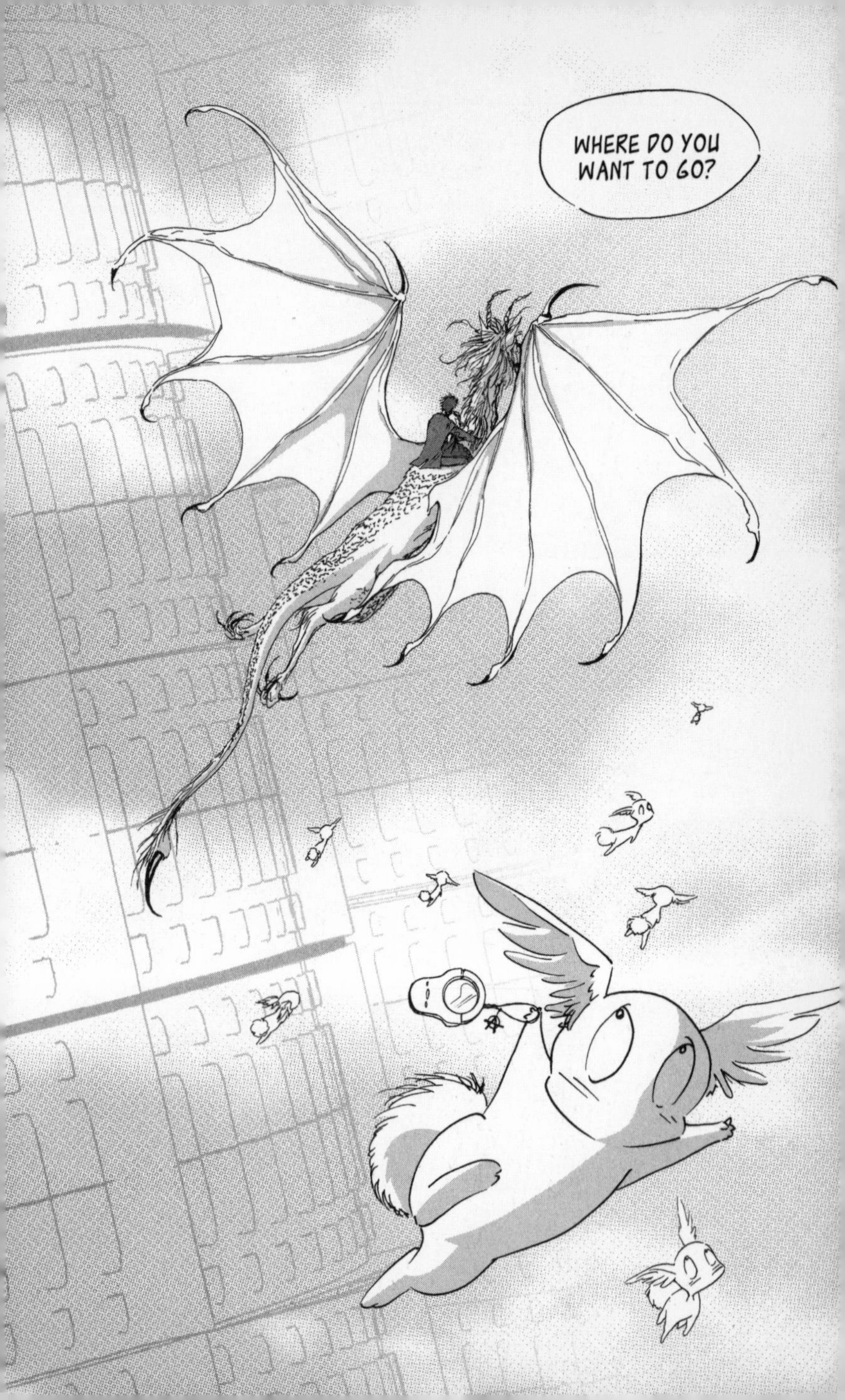
WHERE DO YOU WANT TO GO?

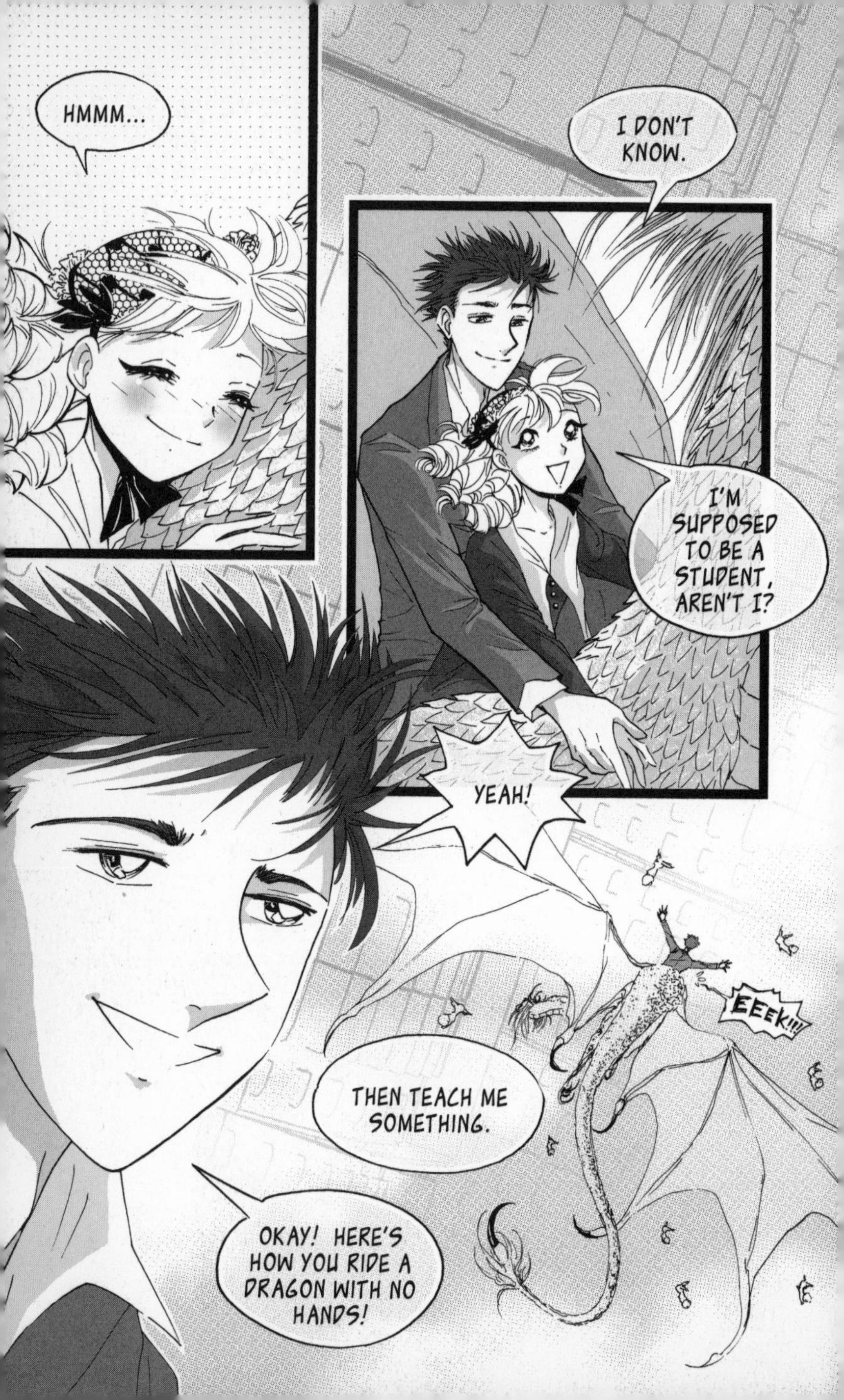
HMMM...
I DON'T KNOW.
I'M SUPPOSED TO BE A STUDENT, AREN'T I?
YEAH!
EEEK!!!
THEN TEACH ME SOMETHING.
OKAY! HERE'S HOW YOU RIDE A DRAGON WITH NO HANDS!

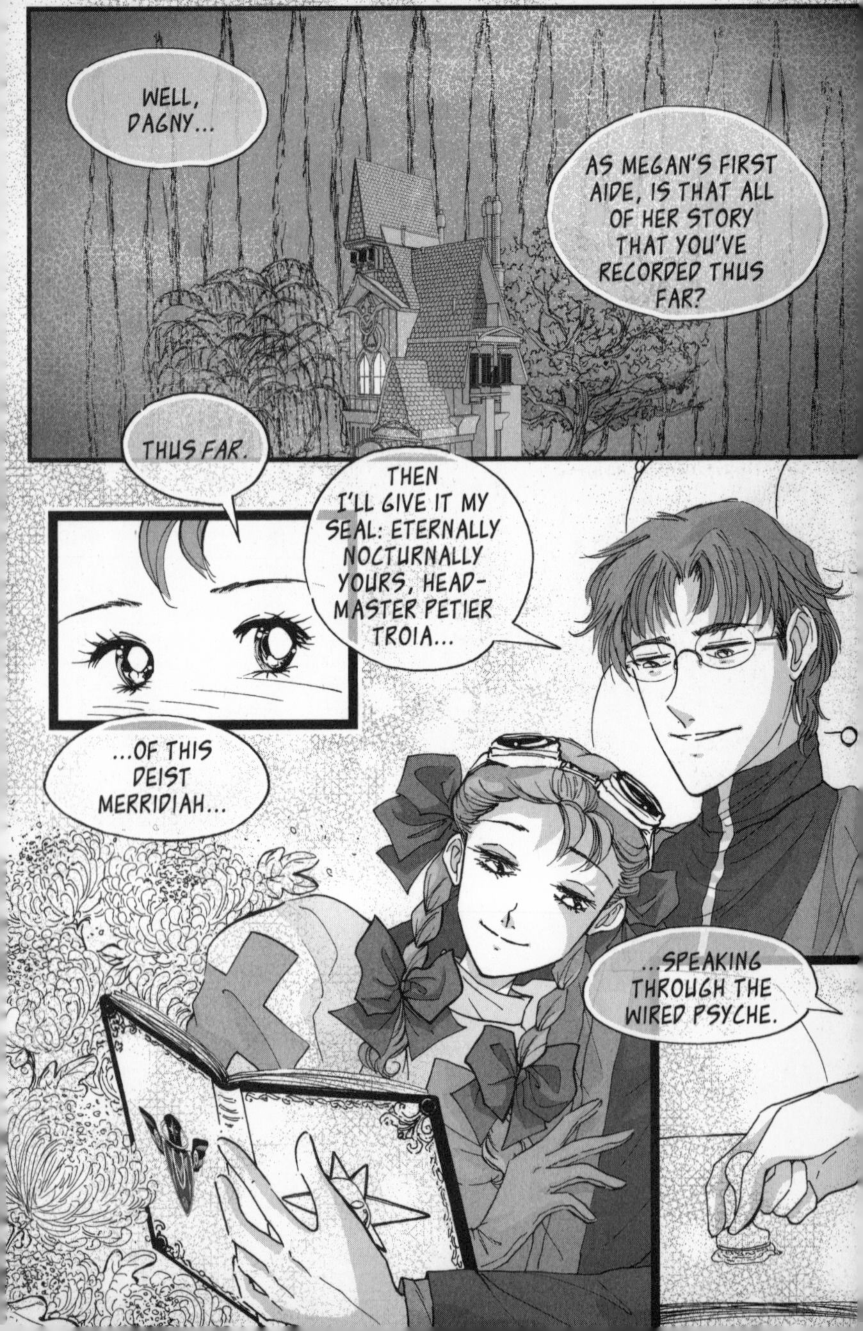
WELL, DAGNY...
AS MEGAN'S FIRST AIDE, IS THAT ALL OF HER STORY THAT YOU'VE RECORDED THUS FAR?
THUS FAR.
THEN I'LL GIVE IT MY SEAL: ETERNALLY NOCTURNALLY YOURS, HEAD-MASTER PETIER TROIA...
...OF THIS DEIST MERRIDIAH...
...SPEAKING THROUGH THE WIRED PSYCHE.

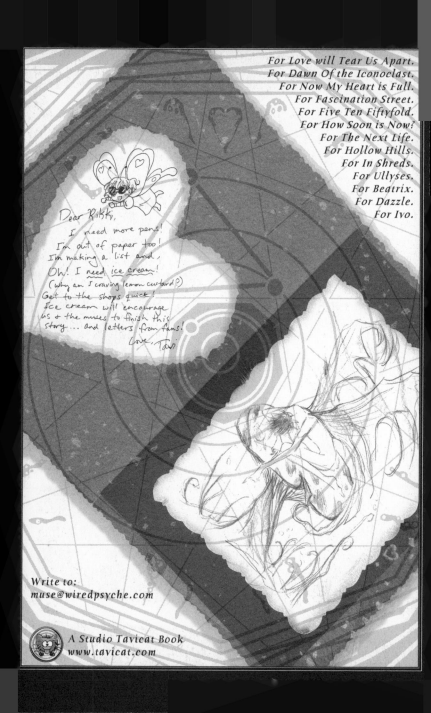

For Love will Tear Us Apart.
For Dawn Of the Iconoclast.
For Now My Heart is Full.
For Fascination Street.
For Five Ten Fiftyfold.
For How Soon is Now?
For The Next Life.
For Hollow Hills.
For In Shreds.
For Ullyses.
For Beatrix.
For Dazzle.
For Ivo.

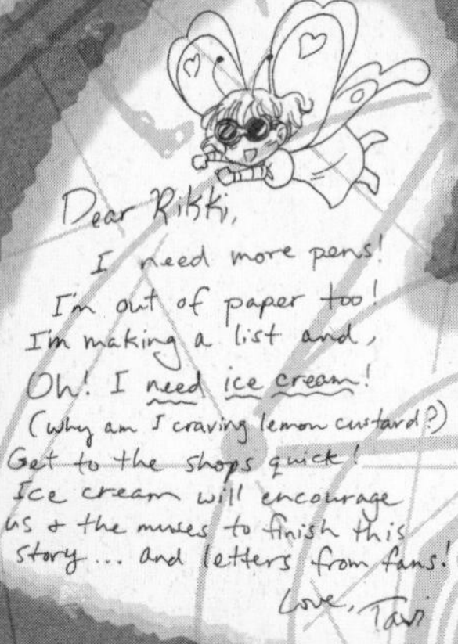
Dear Rikki,
I need more pens!
I'm out of paper too!
I'm making a list and,
Oh! I need ice cream!
(why am I craving lemon custard?)
Get to the shops quick!
Ice cream will encourage
us & the muses to finish this
story... and letters from fans!
Love, Tavi

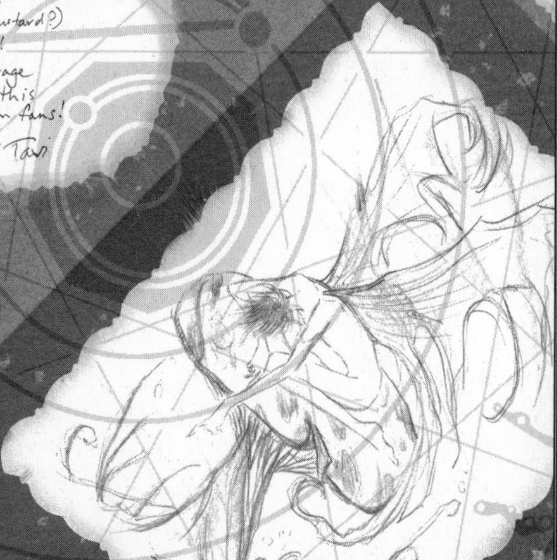

Write to:
muse@wiredpsyche.com

A Studio Tavicat Book
www.tavicat.com

Hello Diary,
I found this picture of Thom. It was in my new den, down in the Well of Armour.

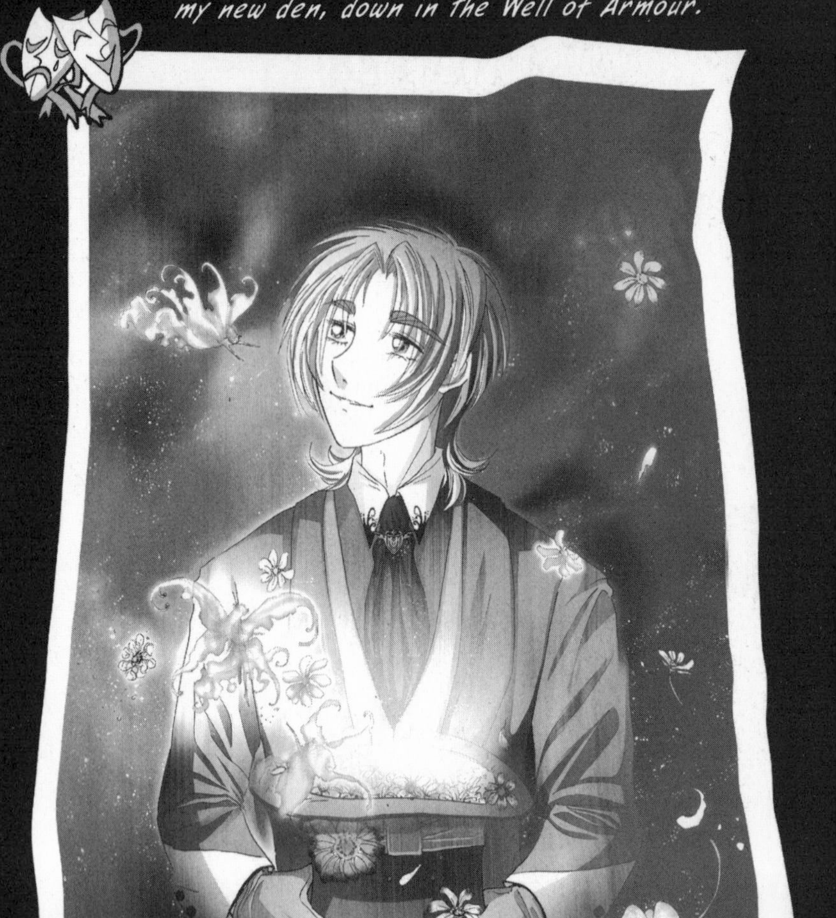

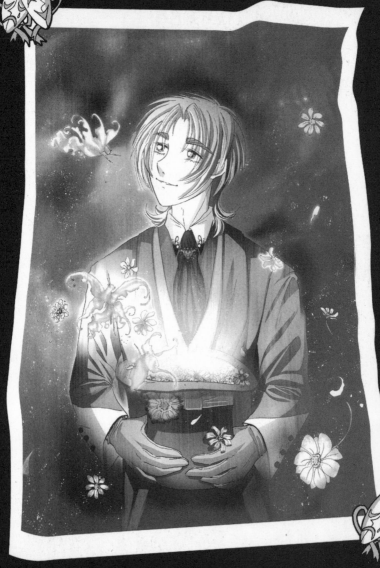

There's nothing written on it but I have to wonder where it was taken. Does Thom keep fairies under his hat? I hope I find out as my story continues...

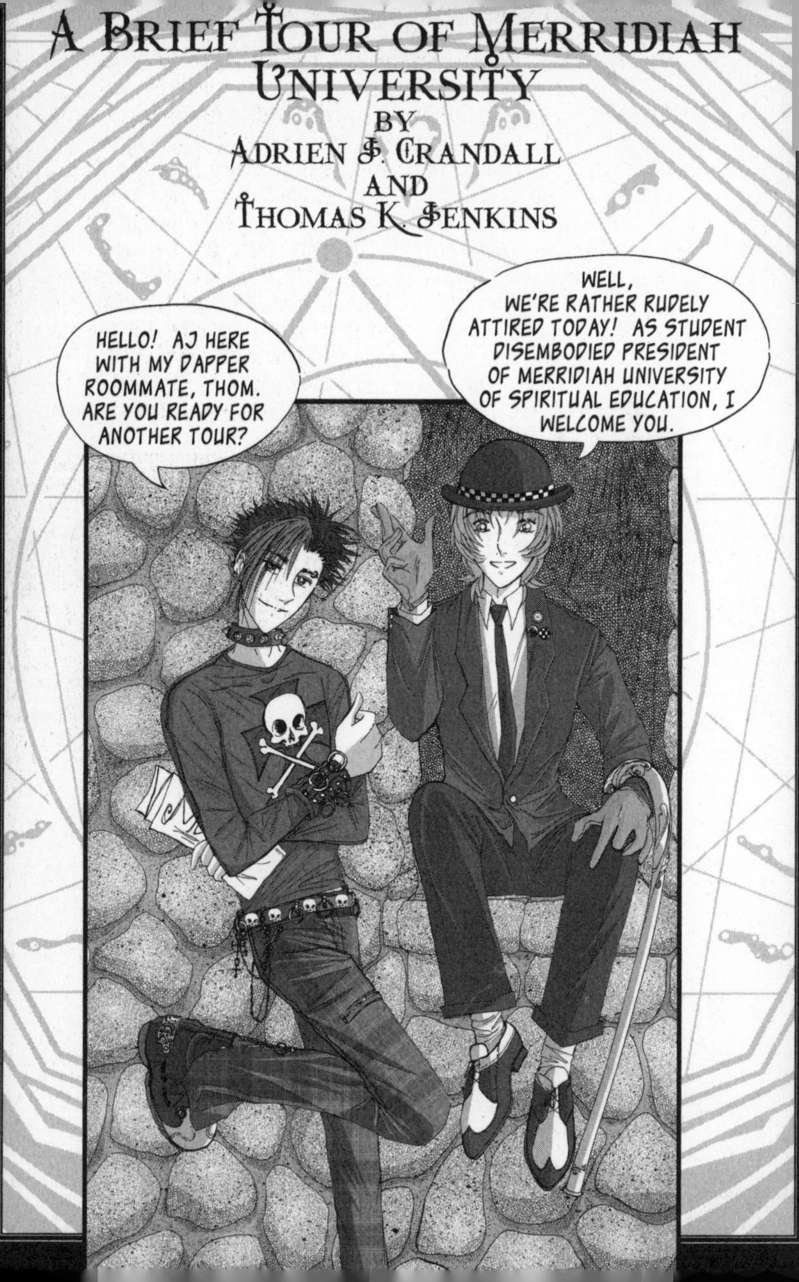
A BRIEF TOUR OF MERRIDIAH UNIVERSITY
BY
ADRIEN J. CRANDALL
AND
THOMAS K. JENKINS
HELLO! AJ HERE WITH MY DAPPER ROOMMATE, THOM. ARE YOU READY FOR ANOTHER TOUR?
WELL, WE'RE RATHER RUDELY ATTIRED TODAY! AS STUDENT DISEMBODIED PRESIDENT OF MERRIDIAH UNIVERSITY OF SPIRITUAL EDUCATION, I WELCOME YOU.

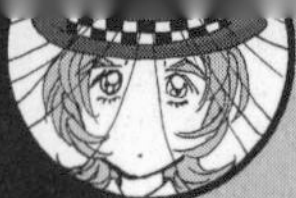

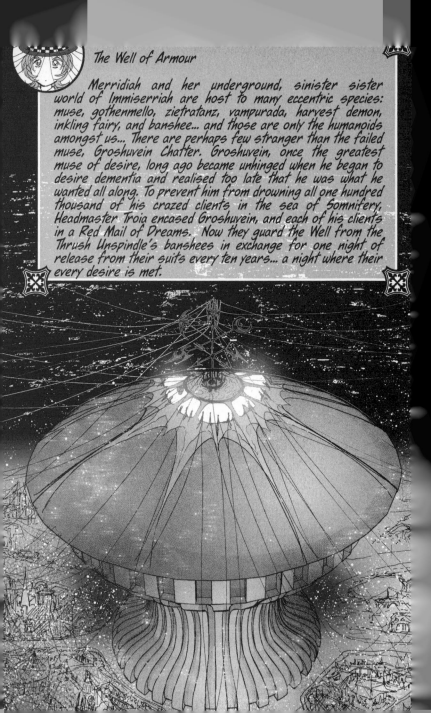

The Well of Armour

Merridiah and her underground, sinister sister world of Immiserriah are host to many eccentric species: muse, gothenmello, zietratanz, vampurada, harvest demon, inkling fairy, and banshee... and those are only the humanoids amongst us... There are perhaps few stranger than the failed muse, Groshuvein Chatter. Groshuvein, once the greatest muse of desire, long ago became unhinged when he began to desire dementia and realised too late that he was what he wanted all along. To prevent him from drowning all one hundred thousand of his crazed clients in the sea of Somnifery, Headmaster Troia encased Groshuvein, and each of his clients in a Red Mail of Dreams. Now they guard the Well from the Thrush Unspindle's banshees in exchange for one night of release from their suits every ten years... a night where their every desire is met.

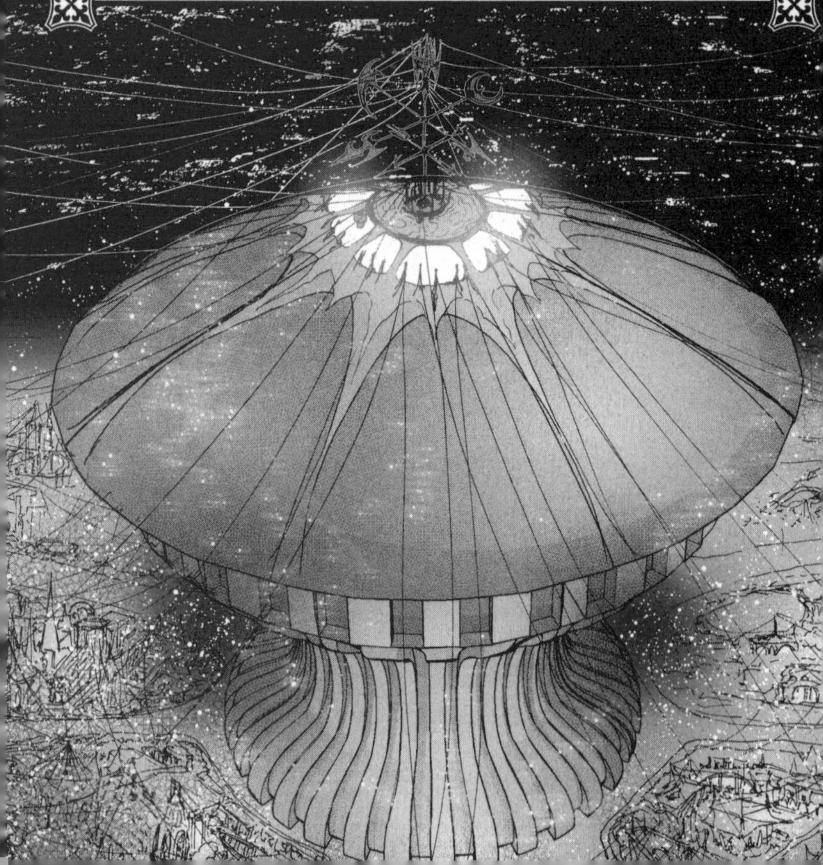

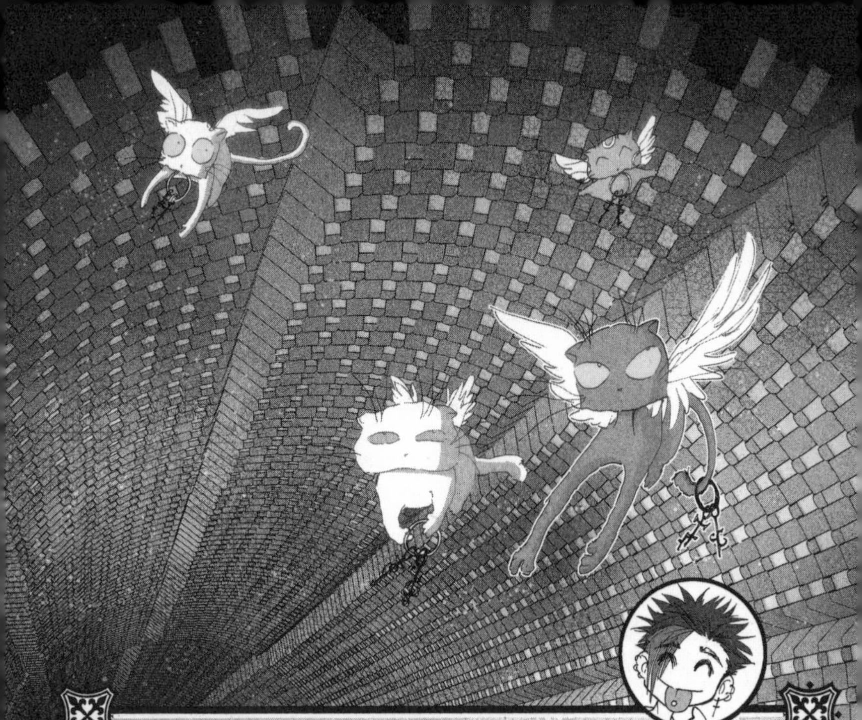

Within the mushroom-shaped structure of the Well of Armour, stretches the monstrous, labyrinthine zero-gravity pit that is the Well proper. The Well stretches at least nine miles from top to bottom, straight through Merridiah's upper crust and into the underground dimension of Immiserriah, the Hourglass Hollow. Not a true entrance to the underground realm, it is guarded at the bottom by ten thousand Red Coats. This is it. This is where the magic happens, so to speak. In short, it works a bit like this: dark roses called inklings grow far underground in Immiserriah. These roses cannot help but to dream of all of humanity's possible futures. Their dreams are collected by the inkling fairies for Groshuvein's Red Coats and forged nightly by the gothenmello into Kagi Crystals. These crystals are then deposited into muse "machines" referred to as Kagi Armours. It's then up to us muses to decrypt the raw data of your lives after we have been assigned Kagi Keys by our personal archangel cats. There we sit within our dens within the Well of Armour, calling you on our halo phones. There are no classes or professors at Merridiah University, and the only subject is you.

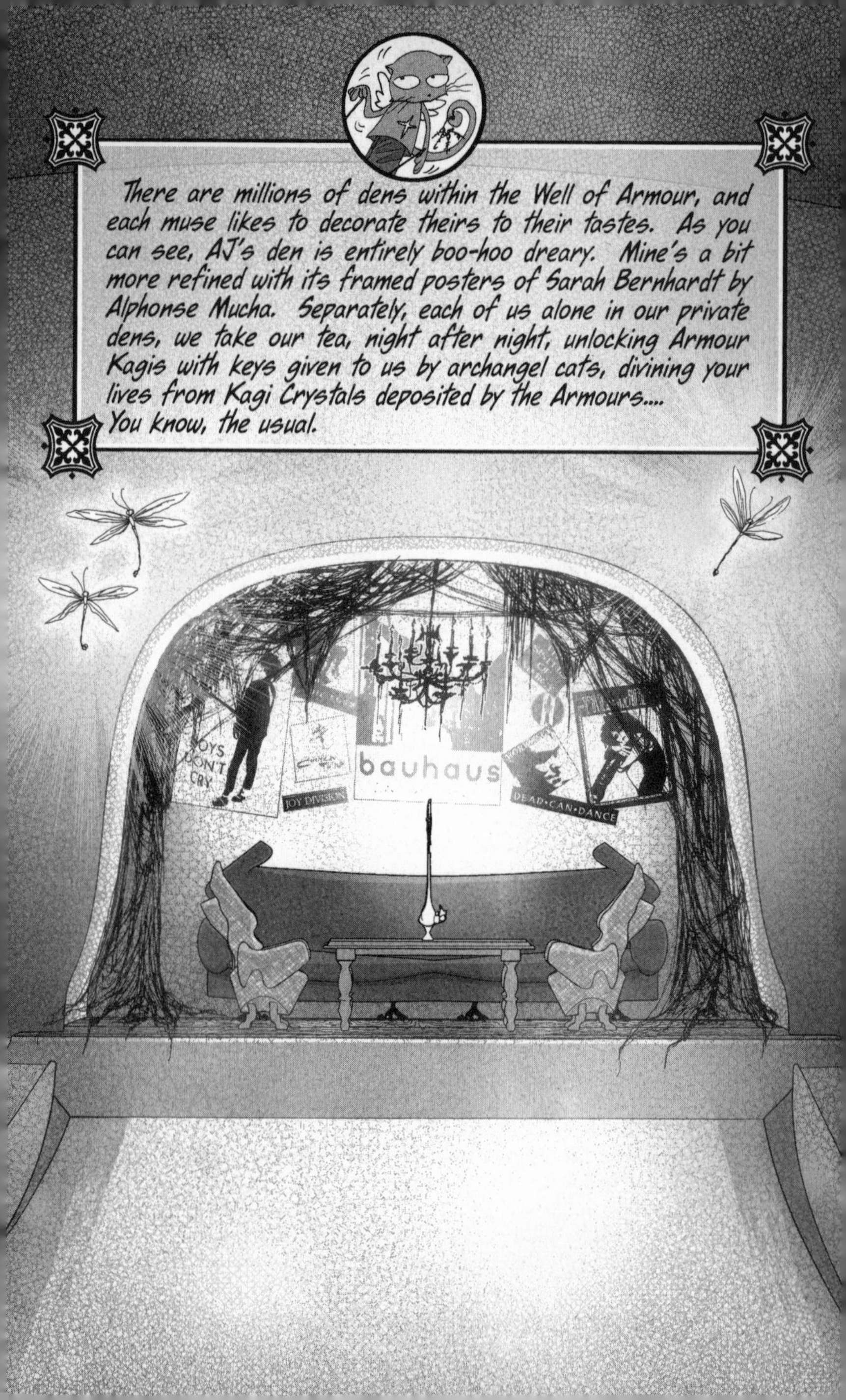
There are millions of dens within the Well of Armour, and each muse likes to decorate theirs to their tastes. As you can see, AJ's den is entirely boo-hoo dreary. Mine's a bit more refined with its framed posters of Sarah Bernhardt by Alphonse Mucha. Separately, each of us alone in our private dens, we take our tea, night after night, unlocking Armour Kagis with keys given to us by archangel cats, divining your lives from Kagi Crystals deposited by the Armours....
You know, the usual.
BOYS DON'T CRY
JOY DIVISION
bauhaus
DEAD·CAN·DANCE

The Muse Kagi

Written in Gothenmello Script

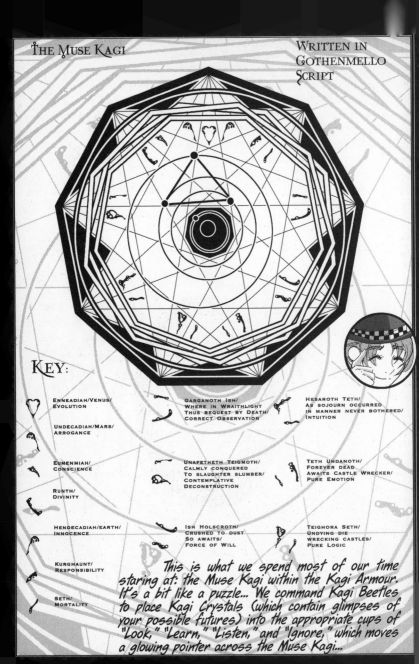

Key:

Enneadiah/Venus/
Evolution

Undecadiah/Mars/
Arrogance

Eumenmiah/
Conscience

Runth/
Divinity

Hendecadiah/earth/
Innocence

Kurghaunt/
Responsibility

Seth/
Mortality

Garganoth Ish/
Where in Wraithlight
Thus bequest by Death/
Correct Observation

Unafetheth Teigmoth/
Calmly conquered
To slaughter slumber/
Contemplative
Deconstruction

Ish Holscroth/
Crushed to dust
So awaits/
Force of Will

Hesaroth Teth/
As sojourn occurred
in manner never bothered/
Intuition

Teth Undanoth/
Forever dead
Awaits Castle Wrecker/
Pure Emotion

Teighora Seth/
Undying die
wrecking castles/
Pure Logic

This is what we spend most of our time staring at: the Muse Kagi within the Kagi Armour. It's a bit like a puzzle... We command Kagi Beetles to place Kagi Crystals (which contain glimpses of your possible futures) into the appropriate cups of "Look," "Learn," "Listen," and "Ignore," which moves a glowing pointer across the Muse Kagi...

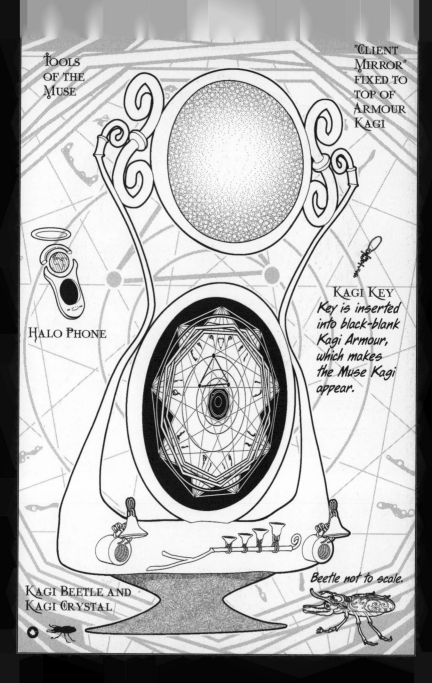

TOOLS OF THE MUSE

"CLIENT MIRROR" FIXED TO TOP OF ARMOUR KAGI

HALO PHONE

KAGI KEY
Key is inserted into black-blank Kagi Armour, which makes the Muse Kagi appear.

KAGI BEETLE AND KAGI CRYSTAL

Beetle not to scale.

A Cutaway Map of Merridiah Revealing Immiserriah: the Hourglass Hollow

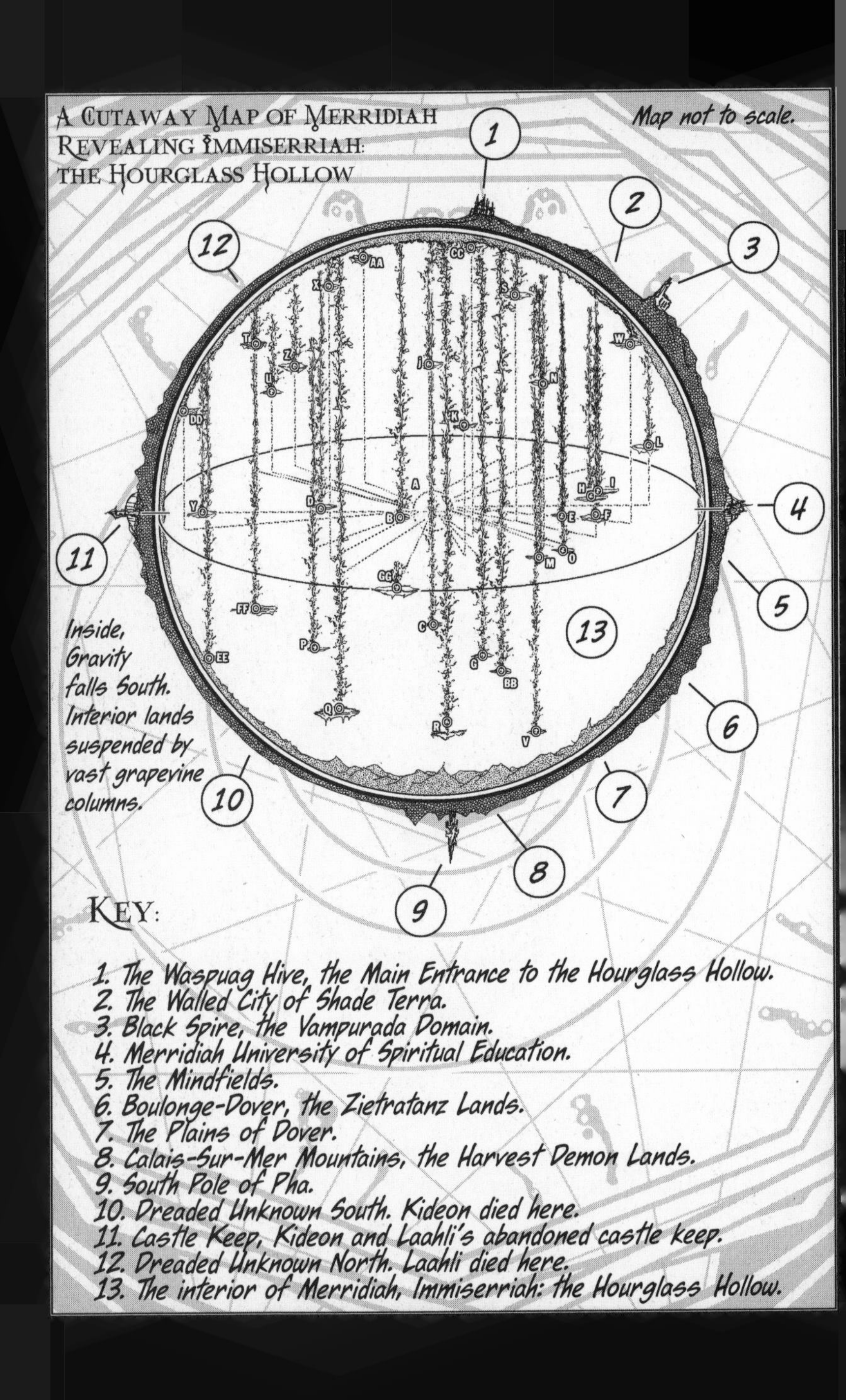

Map not to scale.
1
2
3
12
AA
CC
X
S
T
Z
U
J
W
N
DD
K
L
A
H
I
D
Y
B
E
F
4
11
M
O
GG
5
FF
C
13
P
EE
G
BB
6
Q
R
V
Inside, Gravity falls South. Interior lands suspended by vast grapevine columns.
10
7
8
9

Key:

1. The Waspuag Hive, the Main Entrance to the Hourglass Hollow.
2. The Walled City of Shade Terra.
3. Black Spire, the Vampurada Domain.
4. Merridiah University of Spiritual Education.
5. The Mindfields.
6. Boulonge-Dover, the Zietratanz Lands.
7. The Plains of Dover.
8. Calais-Sur-Mer Mountains, the Harvest Demon Lands.
9. South Pole of Pha.
10. Dreaded Unknown South. Kideon died here.
11. Castle Keep, Kideon and Laahli's abandoned castle keep.
12. Dreaded Unknown North. Laahli died here.
13. The interior of Merridiah, Immiserriah: the Hourglass Hollow.

Immiserriah: The Hourglass Hollow

The Lands:

A. Ambletta Shallow
B. Blinkless
C. Cocteau Corvee
D. Dies Faustus
E. Epimyth Lung
F. Fairy Inkluund
G. Goetee Gravid
H. Holmgang Gag
I. Illude Illocal
J. Jatip Junction
K. Keenspeckle
L. leechfinger
M. Mar Morriss
N. Nanacracker
O. Omingogre
P. Pixic Herile
Q. Quibblish
R. Radia Rashflint
S. Schitzofrettic
T. Terrorbracing
U. Umbracing
V. Vilvolage Vile
W. Wantonflury
X. Xenodregedal
Y. Yearnundone
Z. Zooenpratical
AA. Amon
BB. Bellon
CC. Cibon
DD. Devon
EE. Enon
FF. Frauton
GG. Gigon

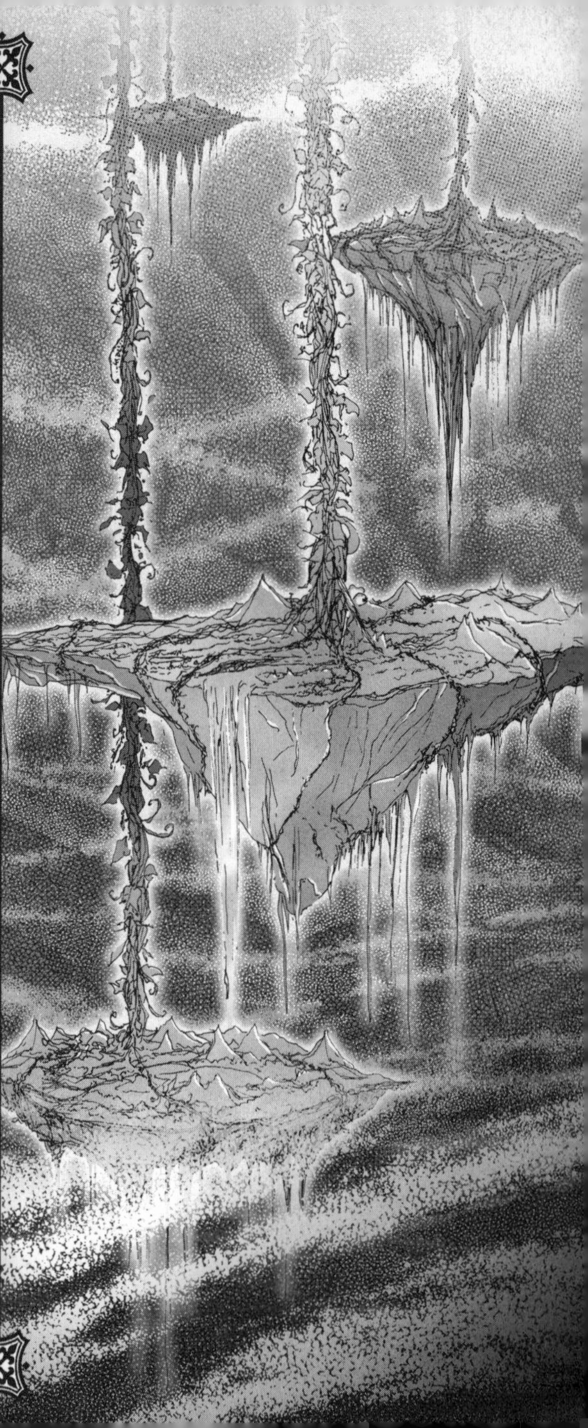

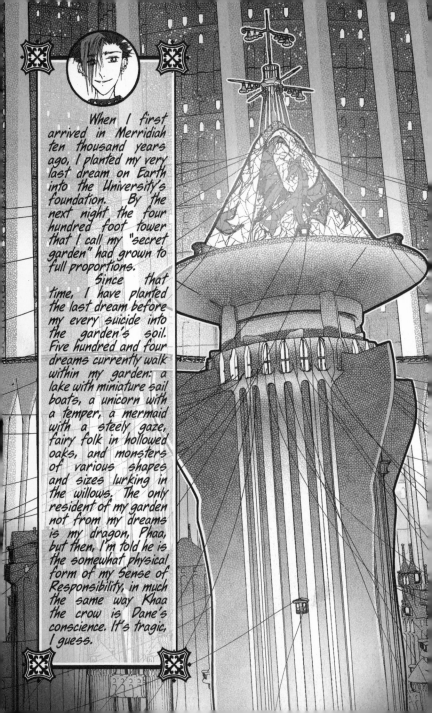

When I first arrived in Merridiah ten thousand years ago, I planted my very last dream on Earth into the University's foundation. By the next night the four hundred foot tower that I call my "secret garden" had grown to full proportions.

Since that time, I have planted the last dream before my every suicide into the garden's soil. Five hundred and four dreams currently walk within my garden: a lake with miniature sail boats, a unicorn with a temper, a mermaid with a steely gaze, fairy folk in hollowed oaks, and monsters of various shapes and sizes lurking in the willows. The only resident of my garden not from my dreams is my dragon, Phaa, but then, I'm told he is the somewhat physical form of my sense of Responsibility, in much the same way Khaa the crow is Dane's conscience. It's tragic, I guess.